The East Somerset and Cheddar Valley Railways

by Richard Harman

The epitome of a West Country branch line in its twilight years; a quiet station proudly displaying its Bristol & Exeter Railway legacy being visited by an 0-6-0 pannier tank coupled to a B-set. The date was 17th February 1962. *Terry Nicholls*

Lodge Hill station, serving the village of Westbury-sub-Mendip. The name was chosen to avoid confusion with Westbury in Wiltshire but possibly did little for a traveller seeking Westbury-sub-Mendip on the railway map. The line's Bristol & Exeter Railway origins were reflected in the ornate detailing of its buildings between Congresbury and Wells.

Copyright Lightmoor Press and Richard Harman 2009

Designed by Tony Miller; Cover design by Neil Parkhouse and Tony Miller

British Library Cataloguing-in-Publication Data. A catalogue record for this book is available from the British Library

ISBN 9781899889 40 2

All rights reserved. No part of this publication may be reproduced, stored in a retrieval system or transmitted in any form or by any means, electronic, mechanical, photocopying, recording or otherwise, without the written permission of the publisher.

Lightmoor Press is an imprint of
Black Dwarf Lightmoor Publications Ltd
Unit 144B, Lydney Trading Estate, Harbour Road, Lydney, Gloucestershire GL15 4EJ
www.lightmoor.co.uk

Printed and bound by T J International, Padstow, Cornwall

Frontispiece - The city of Wells as seen from the top of the Sheldon Jones grain silo on an unknown date but probably in the 1950s. The city was the focal point of three branch lines; from Yatton, constructed by the Bristol & Exeter Railway; from Witham, built by the East Somerset Railway and from Glastonbury, courtesy the Somerset Central Railway. This book expands the story of the railways of Wells.

Gordon Scammell

✤ CONTENTS ✤

Frontispiece		4
Introduction	An Overview	7
Chapter 1	Origins	11
Chapter 2	Somerset Central Railway	14
Chapter 3	East Somerset Railway	19
Chapter 4	Cheddar Valley & Yatton Railway	29
Chapter 5	Takeover by the GWR	39
Chapter 6	1880 to the Present Day	51
Chapter 7	A Description of the Line	79
Chapter 8	Mineral Branches and Tramways	173
Chapter 9	Dulcote and Merehead - - the Foster Yeoman Quarries	181
Chapter 10	Operation of the Line	189
Chapter 11	Goods and Mineral Traffic Operation	209
Chapter 12	Signalling	215
Chapter 13	Accidents	228
Chapter 14	Camping Coaches	231
Chapter 15	Memories of a Branch Line	232
Appendix 1	Strawberry Traffic	240
Appendix 2	Single Line Working	242
Appendix 3	Signal Box Diagrams	245
Appendix 4	Traffic Receipts, 1906 - 1911	257
Appendix 5	Private Traders on the Line	258
Appendix 6	Working timetables	260
Appendix 7	Chronology	266
	Bibliography	268
	Other Sources of Information	269
	Acknowledgements	269
	Index	270

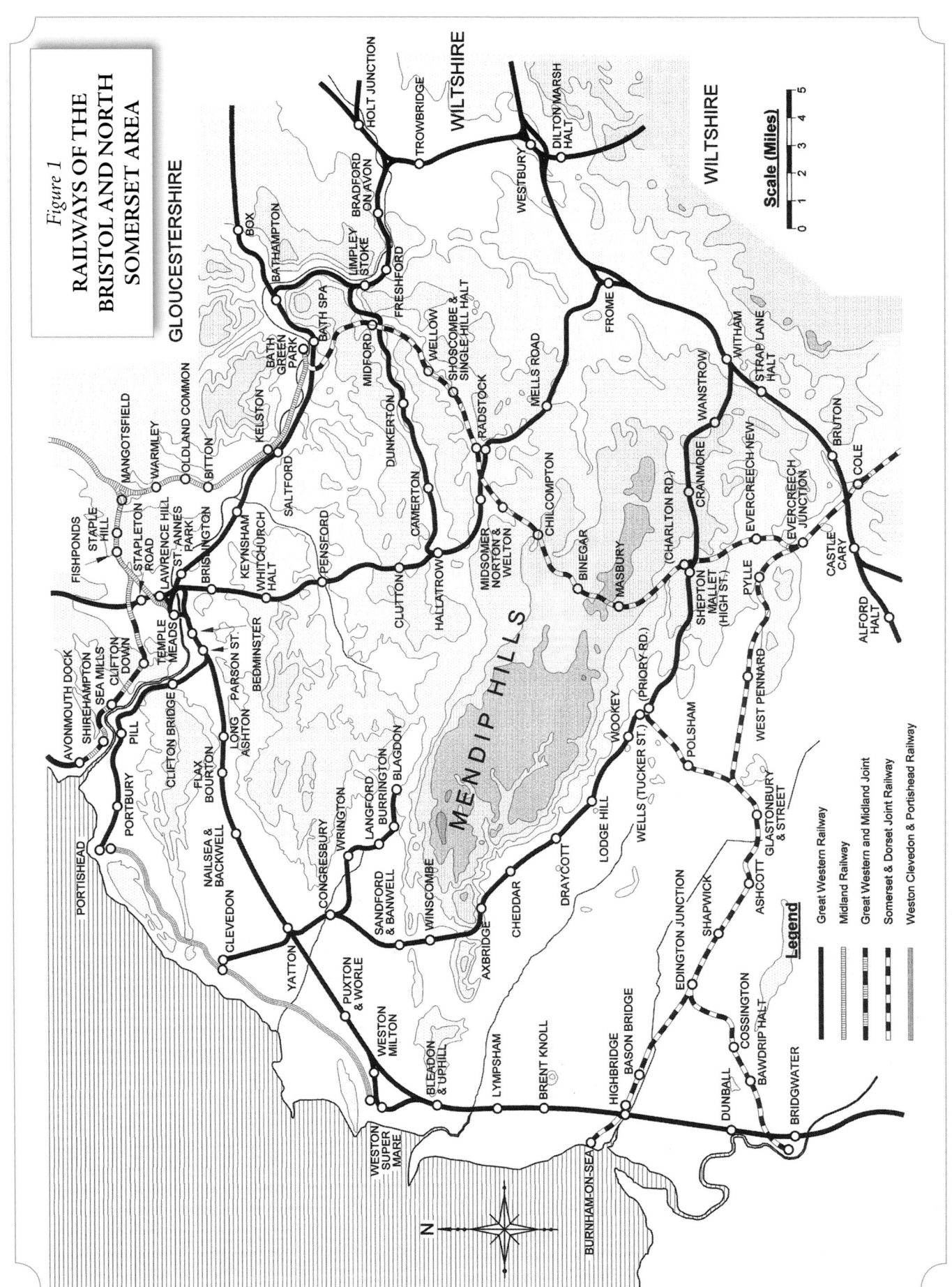

Introduction

AN OVERVIEW

The Yatton to Witham branch of the Great Western Railway originally consisted of two completely separate branch lines both of which terminated in the city of Wells. The western arm of the branch was built as the Cheddar Valley & Yatton Railway which made a junction with the Bristol & Exeter Railway in the village of Yatton about halfway between Bristol and Weston-super-Mare. The eastern arm was built as the East Somerset Railway which made its junction with the Wilts, Somerset & Weymouth Railway at Witham, a few miles south-west of Frome. The history of these two branches, their eventual connection and subsequent operation is a complex affair. Even after the connection was forged and after the appearance in the timetable of trains that ran through between Yatton and Witham, the two branches could still be considered in many ways to be separate entities.

In the great age of railway building during the second and third quarters of the nineteenth century, the county of Somerset was seen as much as a way of getting to a destination as being a destination in itself. The destinations in question were of course Devon and Cornwall, which were experiencing a dramatic growth in tourism in an age when the seaside holiday was rapidly gaining in popularity. In order to get to the seaside resorts in those counties the traveller had to pass through Somerset, there being no through railway lines or major roads to the far south-west via the County of Dorset. This is true to the present day as the local residents who live near the M5 motorway or the A30 trunk road are only too aware and the level of congestion on the roads has, fortunately, resulted in a significant move back to rail travel in recent years. Thus the pattern of railways through Somerset was drawn from the late 1830s through to its completion in the early years of the twentieth century.

Three main lines run through the county, two of which formerly belonged to the Great Western Railway. They converge at Cogload Junction, just east of Taunton. The third belonged to the Southern Railway and, prior to the grouping, the London & South Western Railway. This line was singled for much of its length and reduced to secondary status during the 1960s. However, transport requirements change with time and there are now plans to improve services on the line that will require the restoration of much, if not all, of the line to double track within the next few years. In addition to the main lines there were two cross country routes. The first of these is the Bath to Weymouth route that remains open to this day and runs for part of its length through Wiltshire before joining the West of England main line at Westbury (Wilts). The Weymouth line diverges again at Castle Cary and runs via Yeovil and into Dorset. Secondly, there was the Somerset & Dorset Railway that closed entirely in the 1960s and whose main line ran south from a junction with the Midland Railway at Bath to Poole and Wimborne in Dorset. It cut across the Great Western at a number of places without connection but there was a junction with the London & South Western at Templecombe. The Somerset & Dorset also had branches to Burnham, Wells and Bridgwater.

The Great Western Railway also possessed a number of branch lines in Somerset. Some, such as the Clevedon and Portishead branches, were relatively short and dead-end but there were several longer through branches including the Langport to Yeovil line, and the Bristol and North Somerset. However, not only was the Yatton to Witham a through line, it was also by far the longest in Somerset being over thirty-one miles in length. Arguably the term 'branch line' was not really applicable to the Yatton to Witham line. A branch line, by its very definition, implies one with a terminal station and a service that runs, for the most part, only to and from its junction with the main line. The Clevedon branch was an excellent example of this. The fact that many services on the Yatton to Witham line ran through to other main line destinations beyond the junctions at either end goes against this definition. The main services that spring to mind here are those that worked through between Bristol and Frome. Some of these formed part of a circular Bristol to Bristol service that completed the circle by using the Bristol and North Somerset line between Frome and Bristol via Radstock. If the Yatton to Witham line had had any significant portions of double track it might have had the status of a secondary route but for the severe gradients and axle loading restrictions. As a result the line only had the status of being a branch throughout its existence.

My earliest recollections of the railways in central and north Somerset are of going to Castle Cary on the West of England main line in the mid-1950s with my father when I was still of pre-school age. I can clearly remember seeing the West of England expresses rushing through the station hauled by Castle and King Class locomotives. It was probably this that sparked my railway interest at an early age. We lived on the Mendip Hills just north of Wells and the journey of little more than ten miles to Castle Cary was not without railway interest as it closely followed the Somerset & Dorset main line for much of the way.

The nearest station to my childhood home was Masbury on the Somerset & Dorset and it was this line that really fostered my interest in railways when I was in my early teens. By this time passenger services had already finished on the Yatton to Witham line so I paid little attention to it. The Somerset & Dorset has, of course, been documented in great detail since its still much lamented closure with the number of books on it now running into several dozen. In comparison, the Yatton to Witham line has been largely ignored by railway writers. Until fairly recently a handful of articles and chapters in books of a more general nature represented all that had ever been written about the line although, since 1997, four books have been published. One is a purely photographic book (*referenced as 1*

Plate 1 - Witham represents one end of the journey covered by this book and is just two stations up the West of England main line from Castle Cary, where the author's interest in railways was kindled. This c.1908-10 view from the down platform shows a clerestory carriage in the bay, doubtless ready for its next journey since its tail-lamp is in position. *Roger Carpenter collection*

in the bibliography) and two others are detailed histories only covering specific sections of the line (*referenced as 2 and 3*). The final book (*referenced as 4*) was the first full history covering the entire line and was published in 2001. I started on this work in the 1990s at a time when it seemed that the lack of a full history of the line represented a gap in the history of the railways of Somerset that should be filled as soon as possible. With this work it is my intention to complement the other four titles.

The origins of the Yatton to Witham line and the Somerset & Dorset were inextricably linked. As we shall see, without the Somerset & Dorset and its precursor the Somerset Central, neither the East Somerset nor the Cheddar Valley lines might ever have been built. They certainly would not have taken on the form that they eventually did. So in terms of the amount of information published, the Yatton to Witham line may be seen quite literally as the 'poor relation' of the Somerset & Dorset.

In the end the Yatton to Witham line and the Somerset & Dorset ended up on opposite sides in the long-lasting rivalry between the Great Western on one hand and the Midland and the London & South Western on the other. Following nationalisation and a general decline of rail-borne transport, the two had a shared destiny when both were earmarked for closure by the Beeching report in 1963. The closure of the Yatton to Witham line, for passenger services at least, had already been on the agenda for some years and so was virtually a foregone conclusion. So the end of passenger services in September 1963 was swift. However, those on the Somerset & Dorset suffered an agonising death that lasted for nearly another three years.

Looking back from the twenty-first century, it is difficult to imagine the impact that the coming of the railways had on rural communities such as those in central Somerset. Whilst the business community and land owners for the most part welcomed the railway as they saw the provision of better transport as being advantageous to them (largely for financial reasons, I suspect), much of the rest of the rural population regarded the railways with deep suspicion, at least initially. One spin off that we take for granted these days and think very little about was the adoption of standard time. Since the dawn of agriculture, rural communities had regulated their day by the hours of daylight and darkness and had little need for a system of accurate time keeping. Watches and clocks would have been set by observation of the sun in conjunction with correction tables to allow for the elliptical nature of the Earth's orbit around the Sun. As a result of this, clocks in Somerset would have been a good ten minutes behind those in London. Whilst this fact did not pose a problem for most human activities at that time, it quickly became a problem if you were trying to run a railway, or indeed were planning to catch a train for that matter!

The Great Western Railway was the first to adopt London time in November 1840. This was doubtless due to the fact that it traversed a greater distance in longitude than most other early lines of similar length and so would have suffered from the effects of locally set time to a greater extent. Most other railways had followed suit by 1847 when the Railway Clearing House recommended the adoption of Greenwich Mean Time. By the time that the lines that form the subject of this work were built, Greenwich Mean Time had been more or less universally adopted in Britain.

Another spin off from the railway that benefited the community as a whole was the arrival of the electric telegraph. The development of the telegraph more or less coincided with the spread of railways and it was soon realised that this was the best available means to conduct the safe operation of railways. The telegraph enabled the railways to adopt the 'block' system of signalling that was much safer than the rather haphazard 'time-interval' system. The essence of the block system was to eliminate the chance of collision by ensuring that only one train could be on a particular stretch of line between two stations (or signal boxes) at any one time. Such assurance could not be achieved with the time-interval system of working. The use of the electric telegraph meant that positive information about the whereabouts of trains could be communicated between adjacent points of control thus ensuring that only one train could occupy a particular block section at any one time. This fundamental concept is still an essential part of railway operation today.

The telegraph reached Wells in 1860 and from then it was possible for the general public to send and receive telegrams using the railway telegraph many years before the national telegraphic and telephone services came into being. Telegrams would be delivered by messenger from the receiving end. At the time this must have been a greater leap in information technology than the expansion in the use of e-mail and public use of the Internet one hundred and thirty years later. The arrival of the railway also meant that deliveries of the Royal Mail and London newspapers were earlier than had previously been possible.

At a time when mass travel is part of everyday life it is difficult to appreciate the fact that prior to the coming of the railways the vast majority of people probably never travelled more than a few miles from their birthplace. In fact, it was the railways that gave rise to the phenomenon of mass travel in the first place. So it would have been that, immediately prior to the construction of the Cheddar Valley and the East Somerset lines, many of the local population would have never seen a train even though the main lines that were not very many miles away had already been open for the best part of twenty years. The construction of railways in rural areas generated considerable interest and not all of it was favourable. For example, many of those in authority feared that easier access to travel for the masses would undermine their position and the Church hierarchy expressed fears that Sunday excursions would distract the population from their prescribed devotions. In spite of this the novelty of a faster system of transportation than had previously been possible led to great celebrations as the railway network expanded.

Once the advantages of being connected to the national railway network were understood they rapidly became part of the local culture. Pretty soon nearly every town and village had its Station Road, Railway Inn or Hotel, most of which survive to this day even in places where the railway itself is long gone. Once a railway had opened, local traders forgot any earlier misgivings they may have had and were quick to take advantage of improved communications. In the case of the Cheddar Valley line local newspapers were reporting within a few months of the line's opening that a monthly market had been established in Axbridge, and a horse and cattle fair in Cheddar as a direct result of the facilities offered there by the Bristol & Exeter Railway. Excursion traffic, both incoming and outgoing, was quickly established and remained part of the local railway scene until the rundown of the 1950s.

Over the years the railways became very much a part of the landscape through which they passed. To my mind this was almost a symbiotic relationship in which the railway enhanced the countryside as much as the countryside enhanced the railway. This was particularly true for the rural branch line with just a few trains each day in that those living or working close to the line would be able to tell the time of day by the passing of a train without needing to look at the clock. Also the routines of many country folk were dictated by the railway timetable with the need to get their produce on the first available train to a market in a far-away city whilst still fresh.

The motorways and trunk roads that have now replaced much of the railway network have no such relationship with the countryside through which they pass. They cannot in any way be said to enhance the countryside and for the most part detract from it. The closure of so many rural branch lines has been a great loss to the countryside but at least those that do remain, particularly the preserved ones that still operate steam-hauled trains, enable us to once again enjoy the wonderful atmosphere of the rural railway.

Before moving on I would like to clarify the various names used for the branch. In this work the term 'Yatton to Witham line' is generally used to refer to the entire line between the two main line junctions. In official railway publications, such as working timetables, the term 'Wells Branch' was normally used to refer to the entire line. In many other documents, such as the original plans and gradient diagrams pertaining to the original companies, they were referred to under their original names (ie. the East Somerset Railway, the Cheddar Valley & Yatton Railway or just The Cheddar Valley Railway).

Incidentally, the term Cheddar Valley Railway was frequently used to refer to the entire line between Yatton and Witham but this was historically incorrect as we have already seen. At the risk of being pedantic the name Cheddar Valley was also geographically incorrect. There is no geographical feature with the name 'Cheddar Valley' and the village of Cheddar was not really in a valley in any case! To the south of Cheddar lay a broad expanse of low lying land though which flowed two rivers. Firstly, there was the River Axe whose source was in the well known caves at Wookey Hole. The river flowed in a westerly direction and into the Bristol Channel at Uphill, a few miles south of Weston-super-Mare. The other river was the Cheddar Yeo (there are several Rivers Yeo in the area) whose source was in the Cheddar Gorge and cave system. The Cheddar Yeo flowed into the River Axe near Loxton, about five miles west of Cheddar. Five miles or so south of Cheddar the Wedmore ridge rose out of the moors but it did not compete with the Mendips for height, being no more than 190 feet above sea level (near Stone Allerton).

The line was affectionately known as 'The Strawberry Line'. The southern slopes of the Mendips around Draycott and Cheddar with its well drained soil and relatively mild climate provided ideal conditions for the growing of strawberries and vast quantities were dispatched by rail from the local stations during the growing season. Now to examine the origins of the North Somerset railway network and the Yatton to Witham line in particular.

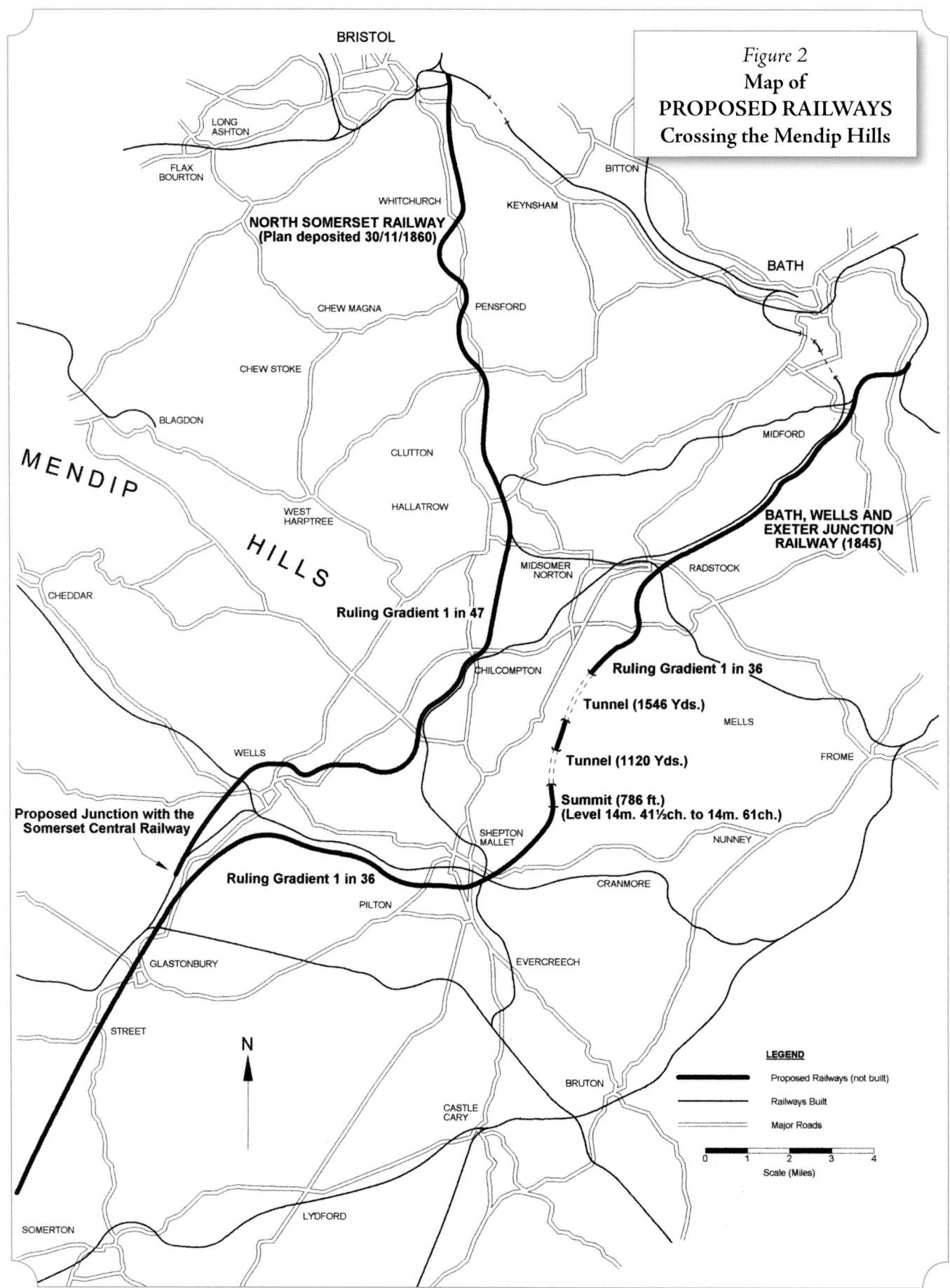

Chapter One

ORIGINS

Before the Coming of the Railway

As with many other parts of the West Country the railway map of Central Somerset was largely drawn by the gauge war. This was fought between the Great Western Railway and its allies who supported Brunel's broad gauge of 7ft 0¼in and the London & South Western Railway and the Midland Railway, both of which were built to the standard gauge of 4ft 8½in. The broad gauge was of course devised by Brunel himself but the origins of the standard gauge are obscure. Another significant influence in the development of the local railway network was that of geography. To the south of a line drawn roughly between Wells and Weston-super-Mare lies a vast area of low lying land, generally known as the Somerset Levels, that extends well into the south of the county. Much of this area is below the high water mark in the Bristol Channel and, despite several centuries of drainage work, flooding is still common even in the twenty-first century.

Immediately to the north of the Levels stands the steep limestone escarpment of the Mendip Hills that rise to over 1,000 feet above sea level in a number of places. Further north lies an area of undulating hill country cut by a number of deep and wide valleys until eventually the Avon Valley is reached. This marked the northern boundary of the pre-1971 county of Somerset and along it ran the lines of communication between Bristol and London. Before the coming of the railways these consisted of the turnpike road (now the A4) and river itself that gave access to the Kennett and Avon Canal at Bath. Within a very few years of the opening of the Great Western Railway it was realised that the high ground south of the Avon Valley would provide a challenge to any attempt to engineer a railway into central Somerset.

During the period of railway construction in central Somerset Wells had a population of about 7,500. The population today is still less than 10,000 making it the smallest city in England. Even so, Wells was always the focal point of both the Cheddar Valley and East Somerset lines and was, in fact, served by a third branch that was also the first to open and the first to close. This was the Somerset & Dorset branch from Glastonbury originally constructed by the Somerset Central Railway. The result of this was that prior to 1878 Wells had three separate railway stations owned by different companies all within a few hundred yards of one another. The Somerset Central and East Somerset stations in fact faced one another on either side of Priory Road, the main road from Wells to Glastonbury. Even up until nationalisation in 1948 the railways of Wells were still the concern of three out of the four groups, with the Yatton-Wells-Witham line being part of the Great Western and the Somerset & Dorset branch being jointly owned by the LMS and Southern Railways. There can be few other small towns in the country which could boast being served by three out of the four groups. One other that springs to mind is Highbridge which is within 20 miles of Wells and was also served by the same railway companies. So it was that a visitor to Wells could see Derby-built locomotives alongside the products of Swindon Works, and London & South Western signals alongside those of the Great Western.

From the earliest days there were proposals to construct railways though North Somerset. In 1830 Isambard Kingdom Brunel set out a prospectus to construct a line from the proposed Great Western Railway at Bath to Exeter. This line would have passed through Wells, Glastonbury, Bridgwater and Taunton although these were probably not his main objective. The plans did not go far enough to show how he would have tackled the problem of getting over the Mendip Hills with a summit of over 800 feet above sea level. The most difficult section would have been the descent from the summit into Wells. No doubt the gradients and banks involved would have rivalled those of Brunel's later South Devon Railway between Newton Abbot and Plymouth. The need for gradients steeper than 1 in 40 seems to have been a distinct probability and who knows, had this line been constructed, this may have been the test-bed for the ill-fated atmospheric system of propulsion that was pioneered on the South Devon line.

During the height of the railway boom there were a number of schemes that never materialised. They included the London & Falmouth (The Direct Western Railway), the London, Devizes & Bridgwater Railway, the Bath, Wells & Exeter Railway, the Somersetshire Railway, the Bristol, Wells & Poole Railway, the Somerset Midland Railway, the Bristol & English Channel Direct Railway (Watchet to Bridport), the Bristol & English Channels Connection Railway (Bridgwater to Lyme Regis) and the South Midland Union Railway. Looking back from the twenty-first century we can only hazard a guess as to how much speculative capital was sunk into these abortive schemes. One thing that we can be sure of is that the only beneficiaries of these schemes were the lawyers, surveyors and also, no doubt, the promoters, many of whom were unscrupulous.

Of these, the planned Bath, Wells & Exeter scheme *(Figure 2)* is particularly interesting if only for the fact that a copy of the deposited plans of 1845 exist in the Somerset County Record Office in Taunton. Leaving the Avon Valley north of Limpley Stoke, the line would have reached Radstock via Midford and Wellow, more or less along the course of the later Cam Valley and Somerset & Dorset Bath Extension lines. Passing to the east and south of Radstock the line would have climbed on a ruling gradient of 1 in 36 to reach the summit of 786 feet above sea level somewhere near Stoke St. Michael. The ascent included tunnels of 1,546 and 1,120yds that would only add to the difficulties of working the line. From the summit an equally precipitous descent would have taken the line east of Shepton

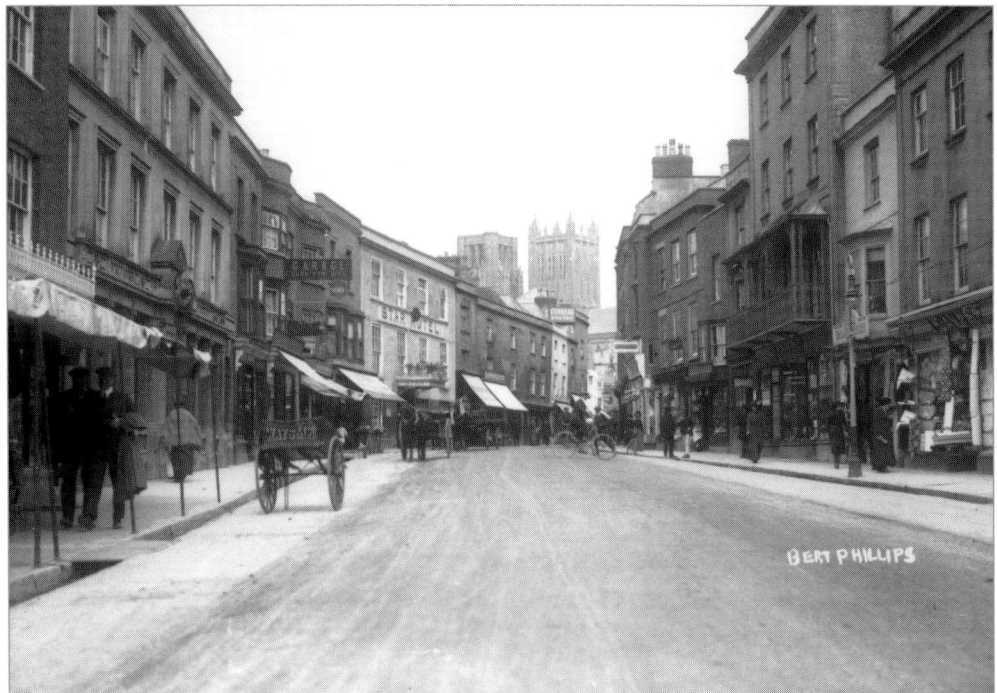

Plate 2 - Wells High Street, probably c.1906, nearly 50 years after the arrival of the railway in the city. The High Street leads to the market square with its gated entrance to the cathedral green.
Wells and Mendip Museum

Because of the high ground to the south of Bristol that has already been described, the only practical route from Bristol to Taunton and Exeter was along the fairly narrow coastal plain that lies to the north-west of the main rampart of the Mendip Hills and the Bristol Channel. This area is known as the Somerset Northmarsh and is generally low lying, just a few feet above sea level. Minimal earthworks were required for this line apart from the cutting and short tunnel between Long Ashton and Flax Bourton, just west of Bristol, and the deep cutting at Uphill, south of Weston-super-Mare, where a western arm of the Mendip Hills reaches the sea.

The railway at the other end of what was to become the Wells branch had a somewhat more protracted beginning. The Wilts, Somerset & Weymouth Railway was authorised in 1845 as a broad gauge line leaving the Great Western main line at Thingley Junction, a few miles on the Bath side of Chippenham. The construction of this railway was beset with problems. Delays caused firstly by the adverse reaction to the Railway Mania of 1845 and the subsequent onset of financial depression, meant that by 1848 only 14 miles from Thingley Junction to Westbury (Wilts) had been completed and were ready for opening. Over one hundred miles of authorised railway remained unopened, and incomplete earthworks abounded along the authorised routes from the junction at Westbury towards Weymouth and Salisbury.

This was the situation that endured until the Wilts, Somerset & Weymouth was taken over by the Great Western in 1850. Later that year the single line was extended and opened as far as Frome. Further progress was halted again because the financial resources of the Great Western itself had become somewhat strained. Legal proceedings were taken in order to compel the Great Western to complete all of the lines authorised under the original Act, but these only succeeded in forcing the construction of the Bradford-on-Avon to Bathampton section. Eventually the Great Western saw that the Yeovil area was under threat by the westward extension of the standard gauge from Salisbury by the nominally independent Salisbury & Yeovil Railway which, in reality, was under the wing of one of the Great Western's great rivals, the London & South Western Railway. Powers were renewed in 1854 to complete all of the lines originally authorised in the 1845 Act and the single line was extended to Yeovil in 1856.

Mallet and then to the south of the future Wells Extension of the East Somerset Railway. Then turning south of Wells the line would have passed Glastonbury, Street and Somerton on its way to Exeter.

Another line that was never built did make it as far as an application to Parliament for authority to construct but failed to get any further due to an inability to raise sufficient capital. This was the South Wales & Southampton Railway of 1854. The line would have left the Bristol & Exeter Railway at Bleadon, near Weston-super-Mare, and run along the southern slopes of the Mendips to Wells, much along the line of the later Cheddar Valley & Yatton Railway. From Wells the line would have run through North Wootton, Pilton, Evercreech, Bruton and Wincanton to join the Salisbury & Yeovil at Buckhorn Weston on the eastern side of Blackmore Vale near Gillingham. It seems that the planning of this line probably did not discuss the gauge to which it should be built. This would have required some thought as the scheme would have linked a broad gauge line at one end with a standard gauge line at the other.

The Railway reaches Somerset

The first railway actually to be constructed in Somerset was the Great Western Railway, whose broad gauge main line was opened from London to Bristol in 1841. Further developments in this area followed rapidly. The Bristol & Exeter Railway, like the Great Western, was also built to the broad gauge and opened from Bristol to Bridgwater in 1841, was extended to Taunton in 1842 and finally reached Exeter in 1844. The Great Western had a considerable interest in the Bristol & Exeter, not least because it would become an important source of traffic. As a result, the Bristol & Exeter was worked by the Great Western from the outset. Once well established, the Bristol & Exeter wished to exert some degree of independence and took over working its own line in 1849.

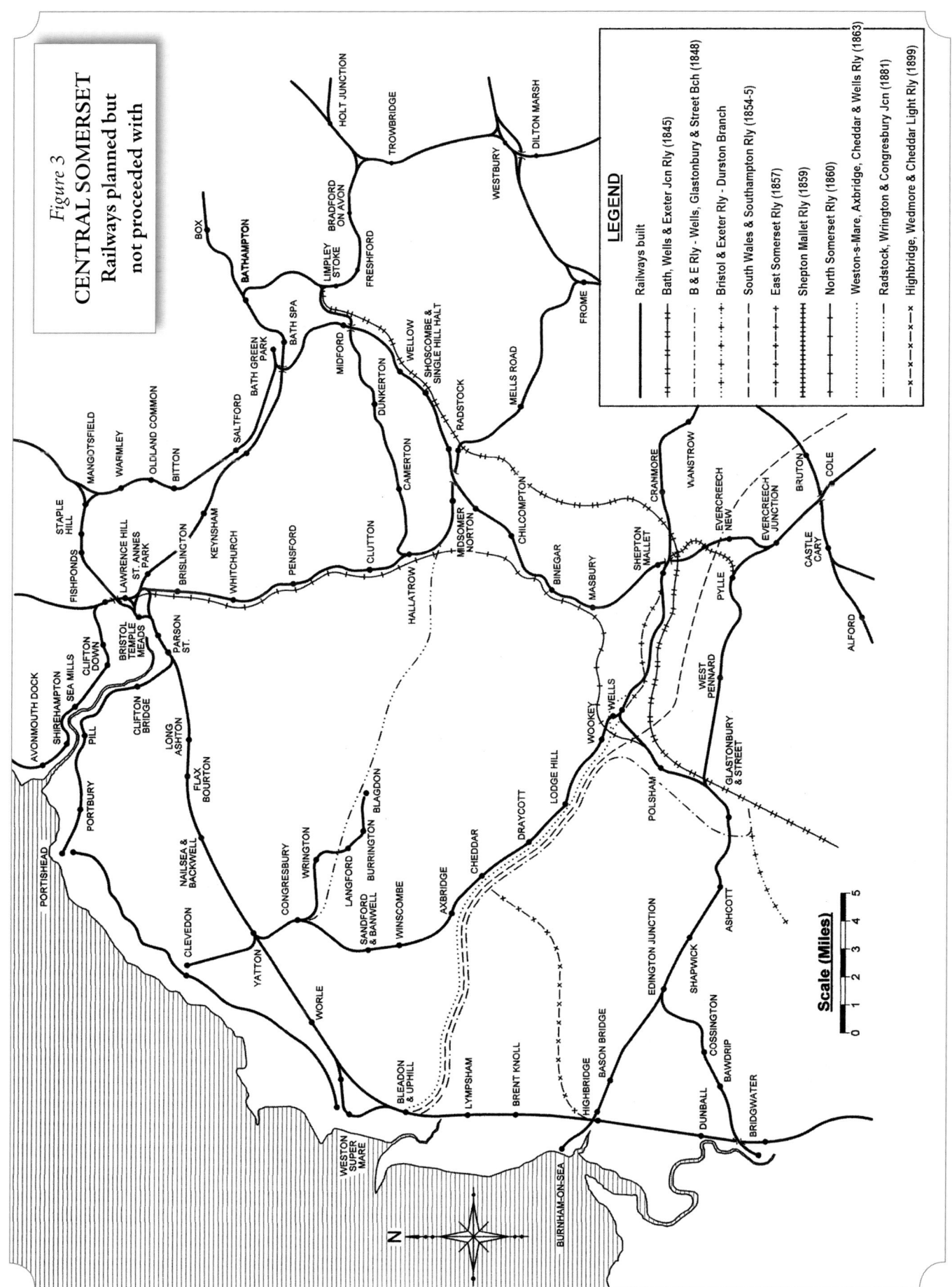

Figure 3 CENTRAL SOMERSET Railways planned but not proceeded with

Chapter Two

THE SOMERSET CENTRAL RAILWAY

Highbridge to Glastonbury and Extension to Wells

In the early 1850s central Somerset still had no railway communication and centres of population like Wells, Shepton Mallet and Glastonbury were well off the railway map. It was not until 1854 that the first railway ventured into this area. This was the broad gauge Somerset Central Railway that bravely crossed twelve miles of the Somerset Levels between Highbridge, on the Bristol & Exeter Railway, and Glastonbury. This railway was sponsored by local business interests including James and Cyrus Clark whose family, although starting off as tanners making leather, are best remembered for shoe manufacturing in the area. The line followed the course of the earlier Glastonbury Canal and was worked by the Bristol & Exeter from the outset. The latter company provided locomotives and rolling stock as well as operating the trains themselves. In return it paid a dividend to the Somerset Central shareholders of 4% of capital value. Interestingly at this time, it had only been five years since the Bristol & Exeter had taken over the running of its own railway from the Great Western. No doubt the working of the Somerset Central, which was unlikely to generate a good return on expenditure, must have put some strain on the resources of the Bristol & Exeter. On the other hand, whilst the arrangement was still in force the Somerset Central was unlikely to fall into the hands of a competitor who would then have gained a foothold in the heart of Bristol & Exeter territory.

The Somerset Central was an ambitious concern that had plans for expansion virtually from the day it opened. Initially the plan was to build an extension via Wells and Shepton Mallet to reach the Wilts, Somerset & Weymouth at Frome. Powers were obtained for the Wells extension by an Act of 30th July 1855. The cost of this line was estimated to be £35,000. The Act also included powers to extend the other end of the line from Highbridge to Burnham-on-Sea. The company soon had other ideas because almost immediately it began to consider a less expensive route that would meet the Wilts, Somerset & Weymouth near Bruton instead. A special meeting of Somerset Central shareholders was held in October 1855, at which it was suggested that the Bruton line would cost £8,000 per mile to construct as opposed to £15,000 per mile for the Frome line with its heavy earthworks and severe gradients.

The Somerset Central obtained an Act on 21st July 1856 to extend its broad gauge line from Glastonbury to a junction with the Wilts, Somerset & Weymouth at Cole, about one mile south-west of Bruton. Powers under this Act permitted the Somerset Central to raise additional capital of £100,000 plus a further £33,000 in loans in order to pay for the construction of the extension. This scheme was supported by the Bristol & Exeter Railway, as it saw this line as a way to further its own interests. The outcome of this was that the Somerset Central reached Wells in 1859 by a dead-end branch instead of the originally planned through route. In the end, even this was only built under pressure from the Somerset Central shareholders representing the city plus the threat imposed by the embryonic East Somerset Railway. The formal opening of the line took place on 3rd March 1859 and was accompanied by the usual festivities. The initial service worked by the Bristol & Exeter consisted of seven trains daily from Highbridge to Wells and six in the opposite direction. There was also a Sunday service of two trains each way.

Enter the Somerset & Dorset Railway

The Somerset Central had a change of heart, the full intentions of which became clear in its Bruton Extension Act of 1861. The plan was to build the extension to the standard gauge and convert the line from Wells to Highbridge to mixed gauge by adding a third rail. The Somerset Central had set its sights on meeting up with the Cole to Templecombe extension of the Dorset Central, whose original standard gauge line from the London & South Western at Wimborne, near Poole, had opened to Blandford Forum in 1860. This would therefore establish a standard gauge route from the South Coast to the Bristol Channel once the missing link between Templecombe and Blandford Forum was completed. The originally planned connection with the Wilts, Somerset & Weymouth was also to be abandoned under this proposal. The Bristol & Exeter retaliated to this proposed standard gauge invasion deep into its territory by insisting that the Bruton extension should be constructed as a mixed gauge line and that a connection should be established with the Wilts, Somerset & Weymouth line as was orginally planned. Following this the Bristol & Exeter gave notice that it would not renew its lease of the Somerset Central that was due to expire on 28th August 1861. At that time the Somerset Central was experiencing financial difficulties and so the Bristol & Exeter continued to hire locomotives and rolling stock for a few more months until the former company managed to sort itself out. No doubt the Bristol & Exeter thought that this magnanimous gesture might ensure the continued existence of the broad gauge on the Somerset Central, at least for the time being. The Somerset Central then laid a third rail between Burnham and Wells so that it could run standard gauge trains.

The Somerset Central and Dorset Central railways amalgamated in 1862 to form the Somerset & Dorset Railway. Approval of the shareholders was obtained at a meeting on 9th May and an Act was drawn up that received Royal Assent on 7th August. The effective date of amalgamation was 1st September 1862. The insistences of the Bristol & Exeter were short-lived as the third rail was removed from the system by about 1870

Plate 3 - A 1928 or later view of Wells Priory Road station, originally the terminus of the Somerset Central Railway branch from Glastonbury, opened in 1859. The carriage is an auto-train driving trailer converted from a non-corridor bogie third. *Lens of Sutton Association*

making it a purely standard gauge line. The connection with the Wilts, Somerset & Weymouth where the two lines crossed at Cole was certainly never used, even if it was ever completed in the first place, although work on it was certainly started. The earthworks of this abortive connection were still plainly visible in the 1960s.

The missing link between Templecombe and Blandford Forum finally opened on 31st August 1863 and the Somerset & Dorset soon began to advertise itself as a coast to coast route. In fact, the company was actively seeking to become the link in a through service between Northern France and South Wales. A short-lived passenger steamer service was established by a nominally independent company between Poole and Cherbourg in the mid-1860s. A somewhat longer lived service was also established between Burnham and Cardiff whilst cargo traffic to Highbridge Wharf lasted until the 1930s. Perhaps some of the difficulties the company experienced with its shipping enterprise caused it to set its sights further afield on the English side of the Bristol Channel in order to tap new sources of traffic. Earlier expectations that the Bristol & Exeter would lay a third rail between Highbridge and Bristol in return for insisting that the Somerset Central lay it on the Bruton Extension came to nothing. Access to Bristol would give the Somerset & Dorset a direct connection with the Midland Railway, whose standard gauge route to the midlands and the north would provide the former company with much needed traffic. In the event the line between Bristol and Highbridge did become mixed gauge, but that was on 1st June 1875, by which time it was of no use to the Somerset & Dorset.

A LINE ACROSS THE MENDIP HILLS

The Somerset & Dorset now found itself in the position of having to promote its own line to Bristol if it wished to attract traffic from that direction. The geographical difficulties of constructing a direct line north from Wells to Bristol have already been outlined. Whilst it would have been possible to construct such a line, it would not have been without considerable cost brought about by the civil engineering work required. Once constructed, it would have been a difficult line to operate because of severe gradients. As a result, any such line would have been totally uneconomic. The Bristol & Exeter found a suitable gap at Uphill, only a mile or so inland from the Bristol Channel. There was another suitable gap at Shute Shelve just west of Axbridge through which the Bristol to Bridgwater turnpike (now the A38) already passed.

Relations between the Bristol & Exeter and the Somerset & Dorset had become sour, for it seems that the former company revived plans to build a line for which it had received the sanction of Parliament as far back as 1848. The Bristol & Exeter Railway Act that included this line, amongst others, received Royal Assent on 22nd July of that year and was known as 'The Branch from Bleadon to Wells, Glastonbury and Street'. The line was to have left the main Bristol to Taunton line south of Uphill Cutting and run in a more or less easterly direction to Axbridge, Cheddar and Wells and then south to Glastonbury and Street where it was planned to join up with another branch from Durston, near Taunton. Capital was to have been £230,000 and seven years were allowed for completion.

In response to the Bristol & Exeter proposals, the Somerset & Dorset promoted a line from Wells to Yatton via Shute Shelve in 1863. Parliamentary powers to construct this railway were obtained by the Somerset & Dorset Railway under the Cheddar Valley & Yatton Railway Act (27 & 28 Vic., Cap. clxxxi) of 14th July 1864. This Act authorised the construction of three railways; Railway No.1 from the existing Somerset & Dorset station in Wells to a point near Tucker Street, where it made an end on junction with Railway No.3 that continued to Yatton. Railway No.2 formed the third side of the triangle between Tucker Street and a point on the existing Somerset & Dorset line south of the Somerset & Dorset engine shed. This arrangement would enable trains to travel directly from Glastonbury to Yatton without the need to reverse at the Somerset & Dorset station in Wells. Five years were allowed for the completion of the line and authorised capital was £170,000 with borrowing powers of £56,000. A contemporary newspaper report stated that the authorised capital for earthworks and purchase of land, but not including permanent way or buildings, was £100,000.

The two parties entered into negotiations and under the resulting agreement dated 27th May 1864, the Bristol & Exeter was authorised to subscribe up to £100,000 of the share capital within six months. Furthermore, if the Bristol & Exeter decided within that period that it wished to subscribe more than £100,000 up to an amount equal to the total authorised capital, then it was obliged to state its intention and both parties were to reach an agreement on the matter. In other words, the way was now open for the powers to build the Cheddar Valley & Yatton Railway to be transferred from the Somerset & Dorset to the Bristol & Exeter Company.

The Bristol & Exeter exercised its rights under the agreement and powers to construct the Cheddar Valley & Yatton Railway were transferred to the company under Section 140 of the Bristol and Exeter Railway Additional Powers Act (28 Vic., Cap. xcvii) of 19th June 1865. The Act authorised the line to be built to the broad gauge. Under the Articles of Agreement dated 6th March 1865, attached to the Act, the Bristol & Exeter abandoned the proposed line from Uphill and agreed not to encroach further into Somerset & Dorset territory. Interestingly, under a clause of the Act, the Bristol & Exeter had the option to make either only one or both of the junctions with the Somerset & Dorset that were authorised by the original 1864 Act as Railway Nos.1 and 2. In fact Railway No.2 was never constructed, its usefulness ceasing once the Cheddar Valley & Yatton had been taken over. Even Railway No.1 did not materialise for many years, a story which will be related later.

The Act also authorised the construction of a broad gauge connection with the East Somerset Railway at Wells. The Bristol & Exeter company would have use of the Somerset & Dorset station at Wells but with their own booking facilities. For this they would be liable to pay rent of £400 per annum to the Somerset & Dorset.

Interestingly, the triangular junction at Wells appeared on a contemporary one-inch Ordnance Survey map (*Figure 4*, sheet number XIX). The original engraving for this map was dated 1817 and the map is annotated as being '*updated for railways to October 1890*'. It seems that the amendments were drawn from parliamentary plans rather than from a survey of what had actually been constructed. Another section of line that was enacted but never completed is also shown on the map. This was the connection between the Somerset & Dorset and the Great Western at Cole, to which reference has already been made.

Figure 4 - This Ordnance Survey map, originally of 1817 but '*updated for railways to October 1890*', shows a non-existent triangular junction at Wells. Presumably the cartographer relied on parliamentary plans rather than a survey of actual construction.   *Crown copyright reserved*

THE EAST SOMERSET AND CHEDDAR VALLEY RAILWAYS

Plate 4 - The junction just to the west of Wells Priory Road station in March 1932. On the right, the Great Western train - the engine number is not quite legible - has recently departed the GWR's Tucker Street station and is running over the junction with the Somerset & Dorset line. The S&D train, having arrived some time before and completed its station duties, has been shunted into a siding to allow the GW train to run through the S&D station. GW trains did not stop at Priory Road before 1934. *Brunel University, Clinker collection*

At that time the ambitions of the Somerset & Dorset had caused it to get into severe financial difficulty, the company being in receivership between 1866 and 1870.

In 1870 the Midland Railway opened a branch to Bath that made a junction with that company's existing line from Bristol to Gloucester at Mangotsfield, a few miles north-east of Bristol. Although the line to Yatton had been lost to the Somerset & Dorset, it had not been diverted from its goal of expanding in that general direction. The fact that the Midland Railway had reached Bath caused it to set its sights in that direction. To the east of Wells the hills are generally lower and rise less abruptly from the lowlands making a north-south rail link a more practical proposition. The Somerset & Dorset obtained its Bath Extension Act in 1871. Construction proceeded rapidly and the line was opened from Evercreech Junction to Bath Junction in 1874. With twelve viaducts, four tunnels, a summit at 810 feet above sea level and many miles of 1 in 50, this was massive undertaking for a relatively small company. As a result the finances of the company were so strained following the completion of the Bath Extension that the company made approaches to neighbouring railways with the view to selling out to a larger concern.

The first approach was made to the Great Western who immediately turned the idea down flat. Following that a secret meeting was arranged with the London & South Western Railway at Waterloo who suggested an approach to the Midland. Finally, an agreement was reached with the Midland and London & South Western Railways to lease the entire line for a term of 999 years as both larger companies could see a benefit in this arrangement for their own ends. The lease was confirmed by an Act of 13th July 1876. The line then took on the familiar title of the Somerset & Dorset Joint Railway and was well known for the fact that it retained much of its own identity until closure. After losing the Wells to Yatton line to the Bristol & Exeter, the Somerset & Dorset played no further part in the development of the Cheddar Valley and East Somerset Railways.

Another railway that invaded North Somerset at this time was the Bristol & North Somerset, whose line from Bristol to Radstock was opened in 1873. Of the many schemes promoted to run south from Bristol into Somerset, this was the only one actually to be constructed. Most, if not all, of the others could never have been viable. This was due, at least partly, to the way in which they intended to cross the Mendips into the lowlands of mid-Somerset, the difficulties of which have already been described. As an example, one proposal that has come to light was the North Somerset Railway of 1860 *(Figure 2)* whose plans were deposited on 30th November of that year. It would have taken the route of the Bristol & North Somerset line as built as far as Farrington Gurney. From there it would have continued south towards Morewood, where it would have followed the course of the Somerset & Dorset Bath Extension as far as Masbury. There would then have been a steep descent westwards along the Mendip escarpment though East Horrington and to the north of Wells. Turning south between Wells and Wookey the line would have made a junction with the Somerset Central Railway's Wells extension near Coxley. Needless to say, the ruling gradient was steep at 1 in 47. In the unlikely event that this railway had been built, the subsequent history of the railways in Wells could have been entirely different. As we shall see, the Bristol & North Somerset later became part of the route taken by the circular Bristol to Bristol local passenger services that ran via the Yatton to Witham line.

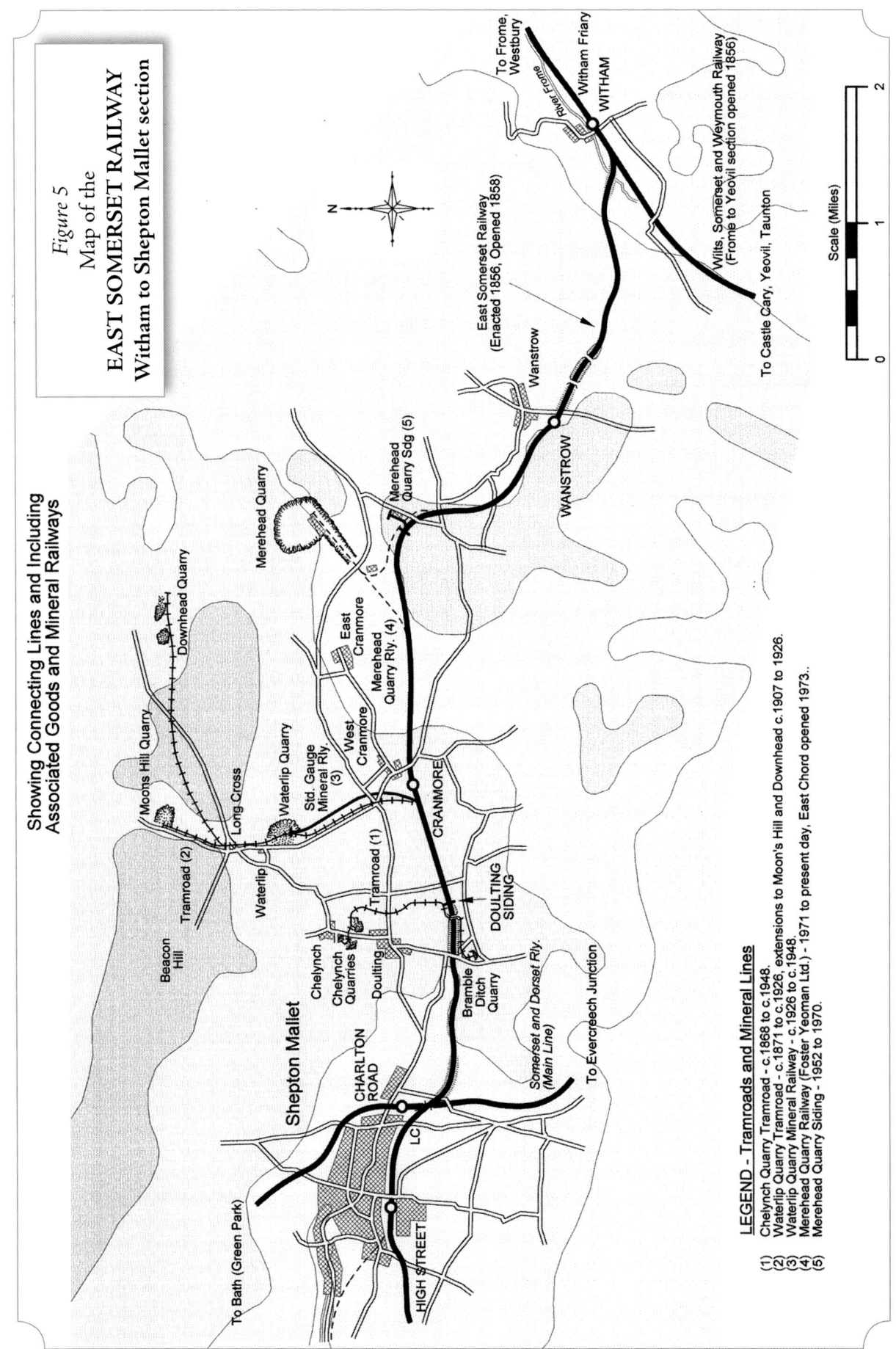

Chapter Three

THE EAST SOMERSET RAILWAY

WITHAM TO SHEPTON MALLET

The origins of the East Somerset Railway date back to 1855 when the Somerset Central abandoned its plans to extend from Wells to Frome in favour of the Bruton Extension and the link with the Dorset Central. A newspaper article in the *Taunton Courier* of 8th August 1855 was critical of the change of mind by the Somerset Central and advocated the construction of what became the East Somerset Railway. Another article in the same edition discussed the various proposals for railways to serve Wells including the Somerset Central and the East Somerset. It went on to conclude that a route through Wells would be the most advantageous and suggested that the two companies unite in their efforts to construct the line. Goods traffic would be generated by the cheese industry in Wells, the Shepton Mallet corn market, Doulting stone quarries and the breweries at Oakhill, Charlton (Shepton Mallet) and Holcombe. The asylum and assize courts in Wells and tourists to the Cathedral would also contribute to the passenger traffic at Wells.

A meeting took place in Shepton Mallet on 29th September that led to the formation of the East Somerset Railway Company. A further meeting took place at the assembly rooms in the George Hotel at Frome on 27th October with Lord Dungarvon in the chair at which alternative routes for the proposed railway were discussed. The attendees of the meeting resolved to support the railway and look into the various alternative routes discussed, including one that joined the proposed North Somerset Railway near Mells. The alternative routes were surveyed by I. K. Brunel and the one eventually decided upon ran from Shepton Mallet to a junction on the Wilts, Somerset & Weymouth at Witham, a few miles south-west of Frome. This route was chosen over a more direct route to Frome on the grounds of cost. The East Somerset Railway Act (19 Vic., Cap. xvi) received Royal Assent on 5th June 1856.

Although it was the company's intention to provide rail communication between Witham and Wells, it was felt expedient at this time to obtain authorisation for the construction of the line from Witham to Shepton Mallet. The Act allowed capital of £75,000 to be raised in £10 shares and provided for additional borrowing powers of £25,000. The line was to be built to Brunel's broad gauge. The Act stated the names of eight directors: The Viscount Dungarvon, The Hon. Henry Thynne, Edward Charles Chetham Strode, John Moore Paget, James Curtis Somerville, Edmund Hugh Clerk, John Wason and William Chester Berryman the Younger.

Deposited plans of 1855 included an amendment dated March 1856 showing a deviation of the line where it passed through parts of the estate of Sir Edward Strode Knight in the parish of West Cranmore, the planned deviation being made at the request of the landowner. The Act authorised the company to construct level crossings over public roads at Witham and Shepton Mallet (Kilver Street) but included the usual clause whereby the Board of Trade retained the right to require bridges to be constructed instead as it felt necessary. Four years were to be allowed for the construction of the line. The junction at Witham was to be laid out in an 'approved manner' and to the satisfaction of the engineer of the Great Western Railway. Under the Act the Great Western was granted running powers over the East Somerset, initially for a period of ten years, with the option to extend them after that period as required. In the event, the line was worked by the Great Western from the opening, the arrangement being formalised by an agreement between the two companies dated 21st June 1861.

Rowland Brotherhood of Chippenham signed the contract to build the line on 6th February 1857. The price was agreed at £64,500. The work was planned to start in early April 1857 and was due to take eighteen months to complete. The main problem encountered during construction seems to be that of delay caused by landowners haggling over the price of land. The construction of the line involved a considerable amount of earthworks, most notably the deep rock cutting either side of the summit south of Doulting. The total amount of material excavated was in the order of 300,000 cubic yards. Nevertheless the railway was complete by the autumn of 1858 and ready for inspection by the Board of Trade. Colonel Yolland was generally satisfied with the works but indicated that there were a number of items that needed attention. He required distant signals to be erected at Witham and Shepton Mallet, a crossing keeper's lodge at Kilver Street (as was required by the original Act) and a platform ramp at Shepton Mallet.

Apart from these his main concern was over a lack of any undertaking as to how the line was to be worked. As both the East Somerset and the Wilts, Somerset & Weymouth were only single track, he was concerned about potential hazards in operation at Witham. If the East Somerset was to be worked as a separate concern then a turntable would be required at Witham in addition to the one already at Shepton Mallet that would otherwise be useless. If trains were to work through to Frome then the turntable there would be sufficient. With no undertaking as to how the line was to be worked, combined with his other requirements, permission to open was refused.

In response to this the East Somerset signed an undertaking that the line would only be operated by tank engines and that only one engine would be on the line at any one time. The Board of Trade then consented to the opening that finally took place on Tuesday, 9th November 1858, although Colonel Yolland continued to argue the case for a turntable at Witham. In his view even tank engines worked better running forwards than backwards. The first train to arrive at Shepton Mallet was hauled by a 4-4-0 saddle tank by the name of *Homer* (Great Western

Plate 5 - Wanstrow station, opened in January 1860 and maybe largely in its original state? The platform is still very short - it was subsequently extended as will be seen in later illustrations - but here it can be barely more than a carriage-length. Bridge rail and transoms form the basis of the possibly broad gauge trackwork, although the original print does not extend far enough to the right to establish the track gauge. The GWR trespass sign is supported by bridge rail. There is evidence of longitudinal cracking of the building wall about five courses of stonework above the 'Pears' advertisement; perhaps some settlement had occurred.
John Alsop collection

broad gauge locomotives were not yet numbered) which was driven by R. J. Ward, the company's engineer. The locomotive was constructed as a member of the 'Bogie' or 'Corsair' Class in August 1854. Although designed by Gooch this particular member was built by R. & W. Hawthorn. It remained in service until August 1873 when its career was terminated by 'a mishap' after which it was officially withdrawn in December of that year. By this date, largely due to the conversion of the South Wales Railway, the Great Western had a surplus of broad gauge motive power. It seems that *Homer* spent its whole working life in the Bristol area.

There was also some further controversy over the Kilver Street level crossing before the line opened for traffic. The Turnpike Trustees wished to replace the level crossing by a bridge. Colonel Yolland considered that a bridge was impractical and that there was nothing wrong with the level crossing. A public meeting was held opposing the bridge plan on 11th August 1858, at which the general view was that it would impede traffic. The approach to the crossing from the crossroads at Charlton Road was already fairly steep and the additional gradient on the approach to the proposed bridge would have indeed been harzardous to traffic. In the event the bridge was not built and the level crossing remained until the closure of the railway.

At 10.00am on the opening day a procession that included members of the Ancient Order of Foresters was made around the town. Alms were distributed to the poor in the Market Place. That evening a celebratory dinner was held at the George Hotel and was presided over by Arthur C. Phipps, Esq., the Chairman of the railway, Lord Bath, and four directors of the railway, J. M. Paget, J. G. Somerville, Edward Clarke and T. S. Foxwell were also present, as was the contractor Rowland Brotherhood, the company's engineer Mr. R. J. Ward and the East Somerset Railway Company Secretary, Mr. G. M. Mackay.

Connection with Wells was provided by a horse bus that took 35 minutes to complete the journey. The opening of the East Somerset Railway caused the cessation of the last Royal Mail coach out of Bath that had run to Wells via Shepton Mallet.

The original permanent way was laid with 61½lb/yd bridge rail in lengths of about 24 feet on longitudinal sleepers with transoms every eleven feet. Maintenance of the permanent way was carried out by Brotherhood for the first year after opening for a price of £900, his original asking price being £1,011.11s.3d. After this the permanent way was maintained by the Great Western. The final cost of construction of the railway was £85,258, a sum that included £2,422 for parliamentary expenses, £4,695 for legal and professional expenses and £15,289 for land and compensation. The main contract had accounted for £59,020, which left £5,480 over from the original contract.

A station was opened at Wanstrow in 1860. Because the railway company could not afford to construct it, the money was raised from the local inhabitants. Even so, it was no more than a halt and remained unstaffed until 1909.

The initial service consisted of five trains each way daily, 25 minutes being allowed for the journey between Witham and

Shepton Mallet. The line did not enjoy this level of service for very long because, within a few weeks on 1st December, the service was cut back to four trains a day each way. There was another alteration to the timetable in February 1859 when the 11.40am down train from Witham was retimed to start at 1.20pm. With the arrival time at Shepton Mallet now being 1.45pm and the departure time of the return working to Witham being 1.55pm there was no time available for the locomotive to carry out any shunting work. As a consequence a horse was hired at an additional expense of £6 per month to carry out the prescribed shunting duties. When Wanstrow station opened in January 1860 it was only served by the first up and last down trains, which was only convenient for passengers who wished to travel to Witham or Frome. Friday was market day in Shepton Mallet and so the first down and last up trains called at Wanstrow on Fridays for the convenience of passengers wishing to go to the market. The overall timings of these trains remained unaltered in spite of the additional stop.

THE WELLS EXTENSION

Meanwhile, having been spurned by the Somerset Central, the citizens of Wells were anxious to promote an extension of the East Somerset to their city as soon as possible. The East Somerset directors wished to gauge the level of support and required the subscription of £12,500 before proceeding. By October 1856, the subscription list amounted to £12,090 and the East Somerset agreed to go ahead. The route was surveyed by Brunel and plans were deposited in November 1856. There was also an added bonus for Brunel when, during the survey, he discovered that the stone of Dulcote Hill was very suitable for railway track ballast. A quarry was established at Dulcote Hill some years after the opening of the line and quarrying activity has continued down to the present day. The commencement and subsequent development of quarrying at Dulcote is taken up in a subsequent chapter.

The East Somerset Railway Extension to Wells Act (20 & 21 Vic., Cap. cv) received Royal Assent on 27th July 1857. The estimated cost of the extension was £50,000 and the Act permitted the raising of an additional £40,000 with borrowing powers of £13,300. The Act authorised the extension to be constructed to the same gauge as the already authorised line from Witham to Shepton Mallet. The fact that the Extension Act did not specify the actual gauge to be used, whereas the original East Somerset Act of 1856 did, could be interpreted as a growing feeling amongst the local railway promoters that the broad gauge might be abandoned within a few years, as indeed it was.

The Act also authorised the construction of two level crossings at Wells (Gate Lane and Priory Road) and a junction with the Somerset Central Railway at Wells to be made in agreement with that company *(see Figure 7)*. Three years were allowed for construction. The level crossing at Gate Lane was later closed by a further Act of Parliament.

After a meeting of the East Somerset Railway Board on 13th October 1858, a Prospectus for the Wells Extension was issued:

Plate 6 - An undated view of Cranmore station and its staff. The station was opened with the line on 9th November 1858 and was provided with just a single platform. The photographer is apparently the same as the one who recorded Wanstrow in *Plate 5*. *Neil Parkhouse collection*

Plate 7 - Shepton Mallet station, with staggered platforms, in the early 1900s with a down train heading towards Wells. The leading brake carriage is partially obscured by the vehicle - a horsebox? - in the loading dock, but the next three form part of a close-coupled 4-wheel set; certainly the coupling between them is closer than that between the brake and the first 4-wheel carriage, a 5-compartment third. The second 4-wheel carriage is a 4-compartment composite. A Great Western iron Mink in the down siding behind the far platform to the left of the picture has 25in high lettering in the style introduced in 1904. *Brunel University, Mowat collection*

'This important line of railway, (i.e. the line from Witham to Shepton Mallet) which, when completed will effect the desired junction between the Wilts, Somerset and Weymouth and the Bristol and Exeter lines will be opened for traffic between Witham Friary and Shepton Mallet in the course of the ensuing month.

The Somerset Central line between Highbridge, Glastonbury and Wells will also be open throughout for traffic about the close of the present year, leaving only the intervening five miles between Wells and Shepton Mallet to be made in order to complete this important chain of communication.

A sufficient amount of share capital to enable the Directors to apply to Parliament, was subscribed and an Act for the extension of the line from Shepton Mallet to Wells was obtained in 1857; and as the line is now complete to Shepton Mallet, they are anxious to proceed with the works on the extension. Before doing this, however, about £25,000 additional share capital is required in order for them to make suitable financial arrangements to meet the necessary outlay and committees have been formed in the towns of Wells and Shepton Mallet, to further this subscription.

The inhabitants of the district between Frome and Wells have already subscribed between £40,000 and £50,000; and the Committees feel assured that when the importance of completing this line is considered, traversing as it will the very centre of the County and forming a direct communication between the towns of Frome, Shepton Mallet, Wells, Glastonbury, Bridgwater and Taunton, the comparatively small amount now to be subscribed will be readily forthcoming.

The Committees therefore earnestly appeal to the Magistracy, Clergy, and the inhabitants generally of the City, for assistance in completing this line and in aid of local efforts; and they would call attention to greatest convenience that will be afforded to all persons whose public duties may call them to attend the Assizes Sessions, Diocesan and other meetings at Wells, and the general saving of great expense to the County by the cheaper transmission of witnesses, prisoners, etc. to the Assize Town.

The Committee have great pleasure in announcing that the Directors have themselves acted upon this view of the importance of the extension of this line to Wells, and at their last meeting upwards of £3,000 was subscribed in the furtherance of the object.

The benefits resulting from this line, moreover, will not be confined to the County of Somerset. A most influential Board of Provisional Directors (including the Marquis of Aylesbury, Lord Ernest Bruce and the Right Honourable T. H. S. Sotheron Estcourt M.P.) has been formed in Wiltshire, and an active canvas is now going on for the purpose of applying to Parliament in the next session for an Act to fill up the gap which now exists in Railway Companies between Hungerford and Devizes. A glance at the map will show that when this extension is completed, the East Somerset Railway will form a part of the shortest and most direct line of communication between the Metropolis and a large proportion of the West of England.'

(Somerset County Record Office; DD\SAS/C795/SE/20/51)

THE EAST SOMERSET AND CHEDDAR VALLEY RAILWAYS

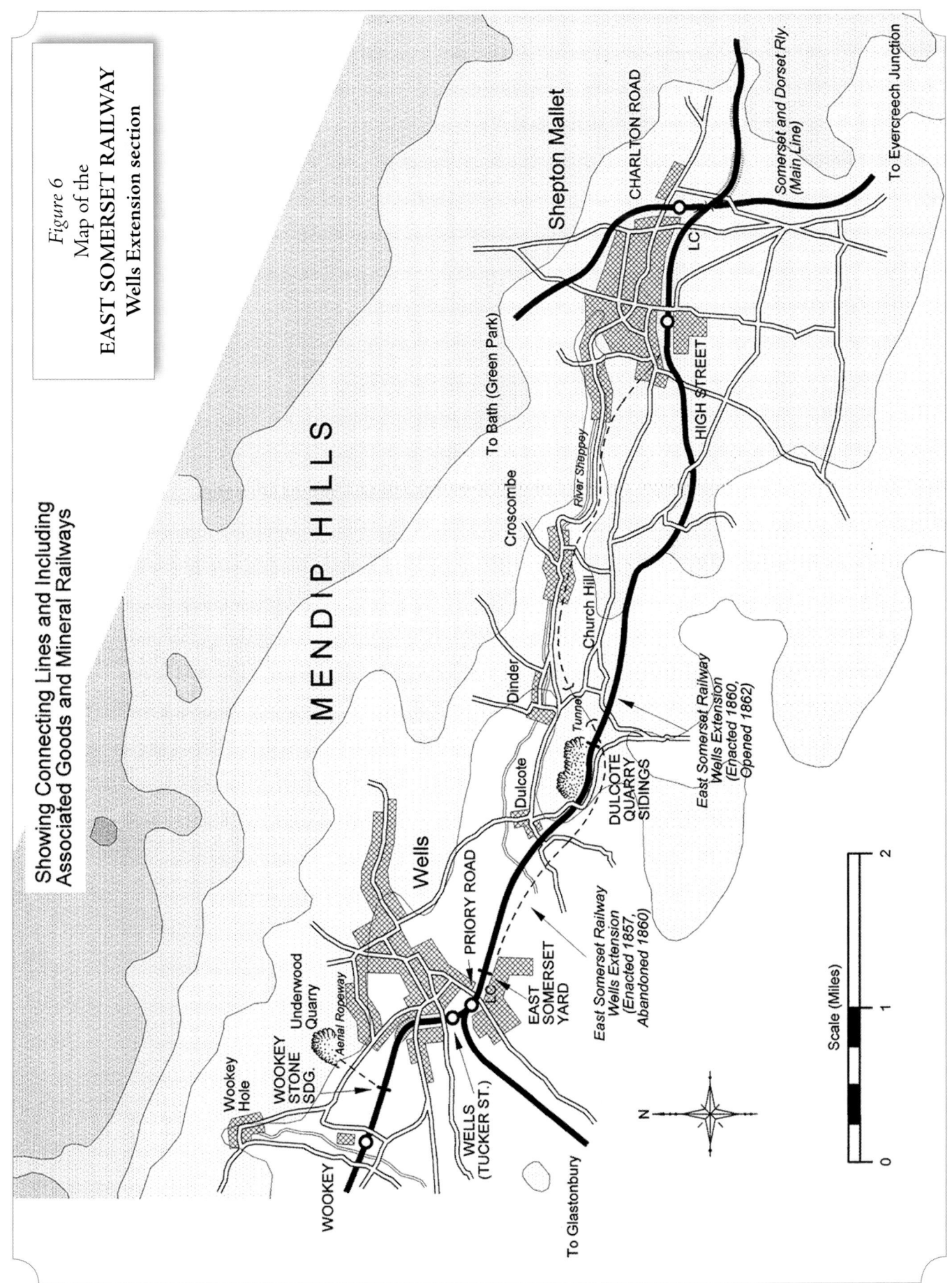

Figure 6
Map of the
EAST SOMERSET RAILWAY
Wells Extension section

Showing Connecting Lines and Including Associated Goods and Mineral Railways

The prospectus must be admired for its optimistic outlook and general pomposity! In November 1859 a letter inviting subscriptions was issued:

'I have to inform you that at a general meeting of the East Somerset Railway Company held at Shepton Mallet on the 28th September Last, it was unanimously resolved to issue five percent Preference Shares, to the amount of £55,000 (in shares of £10 each) for the purpose of completing the extension to Wells.

The Directors have expressed a willingness to take a large amount of these shares, and will be able to complete the work if from £15,000 to £20,000 can be raised from other sources.

You are no doubt fully aware that the making of this portion of line will complete the Railway communication through the centre of the County, and having regard to its importance, I hope you may be disposed to assist the undertaking and shall be obliged by your informing me, at an early date, if I may add your name to the List of Subscribers, and the number of shares you wish appropriated to you.

I remain, Sir,
Yours Faithfully
J. G. Everett
Chairman of the Wells Committee'

(Somerset County Record Office; DD\SAS\C795\SE\20\51)

The East Somerset Railway minute book reveals that there was some competive tendering for the contract to build the Wells extension. The minutes of the Directors' meeting on 29th March 1869 reported that a Mr. Knight, having previously submitted a tender, could not guarantee to complete the line for the sum quoted although the actual figure is not minuted. It was reported that Brotherhood was the preferred contractor in August 1859 but, in December of that year, Smith and Knight submitted a tender to construct the line for £39,500, presumably after some recalculation by Mr. Knight. A month previously Lord Bath had agreed to subscribe £17,000 in preference stock provided that £10,000 was subscribed publicly and the total cost did not exceed £40,000. It could be that potential contractors were urged to reduce their tenders as a result of this. In June 1860 another contractor, Messrs Green and King, submitted a tender but the directors felt duty bound to Smith and Knight. The contract was finally signed with Smith and Knight in July 1860 to build the extension for the sum tendered. However, newspaper reports of the opening say that the contractor was a D. Baldwin of London.

Meanwhile, in May 1859 Wells shareholders complained over a call for £2 per share despite the fact that no land had yet been purchased. It was decided not to start construction immediately partly because of financial worries over the shares not being taken up and partly because of opposition from the Somerset Central. The Directors' meeting of the 8th October 1859 records the reading of a letter from Mr. Bereton reporting the death of Isambard Kingdom Brunel. It was also resolved to appoint Mr. R. J. Ward as Engineer of the company in place of Brunel. In November 1860, out of four tenders submitted for the construction of the station at Wells that of George Beaven of Wells was accepted, his price being £2,411 14s 8d.

Although the Somerset Central Railway had by this time set its sights on expansion in the direction of Bruton, it was not too happy about the East Somerset Railway extending to Wells. A letter to the East Somerset Railway, which was received on 23rd November 1859, proposed a line from Street-on-the-Fosse to Shepton Mallet. Plans for this line were deposited on 30th March 1859 under the name of the Shepton Mallet Railway. The line would have made a junction with the projected Bruton extension of the Somerset Central where that line crossed the

Plate 8 - The Royal Oak hostelry in Wells, probably in late 1906. The licensee was M. Miller, 'retailer of Beer, Ale, Cider and Tobacco - to be consumed on the premises'. The somewhat tired poster in the shop window to the right of the public house is advertising a performance of 'Songs of the West' on Thursday, November 22nd, 1906 by 'Frank Pemberton's Celebrated Costume Concert Party' in Wells Town Hall. *Wells and Mendip Museum*

Fosse Way immediately to the east of the eventual site of Pylle station. From the junction that faced Glastonbury, the line would have struck north then north-east towards Prestleigh. It would then have followed the line of the later Somerset & Dorset Bath Extension, but slightly to the east, until it made a junction with the East Somerset Railway facing Shepton Mallet near to the site of Kilver Street level crossing.

The letter from the Somerset Central was read out at the East Somerset Railway Directors' meeting on 10th December 1859. The Somerset Central proposed that the East Somerset abandon the Wells extension in favour of the line to Street-on-the-Fosse. It also suggested that the line should be jointly owned with both companies taking an equal share of the costs. Application to Parliament would also be made jointly but the line was to be worked as part of the East Somerset company. The East Somerset directors could not agree to this proposal as it was not considered to be in the interests of either the East Somerset Railway or the citizens of Wells. The Directors' meeting of 11th January 1860 records that the Somerset Central had petitioned against the Wells Extension Act as had Mr. Brotherhood, although the reason for the latter is not stated. It seems likely that Mr. Brotherhood was having some difficulty with the contract.

Further legislation followed. The East Somerset Railway Act (23 Vic., Cap. lxxxiii) received Royal Assent on 14th June 1860. The line from Shepton Mallet to Wells authorised by the 1857 Act was abandoned in favour of a line on a different alignment further to the south. The new plans were submitted by R. J. Ward. The primary reason for the realignment was that the original route would have passed within sight of the residence of James Somerville, who was a director and otherwise prominent supporter of the enterprise. Although willing to see the line constructed he did not wish to be able to see it from his home. Obviously the concept of 'nimbyism' was well established by that time although it was not known as such for another hundred years or more. A consequence of the revised route was a saving on construction costs, much of this being achieved by the avoidance of the 286-yard tunnel under Church Hill at Dinder that the original plans necessitated. However, this was done at the expense of steepening the ruling gradient from a relatively easy 1 in 61 to 1 in 46. Also the new alignment was twenty chains shorter than the original, its total length now being 4 miles 62 chains.

The line was authorised to be the same gauge as the Witham to Shepton Mallet section and powers were included to lay a third rail, thus providing more evidence that the arrival of the standard gauge in the area was inevitable. Four years were allowed for completion of the extension. As in the original Act, provision was made for a junction with the Somerset Central at Wells although some sources claim that it was not made at this time. This may relate to the fact that Colonel Yolland seemed to have a dislike of level crossings in general and was opposed to the one planned at Priory Road in particular, this crossing being an essential part of the junction.

In the event, the Act was passed with the planned junction and level crossing still intact. Clauses were inserted into the Act to allow for the replacement of the crossing by a bridge if required. Had the Colonel's view prevailed then either the junction would not have been made or a bridge would have been required in place of the level crossing. Problems with the crossing were to come to a head in the years to come and the matter is explored in some detail in a later chapter. As we shall see, had a bridge been constructed, it would have presented its own problems.

We are now at a convenient point in the history of the East Somerset Railway to consider the exact nature of the junction with the Somerset Central. When the latter company opened its line from Glastonbury to Wells in 1859, its single platform terminus lay immediately to the west of Priory Road. This road was the main turnpike road from Wells to Glastonbury, now the A39. The East Somerset station at Wells was to be to the east of Priory Road immediately opposite the Somerset Central

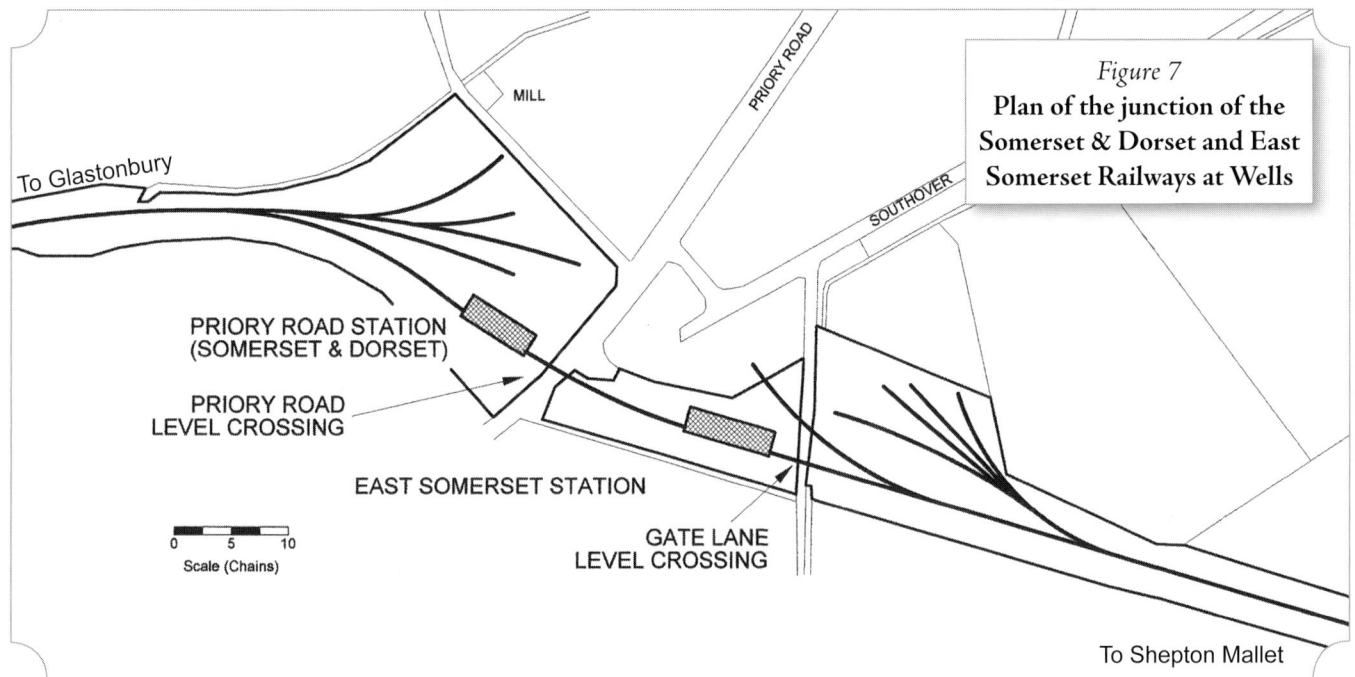

Figure 7
Plan of the junction of the Somerset & Dorset and East Somerset Railways at Wells

Plate 9 - The former East Somerset Railway station building at Wells, which opened for traffic in March 1862 and subsequently closed in January 1878, the GWR's East Somerset section traffic being concentrated at Tucker Street. At the time of the photograph the building was in the hands of Marsh & Adlam, cheese factors, being used as a cheese store; note the pile of baskets at the near corner, behind the two workmen. Differences in the design of the two horse-drawn vehicles are evident, too. The composition of the photograph, the prominence given to the posed GWR delivery vehicles, to Marsh & Adlam's name, both on the nameplate and on the brickwork, and even the photographer's name invite the conclusion that this was a publicity photograph. But for whom? *Wells and Mendip Museum*

station. Thus the junction between the two would be little more than a short connection across Priory Road. Since the East Somerset Act had included a level crossing at Priory Road this was how the junction would be established despite the calls from Colonel Yolland for a bridge at this location. The junction and level crossing were constructed at the same time as the East Somerset line from Shepton Mallet to Wells.

At the East Somerset Directors' meeting of 14th December 1861, the secretary read a letter from Mr. Bernard of the Wells Turnpike Trust complaining about the way that the road had been crossed by the railway. There was also a letter from a Mr. C. Berryman claiming compensation for damage caused by the road not being properly made. The exact nature of the damage was not specified. Both letters were referred to the engineer for report with instructions to require the contractor to '... *remedy the state of things complained of by Mr. Berryman.*'

On 11th January 1862 the engineer reported that the level crossing had been altered as required and that the contractor had arranged with Mr. Berryman for the compensation claimed by him to be paid.

The line was ready for inspection by February 1862 but Colonel Yolland refused to allow the line to open. He was concerned over the incompleteness of the work and required a turntable to be installed at Wells. He also proposed that the Shepton Mallet turntable, now useless in that place, should be moved to Witham. He also required a clock to be installed at Wells in such a position that it could be seen from the platform.

The Board of Trade withdrew its objections to the opening of the Wells Extension after a guarantee was made by the East Somerset Railway Secretary to work the line under one engine in steam regulations and to install a turntable at Wells as and when the traffic warranted it. As traffic developed, the limitations of only having one train on the line at any one time became apparent. Eventually the long section between Witham and Wells would have to be broken up into two or three sections and block working introduced. This was, however, after the independent existence of the East Somerset Railway had come to an end and is dealt with in more detail in a later chapter.

The ceremonial opening of the line took place on 28th February 1862 with public services beginning on the following day, 1st March. On the opening day officials of the Railway, including the Marquis of Bath and other directors, were conveyed from Shepton Mallet to Wells by special train. They were received at the East Somerset station by the Mayor and other leading citizens from where they proceeded to the Swan Hotel for a celebratory luncheon at which the Mayor presided. So Wells now had two stations within one hundred yards of each other on either side of Priory Road, and although there was a connecting link it was not, as yet, put to very much use.

With the existing service between Witham and Shepton Mallet being only four trains each way daily it was quite easy to graft the extension of the service to Wells from 1st March 1862 onto the existing timetable. Thus there were no changes to the departure times of trains from Witham or Shepton Mallet.

Plate 10 - Looking towards Shepton Mallet from East Somerset signal box on an undisclosed date. The mound to the left of the single line marks the site of the East Somerset Railway station. Note the tank wagon at the stop block in the left middle ground. *Rex Conway collection*

Trains left Wells 15 minutes before their booked departure time from Shepton Mallet. Although he had not built the line, Mr. Brotherhood was still involved. A Directors' meeting minute of 16th December 1862 recorded that he had been paid £337 16s 10d for station fittings.

In 1866 the first proposals were made for a siding at the summit of the line near Doulting in order to tap stone traffic from the nearby quarries. From the summit the line fell at 1 in 56 towards Shepton Mallet and at 1 in 70 towards Cranmore and, in view of the potential for runaways, the Great Western, who were operating the line at the time, required the summit to be levelled in the vicinity of the siding. This was duly carried out early in 1868 and the siding opened for traffic on 10th July 1868. The cost of levelling the summit and installing the siding was met by the owner of Chelynch Quarry (a Mr. Paget who was also a director of the East Somerset Railway) who subscribed £471.0s.0d, the Great Western Railway and the East Somerset Railway who subscribed £282.12s.0d and £188.8s.0d respectively. It was planned that the cost would be repaid by a rebate on generated traffic which, from the opening until 28th December 1868, had amounted to £365 before deducting the necessary rebate.

Plate 11 - Taken from East Somerset down home signal, this modern view shows Priory Road crossing, the turntable and the train shed of Priory Road station just beyond. *Brian Hillier*

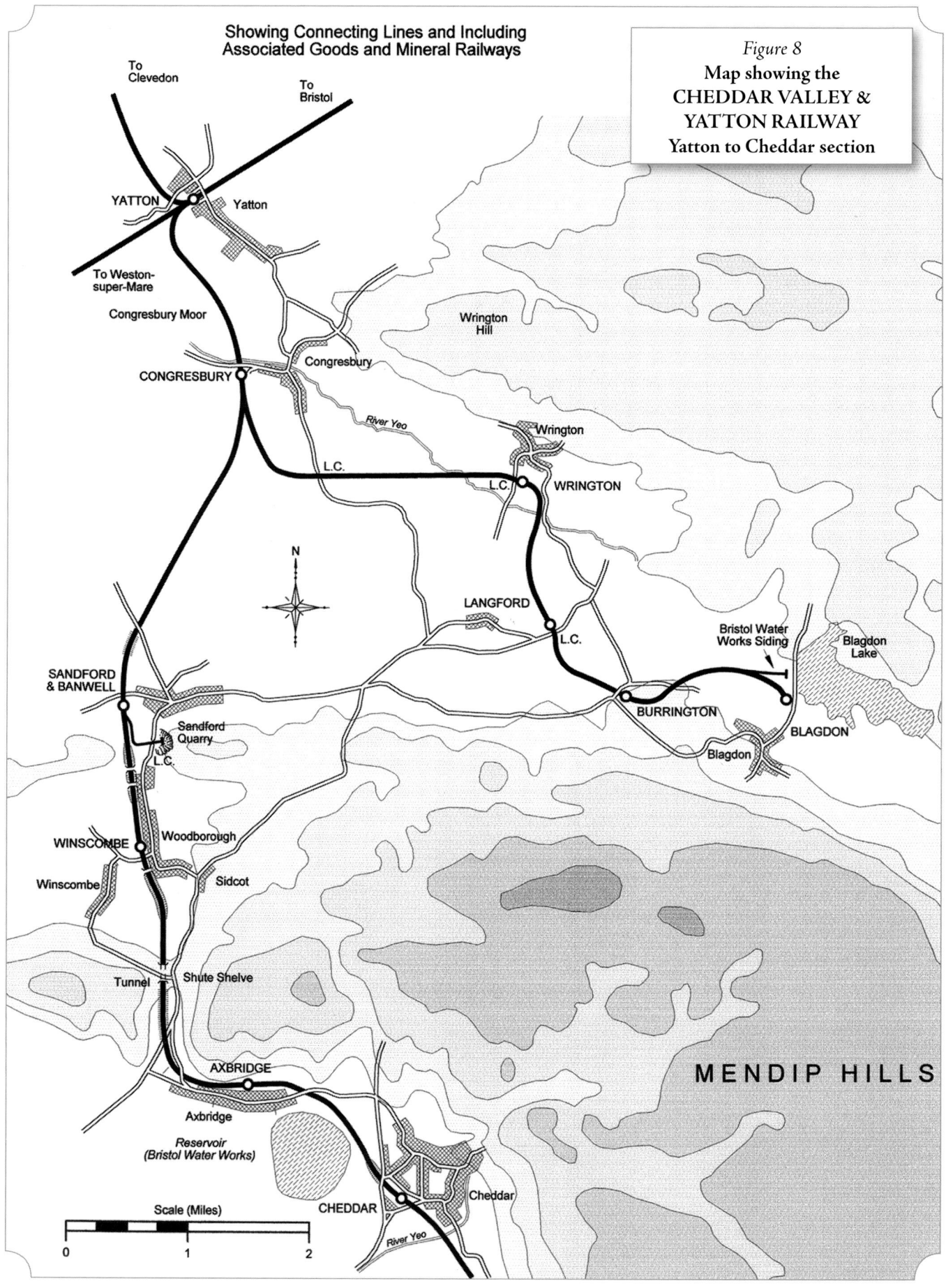

Chapter Four

THE CHEDDAR VALLEY & YATTON RAILWAY

Construction and Opening to Cheddar

The origins of the Cheddar Valley & Yatton Railway have already been outlined. Once the proposed line had been taken over by the Bristol & Exeter Railway the plan was altered to make it a broad gauge line. It was to leave the parent company's line at Yatton and proceed via stations at Congresbury, Sandford, Woodborough and Axbridge to reach Cheddar. Construction of the line began with the cutting of the first sod at Shute Shelve Hill by Mrs. Yatman of nearby Winscombe Hall on Tuesday, 26th February 1867. Interestingly the Yatman family had moved to the area in 1859 in order to escape railway developments elsewhere in the country. Their views must have mellowed during the intervening years in order to be able to support a venture that was to drive a railway tunnel virtually underneath their recently constructed home.

Also present at the ceremony were the Mayor and Corporation of Axbridge plus a large number of spectators. The line was engineered by John Hingston Fox who was not particularly enthusiastic about the ceremony surrounding the commencement of construction work. This fact is born out by the following letter written by John Fox to the Bristol & Exeter Company Secretary, Arthur Moore, shortly before the sod cutting ceremony:

'Bristol and Exeter Railway, Engineer's Office Axbridge

Feb. 21st. 1867

Dear Sir

The Mayor and Corporation of this Town and influential inhabitants of the district seem quite determined to inaugurate the commencement of the works on this branch by a ceremonial gathering - turning the first sod luncheon etc. etc. I have done all that I could to dissuade them from making such an unnecessary fuss about the matter but to no purpose.

Though the Directors do not initiate such an affair I suppose they would not object to its taking place.

Tuesday next at 2p.m. is the hour named and I must wish that yourself and some of the superior officers of the Company could have represented them on this occasion.

I am, dear Sir

Yours truly
John Fox.

A Moore Esquire.'

John Fox's reluctance over any form of celebration was no doubt due to his Quaker upbringing. An engineer's office had been set up in Axbridge for the duration. It is worth noting that John Fox's brother, Francis, was Engineer to the Bristol & Exeter Railway and that John was his assistant. In modern terms John 'project managed' the construction of the Cheddar Valley line under the direction of his brother. Francis Fox was Engineer for the Bristol & Exeter from 1854 until April 1876 when he resigned, four months after the company had been taken over by the Great Western.

The day of the cutting of the first sod was one of great celebration in Axbridge which was then still a borough, a position that it had enjoyed since Saxon times but would only retain until 1886. The weather must have dampened the occasion somewhat as was reported in the *Somerset County Herald*:

'The weather however proved unpropitious, as a thick mist descended during the whole of the day and occasionally it thickened into a drenching rain, through which every object presented a woeful aspect.'

In spite of this the Mayor and the Corporation of Axbridge emerged from the town hall and proceeded to Shute Shelve to witness the event. One of Ronald Bailey's 'Mendip lore' articles in the *Weston Mercury* published in 1949 paints a wonderful picture of the procession.

'On this particular day in 1867, however, they are out in all their regalia, headed by the Mayor, Ald. Trew, in his robes, attended by the sergeants-at-mace, in their cocked hats and long blue frocks. A procession is formed. The members of the Weare Band fill their lungs, and to the accompaniment of sounding brass and tinkling cymbal, the march out of the town to Shute Shelve Hill is begun.

Behind the Weare musicians walks the Mayor in solitary state, followed by the churchwardens, the Lord Bishop of Newfoundland, Preb. Fagan (Rural Dean and Rector of Rodney Stoke), the Rev. W Littlehayes (Vicar of Compton Bishop), Mr Fox (Engineer to the Bristol and Exeter Railway Company), Mr G Millard (Town Clerk of Axbridge), the Sergeants-at-Mace, members of the Corporation, about a hundred local big-wigs, the Axbridge Union Fife and Drum Band, the local school children, and finally a long trail of general spectators.'

On arrival at the appointed place the gathering was treated to the usual round of speeches by local dignitaries and members of the clergy as well as the actual cutting of the first sod itself. It seems that the only representative of the Bristol & Exeter Railway Company was Francis Fox. His brother John's letter

Plate 12 - Yatton station, the western end of the Cheddar Valley branch and junction with the main Bristol to Taunton line. What appears to be GWR steam railmotor No.37 in the Clevedon branch bay platform is just visible at the left edge. This view of the station facilities, taken in the early years of the 20th century, belies the complexity of the junctions sited to the south. *Neil Parkhouse collection*

to the Company Secretary had not encouraged any of the directors to attend. John himself may also have been there but contemporary newspaper reports neglect to mention it. Two hundred and fifty of the poor of Axbridge were treated to a dinner by the Mayor and other principal inhabitants.

Construction of the line started shortly afterwards and the engineering works were not great apart from a short tunnel and rock cuttings at Shute Shelve between Woodborough and Axbridge. The contract for the construction of the line was let to Messrs William and John Pickering of No.14 Chatham Place, Blackfriars, London at a cost of £100,000. Interestingly, the contract only covered the cost of the earthworks, bridges, culverts and the tunnel. The cost of land purchase, permanent way and buildings were not included. Although the line was to be laid as single track, sufficient land was purchased to enable a second track to be laid if the traffic warranted it. Bridges over the line, except for the tunnel, were constructed with enough clearance for double track whereas those under the line were only built for a single track.

Following completion of the line, it was inspected by Colonel Yolland on behalf of the Board of Trade and, in his report dated 31st July 1869, he indicated that he was satisfied with the work and recommended that the line be opened for traffic. His only requirement was the interlocking of facing points with the starting signals at a number of locations. The report states that the permanent way was laid with flat bottomed rails weighing 70½lbs/yd with an average length of 22 feet, fixed to transverse sleepers with fang bolts. The sleeper spacing was 2 feet at the joints and 2 feet 8 inches elsewhere. A brief mention was made of the existence of a turntable at Cheddar as well as at Yatton. This seems strange in view of the fact that Cheddar was to be only a temporary terminus whilst the line to Wells was completed. The location and subsequent history of the Cheddar turntable remains a mystery. An undertaking that the line was to be worked by train staff in conjunction with the block telegraph, signed by the Chairman and the Secretary of the railway company, was attached to the Colonel's report.

During the preparation of this work the writer uncovered a number of different figures for the length of the tunnel at Shute Shelve. The original plans submitted by the Somerset & Dorset Railway in 1864 gave the length of the tunnel as 120 yards. A report of the cutting of the first sod in the *Somerset County Herald* dated Saturday, 2nd March 1867 gave the length at 154 yards. Official railway records give the length as 180 yards, R. A. Cooke's maps state 198 yards and the inspecting officer's report gives the length as 200 yards. The discrepancies were deemed to be sufficiently large that the writer instigated a re-measurement of the length of the tunnel. This was duly carried out by a local railway historian using a pedometer and produced a result of 200 yards. It is clear from a comparison of the sections contained in the original plans with the official gradient profile that alterations were made during construction. It therefore comes as no surprise that the actual length of the tunnel differs from that stated in the plans. It is also of no surprise that the press

Plate 13 - A general view of Axbridge taken from an early colour postcard. The train is comprised of at least six carriages, apparently made up of two sets of three close-coupled vehicles.   *John Alsop collection*

reports are incorrect but one wonders why the official records differ from the actual figure by almost one chain.

The line opened on 3rd August 1869. A special train left Bristol at 11.00am conveying the directors and other guests to Cheddar, returning to Axbridge for further celebrations, including lunch. It seems that the Bristol & Exeter made up for its lack of support at the ceremony of the cutting of the first sod. Most of the directors attended the opening ceremony including the Chairman, the Earl of Devon. Contemporary reports describe the weather as being 'unpropitious', no doubt reminding many of the day of the cutting of the first sod. On arrival at Cheddar the directors and others who had travelled down from Bristol on the first train were received in the goods shed, the station building being incomplete as yet. On their return to Axbridge they were received by the Mayor and Corporation of the borough. A parade through the town was accompanied by Mr. Weymouth's Brislington Band and the Axbridge Poor House Fife and Drum Band. A 'sumptuous repast' was laid out in the Town Hall. In spite of the rain there were rural sporting activities in the afternoon. Two hundred poor people of Axbridge were treated to a dinner and tea paid for by local inhabitants as part of the Celebrations. Such festivities were not to be repeated one hundred years later to mark the opening of the M5 motorway.

Plate 14 - Station staff pose for the camera at Congresbury, date unknown. This was the junction for the Wrington Vale Light Railway to Blagdon, which opened on 4th December 1901. That line also served a Bristol Waterworks depot in connection with Blagdon Lake.   *John Alsop collection*

Train Services in the Early Days and Completion of the Line to Wells

At that time the Bristol & Exeter Railway issued a new working timetable each month and that for August 1869 showed the commencement of services on the branch as far as Cheddar. The passenger service consisted of five down and six up trains Monday to Saturday. There were no Sunday services as was in keeping with the policy of the railway company. Intermediate stations were served by all trains and most provided good connections at Yatton with services to and from Bristol. In fact two of the up trains worked through to Bristol. In the down direction departures from Yatton were at 9.20am, 11.05am, 1.00pm, 3.50pm and 6.35pm with corresponding arrival times at Cheddar of 10.00am, 11.45am, 1.40pm, 4.30pm and 7.15pm. In the up direction departures from Cheddar were at 8.15am, 10.10am, 12.05pm, 2.15pm, 5.00pm and 7.45pm with corresponding arrival times at Yatton of 8.55am, 10.50am, 12.45pm, 2.55pm, 5.40pm and 8.25pm.

The timetable shows one goods train and gives times for the down direction only. The train was booked to depart from Bristol at 6.40am and arrived at Yatton at 7.10am before proceeding onto the branch at 7.15am. The time allowed for the journey to Cheddar was 45 minutes, only five minutes longer than that for passenger trains, so it is unlikely that shunting was carried out at intermediate stations. Also as the line had only very recently opened, it is unlikely that there would have been very much goods traffic at the intermediate stations. The up goods would probably have worked as traffic demanded and to fit in with the passenger train timetable. This being the case its timing would have been at the discretion of a local official rather than being determined centrally by the means of the working timetable. One reason for including the down goods in the working timetable as the first train of the day would be to prove that the line was safe for subsequent passenger trains.

The rest of the line to Wells was completed in eight months and this section opened without ceremony on Tuesday, 5th April 1870. At Wells, the Bristol & Exeter Railway had been forced to construct its own station at Tucker Street, more or less at the junction of the three lines of railway authorised by the Somerset & Dorset's original Act of 1864. At this time it was not connected with either of the other two stations in Wells for reasons that will become clear later. The line had been inspected on the previous Saturday, 2nd April by Captain Tyler who pronounced the works to be satisfactory apart from a few unfinished details at the Wells end. He also required the replacement of fish bolts at various locations where the existing ones were deemed to be too short. The permanent way was of the same construction as the line from Yatton to Cheddar.

The haste with which the line was opened following the inspection meant that there was insufficient time to organise a proper celebration, much to the disappointment of those who felt that they were missing out on a free lunch. No doubt John Fox did not share in this disappointment. However, it seems that the Councillors of the City of Wells were none too pleased as they complained about the lack of 'a Celebratory Luncheon'. It seems that the rush to open the line was brought about by the fact that the County Quarter Sessions were being held in Wells that week and the railway expected to receive a good number of passengers as a result.

There were intermediate stations at Draycott and Lodge Hill. The station at Wookey was a later addition but it must have been anticipated as it appeared in the working timetable right from the opening day, although of course without any times against it. Most sources, including Charles Clinker, give the opening date as 1st August 1871 but according to a contemporary Bristol & Exeter working timetable the station was opened on 1st February 1871.

Following the opening throughout to Wells the passenger train service was revised to six passenger trains each way daily with of course no Sunday service. Down passenger trains departed from Yatton at 7.45am, 9.25am, 11.53am, 1.10pm, 4.15pm and 6.00pm. These services stopped at all stations except the 11.53am which did not stop at Lodge Hill and the 6.00pm

Plate 15 - This picture of a broad gauge mixed train at Cheddar has been described as recording the opening day of the Yatton & Cheddar Valley Railway in 1869. However, the station building at Cheddar was not ready then, so the event is quite likely to be marking the opening of the section between Cheddar and Wells in 1870. *L&GRP*

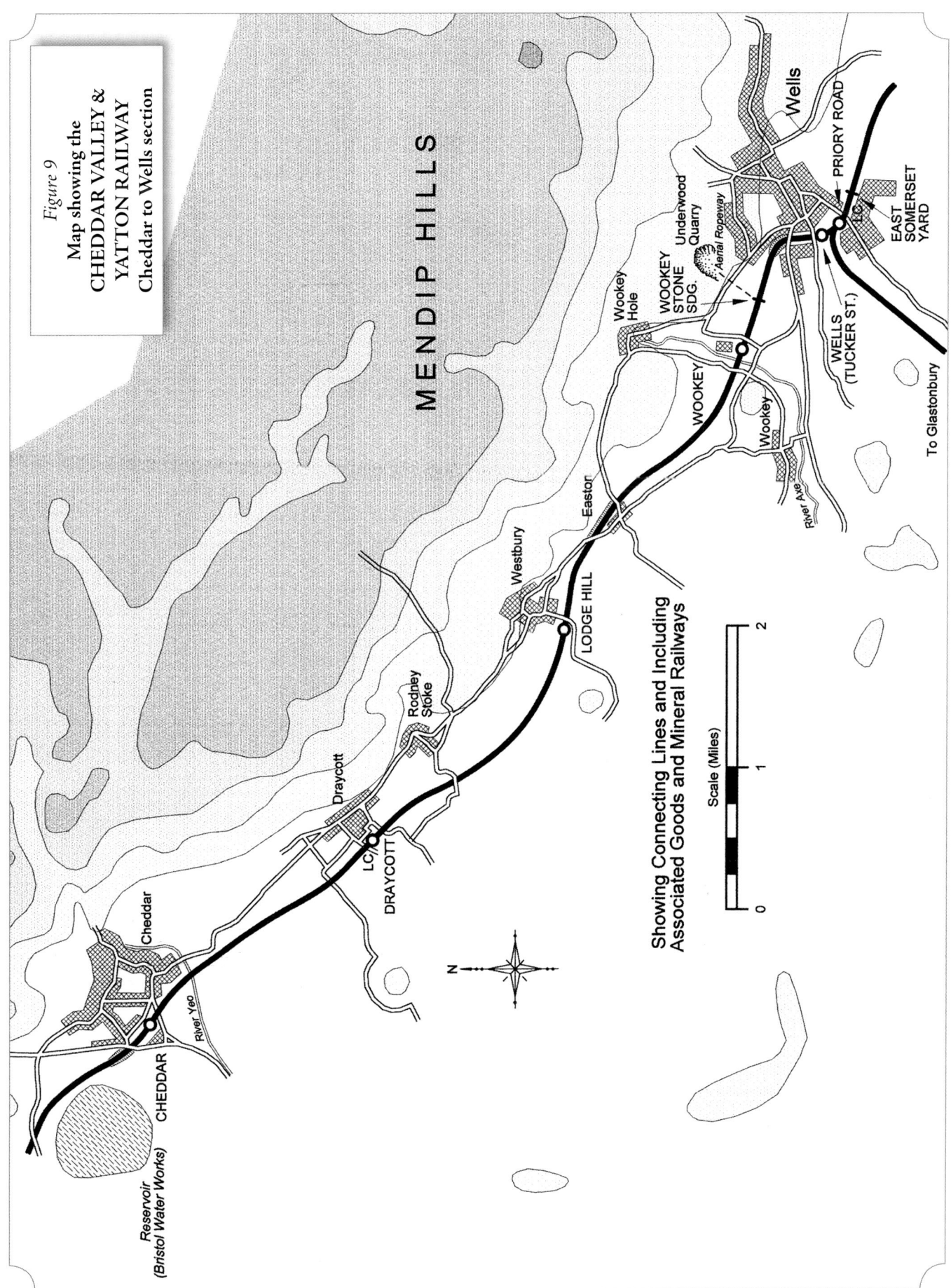

Plate 16 - The station serving Westbury-sub-Mendip village was named Lodge Hill to avoid confusion between it and Westbury (Wilts). This view shows the station's position relative to the village. *Ivan Beale*

which did not stop at either Congresbury or Lodge Hill. The corresponding arrival times at Wells were 8.55am, 10.35am, 12.55pm, 2.20pm, 5.25pm and 7.30pm. The 7.45am, 11.53am and the 5.15pm departures from Yatton originated from Bristol, from where the departure times were 7.15am, 11.20am and 3.45pm respectively. Connecting services from Bristol were available for the other three services that started from Yatton.

Up trains departed from Wells at 7.45am, 9.35am, 12noon, 1.10pm, 5.40pm and 7.50pm. Of these only the 7.45am, the 1.10pm and the 7.50pm called at all stations (except Wookey for reasons already explained). The 9.35am called only at Cheddar, Axbridge and Sandford and Banwell. The mid-day train did not call at Lodge Hill or Congresbury and the 5.40pm called only at Cheddar, Axbridge and Winscombe. Arrival times at Yatton were 8.55am, 10.23am, 12.53pm, 2.19pm, 6.25pm and 8.59pm. The 9.35am, 1.10pm and 7.50pm departures from Wells ran through to Bristol arriving at 10.50am, 2.50pm and 9.35pm respectively. Connecting services to Bristol were available for the other trains that terminated at Yatton.

All trains on the branch conveyed both first and second class passengers. Connecting services to and from Weston-super-Mare and Clevedon were also advertised. The working of goods traffic was completely reorganised with the opening of the line throughout to Wells with one goods train in each direction daily. During May 1871, the down goods departed from Yatton at 5.35am and arrived at Wells at 7.45am, just in time for the departure of the first up passenger train. The goods train originated from Bristol having departed from there at 5.00am. According to the working timetable all intermediate stations except Congresbury and Winscombe were served by this train. The up goods departed from Wells at 1.13pm calling at all stations except Wookey, Lodge Hill, Sandford and Banwell and Congresbury. There was a booked stop of ten minutes at Cheddar where it crossed the 1.10pm down passenger departure from Yatton. The arrival time at Yatton was 2.43pm, where it remained until 3.05pm before departing for Bristol with booked arrival time of 3.40pm. Interestingly, Congresbury was not served by the goods trains in either direction, possibly because there were no facilities for handling goods traffic at the time. Whatever the reason this had been rectified by 1874 because by that date all stations were served by both the up and the down goods trains.

As a result of there being no physical link between the East Somerset and Cheddar Valley sections some of the train connections at Wells, if they could be called that, were very tight indeed. In fact only one minute was allowed for passengers to transfer between the East Somerset and Cheddar Valley stations, a distance of some six hundred yards. In the event the authorities introduced a more 'user friendly' timetable that allowed five minutes for the transfer. When one considers that the present day timetable suggests that passengers should allow ten minutes in order to make a connection at Bristol Temple Meads station it does not seem to be anything like a sufficient length of time. Getting off one train, walking (or more likely running) five hundred yards and boarding another train within five minutes is no mean feat even for a fit and able bodied person, let alone someone who is elderly, infirm or encumbered with luggage or children.

Shortly after opening, the station at Sandford was renamed Sandford and Banwell. The writer is not sure of the exact date but it was definitely before the opening of the extension to Wells as the timetables printed at the time show it with its new name. Banwell village lay just over one mile to the west of the station whereas Banwell station on the Bristol & Exeter main line between Yatton and Weston-super-Mare was well over two miles away. The latter station was renamed Worle in order to prevent any confusion. This station underwent two more renamings, becoming Puxton in 1884 and finally Puxton and Worle in

1922. Readers should note that this was on a different site from the present day Worle station that opened in the 1990s.

In spite of being geographically more correct, Woodborough was renamed Winscombe on 30th October 1869 after the adjacent village that stood half a mile or so to the south-west. The reason was to avoid confusion with another Woodborough station situated on the Great Western line beween Savernake and Westbury in Wiltshire. It seems that the name board here caused problems that were only compounded when the station name was changed. F. A. Knight records in his book *A History of Sidcot School* that the man sent to erect the original Woodborough name board could not read and, as a consequence, fixed it upside down. The late Orion Charles Caple gave an account in his reminiscences of what happened when the name changed to Winscombe. He states that the letters arrived in a crate only requiring to be fixed to the name board. It seems that whoever completed the job was illiterate because the letters were apparently fixed to the board with the 'E' on the left and the 'W' on the right (presumably spelling EBMOCSNIW if all of the intermediate letters were in their correct positions). One can only assume that the mistake was noticed fairly quickly. In any case the account goes on to say that it was duly noticed and that the letters were replaced in their correct position. How much truth there is in either of these accounts we shall probably never know. The writer regards both with a certain amount of scepticism but would not wish to dismiss them out of hand.

Although built to serve the village of Westbury-sub-Mendip, the station there was named Lodge Hill after a nearby topographical feature, an outlying hill of the Mendips in the middle of the moorland. There are a number of similar hills that rise out of the low lying moorland in the area including the well known Glastonbury Tor. The name of Lodge Hill was probably chosen because at the time of construction of the Cheddar to Wells line, Westbury (Wilts) was already well established, although not yet the important junction it eventually became, and there was an obvious need to avoid confusion for passengers and booking clerks alike.

Difficulties at Wells

It was originally intended under the 1865 Act that the Bristol & Exeter trains from Yatton would connect with those of the East Somerset Railway at the latter company's own station and, in fact, a draft proposal was raised to that effect. In order to connect with the East Somerset, the Bristol & Exeter would have to pass through the intervening goods yard and passenger station belonging to the Somerset & Dorset. An agreement was made between the Bristol & Exeter and the Somerset & Dorset railways for such an arrangement. A rent of £400 per annum would be payable to the latter company for the right to cross the goods yard and the maintenance of mixed gauge track at Priory Road. Of this, £200 was for the provision and maintenance of the connection itself whilst the other £200 was in payment for the use of the Somerset & Dorset station, its staff and other facilities.

It is clear that even as late as the spring of 1869, with the impending completion of the line at least as far as Cheddar, no final decision had been made over the arrangements at Wells. Francis Fox, the Bristol & Exeter's engineer, wrote to the company Board in order to focus their attention on this important detail. His letter dated 26th April outlined the various agreements included in the 1865 Act. He then went on to describe the three options open to the company. The first option would be to construct a new station west of the existing Somerset & Dorset station without any connection to the latter company's line. The disadvantage of this would be that there would be no connection with the existing railways at Wells and it would involve the cost of a complete station. This cost would probably exceed the rental payable for the use of either of the existing stations and facilities by a considerable amount. The second option would be to honour the agreement made with the Somerset & Dorset and pay the £400 per annum for the use of their station. The Bristol & Exeter would obtain sufficient station accommodation at a moderate outlay with the additional advantage of less complexity with regard to the signalling than would be the case if trains worked through to the East Somerset station. However, the interchange of passenger traffic between the broad gauge systems was something that he considered extremely desirable. The final course would be to run through the Somerset & Dorset station to link up with the East Somerset. Of course, £200 per annum would still be payable to the Somerset & Dorset for the maintenance of the connection and presumably an equivalent amount would be due to the East Somerset company for the use of their station and facilities.

Francis Fox's view was that the most desirable arrangement would be to exchange traffic with both the Somerset & Dorset and the East Somerset companies at their respective stations as required and he urged the Bristol & Exeter Board to settle the question as soon as possible.

The Board of Trade was quick to realise that a connection to the Somerset & Dorset running through the latter company's goods yard could lead to hazardous operation and refused to sanction use of any connecting line east of the site where the Bristol & Exeter had the option to build its own station. In spite of this refusal, the Somerset & Dorset insisted that the agreement was still binding and demanded the payment of rent. As a result of this dispute the two parties ended up in court and the case was won by the Somerset & Dorset. In view of the fact that this litigation took place at a time when the Somerset & Dorset company was in serious financial difficulties, it must have been very sure that the outcome would be in its favour.

The provision of the £400 per annum in rental was made under Article 12 of the Bristol & Exeter Railway (Additional Powers) Act of 1865. This was, of course, the same Act that transferred the powers to build the Cheddar Valley & Yatton Railway from the Somerset & Dorset to the Bristol & Exeter in the first place. Under the terms of this article, payment of the rental became due as soon as the Bristol & Exeter 'broke ground' within six feet of the Somerset & Dorset permanent way. In 1870 the Bristol & Exeter engineer temporarily removed two rails from Somerset & Dorset track in order to take levels. As a consequence of this, the latter company felt that it should request the payment irrespective of the fact that use of the

Figure 10
WELLS - 1870
PLANNED CONNECTION

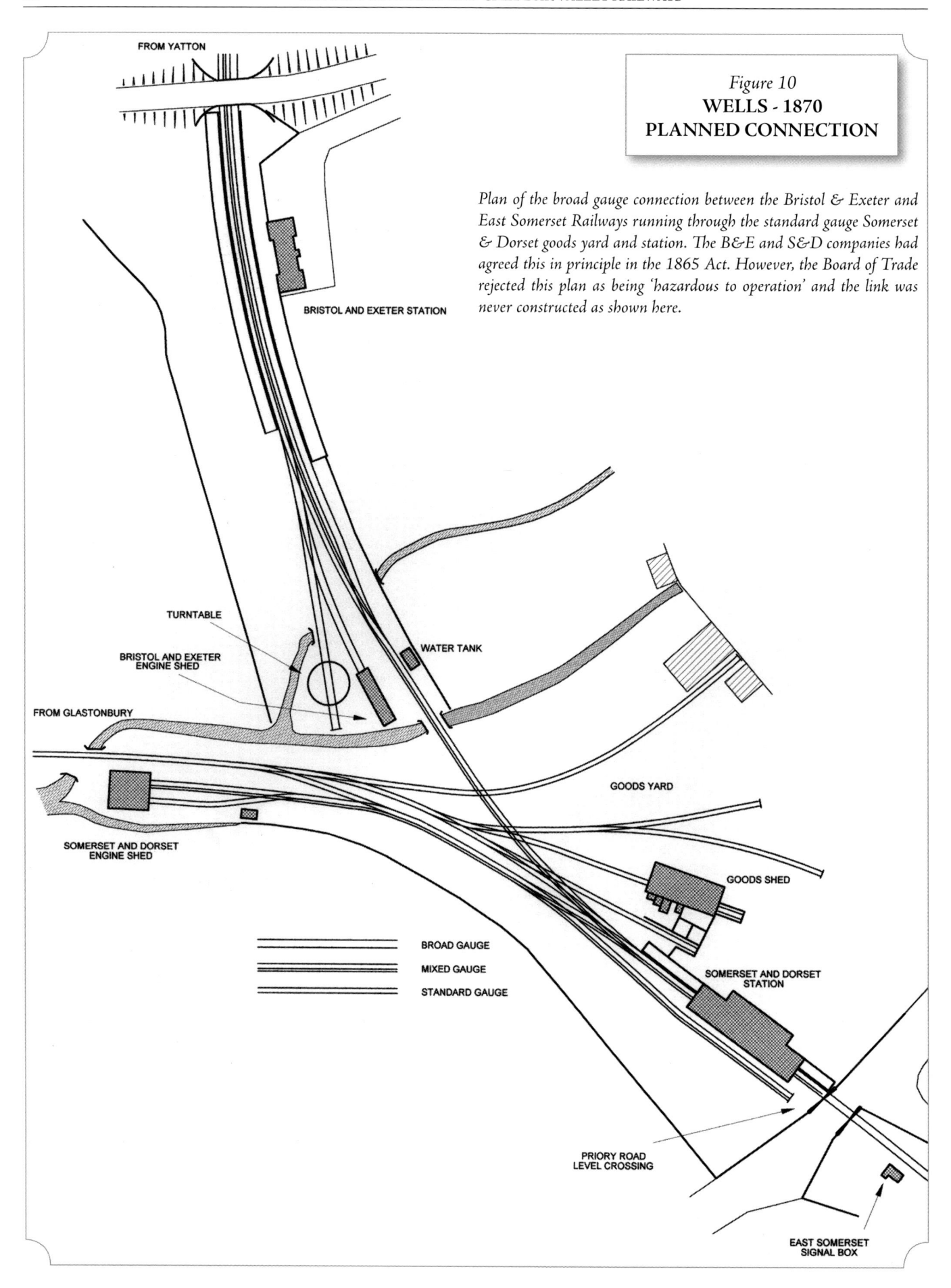

Plan of the broad gauge connection between the Bristol & Exeter and East Somerset Railways running through the standard gauge Somerset & Dorset goods yard and station. The B&E and S&D companies had agreed this in principle in the 1865 Act. However, the Board of Trade rejected this plan as being 'hazardous to operation' and the link was never constructed as shown here.

connection had not been permitted by the Board of Trade. The Bristol & Exeter was insistent that the connection, even if constructed, could not be used and so claimed relief from payment on those grounds. Their claim was not upheld by the court. At least part of the reason for this may have been the discovery of a number of inaccuracies in the original plans. The parliamentary committee that had considered the original Bill would have had access to these plans.

Thus the Bristol & Exeter was obliged to construct its own station at Tucker Street as a terminus. This station was about six hundred yards from the East Somerset station and three hundred yards from the Somerset Central one. As well as providing facilities for passenger traffic, the station at Tucker Street also had its own goods yard and engine shed since those constructed for the other two railways were, at least for the time being, inaccessible. The engine shed was equipped with a 44 foot turntable.

The search for the solution to the problem of providing a satisfactory connection between the East Somerset and the Cheddar Valley lines that would be acceptable to all of the parties involved must have absorbed a considerable amount of effort at this time. It seems that someone had had a premonition that there would be difficulties in providing this link. Just four months after the original Act for the Cheddar Valley & Yatton Railway was obtained by the Somerset & Dorset, plans for the East Somerset & Cheddar Valley Junction Railway were deposited on 30th November 1864 (*Fig.11*). From a junction with the Cheddar Valley & Yatton's Railway No.3 somewhere near the Portway overbridge to a junction with the East Somerset Railway just west of Park Wood, this line would have bypassed the Somerset & Dorset goods yard altogether. From its western end the line would have risen on a gradient of 1 in 75 before passing over Tucker Street near to the Cheddar Valley Inn. Tucker Street itself would have been lowered by nine feet. The line would have levelled out just before passing over Priory Road which would also have been lowered by seven feet. Now descending on a gradient of 1 in 88, the line would have passed over Southover before making its junction with the East Somerset. All three roads would have been crossed by overbridges with a head room of 16 feet. The plans contain no indication of any passenger station so it is probable that trains would have had to reverse into or out of the East Somerset station. Readers familiar with the Somerset & Dorset line will know that through trains from the north would undertake a similar manoeuvre at Bath Green Park and all trains running through between Bath and Bournemouth would also have to reverse to serve Templecombe station. In fact this method of working still happens today at Killarney in the Republic of Ireland. No other information on East Somerset & Cheddar Valley Junction Railway has come to light, so it remains something of an enigma, particularly when one considers that it predates the main battle over the connection by several years.

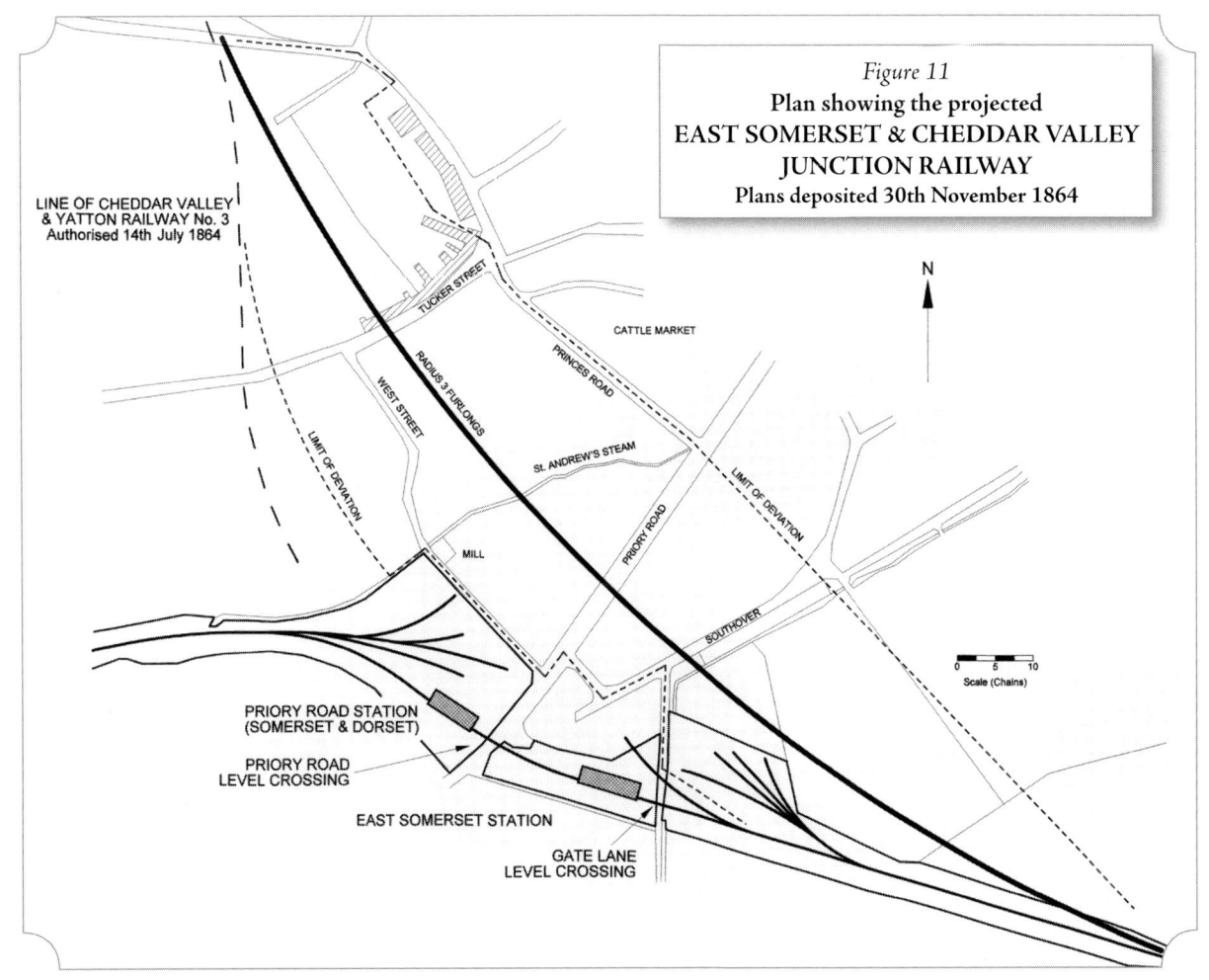

Figure 11
Plan showing the projected
EAST SOMERSET & CHEDDAR VALLEY
JUNCTION RAILWAY
Plans deposited 30th November 1864

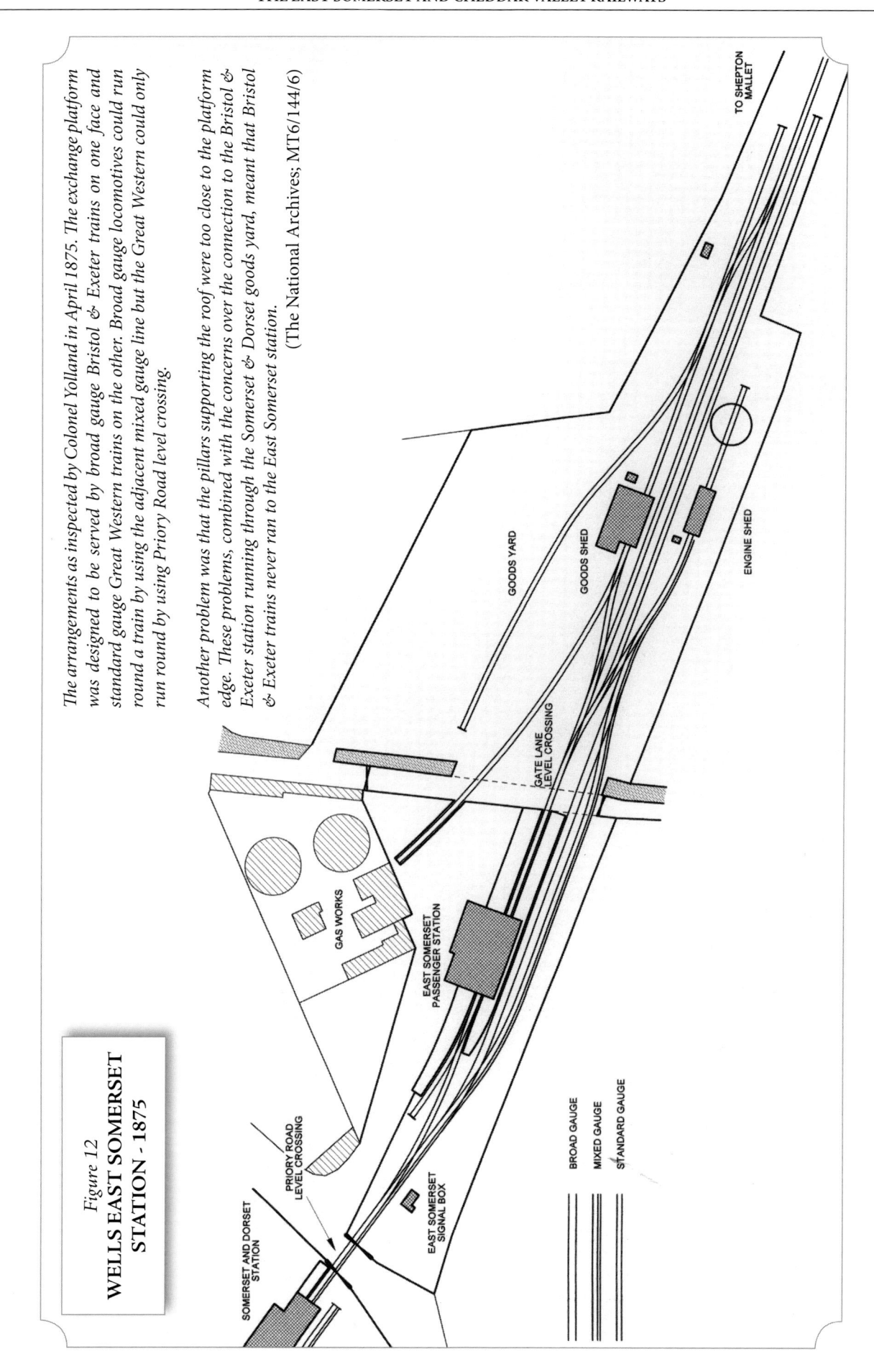

The arrangements as inspected by Colonel Yolland in April 1875. The exchange platform was designed to be served by broad gauge Bristol & Exeter trains on one face and standard gauge Great Western trains on the other. Broad gauge locomotives could run round a train by using the adjacent mixed gauge line but the Great Western could only run round by using Priory Road level crossing.

Another problem was that the pillars supporting the roof were too close to the platform edge. These problems, combined with the concerns over the connection to the Bristol & Exeter station running through the Somerset & Dorset goods yard, meant that Bristol & Exeter trains never ran to the East Somerset station.

(The National Archives; MT6/144/6)

Figure 12
WELLS EAST SOMERSET STATION - 1875

Chapter Five

TAKE-OVER BY THE GREAT WESTERN

The Gauge Conversion and the Completion of the Missing Link

England's smallest city now had three separate stations on three independent lines all within half a mile of each other. Although the East Somerset and the Somerset & Dorset stations were connected by the short line over Priory Road level crossing there was no passenger traffic between the two. It is difficult to imagine what exchange traffic did use the connection in the early 1870s as the Somerset & Dorset was a purely standard gauge line by then and the East Somerset was still broad gauge. However, because of the cramped layout at East Somerset station the level crossing would have to have been occupied by locomotives running round. The writer has not been able to determine whether the link was mixed gauge at this date. The level crossing was also a cause of concern to the local population at this time. An East Somerset Railway Directors' meeting minute of 22nd July 1868 also refers to a letter from the Turnpike Trust complaining about the dangerous state of the crossing. A minute of a Wells Turnpike Trust meeting dated 29th June 1869 refers to complaints made that the rails at the crossing between the East Somerset Railway and the Somerset & Dorset Railway were insufficiently guarded and had caused accidents. The Clerk was directed to write to the Secretary of the East Somerset Railway and request that the matter be immediately attended to. Another minute of the Turnpike Trust meeting of 30th June 1873 reports that a grating (*sic*) on the level crossing was *'greatly out of repair and dangerous to traffic on the turnpike road'*. The clerk was ordered to write to the Secretary of the Great Western Railway (which was responsible for maintenance even before the take-over) requesting that *'the grating be repaired in a proper manner'*. Thus it seems that the concerns over the crossing lasted for some years.

In addition to having completely separate passenger services, each station also had its own goods and locomotive servicing facilities. This somewhat farcical situation did not go down well with the public. The East Somerset suffered as a result of the opening of the Bristol & Exeter branch because the latter afforded a much easier route to Bristol. Consequently the East Somerset approached the Great Western and in 1872 offered to sell out to the larger company for a figure of £86,680. The Great Western was certainly interested in acquiring the East Somerset but considered the asking price to be too high and negotiations were wound up in June 1873.

Not long after this the Great Western Railway announced its intention to convert the entire length of the Wilts, Somerset & Weymouth line to standard gauge. The East Somerset would have no choice other than to follow suit but the estimated cost of conversion at £7,390 was more than the little company would be able to find. It would have been possible to claim that the Great Western should bear the cost but again the East Somerset had neither the funds nor the will to take the much larger company to court. The only viable option was for the East Somerset to approach the Great Western with the view to reopening negotiations for a buy out. The larger company was now able to name its price and the East Somerset was sold to the Great Western for £67,442. The take-over was sanctioned by Act of Parliament (37-38 Vic., Cap. lxxiv) of 14th June 1874. By the time the formal take-over took place in December, the line had already been converted to standard gauge. The conversion was completed in a single weekend from the evening of Friday, 19th June to Sunday, 21st June ready for normal working to resume on the Monday morning using standard gauge stock. It has been remarked that such an operation would not be possible today, modern health and safety requirements would make it impossible to achieve such a task in so short a time.

In 1874 there were six passenger trains in each direction between Witham and Wells. In the down direction passenger trains departed from Witham at 8.45am, 10.55am, 12.43pm, 3.40pm, 6.40pm and 9.00pm arriving Wells at 9.30am, 11.40am, 1.15pm, 4.25pm, 7.30pm and 9.40pm respectively. Of these the 8.45am and the 6.40pm were mixed. Wanstrow station was only served by the 10.55am and 3.40pm and the 12.43pm did not call at Cranmore. In the up direction passenger trains departed from Wells at 6.30am, 9.55am, 12.05pm, 1.25pm, 5.30pm and 7.40pm arriving at Witham at 7.05am, 10.35am, 12.40pm, 2.05pm, 6.20pm and 8.20pm respectively. The 6.30am, 5.30pm and 7.40pm departures were mixed. The only trains booked to call at Wanstrow were the 9.55am and 5.30pm, the latter only calling there as required. The 12.05pm departure from Wells did not call at Cranmore.

There was a daily goods only train to Wells that started from and returned to Oxford. This train departed from Witham at 8.00am and was booked to arrive at Wells at 8.55am serving Cranmore and Shepton Mallet en route. The return working departed from Wells at 9.40pm and arrived back at Witham at 10.40pm. This train also served Cranmore and Shepton Mallet. In spite of the gradients the working timetable does not contain any details as to how the intermediate sidings at Dulcote and Doulting were worked. According to the working timetable, the Sunday service consisted of only one train from Witham to Wells with no return working. This ran as a mixed train and departed from Witham at 8.00am, reaching Wells at 8.55am.

The service on the Cheddar Valley section in 1874 (August) consisted of six down and seven up passenger trains each day. Up passenger trains departed from Wells at 5.45am, 7.45am, 9.40am, 11.53am, 2.20pm, 5.30pm and 7.50pm, arriving at Yatton at 6.45am, 8.45am, 10.40am, 12.51pm, 3.18pm, 6.30pm and 8.50pm respectively. Two of these services did not call at Wookey and one did not call at Congresbury. Other than that,

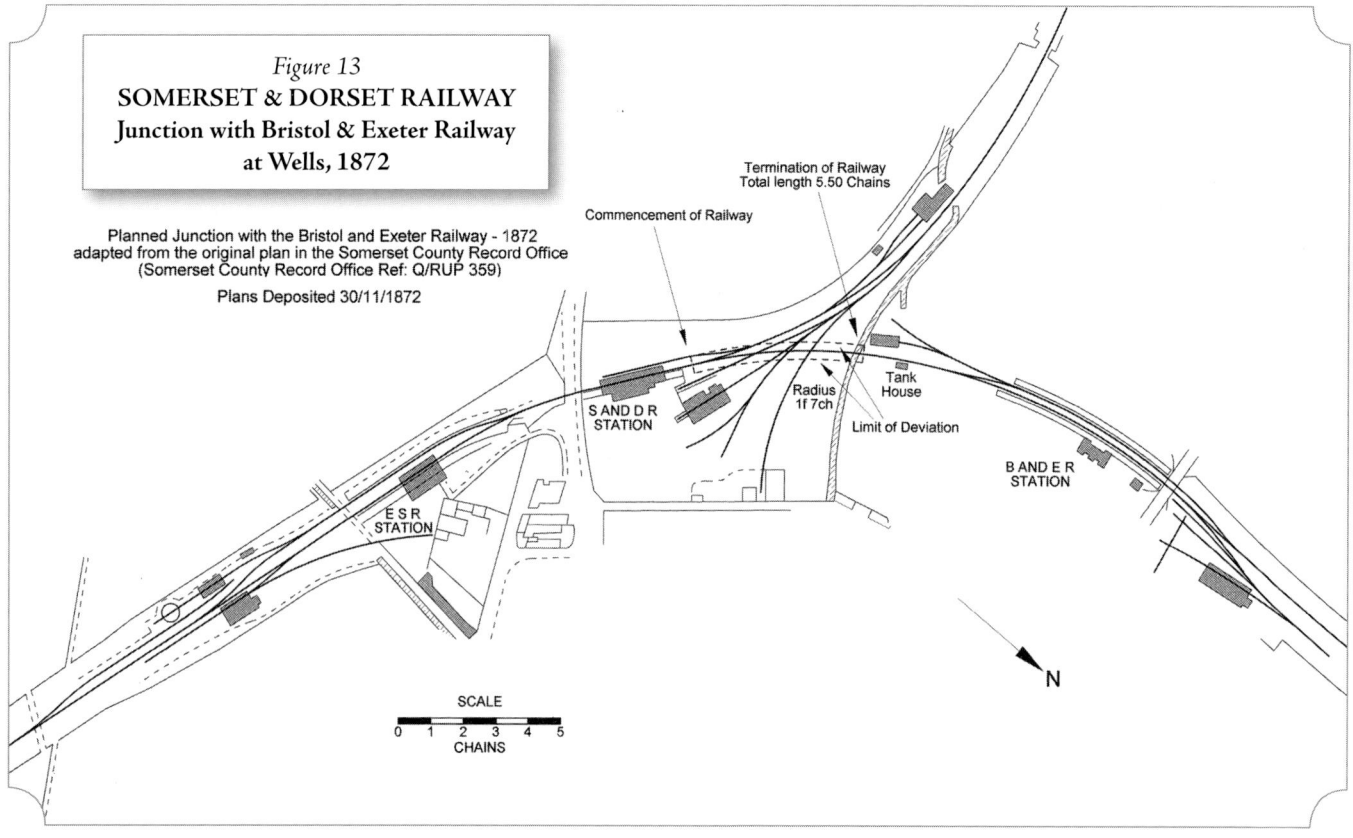

Figure 13
SOMERSET & DORSET RAILWAY
Junction with Bristol & Exeter Railway at Wells, 1872

Planned Junction with the Bristol and Exeter Railway - 1872 adapted from the original plan in the Somerset County Record Office (Somerset County Record Office Ref: Q/RUP 359)

Plans Deposited 30/11/1872

trains called at all intermediate stations. In the down direction passenger trains departed from Yatton at 9.30am, 11.55am, 1.10pm, 4.23pm, 6.45pm and 9.18pm arriving at Wells at 10.42am, 12.55pm, 2.10pm, 5.23pm, 7.45pm and 10.18pm respectively. All trains called at all intermediate stations. There was also one daily goods train in each direction between Bristol and Wells. The down goods started from Bristol at 5.30am and arrived at Yatton at 5.55am. After carrying out any necessary shunting, it left Yatton at 6.32am and arrived at Wells at 9.00am having called at all intermediate stations. Booked times at the intermediate stations were generally around five minutes, except for Cheddar where the train remained for twenty-six minutes during which time it was crossed by an up passenger train.

The up goods departed from Wells at 3.35pm and arrived at Yatton at 6.11pm having called at all intermediate stations. Booked times at the intermediate stations were generally longer than on the down journey. The train went forward from Yatton at 6.33pm arriving in Bristol at 7.00pm. On the first Saturday of each month the down goods ran as a mixed train conveying passengers for Wells Market. There were no Sunday services on the line.

For the purposes of regulating single line working the line was divided into two sections, Wells to Cheddar and Cheddar to Yatton, so that all intermediate crossing movements took place at Cheddar. The 1874 timetable described above required four crossing movements each day. Interestingly, Axbridge had a passing loop right from the opening day but the staff and ticket arrangements in force prevented trains from crossing there. It seems that this situation had been rectified by 1891 as the working timetable shows Yatton to Cheddar as two sections with three crossings movements at Axbridge each weekday.

In January 1876 the Great Western took over the Bristol & Exeter Railway, so the Great Western now found itself owning two of the three stations in Wells. In the meantime, the matter of the connecting link from the Cheddar Valley Railway to the Somerset & Dorset, and therefore to the East Somerset, had not been allowed to die. The Board of Trade eventually lifted its ban and permitted construction of the link to go ahead but it is not certain exactly why or when this change of mind happened. Plans were deposited on 30th November 1872 for a link five and a half chains in length on a curve of radius one furlong and seven chains (*Figure 13*). The commencement of the link was almost immediately at the western end of the Somerset & Dorset station platform. The planned line turned northwards passing right through the Somerset & Dorset goods yard. It was, of course, the proposed crossing of the goods yard lines by a passenger carrying line on the level that was the main reason for the Board of Trade's objection in the first place. The Board of Trade required a safety siding parallel to the connecting link with connections from each of the sidings in the Somerset & Dorset goods yard. The purpose of the safety siding was to protect the connecting link from runaway vehicles in the yard. Francis Fox wrote to the Board of Trade in February 1874 stating that two of the connections to the safety siding would have a radius of less than 120 feet which would be likely to cause derailments and suggested the use of scotches instead. Colonel Yolland disagreed and suggested that check rails should be installed to prevent derailments and that this arrangement would be safer than scotches. The Colonel went on to state that the railway should conduct some tests with check rails and only use scotches if the use of check rails did not prevent derailments. After the goods yard the line was to cross over the St. Andrew's

Plate 17 - This may be a relatively modern view taken on 7th May 1959 but it illustrates admirably the way the connection from the former B&E station, out of picture to the left, cuts a swathe through the S&D goods yard to connect with the S&D running line just this side of Priory Road station, right of centre. The former S&D goods shed and yard is straight ahead and is still busy although the passenger station had been closed since 1951. *Rex Conway collection*

Stream on a bridge and then make an end on junction with the former Bristol & Exeter Railway adjacent to the latter company's locomotive shed.

Once completed, the connecting link was inspected by Colonel Yolland in April 1875. His report dated 23rd April 1875 refused permission to open the link on the grounds of the width of the exchange platform at East Somerset station, insufficient protection of the running line from runaway vehicles in the Somerset & Dorset goods yard and the fact that locomotives running round at East Somerset would need to occupy the level crossing over Priory Road. It is interesting to note that during the time between the plans being deposited in 1872 and the inspection, the East Somerset had been converted to standard gauge and this almost certainly resulted in alterations to the track layout as shown in the original plan. The plans show that the connecting link was of mixed gauge which continued through the up platform of the Bristol & Exeter station. In the other direction, mixed gauge track continued through the Somerset & Dorset station, over the level crossing and into the East Somerset station which, after conversion of the line from Witham, contained a mixture of standard gauge, broad gauge and mixed gauge track (*Figure 12*). The Colonel's report was hand written and is in places quite difficult to decipher. It is interesting to note that whilst the language used in the report would by the standards of the twenty-first century be considered very formal, its presentation as hand written on unheaded note paper would not measure up to today's requirements. The full text of the report follows:

'Sir

I have the honour to report for the information of the Board of Trade in compliance with the instructions contained in your minute of the 15th instant that I have inspected the single line connecting the three stations together at Wells which belong to the East Somerset Branch of the Great Western, the Somerset and Dorset and the Cheddar Valley Branch of the Bristol and Exeter Railway companies which line runs across the goods lines of the Somerset and Dorset Railway Company on the level by the special authority of the legislature. The three passenger stations belonging to the three respective railway companies are all comprised in a distance of about a quarter of a mile and the line crosses an important turnpike road on the level also within the sanction of Parliament at the eastern end of the Somerset and Dorset passenger station by a single line of rails.

An exchange platform has been constructed in the East Somerset station yard for passengers to change carriages who may be proceeding in the narrow gauge trains of the Great Western Railway eastwards or by the broad gauge carriages of the Bristol and Exeter Railway westwards along the Cheddar Valley Railway. Provision is made for the engines of the Great Western Railway Company to run round their trains after arriving at their Wells station from the east by means of a mixed gauge loop line lying south of the Bristol and Exeter passenger line which is also used by the engines of the latter company.

From the position of the points etc., the Great Western engines cannot get from the western to the eastern end of their trains without first closing the level crossing gates, partly crossing the turnpike road and then shunting back along the loop line; and it is quite possible that hereafter complaints may be made on this subject by the road authorities.

The arrangements thus carried out, comply with the requirements of the Board of Trade and great pains have been taken to make such arrangements of the siding points and their connection with the signals by interlocking etc. as to provide against the danger inherent in crossing so many goods lines on the level, but it must be distinctly understood that these arrangements are not suitable for working the passenger trains through Wells as a through station.

I should however state that the Pillars which support the roof that covers the exchange platform in the East Somerset station yard are placed at a distance of from about 4 feet 8 inches to 5 feet of the south edge of this platform. The requirement of the Board of Trade being 6 feet.

Plate 18 - It may be a poor postcard of the platform side of the station building at Wells Tucker Street station, but is included because it is the only one available of this side of the building in this era, c.1912.   *Lens of Sutton Association*

This may be recognised as a mere temporary arrangement, on receipt of an understanding from the Great Western Railway Company to alter the position of the pillars and to give the required width in the course of six months; but in the absence of any undertaking I must report that this single line cannot by reason of the incompleteness of the works be opened for passenger traffic without danger to the public using the same. I must not moreover be understood to assent to the present construction of this station so far as it renders it necessary to shunt engines etc., across the turnpike road.

A good deal has been done by the Bristol and Exeter Railway Company in carrying out these works to render the working into and out of the Somerset and Dorset passenger station safe but there are still sidings lying south of their passenger lines which are not provided with blind sidings or throw off points to prevent vehicles from being brought out of them without the sanction of the signalman on duty.

I have requested that a tracing of the three stations should be provided.

*I have etc.
W. Yolland
Colonel'*

(The National Archives; RAIL 253/707)

Thus the saga of the connecting link between the three stations at Wells was destined to drag on for a few more years. Its use was no doubt further delayed by the imminent conversion of the Cheddar Valley line to the standard gauge which would render the alterations obsolete and would in any case require a further inspection. It does seem, however, that the Great Western made alterations to the pillars as requested in the report. The general manager of the railway wrote to the Board of Trade in September 1875 confirming that the alterations had been made. In the same month Colonel Yolland requested a new copy of the drawing (referred to as a tracing) as he considered that the one sent following his request in the April report was not accurate. The new drawing was received later in the month and the Colonel noted that,

'The new tracing now represents what I believe to be the true state of the East Somerset station yard and materially differs from the former tracing.'

The mixed gauge rails on the Somerset & Dorset had remained in use until 1868, there being a broad gauge Bristol & Exeter goods train that ran daily from Bristol to Wells via Highbridge up until that time. Quite what happened to that traffic in the intervening period up until the opening of the Bristol & Exeter Railway into Wells is not certain.

Although the broad gauge had now gone from the three lines into Wells evidence of its existence remained. The platform spacings at Wells, Cheddar and Axbridge were obviously wider than those at Congresbury, Shepton Mallet and Cranmore. The first three stations had two platforms and passing loops during the broad gauge era whereas the latter three had their second platform and loop added some years after the gauge conversion. According to local folklore in Wells, the unused length of rail was left in place in the roadway at Priory Road level crossing following the gauge conversion. It seems that it remained there until at least the 1930s. Since the line over the crossing was of mixed gauge at the time, no work was actually needed to be done to the road surface during the gauge conversion. The various authorities may have decided to leave the crossing as it was until such time as maintenance was required in order to minimise the disruption to both road and rail traffic.

Problems with permanent way during the 1870s were not confined to the Cheddar Valley section of the Bristol & Exeter Railway. In 1876 there was a derailment at Flax Bourton, between Yatton and Bristol, largely caused by the condition of the track. As engineer, Francis Fox was blamed although his assistant, none other than John Fox, had been appointed as deputy to oversee track matters. Francis wrote a rule book for permanent way maintenance some three years earlier that seems to have been largely ignored by all those who should have complied with it.

The problems that prevented the opening of the connecting link between the former East Somerset and Cheddar Valley stations remained unresolved. This resulted in a number of operating practices and specific incidents that soon attracted the attention of higher ranking officials of the Great Western Railway. Following a visit to Wells on 2nd November 1876, Alexander Wood, the Great Western Deputy Chairman, issued a report highlighting a number of problems he found there. The full text of Mr. Wood's report is as follows:

'The first thing which attracted my attention was a new First Class Coach, sent from Swindon upon the order of Mr. Stephenson. I subsequently learned that, at Wells, there was no advice of this vehicle's arrival, and that being destined to relieve a Bristol and Exeter coach it had been sent to the wrong station at Wells; and to reach the right one it had to go via Bristol! I merely mention this as a forcible illustration of the very great importance of connecting our two Wells Stations at the earliest moment.

The next thing in the Station yard that attracted my attention was the Cattle Pens. They evidently had been disused for some time. As much as four months previously the Government Inspector, in consequence of the pens not being paved, had condemned them and prohibited their use.

The only cattle passing to or from the Great Western Railway system at Wells station, on the Witham branch is loaded or unloaded at the Passenger Station and on the Passenger Platform. It certainly seems to me to be a most objectionable arrangement.

As regards the general goods, the South Western and Midland goods were delivered regularly between 9 and 10am, but ours remain undelivered until between 2 and 3pm.

As regards the passenger traffic, our best train is the 1.10, timed to run in 4 hours and 40 minutes. By our morning train run from Swindon at express fares, passengers are on the road upwards of five hours, while if they do not pay express fares from Swindon, upwards of six hours. The South Western convey their passengers to London at a more convenient time than ours, accomplishing the journey without express fares, and in very little over 4 hours.'

Looking at it from the present time it is quite difficult to understand why such incidents, although not of a totally trivial nature, would command the attention of such a high ranking official. Perhaps in these days of delegation of responsibility and empowerment of the individual we forget the control that the most senior levels of management took in the day to day running of the railways at this time. Railway managements today are more concerned with the issues of business and finance and would have little understanding of day to day operational problems such as these. Mr. Wood's comments on the importance of the connecting link are also interesting because, of course, the link was already in existence. The amount of work to bring the link up to the standard required by the Board of Trade was not great but it was to be more than a year before the problem was finally resolved. However, Mr. Wood's observations on goods traffic brought a much swifter response. John Grant, the Chief Goods Manager of the Great Western replied as follows:

'The late delivery of the London Traffic at Wells has for some time past been complained of, and although there is now some improvement I am not satisfied that it will continue.

The London traffic for Wells is conveyed by the 11.35pm train which is due at Witham at 8am. The Witham branch goods train leaves at 8.35, and if the London train keeps proper time the goods would be at Wells at 9.20am. The London train is, however, frequently late, so that the branch train has to leave without the London goods, which are detained at Witham until 12 noon which reaches Wells at 12.40pm.

Formerly the Weymouth train which conveys the Wells traffic to Witham started at 11.15am and reached Witham

Plate 19 - The photographer is standing on Priory Road platform c.1949 with the S&D signal box in the centre of the picture. The link to Tucker Street station curves away to the right, crossing the S&D goods yard lines. The left-hand starter signal on the bracket is for the S&D running line; the right-hand signal and distant are for the route to Tucker Street.
J Moss; Roger Carpenter collection

about half an hour earlier than at present, but the time of this train had to be altered and put in later in order that a new and important narrow gauge train from Swindon to Exeter should start at 11.15am.'

In January 1877 a report was issued by James Grierson, the Great Western's General Manager, on the workings of Wells station. It seems that as a result of pressure of work on the company's engineering staff, the delays in making improvements to the crossing arrangements in order to satisfy the Board of Trade had been '*summarily excused*'. The report also commented on the matter of cattle traffic raised by Alexander Wood the previous year. Grierson concluded that the cattle business at Wells was '*a very small traffic*'. The receipts for the years 1874, 1875 and 1876 were given as £448, £500 and £474 for the Great Western (at East Somerset) and £185, £202 and £345 for the Bristol & Exeter (at their station) respectively. An extract from the report on this matter is as follows:

'*.... With regard to the GWR cattle pens having been closed by the cattle inspector .... an estimate was submitted for paving the pens, but it was considered undesirable to recommend the Board incur the expenditure estimated at £44.4s.6d.*

From the memorandum of the Deputy Chairman, he seemed to be under the impression (1) that the cattle trade of Wells is a large trade and (2) that this Company lost a considerable proportion of it because the pens were closed. ....'

Grierson moved on to consider the working of a through service between Yatton and Witham:

'*.... owing to the difficulty of meeting the through trains at Witham and Yatton by running the engines and trains through between those stations, there not being sufficient traffic to justify the running of increased mileage.*'

The line from Yatton to Wells was converted to standard gauge between Monday, 15th and Thursday, 18th November 1875. No work on the conversion was carried out at the weekend because the directors did not believe in Sunday working. It was some time before an inspection was made by the Board of Trade, this not being until September 1876 when the line was inspected by Captain Tyler. It could be argued that gauge conversion was little more than a relaying or permanent way maintenance exercise and would therefore not require to be inspected. In any case it seems to have been treated as being of low priority. It was found that the conversion had been done by simply moving one rail inwards to provide the correct gauge. As a consequence of this the length of sleeper outside the rail was over two feet more on one side that the other. The inspector did not approve of this and recommended that the rails should be placed in the middle of the sleepers and the extra two feet or so should be cut off. He reported that

'*... better arrangements are needed to prevent needless multiplication of cases where rails of different sections meet.*'

The track was laid with a mixture of 72lb/yd and 75lb/yd flat bottomed rails (Vignoles) and his remarks imply that the two different sections of rail had been used interchangeably. In addition to this he found that the fishplates were not properly fitted and in many cases the bolts were too short to go through the rails, particularly where rails of different sections met. It was also found that three miles of track were a quarter of an inch under gauge, which it seems had come about under the verbal orders of the engineer, Mr John Fox. It was apparent from this report that the line was generally unsafe but it had been in use for ten months without mishap. Incidentally, this was the only section of the Bristol & Exeter Railway to be converted during the company's independent existence, mainly due to the fact that the line was laid with transverse sleepers in the first place which would have made conversion a simpler procedure. The engineer may have had conversion in mind when the line was first constructed. The use of transverse sleepers rather than baulk road construction meant that the track was laid using flat bottomed rail instead of bridge rail. The latter type of rail requires to be supported along its full length as it is not sufficiently stiff in the vertical plane to support the weight of a moving train. During the same visit Captain Tyler also inspected the mixed gauge on the Bristol & Exeter main line.

Captain Tyler's report also required further work to be carried out on the Cheddar Valley line. A shelter was needed on the down platform at Axbridge and repairs to the fencing were required at various places on the line. Wells station (Tucker Street) was only signalled as a terminus and additional signalling was required before it could be used as a through station for passenger trains. At Yatton the facing points controlling access to the goods loop from the single line were 329 yards from the signal box which was considered to be too far. Captain Tyler required the points to be worked by a ground frame released by the Yatton to Cheddar train staff.

A further inspection was made in July 1877 by Colonel Yolland who reported that the line was generally in good order and that the ends of about 40,000 sleepers had been cut off as requested but that there were places where the gauge was only 4ft 8¼in. The Colonel pointed out that the requirement for a shelter on the down platform at Axbridge and a ground frame for the loop points at Yatton, which had already been stated in Captain Tyler's report of the previous year, had still not been attended to. The Great Western subsequently carried out this work and confirmed that it had been completed in November 1877. The Board of Trade signified that it required no further alterations to be carried out.

As from 1st January 1878 the connecting link between the former East Somerset and former Bristol & Exeter stations was finally brought into use for passenger traffic. The East Somerset station was closed for passengers and the yard became the main Great Western goods depot whilst the former Bristol & Exeter station became the Great Western's passenger station for both the former East Somerset and Cheddar Valley services. Since Colonel Yolland's inspection of 1875, the Cheddar Valley line had been converted to standard gauge and its permanent way had been brought up to an acceptable standard during 1877. This fact, in conjunction with the concentration of Great

Western passenger services at the former Bristol & Exeter station, meant that two of the three objections raised in the inspector's report of 1875 were no longer valid. The exchange platform would no longer be required and there would be no need to run locomotives round and so occupy the level crossing unduly. This just left the matter of the protection of the running line where it ran through the Somerset & Dorset yard. Readers will recall that Colonel Yolland required a '*safety siding*' where the connecting link ran through the Somerset & Dorset goods yard but that Francis Fox thought that scotches would suffice. In the event Colonel Yolland won the argument and the safety siding was put in place with sharply curved slip connections to ensure that any run away vehicle would be diverted onto the safety siding headshunt and not foul the running line. This layout was simplified in about 1921 when the safety siding and slip connections were removed and catch points or traps were put in on the siding connections either side of the running line to protect it from runaways.

Another rationalisation that took place in 1877/78 was the closure of the former Bristol & Exeter engine shed and the transfer of its allocation to the former East Somerset shed, which then became the Great Western's only shed at Wells. The actual date this took place is not certain but there is evidence that it may have been as early as 1876 when the link had actually been completed but was not yet authorised for use by passenger trains. There was no reason why the link it could not have been used for light engine movements or goods trains. In 1879 the former East Somerset engine shed was demolished and a new twin road engine shed was built on more or less the same site to replace it. The turntable at Wells station was taken out at this time only to be reinstated a few years later and it remained in use until the 1920s. Latterly the site of the former Bristol & Exeter shed and turntable was occupied by two carriage sidings.

The Bristol & Exeter station remained as the Great Western and later British Railways (Western Region) passenger station until the end of passenger services in 1963. In spite of the connecting link, the East Somerset and Cheddar Valley sections still maintained much of their own identities as far as timetabling was concerned.

Somerset & Dorset passenger traffic from Glastonbury continued to be handled at its own Priory Road station and was only really affected by the fact that all Great Western services passed through it, although without stopping at this time.

DEVELOPMENTS ON THE EAST SOMERSET SECTION

When the East Somerset Railway was taken over by the Great Western it was still being worked as a single section between Witham and Wells with only one train allowed on the line at any one time. Some consideration had been made in 1872, shortly before the takeover, to introduce the electric telegraph and split the line into two sections, each with its own train staff, and work the line on the absolute block system. The Great Western installed the electric telegraph and wrote to the Board of Trade in December 1874 stating that they wished to cancel the undertaking of 1858 and work the line with the train staff and ticket system. The line would be split into two sections, Witham to Shepton Mallet and Shepton Mallet to Wells. Both Shepton Mallet and Cranmore stations were originally constructed with only one platform. Shepton Mallet station was the original terminus of the line and so had a loop to enable locomotives to run round. It also had a siding with a goods shed on the up side. Cranmore had no siding accommodation when the line opened but a couple of sidings were added in 1873. The Board of Trade required distant signals to be erected to protect the sidings but when the Great Western signed an undertaking that the sidings would only be shunted using a locomotive and not by horses or manpower, the requirement was withdrawn.

A Board of Trade minute of January 1875 favoured the introduction of train staff and ticket working between Witham and Wells but one engine in steam working remained in force until 1880. The reason for this is not clear but it may have been because, until such time that either Cranmore or Shepton Mallet were provided with a second platform and a fully signalled

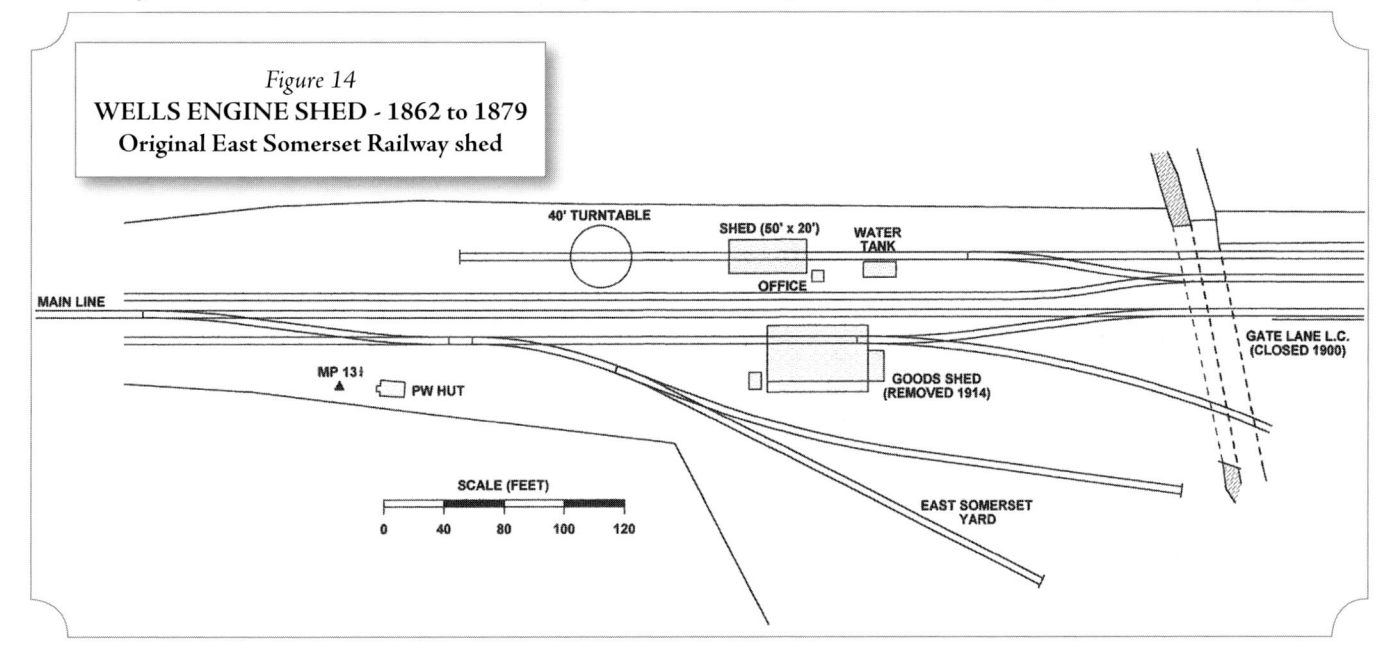

Figure 14
WELLS ENGINE SHED - 1862 to 1879
Original East Somerset Railway shed

Plate 20 - A general, but grainy, view of the facilities at Cranmore in 1933. Just a single line and platform had been provided until 1880, when a passing loop and a second platform were built to enable additional passenger trains to use the line from Wells to Witham.
Brunel University, Mowat collection

passing loop, it would still not be possible to run more than one passenger train on the line at any one time. It seems that plans were drawn up for the construction of passing loops but they were rejected by Grierson on the grounds of cost. The engineer was requested to come up with a more economical solution and it was agreed to dispense with the passing loop at Shepton Mallet for the time being and only construct one at Cranmore.

A passing loop with a second platform and additional sidings to cope with the increasing mineral traffic were brought into use at Cranmore in 1880. A signal box was built on the up platform next to the station building. Some years before, a tramway had been constructed from the nearby Waterlip Quarry to a loading dock and stone crushing plant in the station yard. The tramway is discussed in more detail in a later chapter. The new track layout was inspected by Colonel Rich on behalf of the Board of Trade and his report dated 31st May 1880 required some alteration to the interlocking before the alterations were passed as fit for use. The one engine in steam undertaking of 1858 was cancelled by the Board of Trade on 24th August 1880 when staff and ticket working in conjunction with the block telegraph came into force. The line was now divided into two block sections: Witham to Cranmore and Cranmore to Wells.

Train Services in 1879

Although the connecting link between the Cheddar Valley and East Somerset sections was now in place they were still effectively being operated as separate branches. In the physical sense Wells was now a through station but from the point of view of passenger operation it acted as the terminus for services on both sections of the line. In October 1879 the weekday service on the Cheddar Valley section consisted of five passenger trains in each direction between Yatton and Wells each day. Up passenger trains departed from Wells at 7.50am, 9.55am, 11.43am, 2.40pm and 5.40pm arriving at Yatton at 8.50am, 10.55am, 12.45pm, 3.40pm and 6.40pm respectively. It is interesting to note that the working timetable does not indicate whether any of the services continued through to Bristol. This would, of course, have been possible as the main line had been mixed gauge since 1875. In the down direction passenger trains departed from Yatton at 9.45am, 11.45am, 1.20pm, 4.00pm and 7.10pm arriving at Wells at 10.57am, 12.45pm, 2.20pm, 5.00pm and 8.10pm respectively.

Additional passenger accommodation was afforded by the early Bristol and Wells goods that ran as a mixed train between Cheddar and Wells. This train was the first down train of the day on the Cheddar Valley section. It arrived at Yatton from Bristol at 6.00am and departed again at 6.20am arriving at Cheddar at 7.40am where it crossed the first up passenger train. Leaving Cheddar at 8.15am it was booked to arrive at Wells at 9.15am. The allowance of one hour for a journey of under eight miles must have been very tedious indeed, especially for those in eager anticipation of the day's work ahead. Twenty-five minutes alone of this time were allowed for shunting at Wookey. There was also an evening passenger working between Yatton and Cheddar. This train left Yatton at 5.20pm calling at all stations and was booked to arrive at Cheddar at 5.52pm. On the return journey the train left Cheddar at 8.15pm again calling at all stations and was booked to arrive at Yatton at 8.47pm.

As for other goods traffic on the Cheddar Valley section there was an up train that left Wells at 3.25pm. It was booked to call at all stations except Winscombe and Congresbury which were only served as required. This train spent forty-seven minutes at Cheddar during which time it was crossed by the 4.00pm down passenger train and was due to arrive at Yatton at 6.55pm before departing for Bristol at 7.10pm. There was also the Bristol and Cheddar goods that was timetabled to run on Mondays, Wednesdays and Fridays only. It arrived at Yatton from Bristol at 4.00pm, departed again at 4.10pm and was due at Cheddar at 5.00pm, calling at Sandford and Axbridge en route. After the necessary shunting operations at Cheddar the return working, referred to as the 'Cheddar and Bristol Goods' in the working timetable, would depart at 7.40pm and was due to arrive at Yatton at 8.15pm. All intermediate stations except for Axbridge were only served as required. This train would continue its journey to Bristol, departing from Yatton at 8.25pm.

At this time there was still a separate working timetable for the East Somerset section as if to emphasise its operational

Plate 21 - The two-road engine shed built at Wells East Somerset to replace the original East Somerset Railway shed that was demolished in 1879. The photograph is undated and the LMS-designed 2-6-2T inside is unidentified. *Lens of Sutton Association*

independence from the Cheddar Valley section. Six down and five up passenger trains ran each weekday between Witham and Wells, some running as mixed trains. In the down direction passenger trains departed from Witham at 8.20am, 12.35pm, 2.15pm, 4.25pm, 7.15pm and 9.05pm arriving at Wells at 9.15am, 1.10pm, 3.00pm, 5.15pm, 7.55pm and 9.45pm respectively. Of these trains both the 4.25pm and the 7.15pm were mixed. All stations were served except that the 12.35pm, the 7.15pm and the 9.05pm trains did not call at Wanstrow. In the up direction passenger trains departed from Wells at 6.10am, 9.45am, 3.15pm, 6.00pm and 8.05pm arriving at Witham at 6.50am, 10.30am, 4.00pm, 6.55pm and 8.50pm respectively. All were mixed except for the 9.45am departure. Only the 6.00pm departure called at Wanstrow. There was also a Wednesdays only passenger train that departed from Wells at 1.10pm and arrived at Witham at 1.50pm calling at all stations except Wanstrow. Interestingly, Wanstrow, which at that time was only an unstaffed halt, was served by three down trains but only one up train each day. The timings were such that passengers travelling from Wanstrow to Witham or Frome would be unable to return on the same day.

Goods-only trains on the East Somerset section at that time consisted of two trains in each direction running the full length of the branch and one stone train in each direction between Witham and Shepton Mallet only. The first down goods, known in the working timetable as the 'Yeovil and Swindon Goods', left Witham at 6.50am calling at Cranmore and Shepton Mallet before arriving at Wells at 7.35am. The second down goods, known as the 'Wells and Chippenham Goods', departed from Witham at 7.20am, also calling at Cranmore and Shepton Mallet before arriving at Wells at 8.20am. Neither of these trains appeared to have much time for shunting at intermediate stations. Interestingly, the working timetable shows their arrival at Wells passenger station and neglects to mention any working of East Somerset yard. There was also the 'Stone Train' that left Witham at 11.15am and arrived at Shepton Mallet at 11.50am. Cranmore and Doulting Siding were worked as required. There was no siding at Wanstrow at this time. The booked time for this train at Shepton Mallet was five minutes, which would have left little time for anything other than running round. Having departed from Shepton Mallet at 11.55am the up 'Stone Train' was booked to arrive at Witham at 12.20pm, calling at Cranmore as required but not at Doulting Siding. The two up ordinary goods trains were the return workings of the Yeovil and Swindon Goods that departed from Wells at 10.00am, arriving at Witham at 11.15am, and the Wells and Chippenham Goods that left Wells at 10.00pm and arrived at Witham at 11.15pm. Both trains served Shepton Mallet and Cranmore. The latter was allowed twenty-five minutes for shunting at Cranmore.

Sunday services on both sections of the line were very sparse indeed. On the East Somerset section the only train was a down Chippenham and Wells goods. It departed from Witham at 7.15am and was due to arrive at Wells at 8.30am calling at Cranmore and Shepton Mallet. The writer has not been able to find out whether there were any Sunday services on the Cheddar

Valley section at this date.

Anyone who wished to travel between the East Somerset and Cheddar Valley sections would soon discover that the connections at Wells were far from 'passenger friendly'. The first two departures from Wells to Witham left before the arrival of the first service from Yatton. Thus any passenger travelling from the Cheddar Valley to the East Somerset would be advised to catch the 1.20pm from Yatton in order to connect with the 3.15pm from Wells to Witham. Even this meant a fifty-five minute wait at Wells! The only other reasonable connection in this direction was afforded by the 3.40pm from Yatton which connected with the 6.00pm departure to Witham, albeit with a one hour wait at Wells. For passengers travelling in the opposite direction the connections were better but still far from ideal. The 8.20am from Witham connected with the 9.55am from Wells to Yatton, the 12.35pm from Witham connected with the 2.40pm from Wells to Yatton and the 4.25pm from Witham connected with the 5.40pm from Wells to Yatton. The waiting times at Wells were forty minutes, ninety minutes and forty minutes respectively.

GREAT WESTERN RAILWAY.

CHEAP BOOKINGS TO CLEVEDON AND WESTON-SUPER-MARE

EVERY WEDNESDAY AND SATURDAY,
Commencing on July 4th, 1877, and
UNTIL FURTHER NOTICE,
CHEAP TICKETS WILL BE ISSUED AS UNDER, BY TRAINS

Leaving	A.M.	A.M.	P.M.	FARES TO & FRO CLEVEDON or WESTON
				FIRST CLASS. THIRD CLASS.
WELLS	at 7 45	11 43	or 2 40	
WOOKEY	" 7 50	11 49	" 2 45	
LODGE HILL	" 7 59	11 58	" 2 54	2s 6d 1s 6d
DRAYCOTT	" 8 6	12 6	" 3 1	
CHEDDAR	" 8 13	12 14	" 3 8	
AXBRIDGE	" 8 20	12 20	" 3 15	
WINSCOMBE	" 8 27	12 27	" 3 22	2s 1s
SANDFORD and BANWELL	" 8 32	12 32	" 3 27	
CONGRESBURY	" 8 40	12 40	" 3 35	

Returning from CLEVEDON or WESTON-SUPER-MARE by any Train on the day of issue only.

Children under 12 years of age Half-price.   No Luggage allowed.

The Tickets are not transferable and are not available for any other than the Station marked upon them.

The EXCURSION ROOM at WESTON-SUPER-MARE is open free to all holders of Tickets. Tea and Coffee with other Refreshments may be had on very reasonable terms.

Passengers holding Weston-Super-Mare Excursion Tickets may return by any Train stopping at BLEADON and UPHILL without extra charge.

PADDINGTON, June, 1877.   J. GRIERSON, General Manager.

(5000).   ARROWSMITH, Printer, Quay Street, Bristol.

(Left) Plate 22 - A handbill for the summer of 1877 showing train times and prices for cheap day bookings to the Bristol Channel towns.

PROMOTIONAL LITERATURE of the 1870s

from the author's collection

(Right) Plate 23 - A handbill from July 1878, a year later than that on this page. Whereas the handbill to the left offered cheap day return fares, those listed in this handbill are valid for up to two months, they start from London and are for more adventurous expeditions. Cheddar and Wells (B&E) are listed in the fare table but note that the typesetter cannot decide on the spelling of 'Bridgwater'.

GREAT WESTERN RAILWAY.

ILFRACOMBE, LYNTON AND LYNMOUTH,

Per GREAT WESTERN RAILWAY to Portishead, via Bristol, and thence per commodious Steamship.

DAILY SERVICE
(Sundays excepted).

THROUGH FARES including Railways, Steamers, and all charges on Landing and Embarkation.

LONDON, Paddington, Westbourne Park, and Kensington. [Return and Circular Tickets at London Fares are also issued at Victoria, Uxbridge Rd., Moorgate St., Cook's Office, Ludgate Circus, Farringdon Street, Mansion House, Blackfriars, Charing Cross, Westminster Bridge.]	SINGLE. 1st Class Best Cabin and Promenade Deck.	SINGLE. 2nd Class Best Cabin and Promenade Deck.	SINGLE. 3rd Class Fore Cabin and Main Deck.	RETURN. Available for Two Months. 1st Class Best Cabin and Promenade Deck.	RETURN. 2nd Class Best Cabin and Promenade Deck.	RETURN. 3rd Class Fore Cabin and Main Deck.	CIRCULAR. Forward via Portishead, and return by Coach, and Devon and Somerset Railway or vice versa. 1st Class	CIRCULAR. 2nd Class
	S. D.	S. D.	S. D.	S. D.	S. D.	S. D.	S. D.	S. D.
	29 6	24 6	15 0	43 6	36 0	22 6	49 3	68 0
OXFORD	24 0	20 6	13 0	35 6	29 9	19 6	45 0	36 6
READING	25 6	21 6	13 6	37 6	31 9	20 3	46 0	36 6
WARWICK	32 0	26 0	16 0	47 6	38 3	24 0	54 6	43 0
LEAMINGTON	32 0	26 0	16 0	47 6	38 3	24 0	54 6	43 0
BANBURY	28 6	23 6	14 6	42 6	34 9	22 6	52 0	41 6
STROUD	20 0	17 0	11 0	29 6	24 9	16 0	36 0	30 0
CIRENCESTER	19 6	16 6	10 6	28 0	24 3	15 9	36 6	30 6
SWINDON	18 6	16 0	10 0	27 0	23 3	15 3	35 6	29 6
CHIPPENHAM	15 6	13 6	8 6	23 0	19 6	13 3	31 0	25 6
BATH	11 6	10 6	7 6	17 6	15 6	10 6	26 6	22 6
NEWPORT	15 0	12 6	9 0	22 0	18 6	13 0	31 0	25 6
CHEPSTOW	13 6	12 0	8 6	19 6	17 6	12 6	28 9	24 3
CHEDDAR	...	...	...	19 0	17 0	12 9	23 6	19 6
CLEVEDON	...	...	...	17 6	16 0	11 9	22 0	18 6
HIGHBRIDGE	...	...	...	22 3	19 3	13 6	22 0	18 6
WELLS (B. & E.)	...	...	...	21 0	18 3	14 0	26 6	22 0
WESTON-SUPER-MARE	...	...	...	19 0	17 0	12 3	22 0	18 6
BRIDGEWATER	...	...	...	25 3	22 6	15 0	22 0	18 6

The Steamer will start from Portishead Pier about 1.15 p.m., after the arrival of the Trains leaving Paddington at 9.0 a.m.; Oxford, 9.30; Reading, 9.50; Warwick, 7.36; Leamington, 8.0; Banbury, 8.29; Stroud, 8.7; Cirencester, 7.50; Swindon, 10.55; Chippenham, 9.45; Bath, 11.35; Wells (B. & E.), 9.55; Highbridge, 10.42; Weston-Super-Mare, 10.45; Cheddar, 10.23; Clevedon, 11.0; and Bridgwater at 10.29 a.m.

PADDINGTON, *July*, 1878.   J. GRIERSON, *General Manager*.

Waterlow and Sons Limited, Printers, London Wall, London.

Plate 24 - This aerial view of Wells on 12th May 1933 shows the railway running along the south-west edge of the city. The Great Western station, Tucker Street, is on the line wending its way to the top left-hand corner of the photograph and thence towards Cheddar and Yatton; shunting is in progress since vehicles have been left on the main line near the advanced starter. At the extreme left hand edge is the Somerset & Dorset engine shed with engine and vehicle apparently at rest. The single line branch from Glastonbury passed behind the shed and, curving to the right, joins the line from Tucker Street just before entering Priory Road station, originally the terminus of the Somerset Central Railway's branch. There are some covered vehicles this side of the train shed that constitutes Priory Road station. The two areas that caused concern at Wells are visible in this picture. Firstly, the passage of the former Bristol & Exeter Railway line from Tucker Street to Priory Road which passed through the Somerset & Dorset goods yard and precipitated much correspondence with the Board of Trade, is almost in the middle of this view. Secondly, Priory Road crossing, just to the east of Priory Road station, is on the road stretching from bottom left, past the cheese factory and thence to top right of the picture. The options to reduce the lengthy interruptions to road traffic across this crossing occupied the minds of both the City council and the Great Western company. *English Heritage, Aerofilms collection*

Chapter Six

1880 TO THE PRESENT DAY

Following the opening of the connecting link at Wells and the subsequent rationalisation of the separate facilities originally provided there for the Cheddar Valley and East Somerset sections, the line achieved its final form which it retained until closure. That is not to say that there were no further developments on the line. Improvements to station facilities, the addition of passing loops and sidings and the replacement of signal boxes all took place well into the twentieth century, not least of which was the opening of the Wrington Vale Light Railway in 1901. In fact some of the most far-reaching improvements to the easternmost section of the line did not take place until the 1970s, some years after the withdrawal of passenger services. The chapter on signalling deals with track and signalling alterations at individual stations in some detail.

After its closure to passengers in 1878 the former East Somerset station building in Wells became a cheese store for Marsh and Adlam. The island platform originally constructed for the exchange of traffic with the Bristol & Exeter was demolished, although the position it occupied could be identified by the track layout that existed right up until closure of the line. The platform face on the station building side was still in existence when the line closed. The station building caught fire in the early afternoon of Friday, 21st September 1929 but, despite the efforts of the Wells Fire Brigade and local residents, it was reduced to a burned-out shell within an hour. Paul Fry's book *Railways into Wells* gives an account of the fire and also includes some of the only known photographs of the former East Somerset station building, including that at *Plate 9*.

When the line opened, the goods facilities at Wookey consisted of a single siding on the down side with a goods shed at the Wells end. Access to the siding was via a crossover facing from the Cheddar direction. At the Cheddar end of the siding there was a wagon turntable providing access to another siding at right angles which led into the nearby paper mill. The date that this siding was installed is unknown but in 1880 the Great Western Railway provided improved access to the paper mill site. The crossover was reversed and placed adjacent to the station so that the lead off the running line was adjacent to the station building on the platform. The crossover was now facing from the Wells direction. A new connection, also facing from the Wells direction, ran from the down siding into the paper mill. The Great Western Railway informed the Board of Trade of the alterations, which were inspected by Major General Hutchinson and his reported dated 24th March 1880 recommended that they be brought into use. Interestingly, the drawing which shows the alterations does not include the signal box but does indicate the position of up and down home and distant signals. We can only assume that some form of signal box was in existence but whether it was the same one as was there on the platform in later years is a matter of speculation.

The Joint Station Proposal and Priory Road Level Crossing

The opening of the link between the Cheddar Valley section and the Somerset & Dorset station to passenger traffic led to a rapid increase in rail traffic using Priory Road level crossing. Before this it had only been used for the exchange of traffic. The level crossing was brought into use on the same date that the Wells extension of the East Somerset opened in March 1862. This was in spite of the fact that, when the Act was under consideration in 1860, the Parliamentary Select Committee received a recommendation from Colonel Yolland of the Board of Trade Railway Inspectorate that it should not be sanctioned. The reason given was that level crossings had been found to be '*a great inconvenience*' at places where a passenger station and goods station were on the opposite sides of a level crossing; and it was considered that passenger stations belonging to different companies in a similar position would be equally inconvenient. It seems that insertion of sections into the Act to make provision for replacement of the level crossing by a bridge, should it prove necessary, was sufficient for the objection to be withdrawn.

In addition to its use by service trains travelling between Wells Great Western passenger station and Witham, the crossing also saw use by light engines running between the station and the new Great Western locomotive shed in East Somerset yard. There were also transfer trips between the various goods yards. The gates would also be closed across the road when a Somerset & Dorset train was approaching from Glastonbury. This was because the gates were interlocked with the signals in order to protect the crossing in the event of the train over-running the station. This caused much annoyance to road users who, having no knowledge of the operational requirements of the railway and the safety requirements of the Board of Trade, could not understand why the gates had to be closed when no train was booked to run over the crossing. In Brunel's original survey it was planned to have a road underbridge but the height of the water table precluded this. Complaints about the level crossing were made both to the Somerset & Dorset and the Great Western companies. The responsibility was mainly that of the Great Western although the S&D was partly to blame.

Such was the concern by 1881 that the Town Clerk wrote to the Great Western, the Midland and the London and South Western Railways requesting the construction of a joint station to replace the two remaining stations. The City Council argued that if a joint station were to be constructed on the site of the Somerset & Dorset station then delays at the level crossing would be reduced, particularly when trains were due to cross at Wells. The Great Western Railway responded that the existing Priory Road station would be inadequate and that a new station would have to be constructed at a considerable cost and, even then, some delay at the level crossing would be inevitable. The Great Western issued instructions to their operating staff to ensure that delays were kept to a minimum.

The City Council resolved to press the Great Western to reconsider the matter and asked that they should not be deterred on the matter of cost. The Great Western stated that being a commercial organisation it could not possibly ignore the financial considerations but if the Council were willing to contribute, then the railway company would be prepared to consider the matter further. The City Council retorted that it had no power to devote public funds to a joint station and asked the railway company to furnish them with a plan of what it proposed doing so that it could be laid before the inhabitants of the city. The Great Western said that it had no plans as the directors considered the traffic at Wells to be insufficient to justify the financial outlay of a joint station. The Midland and the London & South Western companies were more favourable but without the backing of the Great Western no further progress could be made.

The Town Clerk wrote to the Board of Trade on 30th January 1882 on the matter of the joint station, the delays at the level crossing and the fact that dialogue with the Great Western Railway was not making satisfactory progress as far as the City Council was concerned. Three questions were put to the Board of Trade for their consideration:

1. Does the Great Western Railway have the powers to close the gates from 15 to 20 minutes at a time?

2. Could the Board of Trade, under the circumstances, compel the railway companies concerned to make a joint station?

3. Could the Great Western Railway be compelled to construct a bridge in place of the level crossing if a joint station could not be made?

The Board of Trade's response was that sections 15 and 16 of the original East Somerset Railway Act of 1860 made provisions for the construction of a bridge in place of the crossing, but the Board had no powers to order the construction of a joint station. It would only order a bridge to be constructed if it could be proved that the level crossing was unsafe but as there had been no fatal accidents there, perhaps it was more a matter of detention and inconvenience rather than of any real danger. The Board considered the appointment of an inspecting officer to look into the matter.

On 24th April 1882, James Grierson, the General Manager of the Great Western Railway wrote at length, stating that a joint station would not relieve the problems of the level crossing and that they would not be prepared to abandon their station for the inferior accommodation of the Somerset & Dorset station. The cost of a joint station could not be justified on the grounds of the expected traffic, which was based on a figure of eleven passengers per train for the year of 1880. The railway company also disputed the City Council's remarks over delays at the level crossing by providing its own figures, which showed that for the month of January 1882 the average delay was five or six minutes and on only one occasion were the gates closed to road traffic for more than eight minutes. This was on 27th January when a locomotive was derailed at a set of catch points and because the gates were interlocked with the points they could not be opened to the road until disconnected. In this case the gates were closed across the road for seventeen minutes.

Colonel Yolland was appointed to enquire into the matter and in his report of 6th July 1882 he outlined the history of the three lines into Wells, how they were subsequently connected and that, having acquired two of the lines, the Great Western Railway consolidated its passenger traffic at the Tucker Street station. Colonel Yolland had travelled to Tucker Street where he met the Mayor, the Town Clerk and a number of officials of the Great Western and Somerset & Dorset companies. Figures for the amount of road traffic over the level crossing were provided by both the Great Western Railway and the City Council as follows:

	GWR	City Council
Pedestrians	463	823
Cattle	65	598
Vehicles	175	499

The figures from the railway company were taken on an unrecorded date between the hours of 6.00am and 8.00pm, whereas those from the City Council were for 6th May, which happened to be a market day thus accounting for the higher numbers. There was also a large variation in the total time that the gates were closed from day to day, whilst on one day the gates had been closed no less that 29 times for light engine movements alone. Colonel Yolland's response was that these figures were proof that the level crossing should never been sanctioned in the first place (as we have seen, it was he who recommended that the crossing should not be sanctioned back in 1860). He added that credit was due to the employees of the railway company that there had been no serious accidents. The Colonel recommended that the level crossing be replaced by a bridge and that three years should be allowed for its completion.

The GWR requested that the order for the bridge be held back until more information could be obtained. On Monday, 25th September 1882 an accident occurred at the crossing when a wagonette (*sic*) driven by a Miss Tasker was struck by one of the gates as it was closing across the road, spilling all five occupants onto the road. Fortunately there were no serious injuries but the vehicle was a write-off. The Great Western alleged that the vehicle had attempted to 'jump' the gates as they were closing (a phenomenon more often associated with modern barrier level crossings) but the owner of the vehicle, Miss Tasker's father, was awarded compensation for damages against the railway company. One point on this matter that was taken up by the *Wells Journal* at the time was that, because of the position of the original East Somerset signal box, it was not possible to see more than about twenty yards up the road towards the city centre, the direction from which Miss Tasker was approaching. This remained the case until 1912 when a replacement signal box

Plate 25 - The 1912 replacement signal box at the crossing of Priory Road, photographed in 1936. The box was named 'Wells East Somerset Box'. Although not fully visible, the oval sign peeking from behind the box says 'ESSO WELLS DEPOT' on three separate lines. Note the boardwalk, to enable the signalman to cross the point rodding and signal wires with some degree of safety, and the lamp for night illumination of the token exchange point.

*Ian Scrimgeour;
Signalling Record Society*

was constructed nearer the crossing, which gave the signalman a better view of the road in both directions.

The Great Western Railway continued to argue that due to the low level of road traffic on Priory Road the bridge was unnecessary and, in support of their statement, quoted much higher road usage figures for level crossings at Peterborough, Doncaster and Lincoln. They also stated that no mention had been made of the level crossing following two inspections made after the conversion of the link from Tucker Street to standard gauge. They concluded that there would be considerable difficulties in constructing a bridge and that it would cost in the region of £13,000. A further letter from James Grierson to the Board of Trade quoted road usage figures for Commercial Street level crossing in Newport as 14,026 pedestrians, 1,151 vehicles and 1,240 horses as well as other traffic over a twelve hour period from 6.00am to 6.00pm on 29th November 1882.

In the event, the Board of Trade issued the order for the construction of a bridge at the expense of the Great Western Railway on 25th January 1883 and allowed three years for its completion. On 13th February Grierson replied on behalf of the directors who wished to express their regret that the Board of Trade felt it necessary to make the order. The whole matter dragged on whilst the Board of Trade and the railway company continued to disagree. The Great Western applied for an extension of time but the Board of Trade, and Colonel Yolland in particular, were adamant that an extension should not be granted. Colonel Yolland died shortly before he was due to retire in 1885 and it seems that the Board of Trade became more amenable to negotiation. An extension of two years was granted in November 1885, no actual work on the bridge having been carried out up until then.

Major General Hutchinson was appointed to make a further enquiry, which took place on 30th April 1886. The Great Western Railway listed four reasons why the Board of Trade should reconsider the bridge order:

1. Public opinion in Wells was opposed to the bridge;

2. The absence of a serious accident since the last enquiry;

3. The cost of the bridge and its approaches;

4. The adoption of certain remedial measures that would reduce delays at the crossing.

The general opinion expressed by the Mayor and other influential citizens was that they were more in favour of getting the delays at the crossing reduced than the erection of a bridge to replace it. The remedial actions discussed at the meeting were:

1. The erection of a footbridge at the level crossing;

2. The realignment of sidings and connections in East Somerset yard to reduce the need to shunt over the crossing;

3. Alterations at Priory Road station so that the Somerset & Dorset platform line terminated at a buffer stop.

The latter action would have removed the need to close the gates over the road when a Somerset & Dorset train was approaching from Glastonbury. However, it would have required considerable alterations to allow Great Western trains to continue to run over the level crossing and was eventually dropped from the plan. The Great Western wished to limit any remedial work to the track alterations in East Somerset yard. The City Council was not satisfied with this and continued to press for the bridge. The Great Western was asked to make further concessions and it agreed to put in a coal stage and turntable at Tucker Street in order to reduce light engine movements over

This newspaper report was discovered in Wells and Mendip Museum. The name of the newspaper is not disclosed but it is probably the *Wells Journal* and appears to report on discussions of the Town Council in respect of a GWR response.

'The Level Crossing

A letter was read from the Board of Trade enclosing the following communication from the Great Western Railway Company, stating the arrangements they were prepared to adopt at the level crossing, and saying that the Board thought it would be desirable, as an experiment, that the proposed alterations should be carried out:

Great Western Railway, Paddington Station, 21st July, 1887. - My dear sir, - Referring to your letter of the 6th inst., respecting the level crossing at Wells, I have to state the views of the Directors have in no degree changed from those already expressed, viz., that there is no real necessity for any outlay to be incurred in altering the present arrangements, but to meet the views of the Board of Trade and the wishes of the inhabitants of Wells, they are willing to carry out the following works, namely (1) To construct new road gates to the crossing interlocked with the signal box and to provide new wickets for pedestrians. (2) To construct new sidings on the south-east side of the station for shunting purposes, and (3) to remove the turnstile (sic) and coal stage to the Tucker-street station side of the crossing. The new road gates being locked with the signals will keep delays to vehicles down to a minimum, and the provision of wicket-gates will reduce the time of detention to pedestrians very considerably.

The sidings on the south-east side of the station will virtually put a stop to the fouling of the crossing during shunting operations, and materially diminish the number of times that the gates have to be closed. The removal of the turntable and coal stage will also further reduce the number of times that the gates have to be closed across the road.

The footbridge suggested by the Wells Town Council cannot possibly be necessary if wicket gates are provided; indeed, our experience elsewhere is that it would be scarcely used, whilst it is admitted that it would be very unsightly, and although the cost of its construction would not be great, the outlay would be practically wasted. With regard to the removal of the engine shed, also asked for by the Wells Town Council, I may state that the present site is by far the most convenient, and I am informed that if the shed were removed to the site suggested on the Tucker-street side of the crossing, which is close to the town, complaints would be made by the inhabitants of the adjacent houses of the nuisance caused by the smoke emitted from the engines during the time that they are being got ready for work. The placing of a stop block in the Somerset and Dorset Station, as also urged by the Town Council, would break the connection between the lines of the Somerset and Dorset and this Company, and would prevent the direct transfer of any passengers to and from the Somerset and Dorset line who might under special circumstances require such accommodation. If, however, it should be considered necessary that the lines should be disconnected, and a stop block placed at the end of their line (but I trust this view will not be adopted), I submit that the work ought not to be done by this company, but by the Somerset and Dorset, inasmuch as the closing of the gates across the road on the approach of their trains, although they do not {normally} pass over the level crossing, is in no way rendered necessary by any arrangements of this Company. I beg for these, among other reasons, to submit to the Board of Trade that the works proposed by the Company even from the point of view of some of the inhabitants of Wells, are all that can reasonably be asked for, they being in fact more than the circumstances and the limited user (sic) made of the crossing render necessary; and I trust that they may be accepted as a settlement of the question at issue. - I am, &c., J. GRIERSON.

- H. G. Calcraft, Esq., C.E., Railway Department, Board of Trade.

Mr. Vonberg said he had no doubt it would reduce the inconvenience to a large extent. He supposed that wicket gates would be regulated by the man in the signal box as the gates are now; if the wickets were not locked the danger would be increased.

Mr. P. Fry: The letter stated they would be.

Mr. Harte did not see the good of the wicket gates.

Mr. Tate thought it would be only fair to give the proposed alterations a good trial, but from his experience of wicket gates at other level crossings, he should strongly advise their omission. They would be a source of the greatest danger. It would be impossible to say when the engine was close to the spot, a child may stray on to the line, and while she was being called to she might be knocked down by the engine. He proposed that the alterations as submitted by the Board of Trade be given a trial.

Mr. Holloway: What do they mean by the south-east?

The Mayor (looking at the plan): According to this old plan, the Witham side would be the south-east.

Mr. Holloway: They say south-east of the station of the Great Western Railway; they have only a right to speak of one station - Cheddar Valley.

The Mayor: There is no room on that side.

Mr. Holloway: If they put it on the side of the Cheddar Valley station, he could quite see it would lessen the traffic across the level crossing, but if they put it on the East Somerset side he could not see that it would lessen it very materially.

Mr. Fry: They mean the East Somerset side.

After further reference to the plan.

Mr. Holloway said he thought it really a matter for the Board of Trade, who originally ordered a bridge to be constructed, and if they wished what was now suggested to be tried as an experiment, they were out of the question altogether.

Mr. Tate would like to suggest to the Company the necessity of placing a footbridge over the line at the Cheddar Valley station from one platform to the other, but the Mayor ruled that he was out of order.

At the suggestion of Mr. Holloway, Mr. Tate agreed to accept the following form of resolution in place of the one he proposed: "That this question having been referred to the Board of Trade for their decision, and the Board of Trade having originally ordered a bridge to be constructed in lieu of the level crossing, this Council has no objection to the arrangement suggested as an experiment only."

Mr. Holloway seconded the motion.

Mr. Manning protested against the wicket gate, which he thought would be very dangerous. They kept the gates closed against a horse and cart that could get through quickly, and would open the wicket to a child or a nurse-girl with a perambulator. If it were not safe for a horse and cart to go through, it was not safe for children or nurse-girls with perambulators.

Mr. Barnes said those who would use the wicket would not be confined to children or nurse-girls, and he thought it would be a convenience to passers-by.

On the motion being put to the meeting, it was carried.'

Plate 26 - An Edwardian view of passengers and luggage being loaded at Wookey. *Neil Parkhouse collection*

the crossing. The requirement for the footbridge seems to have been dropped at some point and was replaced by wicket gates on the Somerset & Dorset side in order to make the crossing safer for pedestrians. At this point the order for the bridge was withdrawn and the Great Western Railway carried out the following improvements:

1. A turntable and locomotive servicing facilities at Tucker Street;

2. New gates at the level crossing and the addition of wicket gates for pedestrians;

3. Additional sidings and a relocated connection to the running line controlled by a ground frame in East Somerset yard;

4. Signalling alterations in the vicinity of the level crossing and at Tucker Street station.

Major General Huchinson inspected the work in October 1888 and following some minor alterations to the signalling passed the new arrangements in January 1889. Ironically there had been a turntable and locomotive servicing facilities at Tucker Street when the Cheddar Valley section first opened but these had been taken out when the connecting link was opened along with the new locomotive shed at East Somerset in 1878.

It seems that there were still complaints about the level crossing but it remained in situ until the complete closure of the railway through Wells in 1969. The Great Western did act upon one complaint however. One City Councillor complained in a council meeting that the level of the rails stood out above the stone cobbles in the crossing to such an extent that the acetylene lights of his bicycle were put out by the shock of crossing and he was concerned that he would be summonsed by the police for riding without lights. Oh! that cyclists today would be so conscientious over the matter of lights; and when was the last time you saw a politician riding a bicycle? In response, the Great Western agreed to tarmac over the cobbles so that the rails were level with the road surface.

Train Services in 1886

The two remaining stations at Wells will be referred to as Priory Road (Somerset & Dorset) and Tucker Street (Great Western and British Railways Western Region) where necessary in order to avoid confusion although the name 'Wells (Tucker Street)' was only applied to the latter for the thirty year period between 1920 and 1950. The Somerset & Dorset station was given the name 'Wells (Priory Road)' in 1883.

Goods trains generally arrived at or departed from Wells East Somerset yard whilst Tucker Street station retained its own goods facilities at the small yard on the opposite side of Burcott Road bridge from the passenger station. Goods traffic was generally tripped between Tucker Street and East Somerset. There was also exchange traffic between East Somerset yard and the Somerset & Dorset at Priory Road.

In 1886 the major changes to the timetable since 1879 were the introduction of one passenger and one goods service running through from Yatton to Witham, two goods services running through in the reverse direction and the opening of a signal box, passing loop and a second platform at Cranmore. Thus the line between Wells and Witham was divided into two sections with Cranmore as the intermediate passing place.

GWR Service Timetable - 1886

WELLS BRANCH. (Single Line.) Narrow Gauge.

Down Trains. YATTON TO WELLS.—Week Days. Sundays

Miles from Yatton.	STATIONS.	1		2		3	4		5	6		7		8		9		10		Sun. 1	
		Bristol and Wells Goods. A		Passenger.		R R Goods.	Passenger.		R R Goods.	Passenger.		Bristol Goods.		Passenger.		Passenger.				Passenger.	
		arr.	dep.	arr.	dep.	dep.	arr.	dep.	dep.	arr.	dep.	arr.	dep.	arr.	dep.	arr.	dep.			arr.	dep.
		A.M.	A.M.	A.M.	A.M.	A.M.	A.M.	A.M.	P.M.	P.M.	P.M.	noon.	P.M.	P.M.	P.M.	P.M.	P.M.			A.M.	A.M.
	Yatton	5 40	6 0	....	9 55	....	....	11 45	12 50	—	1 15	12 0	1 25	—	4 0	....	7 5	....	....	10 0	10 10
1½	Congresbury	6 8	6 21	9 59	10 0	..	11 49	11 50	—	1 19	1 20	1 32	1 40	4 4	4 5	7 8	7 9	..	..	10 14	10 15
4½	Sandford	6 31	6 42	10 6	10 8	....	11 56	11 57	—	1 26	1 27	1 50	2 0	4 11	4 12	7 14	7 15	....	....	10 21	10 22
5¾	Winscombe ..	6 50	7 5	10 12	10 13	..	12 1	12 2	—	1 30	1 31	C R		4 15	4 16	7 19	7 20	..	..	10 25	10 26
8	Axbridge	7 13	7 25	10 18	10 20	....	12 6	12 8	—	1 35	1 37	2 15	2 25	4 21	4 22	7 24	7 25	....	....	10 30	10 32
9¾	Cheddar ..	7 35	X8 0	10 24	X10 26	..	12 12	X12 14	*1 20*	1 41	1 43	2 30	X3 5	4 26	4 28	7 30	7 32	..	..	10 36	10 38
11¾	Draycott	8 6	8 12	10 32	10 33	..	12 21	12 22	*Weds. only.*	1 47	1 48	—	—	4 33	4 34	7 38	7 39	....	....	10 42	10 43
14	Lodge Hill ..	8 19	8 25	10 38	10 39	..	12 29	12 30		1 52	1 53	—	—	4 39	4 41	7 44	7 45	..	..	10 47	10 48
16½	Wookey	8 31	8 55	10 46	10 47	*11 35*	12 37	12 39		1 59	2 1	3 20	3 45	4 48	4 50	7 52	7 55	....	....	10 54	10 56
17½	**Wells** ..	9 0	..	10 52	..	*11 40*	12 45	12 55		2 5	—	3 50	4 10	4 55	—	8 0	—	..	..	11 0	—
31¾	Witham	—	—	—	—	—	1 40	—		—	—	5 30	—	—	—	—	—	....	....	—	—

Up Trains. WELLS TO YATTON.—Week Days. Sundays

Miles from Wells.	STATIONS.	1		2		3	4		5		6	7		8		9		10		Sun. 1	
		Passenger.		Passenger.		R R Goods.	Passenger.		Passenger.		R R Cattle.	Bristol Goods.		Passenger.				Bristol Goods.		Passenger.	
		arr.	dep.	arr.	dep.	dep.	arr.	dep.	arr.	dep.	dep.	arr.	dep.	arr.	dep.			arr.	dep.	arr.	dep.
		A.M.	A.M.	A.M.	A.M.	A.M.	A.M.	A.M.	P.M.	P.M.	P.M.	P.M.	P.M.	P.M.	P.M.			P.M.	P.M.	A.M.	A.M.
14¼	Witham ..	—	—	—	—		—	—	—	—		—	12 55	—	—	....	....	—	6 10	—	—
	Wells	....	7 20	....	10 0	*10 55*	—	11 50	—	2 35	*Wednesdays only.*	2 10	5 0	—	5 40	..	..	7 20	8 5	—	11 20
1	Wookey ..	7 23	7 24	10 3	10 4	*11 0*	11 54	11 55	2 38	2 39		5 5	5 20	5 43	5 44	....	....	8 10	8 20	11 23	11 24
3½	Lodge Hill	7 30	7 31	10 11	10 12	..	12 0	12 1	2 45	2 46		C R		5 50	5 51	..	..	—	—	11 30	11 32
5¾	Draycott ..	7 35	7 36	10 16	10 17	..	12 4	12 6	2 50	2 51		—	—	5 57	5 58	....	....	8 31	8 38	11 36	11 37
7¾	Cheddar	7 40	X7 41	10 22	X10 24	....	12 11	X12 14	2 55	X2 56	*3 5*	5 50	•6 14	6 3	•6 6	..	..	8 45	8 50	11 42	11 44
9½	Axbridge ..	7 47	7 48	10 28	10 30	..	12 18	12 20	3 1	3 3	*3 20*	6 19	6 35	6 11	6 13	....	....	C R		11 48	11 50
11¾	Winscombe	7 53	7 54	10 36	10 37	....	12 26	12 27	3 8	3 9	*3 30*	C R		6 19	6 20	..	..	9 5	9 15	11 55	11 57
13	Sandford ..	7 57	7 58	10 41	10 42	..	12 31	12 32	3 12	3 13	*3 40*	—	—	6 24	6 25	....	....	9 21	9 35	12 0	12 2
16	Congresbury	8 4	8 5	10 48	10 50	....	12 38	12 40	3 19	3 20	—	—	—	6 31	6 33	..	..	9 44	9 55	12 8	12 10
17½	**Yatton** ..	8 10	8 13	10 55	..	..	12 45	..	3 25	..	*3 50*	6 55	7 10	6 38	..	....	....	10 0	10 20	12 15	....

A Goods and Passengers from Cheddar.

CROSSING ARRANGEMENTS BETWEEN YATTON AND WELLS.

The 6.0 a.m. Train from Yatton will cross the 7.20 a.m. from Wells at Cheddar.
The 9.55 a.m. Train from Yatton will cross the 10.0 a.m. Train from Wells at Cheddar.
The 11.45 a.m. Train from Yatton will cross the 11.50 a.m. Train from Wells at Cheddar.
The 1.25 p.m. Goods from Yatton will cross 2.35 p.m. ex Wells at Cheddar.

Single Line worked by Train Staff. The Staff Stations are Yatton, Cheddar and Wells.

TRAIN STAFF AND TICKETS:—

SECTION.	COLOR OF STAFF AND TICKETS.		SHAPE OF STAFF AND TICKETS.	
	Staff.	*Tickets*	*Staff.*	*Tickets.*
Wells and Cheddar	Green	Green	Square	Square
Yatton and Cheddar	Red	Red	Round	Round

Plate 27 -
Great Western 1886 working timetable.
Author's collection

Plate 28 - An undated view of strawberry traffic being loaded at Cheddar, probably in Edwardian times. The engine is an unidentified outside-framed (probably) Class 360 or 388 Standard Goods with Belpaire boiler whilst the vehicles are predominantly 6-wheeled Siphons, although at least two passenger vehicles are at the rear of rake.
Neil Parkhouse collection

On the Cheddar Valley section there were departures from Wells in the up direction at 7.20am, 10.00am, 11.50am, 2.35pm and 5.40pm arriving at Yatton at 8.10am, 10.55am, 12.45pm, 3.25pm and 6.38pm respectively. The timetable now showed that the first of these departed from Yatton at 8.13am to work through to Bristol. In the down direction trains departed from Yatton at 9.55am, 11.45am, 1.15pm, 4.00pm and 7.05pm arriving at Wells at 10.52am, 12.45pm, 2.05pm, 4.55pm and 8.00pm respectively. The second of these worked through to Witham, departing from Wells at 12.55pm and arriving at its final destination at 1.40pm. This was the only through passenger service to work over both sections of the line. Throughout the history of the line trains which nominally ran though between Yatton and Witham were subject to a 10 minute wait at Wells.

So it was argued by some that it was not a through working at all but two distinct services that happened to utilise the same locomotive and rolling stock. The evening passenger working from Yatton to Cheddar and return that existed in the 1879 timetable had been withdrawn by 1886.

The early Bristol and Wells goods was now timed to depart from Yatton at 6.00am and arrived at Cheddar at 7.35am. This train was still mixed from Cheddar with its departure now 15 minutes earlier and a booked journey time of one hour to Wells as before.

Other goods traffic was provided by a later Bristol and Wells goods in the down direction. This train arrived at Yatton from Bristol at 12noon and departed again at 1.25pm. It called at all stations except Draycott and Lodge Hill. Winscombe

Plate 29 - A rake of A. Perry private owner wagons being shunted in Cheddar goods yard. The firm Alfred Perry of 'Nyland View', Station Road, Cheddar were coal merchants between about 1896 and 1927.
P Gardner

was served only as required. During shunting operations at Cheddar it was crossed by the 2.55pm up passenger train from Wells. Its booked arrival time at Wells was 3.50pm, from where it departed at 4.10pm to arrive at Witham at 5.30pm. In the up direction there were two daily goods trains from Wells to Yatton and Bristol. The first of these departed from Wells at 5.00pm and was booked to call at Wookey, Cheddar and Axbridge only before arriving at Yatton at 6.56pm. Stops at Lodge Hill and Winscombe would be as required. This train also worked over the East Somerset section, having departed Witham at 12.55pm and arriving at Wells at 2.10pm, which left nearly three hours for shunting before continuing. On arrival at Yatton it departed for Bristol at 7.10pm. The second up goods departed from Wells at 8.05pm calling at all stations except Lodge Hill and only at Axbridge as required. It arrived at Yatton at 10.00pm and departed for Bristol at 10.20pm. Again this train worked the East Somerset section, departing from Witham at 6.10pm arriving at Wells at 7.20pm.

There was a trip working from Wells to Wookey Paper Mill which ran as required. This was scheduled to depart from Wells at 10.55am and five minutes was allowed for the run to Wookey. The return working left Wookey at 11.35am arriving back in Wells at 11.40am. Another trip working left Yatton at 12.50pm and was booked to arrive at Cheddar at 1.20pm without calling at intermediate stations. The return working was described as 'Cattle' in the working timetable and departed from Cheddar at 3.05pm, calling at all stations except Congresbury and arriving at Yatton at 3.50pm. These two workings were listed in the working timetable to run Wednesdays only, as required.

Sunday workings were restricted to one train in each direction, run principally for the collection of milk although it was described in the working timetable as 'Passenger'. The down train left Yatton at 10.00am calling at all stations and arrived at Wells at 11.00am. The return train left Wells at 11.20am again calling at all stations and arrived back at Yatton at 12.10pm.

On the East Somerset section, down passenger services left Witham at 8.15am, 12noon, 2.05pm, 4.50pm and 7.23pm arriving at Wells at 9.10am, 12.45pm, 2.50pm 5.35pm and 7.58pm respectively. The first of these ran mixed. In the up direction passenger services departed from Wells at 6.10am, 9.40am, 12.55pm, 3.15pm and 6.00pm arriving at Witham at 6.45am, 10.13am, 1.40pm 3.55pm and 6.55pm respectively. The 12.55pm departure from Wells originated from Yatton as described earlier. Shepton Mallet and Cranmore were served by all trains in both directions. Wanstrow was only served by three trains in each direction, which was something of an improvement over earlier timetables.

Goods workings in the down direction consisted of four trains daily between Witham and Wells in addition to the mixed train already described. Departures from Witham were at 6.45am, 7.45am, 12.55pm and 6.00pm arriving at Wells at 7.50am, 8.45am, 2.10pm and 7.15pm respectively. The first originated from Chippenham and the second from Yeovil, whilst the last two ran through to Yatton as described above, leaving Wells at 5.00pm and 8.05pm respectively. Cranmore and Shepton Mallet were served by all four trains. At this time the sidings at Dulcote Quarry appear to have only been worked in the up direction. The working timetable makes no mention of Doulting Siding. The first goods in the up direction was the return working of the down goods from Yeovil that had arrived in Wells at 8.45am. This

Plate 30 - Shepton Mallet early in the 20th century looking towards Cranmore. Neither the engine on the approaching passenger train nor the 0-6-0ST taking a break from shunting can be positively identified. The footbridge, as well as siding alterations and a new signal box, was installed in 1894/95.
John Alsop collection

Plate 31 - Cranmore after the extension of the platforms, the join of which can just be seen. Note the diverted footpath, which was mentioned in the text, at track level at this end of the platforms.
John Alsop collection

train departed from Wells at 10.15am and arrived at Witham at 11.55am before continuing its journey to Swindon. A second up goods departed from Wells at 11.15am arriving at Witham at 12.35pm. This train served Dulcote Siding and also crossed a down passenger train at Cranmore. The final up goods departed from Wells at 4.10pm and was booked to arrive at Witham at 5.30pm. This was the 1.25pm departure from Yatton that had originally started from Bristol as noted above. It also crossed a passenger train at Cranmore. Shepton Mallet and Cranmore were served by all goods workings.

The Sunday service consisted of one train only in each direction. It was described in the working timetable as the Wells and Chippenham Goods although it may have been mixed. Its main purpose was the collection of milk traffic. The down working departed from Witham at 6.45am and arrived at Wells at 7.50am. The return working departed from Wells at 8.35am and arrived at Witham at 9.35am. Shepton Mallet and Cranmore were served in both directions.

With the area being mainly agricultural the railway became an important source of employment. The 1891 census showed that in excess of 70 men in Wells had declared themselves as being railway workers. When one considers that they would have supported more than 200 dependants it will be seen how important the railway was to the local economy.

Developments at Shepton Mallet and Cranmore

We have already seen that plans for a passing loop and second platform at Shepton Mallet had been proposed as far back as the 1870s and that Cranmore had received this treatment in 1880. The Great Western Railway wrote to the Board of Trade on 24th June 1893 to submit a plan of proposed work at Shepton Mallet station and requested the sanction of the Board to proceed. The plans were for a second platform on the down side with a loop siding running behind, a new signal box on the down side at the Wells end of the station, various other alterations to sidings and connections with the running line, and covered footbridge. Major Marindin inspected the new layout on 7th March 1895 and passed it as fit for use.

During the early years of the twentieth century the Great Western Railway was planning a further extension of the siding accommodation at Cranmore in order to be able to handle the increasing mineral traffic from nearby quarries. The passing loop and second platform had been put in place in 1880 but both platforms were very short, which proved to be inconvenient for passengers and operating staff alike. Either the train had to draw up twice or else alighting passengers faced a descent to track level. Part of the problem was the existence of a footpath across the railway at the Witham end of the platforms which would be affected by any lengthening of the platforms. Shepton Mallet Rural District Council requested extension of the platforms and the provision of a footbridge for both railway passengers and users of the footpath. The Great Western Railway proposed to lengthen the platforms but planned to divert the footpath instead of providing a footbridge as it considered that it could not justify the cost on the grounds of the volume of railway traffic. The powers for the diversion were included in the railway company's Bill under consideration at the time.

There were local objections to the proposed diversion of the footpath and the council threatened to petition against the Bill unless the railway company provided the footbridge. The GWR retaliated by deleting the powers for the diversion of the footpath and platform extension from the Bill, thereby limiting the alterations at Cranmore to the sidings alone. The Council complained to the Board of Trade that in actual fact the platforms had been shortened. The railway company went ahead with its siding alterations which included new sidings, alterations to the passing loop and a new signal box on the down side of the line at the Shepton Mallet end of the passenger station. Major Pringle reported for the Board of Trade on 22nd June 1905 and whilst he was satisfied with the siding alterations and signalling, he was critical of the passenger accommodation. He stated that the platforms were only about 100 feet long, which was not long enough to accommodate an ordinary branch passenger train of four coaches.

A compromise was reached eventually in which the footpath was diverted to allow the platforms to be extended but the path still crossed the railway on the level, a footbridge not being provided. This all took some time to achieve as the lengthened platforms were not brought into use until February 1912.

Plate 32 - Congresbury, c.1935 and 'junction for the Wrington Vale branch', to quote the station running-in board, in spite of the closure of the branch to passenger trains four years earlier. The station was significantly altered in 1901 as a result of the construction of the Wrington Vale Light Railway to Blagdon and the construction of a new reservoir.
Brunel University, Clinker collection

The quarry tramroad was realigned and upgraded to a standard gauge line in 1927. Further extension to the sidings on the up side at Cranmore were made at this time, which included a wagon repair shop and a new connection from the running line at the Shepton Mallet end of the layout which was controlled by an in-section ground frame.

Gate Lane Level Crossing

When the East Somerset Railway was built there was a second level crossing in Wells in addition to the one at Priory Road. This was at Gate Lane, which was just on the Shepton Mallet side of the former East Somerset passenger station. The Great Western Railway closed this crossing in 1900 as one of the various works included in its Act of 30th December 1899. After closure of the crossing, access to the houses, laundry and Park Farm in this otherwise isolated section of Gate Lane south of the railway was afforded by extending the eastern end of Rowdens Road by about two and a half chains.

The Wrington Vale Line

The Wrington Vale Light Railway was opened on the 4th December 1901 from its junction on the Cheddar Valley section at Congresbury to Blagdon, with intermediate stations at Wrington, Langford and Burrington. Although the line was constructed by the Great Western, it was a combination of the Light Railways Act of 1896 and the proposed construction of a reservoir at Blagdon for the Bristol Waterworks Company that made it a viable proposition. Agricultural produce was seen to be a major source of traffic and this was by no means the first line to be projected through the Chew Valley area. In 1881 a company was formed to build a line from Congresbury to Farrington Gurney on the Bristol & North Somerset Railway and an Act was obtained on 18th August 1882. The Great Western agreed to work the line for 50% of the gross receipts but the necessary capital was not forthcoming, so the undertaking was abandoned by a further Act of 4th June 1886.

The only section of the Cheddar Valley line that was really affected by the coming of the Wrington Vale line was that between Congresbury and Yatton. Major alterations were made at Congresbury station including a passing loop, a second platform on the up side, a new signal box and a scissors crossover forming a junction with the Wrington Vale line. These alterations are described in more detail in subsequent chapters. Colonel Yorke inspected the alterations on behalf of the Board of Trade and his report of 19th December 1901 found the work to be satisfactory. Blagdon trains generally started from or terminated at Yatton primarily because Congresbury had no bay platform, but during the 1920s on peak summer Saturdays trains would start from or terminate at Congresbury in order to avoid congestion at Yatton.

Alterations at Yatton

The down platform at Yatton was extended in 1885, which also affected the Cheddar Valley bay since some realignment of the track leading out of the bay was undertaken. More extensive alterations to the layout of the junctions took place in 1898. Prior to this, the junction consisted of single trailing connections from each branch to the up main on the Weston-super-Mare side of the station. This meant that through trains from Bristol had to reverse at Yatton in order to gain access to either branch. Both junctions were upgraded to double line running junctions and the sidings on both sides of the line were extended. Yatton Junction signal box was considerably enlarged and a new 135-lever frame was installed. There was also a short extension to the Clevedon bay platform. Colonel Yorke inspected the alterations and reported on 24th September 1898 that he was generally satisfied with the work and only required a clearance bar on the up Clevedon loop to work with No.70 points. Yatton Junction signal box was renamed Yatton West in April 1925 when Yatton East signal box was opened in conjunction with the opening of up and down goods loops on the Bristol side of the station.

Plate 33 - This undated view of Wookey, looking towards Cheddar, shows the additional cross-over installed in 1900 at the far end of the yard. The siding curving away to the right behind the goods shed leads to the paper mill.
John Alsop collection

The Twentieth Century

A further alteration was made at Wookey in 1900 when a second crossover was installed providing access to the down siding, facing trains coming from Cheddar. The down siding was extended in the Cheddar direction at the same time so that the new crossover was about 150 yards nearer Cheddar than the one taken out in 1880. As the crossover was not in station limits but actually in the Wookey to Cheddar single line section, the crossover was operated by a ground frame released by an Annett's key on the Wookey to Cheddar electric train staff. Unlike the diagram issued for the 1880 changes, the one for 1900 does show the 8-lever signal box on the platform that remained open as a ground frame until 1965. The completed work was inspected by Major Pringle who submitted a satisfactory report on behalf of the Board of Trade on 12th September 1900.

In 1902 a new connection was added at the Sandford and Banwell end of the siding at Winscombe, turning it into a goods loop. The original connection adjacent to the station and the siding itself were realigned at the same time. The two connections were each operated by separate ground frames, the original one still being operated by a ground frame in a hut on the platform.

Major Druitt reported on behalf of the Board of Trade on 5th September 1902 and was satisfied with the alterations but required that traffic must be worked with the locomotive at the lower (ie. Sandford and Banwell) end of the train.

The Great Western Railway drew up plans in May 1905 to install a goods loop and additional sidings at Sandford and Banwell. The layout was to be controlled by a new 31-lever signal box on the up side, adjacent to the goods loop, and by a ground frame at the Winscombe end. A second platform was not built, so it was not possible to cross two passenger trains there. The new work was carried out in conjunction with the short mineral branch that was opened at about the same time to serve the nearby Sandford Quarry which had recently opened.

Plate 34 - It is quite likely that this undated view of Sandford and Banwell was taken shortly after the construction of the new passing loop, opened in 1906. As noted in the text, the work coincided with the construction of a line to the newly-opened Sandford Quarry and, as well as the passing loop, included a new signal box. *John Alsop collection*

Plate 35 - An early postcard view of Axbridge, showing the open footbridge added in 1908. The continuation of the bridge to the right - to join Horne's Lane - is visible above the waiting shelter. Note the lamps along the bridge and the wide spacing of the lines through the platforms, a legacy of broad gauge origins. *John Alsop collection*

The branch and the alterations at the station are described in more detail in subsequent chapters. The completed work was inspected by Colonel Yorke who submitted a satisfactory report on behalf of the Board of Trade on 6th December 1906.

Another alteration worthy of mention is the footbridge at Axbridge which was added in 1908. As well as being for the use of railway passengers and staff, it also formed part of a public footpath from Horne's Lane on the north side of the railway down to the town itself. Prior to this, the footpath crossed the railway on the level just off the end of the platforms at the Cheddar end of the station. The platforms also formed part of the right of way. Interestingly, it was the Great Western Railway that instigated the alterations under powers provided by Section 13 of the Railway Regulation Act of 1842. This fact may come as something of a surprise when one considers the railway company's attitude towards the proposal for a footbridge at Cranmore just a few years earlier and also the saga of the level crossing at Wells back in the 1880s.

In 1909 Wanstrow, which hitherto had been no more than an unstaffed halt, attained full station status and had its own station master, albeit at Grade 6 which was the lowest grade. Before 1909 a small single storey stone building with a wooden extension at the Cranmore end was the only structure on the platform. It is not known what purpose this building was used for when Wanstrow was only a halt. It could be that it was just a waiting shelter but surely a cheaper timber structure would have sufficed here, similar to that on the down platform at Cranmore. The platform at Wanstrow was situated on top of an embankment which required both buildings to be supported by fairly substantial retaining walls.

When it was upgraded to a staffed station an additional wooden building was constructed on the platform. A further expansion of the facilities took place on 3rd January 1927 when a goods loop was added to hold up to ten wagons. This was used

Plate 36 - Wanstrow prior to 1909, showing the wooden extension built onto the stone building depicted in *Plate 5*. In 1909 an additional wooden building was added to the platform. It was to be 1927 before any substantial changes to the facilities took place. *John Alsop collection*

to deal with coal, animal feed and livestock that were loaded from two cattle pens made from cut-down sleepers.

The Grouping of 1923 left the Great Western Railway largely unaffected. The Somerset & Dorset, however, found itself under the joint management of the LMS and Southern Railways which had absorbed the Midland and London & South Western Railways respectively. In spite of this, there was still little visible change as the Somerset & Dorset was still locally managed and its locomotives and rolling stock were still to be seen at Priory Road station in their distinctive Prussian blue livery. However, this all changed in 1930 when the nominal independence of the Somerset & Dorset came to an end. By this time road competition was taking traffic away from the railways at an alarming rate and economies had to be made. The Somerset & Dorset Railway's works at Highbridge were closed and the locomotive fleet was taken into LMS stock. The Prussian blue livery disappeared and, whilst many former Somerset & Dorset locomotives survived into the 1960s, 'foreign' locomotives of ex-Midland or LMS design were introduced to replace some of the older former Somerset & Dorset types.

Passenger services on the Wrington line were withdrawn on 14th September 1931. The line remained open to Blagdon for goods traffic which latterly consisted only of coal for the nearby Bristol Waterworks pumping station at Blagdon Reservoir. The steam pumping engines were replaced by electric pumps and the line closed for all traffic beyond milepost 3¼ at Wrington on 1st November 1950. The track was lifted between January and April 1952. The remaining portion to Wrington was retained primarily for coal traffic but this closed completely on 10th June 1963 and was lifted in May 1964.

Another manifestation of the difficult relationship between the Great Western and the Somerset & Dorset was the fact that Great Western trains ran through Priory Road station without stopping. This must have been the cause of great alarm to the uninitiated either on the train or on the platform! The collector of obscure facts was thus provided with two examples of adjacent passenger stations between which it was not possible to travel by a normal timetabled passenger train (Shepton Mallet to Wells Priory Road and Wells Priory Road to Wells Tucker Street). From 1st October 1934, Great Western trains called at both the Somerset & Dorset and Great Western stations. It seems that card tickets were printed for this short journey but there is no evidence that any were ever issued.

Train Services in 1933

By the 1930s both the Cheddar Valley and East Somerset sections of the line were shown on the same working timetable. In the summer of 1933 there were three through passenger trains on weekdays from Yatton to Witham departing from Yatton at 8.00am, 2.52pm and 6.05pm and booked to arrive at Witham 9.49am, 4.22pm and 7.36pm respectively. All three trains originated from Bristol Temple Meads. In the opposite direction, however, there were four through passenger trains from Witham to Yatton. Departures from Witham were at 8.32am, 11.51am, 3.12pm and 6.50pm. Booked arrival times at Yatton were 10.40am, 1.11pm, 5.00pm and 8.54pm. Many of these services stood at Wells Tucker Street station for some time. The 6.50pm from Witham, for example, waited at Wells for fifty-one minutes, so the description of it being a through train was a little dubious. All of the 'through' services called at every station, including Wanstrow.

In addition to the 'through' trains there were a number of passenger services that did not cover the full distance between Yatton and Witham. For the most part they either started from or terminated at Wells. There were two early morning passenger trains to Bristol. The first departed from Wells at 7.22am calling at all stations to arrive at Yatton at 7.59am. The second started from Shepton Mallet at 8.47am calling at all stations except Wookey to arrive at Yatton at 9.39am. Unlike many passenger trains that ran through both sections of the line, this one was only booked to stand at Wells station for three minutes. It also crossed the 7.25am Bristol Temple Meads to Witham at Wells. There was one evening departure that ran daily from Wells at

Plate 37 - The 1.10pm (Saturdays only) from Yatton, hauled by Collett 1400 Class 0-4-2T No.1430 has arrived at Wells Tucker Street on 5th November 1949. *R F Roberts*

Plate 38 - Former Midland & South Western Jct. Railway No.24 as GWR No.1008 passing the Cheddar reservoir workings in 1936. No.1008 was built by Beyer Peacock in 1899 for goods working and withdrawn in December 1936. The class, which numbered ten, generally remained at Cheltenham after grouping, continuing to work the M&SW section. However, Nos.1008, 1011 and 1013 moved to Bristol early in 1936, which probably led to this working over the Cheddar Valley route. *Mike Barnsley*

6.52pm calling at all stations to Yatton and arriving at 7.50pm. This train also conveyed milk and fruit traffic. In addition, on Wednesdays and Saturdays only, a train departed from Wells at 8.48pm calling only at Wookey and Cheddar before arriving at Yatton at 9.19pm. There was also one passenger working from Witham to Wells, departing Witham at 8.43pm and calling at all stations to arrive at Wells at 9.20pm.

In the opposite direction there were four trains each weekday between Yatton and Wells, departing at 9.52am, 11.08am, 4.05pm and 8.45pm and calling at all stations to arrive at Wells at 10.39am, 11.59am, 4.58pm and 9.26pm respectively. The last of these services started from Trowbridge, running via Bath and Bristol. There were two trains from Wells to Frome each weekday that left Wells at 11.02am and 12.35pm to arrive at Witham at 11.37am and 1.09pm respectively. Both trains called at all stations between Wells and Witham.

At this time there was still a considerable amount of goods traffic. For most of the line's existence the first train of the day was a goods train. This was generally the case on lines where the signal boxes closed overnight and had the effect of proving the line to be safe before the passenger services started. There have been instances of lines becoming unsafe overnight due to the track being undermined by flooding, or a similar natural event, that has only been discovered by the first goods train of the day. Sometimes, as in the Sun Bank accident between Ruabon and Llangollen in North Wales in 1945, this has resulted in the deaths of the train crew. Unfortunately, as a result of the demise of the pick-up goods train since the 1960s, there have been a few similar mishaps to passenger trains which have resulted in the death of, or injury to, fare paying passengers.

Many goods trains either started from or terminated at Wells East Somerset yard. On weekdays, the first down goods on the Cheddar Valley section departed from Yatton at 4.45am having originated in Bristol. This train called at all stations except Draycott and Lodge Hill and arrived at Wells East Somerset at 7.43am. Whilst shunting at Wookey the train was crossed by the first up passenger working, the 7.22am from Wells to Yatton.

The Blagdon goods was the next down working from Yatton, departing from there at 7.30am and arriving at Blagdon at 8.50am after a leisurely trip of 80 minutes to travel eight miles and fifteen chains! Admittedly the train had called at all stations en route. The branch from Congresbury to Blagdon had lost its passenger service two years previously. On its return journey this train departed from Blagdon at 9.30am and proceeded to Congresbury in the same leisurely manner to arrive at 10.20am. It waited there for 55 minutes, during which time it was crossed by a down passenger train. Its journey was finally completed when it arrived back at Yatton at 11.21am.

There were two more down goods trains that originated at Bristol. The first departed from Yatton at 10.42am and was booked to arrive at East Somerset yard at 2.40pm having called at all stations. The second departed from Yatton at 1.22pm but this one terminated at Cheddar at 3.26pm, also having called at all stations en route.

In the up direction there was a morning Bristol goods that departed from East Somerset yard at 7.55am, calling at all stations, and was booked to arrive at Yatton at 1.56pm before proceeding to Bristol. In the afternoon there were two up goods trains to Bristol. The first of these started from Cheddar with a departure time of 5.25pm calling only at Sandford and Banwell en route where it was booked to stay for 31 minutes. Here it was crossed by a down passenger train. It then proceeded to Yatton, arriving at 6.31pm before continuing to Bristol. The second afternoon goods departed from East Somerset yard at 5.10pm, calling at all stations and booked to arrive at Yatton at 8.20pm. This train also continued to Bristol.

On the East Somerset section there was one down goods train that ran through to Wells. This train left Witham at 6.40am having originated at Westbury (Wilts). The train called at Cranmore and Shepton Mallet before arriving at Wells East Somerset yard at 8.17am. It then left East Somerset at 8.25am and ran to Tucker Street station where it terminated in the small goods yard on the Cheddar side of Burcott Road overbridge. The working timetable also records stops at Doulting Siding and at the top of the 1 in 46½ gradient between Shepton Mallet and Wells in order to pin down brakes. Stop boards were erected at both places in order to advise the crew of unfitted down goods trains. Similar stop boards for up trains were provided at two places between Cranmore and Witham where steep gradients were also to be encountered.

In the up direction, two goods trains ran through to Witham departing from Wells East Somerset yard at 4.10pm and 6.15pm respectively. The first of these did not call at Doulting Siding or Wanstrow and ran through to Westbury. On alternate Fridays it left Wells at 2.00pm but after arrival at Shepton Mallet all subsequent times were unchanged. Arrival at Witham was at 6.23pm having stopped to pin down the brakes as already described. The second up goods in fact started from Wookey at 5.30pm in order to clear traffic from the paper mill and arrived at East Somerset yard at 5.37pm before continuing on its journey to Witham.

In addition there were a number of shorter goods and trip workings. These were to serve the various quarry sidings on the East Somerset section, principally those at Dulcote Quarry. Loaded mineral wagons were trip worked to Cranmore where they were made up into full loads before being dispatched to destinations elsewhere on the network. Empty wagons and incoming traffic were worked in via Cranmore in similar fashion. On the Cheddar Valley section the only working of note other than those already described was an engine and van that departed from Wells passenger station at 5.00pm and was booked to arrive at Wookey at 5.05pm. Having shunted the goods yard and Paper Mill sidings this formed the 5.30pm goods to Witham as has already been described.

Sunday traffic still consisted of one train in each direction with the primary purpose of collecting milk traffic. The Yatton to Witham working left Yatton at 1.27pm having originated from Bristol at 1.03pm. Having called at all stations it arrived at Witham at 3.48pm thus taking two hours and twenty minutes to complete the journey of thirty-one miles and fifty-five chains. Few, if any, passengers must have ventured out for such a tedious journey! The return working was worse with a departure from Witham at 5.25pm and arrival at Yatton at 8.04pm, making a journey time of two hours and thirty-nine minutes!

WORLD WAR II AND NATIONALISATION

A cold store was opened at Wells during World War II. It was situated on the down side of the single line on the Shepton Mallet side of East Somerset yard. An in-section ground frame known as Gate Lane controlled access to sidings that served the cold store. The sidings were lightly laid using flat-bottomed rail. The store, which still exists although not in use as such any more, was a dark, austere structure built of concrete and is totally out of keeping with the rest of the city. Perhaps we should not judge the needs of the wartime effort in 1942 with the more environmentally conscious standards of the twenty-first century.

(Top) Plate 39 - GWR 2-6-2T No.5512 at Cheddar in May 1948. Note that the leading carriage is an LMS one.

J Moss; Roger Carpenter collection

Plate 40 - Unknown Great Western 2-6-2T in the Wells branch bay at Yatton at the head of what appears to be a two coach 'B' set. Note the gantry of centre-pivoted signals; these would be Yatton West down inner homes. The presence of the road bridge, footbridge and the platform canopy could have caused sighting problems if normal length arms had been spaced across the gantry.

John Alsop collection

Plate 41 - Collecting scrap metal for the war effort. Thorne Colliery, near Doncaster, was under the control of Pease & Partners Ltd, a company with major interests in the coal industry in the north-east of England. Although the loads look precarious, a number of bedstead ends and lengths of railings have been used in the manner of 'coke rails' to restrain smaller items of scrap. Wells cathedral is in the distance, the nearer church being dedicated to St. Cuthbert.

Wells and Mendip Museum

After nationalisation in 1948 the Somerset & Dorset branch from Glastonbury effectively became surplus to requirements. Goods traffic on the branch ceased on 26th September 1949. Passenger traffic on the branch had dwindled to a very low level indeed with rarely more than one or two passengers on each train. The branch finally closed to all traffic on Saturday, 29th October 1951. The final service train on the branch arrived just before 8.00pm and was hauled by 0-4-4T No.58086 hauling an auto-trailer No.M24465. The locomotive was formerly Midland Railway No.1423 and was destined to become the last survivor of a class that had been introduced on the Somerset & Dorset as far back as 1877. The Somerset & Dorset engine shed was rendered redundant by the closure of the line and was itself closed at the same time. Some sources give the engine shed closure date as 1947 but the locally accepted date of 1951 is more likely to be accurate. There are plans in existence suggesting that a four-inch main was installed during World War II connecting the Somerset & Dorset's water tank with that at Tucker Street station, although the reasons behind this are not clear. The goods yard at Priory Road remained open for traffic and so the

Plate 42 - A Yatton-bound ex-GWR railcar approaches Sandford and Banwell, believed to be c.1949-50.

J Moss; Roger Carpenter collection

Plate 43 - A busy period at Congresbury on 23rd June 1953 as 4500 Class 2-6-2T No.5548 restarts an up passenger train. Note the vans loaded with strawberries attached between the locomotive and passenger vehicles. A down train can be seen departing at the same time.
P J Garland;
Roger Carpenter collection

Somerset & Dorset signal box remained in use until such time that alterations were made to control access to the yard from a ground frame released by East Somerset signal box. This work was completed in 1955 and the Somerset & Dorset box was closed but was not demolished until about 1960.

Train Services in 1954

The working timetable for the summer of 1954 showed a broadly similar pattern of services to those that had existed before World War II. There were three through passenger trains on weekdays from Yatton to Witham departing from Yatton at 7.58am, 2.52pm and 6.10pm and booked to arrive at Witham 9.42am, 4.26pm and 7.36pm respectively. The working timetable indicates that only the first of these originated from Bristol Temple Meads, the departure time being 7.25am. All three services ran through to Frome. The 2.52pm departure from Yatton was normally worked by an ex-GWR A.E.C. diesel railcar. In the opposite direction there were four through passenger trains from Witham to Yatton. Departures from Witham were at 8.25am, 10.20am, 3.30pm and 6.53pm. Booked arrival times at Yatton were 9.54am, 11.50am, 5.06pm and 8.58pm. respectively. These services originated at various stations on the main line. The 8.25am from Witham started from Trowbridge at 7.53am, whilst the 10.20am started from Westbury (Wilts) at 9.57am and the 3.30pm started from Frome at 3.20pm. The 6.53pm departure from Witham is described in the working timetable as being the '5.20pm Bristol Passenger'. This train had, in fact, started from Bristol Temple Meads at 5.20pm and had run to Frome and Witham via the Bristol and North Somerset line. Again, describing these trains as 'through' from Witham to Yatton is possibly a little dubious as the 5.20pm from Bristol Temple Meads stood at Wells Tucker Street for forty-nine minutes whilst the other three spent between ten and seventeen minutes there.

On Saturdays only the departure times from Witham of the second and third trains were amended so that the 10.20am became the 10.10am and the 3.30pm became the 3.37pm. Interestingly, the 10.10am times over the Cheddar Valley section were the same as those for the 10.20 on weekdays. This came about because the train stood at Wells for twenty-five minutes on Saturdays whereas on weekdays it only stood there for fifteen minutes. The overall journey time for the 3.37pm on Saturdays was shorter than for the equivalent 3.30pm on weekdays as its arrival at Yatton was four minutes earlier in spite of having left Witham seven minutes later. This was accounted for by shorter waiting times at Wells and Shepton Mallet.

As with previous timetables already described, there were additional passenger services that either terminated at or started from Wells. There were two early morning passenger trains to Bristol. The first departed from Wells at 7.05am calling at all stations to arrive at Yatton at 7.42am. The second departed from Wells at 8.00am also calling at all stations to arrive at Yatton at 8.39am. On Mondays to Fridays there was also an evening departure from Wells at 7.00pm, calling at all stations to Yatton and arriving at 7.44pm. A Saturdays only service departed from Wells at 2.47pm and arrived at Yatton at 3.28pm. There was also one passenger train that worked over the East Somerset section only, departing from Witham at 9.20pm and calling at all stations to arrive at Wells at 9.57pm.

In the opposite direction there were four trains each weekday between Yatton and Wells, departing at 6.55am, 11.12am, 1.11pm and 5.47pm and calling at all stations to arrive at Wells at 7.40am, 11.53am, 1.53pm and 6.28pm respectively. The last of these services started from Bristol. There was one train from Wells to Frome each weekday that left Wells at 12.03pm and arrived at Witham at 12.39pm, calling at all stations between Wells and Witham.

Turning now to goods traffic on the Cheddar Valley section, the early morning goods from Bristol West Depot to Wells still ran very much as it did in the 1930s although slightly retimed. This train left Bristol at 3.55am and after a leisurely trip down the main line departed from Yatton at 4.50am. The train called at all stations except Draycott and Lodge Hill and arrived at Wells

Plate 44 - Still awaiting a smokebox number plate following nationalisation, 2251 Class 0-6-0 No.2220 waits at Cheddar with a Wells to Bristol freight working in May 1948.
J Moss; Roger Carpenter collection

East Somerset yard at 7.31am. Once business at East Somerset was complete the engine and guard were to work the Wells Cold Store Depot as required.

There was a second down goods from Bristol West Depot to Wells, Saturdays excepted. This train departed from Yatton at 10.33am having left West Depot at 9.30am. It called unconditionally at all stations except for Congresbury and Draycott, which were only worked as traffic required. It was booked to arrive at East Somerset yard at 2.50pm.

In the up direction on the Cheddar Valley section, through goods trains departed from East Somerset yard at 7.55am and 4.40pm. Both trains called at all stations en route to Yatton. The first arrived at Yatton at 2.11pm before continuing to Bristol West Depot. The second arrived at Yatton at 7.56pm before continuing to Bristol, its destination being St. Philip's Marsh.

On the East Somerset section two down goods trains now ran through to Wells. The first of these left Witham at 6.35am having originated from Westbury (Wilts) at 5.20am. The train called at Cranmore and Shepton Mallet before arriving at Wells East Somerset yard at 8.17am. It then left East Somerset at 8.25am and ran to the goods yard at Tucker Street. Interestingly, the arrival times in Wells were the same as they had been in 1933. Doulting Stone Siding was out of use by this time but down goods trains still stopped on the running line here in order to pin down brakes for the descent to Shepton Mallet. The positions of the other stop boards on the line, one down and two up, have been described previously. The second down goods left Witham at 1.45pm, calling at Cranmore, Shepton Mallet and Dulcote Siding (as required). This train did not run on Saturdays.

Plate 45 - An early view of Draycott station building and the small signal box, the sharp shadows making for a difficult exposure. The picture is undated but the style of the GWR's 'Holiday Haunts' and Channel Islands posters may give some clues. Below those posters, either side of the door, P. E. Gane, of College Green, Bristol, is also advertising carpets as well as furniture. Free delivery, too. Meanwhile, the chocolate in the Nestlé machine might suffer if the shadow does not protect it. *Lens of Sutton Association*

Plate 46 - 2251 Class 0-6-0 No.3215 passes Lodge Hill with up goods train in 1948/9.

J Moss; Roger Carpenter collection

In the up direction goods trains ran through to Witham departing from East Somerset yard at 11.10am, 4.25pm and 6.15pm. The first of these only ran as required between Cranmore and Witham and only the 6.15pm ran on Saturdays. All three trains called at both Shepton Mallet and Cranmore but only the 11.10am called at Dulcote Siding. The 4.25pm train also called at Wanstrow as required. The scheduled arrival time of the trains at Witham was 1.17pm, 6.41pm and 8.15pm respectively. The 4.25pm worked through to Westbury (Wilts). On Mondays to Fridays only, the 6.15pm started from Cheddar at 4.45pm with an intermediate stop only at the goods yard adjacent to the Wells passenger station before arriving at East Somerset at 5.37pm. The engine and van to work this train left Wells East Somerset at 2.45pm and arrived at 3.09pm in plenty of time to make up the train.

There were still a few shorter goods and trip workings on both sections of the line. A goods train left Yatton on Mondays to Fridays at 7.10am and proceeded directly to Sandford and Banwell arriving at 7.25am to deal with the quarry traffic. The return working departed from Sandford and Banwell at 8.10am and arrived at Congresbury at 8.21am. The train then worked the Wrington Vale line that had by this date been truncated to Wrington itself and was more or less exclusively for coal traffic. The train left Congresbury at 8.45am and arrived at Wrington at 8.55am. After carrying out the necessary duties there, the return working departed from Wrington at 9.25am arriving back at Congresbury at 9.35am and at Yatton at 10.01am. An engine and van departed from East Somerset on Saturdays only at 10.10am, destined for Frome. This working stopped only at Shepton Mallet to cross a down passenger train. During the fruit picking season a train ran from Cheddar to Birmingham (Moor Street) Mondays to Fridays as required. It departed from Cheddar at 9.50pm with intermediate stops for picking up at Draycott and Lodge Hill. It then ran through to Witham arriving at 11.17pm before proceeding to the Midlands, presumably via Didcot and Oxford. The engine and van for this working originated from Frome at 8.20pm arriving at Cheddar at 9.27pm.

Sunday working was very much as it was before with one train in each direction although the times had been altered. The Yatton to Witham working left Yatton at 2.30pm having originated from Bristol at 2.10pm. Having called at all stations it arrived at Witham at 4.36pm, still a very leisurely journey! The return working departed from Witham at 5.40pm and arrived at Yatton at 8.04pm.

EXCURSION TRAFFIC

From time to time special and excursion trains had been worked over the Yatton to Witham line in addition to the normal service trains. On Easter Monday, 17th April 1922 the Great Western advertised day return trips from Wells to Cheddar for one shilling and six pence (£0.08p) and to Clevedon and Weston-super-Mare for three shillings and six pence (£0.17p). The departure time from Wells on the outward journey was 9.00am thus assuring a reasonable amount of time at the chosen destination. The Somerset & Dorset also offered similar excursions that year to destinations that included Burnham-on-Sea, Bath and Bournemouth.

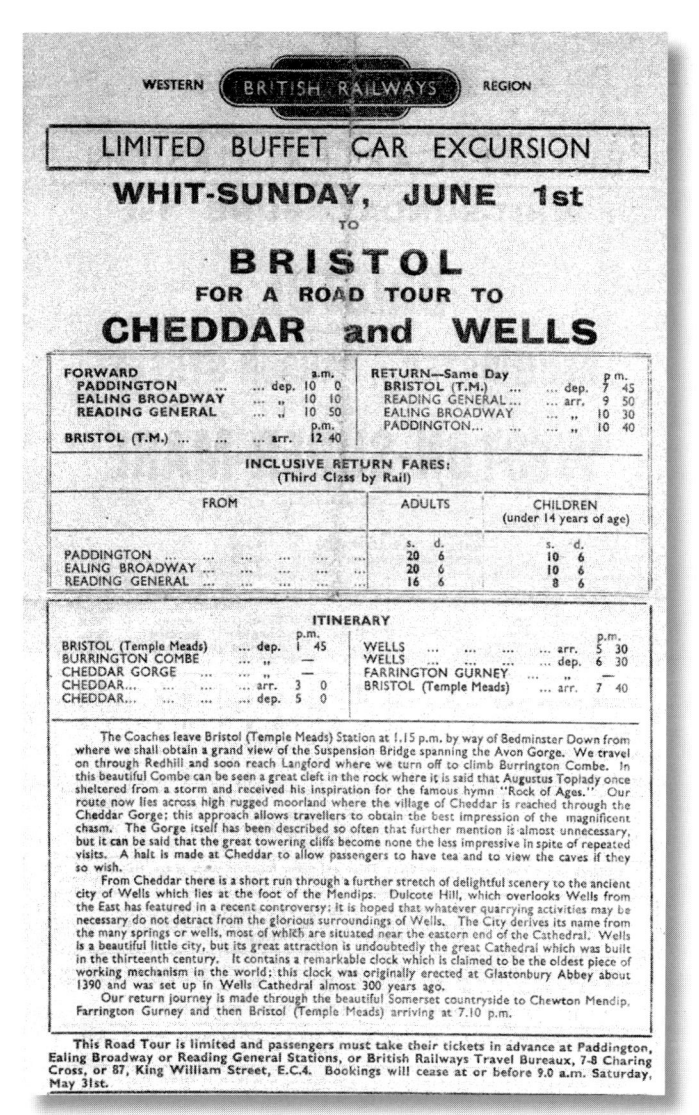

Plate 47 - A Western Region handbill advertising a road tour from Bristol to Cheddar and Wells on Whit Sunday, 1st June 1952. The excursion, from Paddington, Ealing and Reading, offered passengers the alternatives of continuing to Weston-super-Mare by train or taking the Mendip bus tour from Bristol. The handbill described the bus tour itinerary and highlights points of interest along the way. *J Moss; R Carpenter collection*

In April 1939 the Great Western ran specials on three consecutive Saturdays to the Ideal Homes Exhibition in London. Departure time was 9.09am from Wells and the train called at all stations on the branch as far as Witham and was due at Paddington at 11.50am. The return train was due to depart from Paddington at 6.00pm on the same day. The cost of the return trip was between twelve (£0.60) and thirteen shillings (£0.65) depending on the station of departure. On Saturday, 22nd July 1939 cheap trips to London were available priced at thirteen shillings (£0.65) for the return journey. With war being a virtual certainty at that time one wonders how many took advantage of the opportunity to visit London whilst they could. On Sunday, 30th July return trips to Yeovil for three shillings and two pence (£0.16) or Weymouth for four shillings and nine pence (£0.24) could be made with a departure time from Wells at 10.55am. Evening excursions to Weston-super-Mare could be made for one shilling and six pence (£0.08), the train departing from Wells at 4.22pm.

The 1950s were the heyday of the seaside excursion train and the Yatton to Witham line was no exception. In the late 1950s and early 1960s there were Sunday excursion trains to various places including Weymouth, Teignmouth and Barry Island. As on many other lines these trains were well loaded. One train was reported to be so long that when the locomotives were passing Priory Road station, the tail end of the train had not yet left Tucker Street. What a sight that must have been ascending the 1 in 46½ to Shepton Mallet.

The Run-down Begins

After withdrawal of all services on the former Somerset & Dorset branch from Glastonbury, Priory Road passenger station closed altogether there being little point in the Cheddar Valley and East Somerset services calling there any more. However, the goods yard remained open, goods traffic being diverted via the former Great Western lines. In 1951 the Priory Road station buildings became the zoned freight offices for the section of line from Shepton Mallet to Cheddar. The displaced ex-GWR clerks and the remaining former Somerset & Dorset staff administered the accounts from Wells. All 'smalls' traffic was concentrated at Wells, so the Cheddar delivery vehicle came to Wells to fetch the consignments for delivery. No information has come to light as to what happened to the Shepton Mallet deliveries.

Track and signalling alterations in conjunction with the final closure of Wells 'A' signal box were made in 1955 and are described in the section on signalling. The track from the junction at Glastonbury to a point near the Somerset & Dorset engine shed at Wells was also lifted during 1955, the short section from there onwards providing a head shunt for Priory Road goods yard. The overall roof at Priory Road station was removed shortly after closure, presumably for reasons of safety but with the added benefit of giving the signalman at East Somerset signal box a better view of the line towards the remaining passenger station. The rest of the station building and platform remained in place until they were demolished to make way for the Wells relief road.

By the late 1950s road competition had taken a considerable bite out of the traffic on the Cheddar Valley and East Somerset lines. Rationalisation had already begun as Congresbury station had become partly unstaffed on 7th May 1956. The station here was in a slightly unfortunate position. It was only a little further for much of the village to go directly to the junction station at Yatton and catch a train to Bristol, the most likely destination, from there. With the increase in private car ownership this was a more practical proposition for many. Also Yatton, being on the main line, had a better train service and for many of those without access to a private car, the local buses probably provided a more convenient service.

Sunday, 28th April 1957 saw what was probably the last passenger train to visit Wrington. This was an RCTS rail tour that started from Waterloo and ran to Reading via Weybridge. The outward run featured 4-6-0 No.30453 *King Arthur* as far as

Plate 48 - GWR 5100 Class 2-6-2T No.4130 in the sidings at East Somerset yard, Wells, on an unknown date. The train, consisting of at least three vehicles, is carrying Class A headlamps, an unusual occurrence for the branch since none of the booked passenger workings ran as anything other than Class B, 'stopping passenger train'. No.4130 was a long-term resident of the Newport area, ultimately being withdrawn from Severn Tunnel Junction in July 1964, so might the train be a return Sunday excursion in preparation? Note that some of the siding track is supported by concrete blocks under the chairs, the gauge being maintained by transverse tie-rods. *R Told; Wells Railway Fraternity*

Reading where it was replaced by 4-4-0 No.3440 *City of Truro*. From Bristol Temple Meads Ivatt 2-6-2Ts Nos.41202 and 41203 took charge for the run to Wrington, where a certain amount of shunting was required in order to run round. After the visit to the truncated Wrington Vale line, the rail tour ran to Burnham-on-Sea and then over the North Somerset line from Bristol to Frome on its return trip to Paddington. A full account of the trip may be found on page 146 of the May 1957 edition of the *Railway Observer*.

By this time, thanks to competition from road transport, both passenger and goods traffic were in decline with the branch lines being particularly hard hit; the Yatton to Witham line was no exception. This led in 1958 to a rationalisation of both passenger and goods services. Weekday services were cut back and Sunday services ran on the Cheddar Valley section for the duration of the summer timetable only. There were no Sunday services at all on the East Somerset section. Also by this time a speed limit of 35mph for passenger trains and 20mph for goods trains had been imposed over the entire line, presumably to be able to cut down on permanent way maintenance costs! The timetable that came into force on 15th September 1958 amply demonstrates the reduction in services.

There were no passenger trains between Wells and Yatton from 9.05am to 4.20pm Monday to Fridays and goods services also suffered a reduction. On Mondays to Fridays there were four through trains from Yatton to Witham with departures from Yatton at 7.58am, 11.35am, 2.52pm and 6.13pm serving all stations and arriving at Witham at 9.31am, 12.39pm, 4.26pm and 7.40pm respectively. All four trains worked through to Frome. The 7.58am from Yatton was a through train from Bristol Temple Meads starting at 7.25am. There were also two trains that ran from Yatton to Wells only. These trains left Yatton at 6.55am and 5.47pm and called at all stations before arriving at Wells at 7.40am and 6.28pm respectively. The second of these was a through train from Bristol Temple Meads, departing from there at 5.30pm.

On Saturdays there were additional trains departing from Yatton at 11.12am, 1.18pm and 8.08pm. The first of these called at all stations to Witham arriving at 12.39pm. The other two ran only as far as Wells after calling at all stations. Their arrival times in Wells were 2.00pm and 8.50pm respectively.

In the opposite direction during Mondays to Fridays there were now only two through trains from Witham to Yatton. These trains worked through from Frome to Bristol Temple Meads with the departure times from Frome being 8.12am and 3.17pm with corresponding departure times from Witham of 8.21am and 3.28am. Both trains called at all stations en route to Yatton, arriving there at 9.44am and 5.05pm respectively before continuing their journey to Bristol. Two trains ran only from Wells to Yatton, calling at all stations. The departure times from

Plate 49 - It appears to be high summer as 5700 Class 0-6-0PT No.5757 draws the 3.17pm Frome-Bristol Temple Meads train into the down platform on 23rd May 1959.

Hugh Ballantyne

Wells were 7.05am and 8.00am with corresponding arrival times at Yatton of 7.42am and 8.39am. There was also one service from Bristol Temple Meads to Wells via the Bristol and North Somerset line and Frome. The train departed from Bristol at 5.20pm and after a five minute stop at Frome from 6.31pm to 6.36pm it ran down the main line to Witham. Departure from here was at 6.53pm after which all stations were served to Wells where it arrived at 7.29pm. The locomotive from this service worked forward to Yatton leaving Wells at 7.40pm.

On Saturdays there were two additional through trains from Witham to Yatton, both of which served all intermediate stations. Their departure times from Witham were 10.20am and 1.30pm with corresponding arrival times in Yatton of 11.50am and 2.49pm. The first of these originated from Westbury (Wilts) at 9.57am and both trains ran through to Bristol Temple Meads. In addition to these two, the 5.20pm from Temple Meads to Wells via Radstock and Frome was extended to Yatton and effectively provided a third additional through service from Witham to Yatton. Departure time from Wells was 8.15pm, which meant a 46 minute wait so some might argue that it was not really a through service at all! No doubt the wait provided the through passenger with a good excuse to pop into the nearby Cheddar Valley Inn for some suitable refreshment. The arrival time at Yatton was 8.54pm. In 1954 the 5.20pm from Bristol had run through to Yatton on Mondays to Fridays as well as on Saturdays. There was also one additional train over the Cheddar Valley section only that departed from Wells at 2.47pm and arrived at Yatton at 3.28pm calling at all stations.

Apart from the Wrington service, all goods trains on the line either started from or terminated at Wells and strawberry specials would still be run during the season. On the Cheddar Valley section two down goods trains ran daily from Yatton to Wells East Somerset yard, both of which had started from Bristol West Depot. The first of these departed from Yatton at 4.50am (3.50am from West Depot) and was booked to call only at Congresbury, Sandford and Banwell, Cheddar and Wookey en route. Arrival time at Wells was 6.59am. The locomotive and guard were then to work the Cold Store Depot at Wells if required. The second down goods departed from Yatton at 10.33am calling at all stations (Draycott and Lodge Hill as required) and was due to arrive at Wells East Somerset at 2.50pm. Note that the second train also served the goods yard at Wells station, whereas the first one did not.

In the up direction there were also two daily goods trains between East Somerset yard and Yatton. The first train continued to Bristol West Depot whilst the second continued to St. Philip's Marsh. The first train departed from Wells East Somerset at 10.22am and called at all stations (except the goods yard at Wells passenger station and calling at Lodge Hill and Draycott only as required) to arrive at Yatton at 2.11pm. The second train departed from East Somerset at 3.30pm calling at all stations (Wookey, Lodge Hill and Draycott only as required) to arrive at Yatton at 7.56pm. Both trains also ran on Saturdays, but with different timings between Wells and Cheddar although with the same arrival time at Yatton.

The only other goods working on the Cheddar Valley served Congresbury, Sanford and Banwell and Wrington. This working has already been described in detail for the duration of the summer 1954 timetable. The only change in the winter 1958 timetable was that all timings were two hours later (ie. departure from Yatton at 9.10am instead of 7.10am). Possibly the reason for the later start was to allow for the darker mornings during the period of the winter timetable and ensure that all shunting operations were conducted during the hours of daylight.

The East Somerset section was now only served by one goods train in each direction daily. On Mondays to Fridays the down service departure from Witham was at 1.45pm. This train originated from Westbury at 12.50pm and served Wanstrow and Merehead Quarry Siding as required, then Cranmore and Shepton Mallet before arriving at Wells East Somerset at 3.45pm. On Saturdays departure time from Witham was 11.00am (10.15am from Westbury) and arrival time at East Somerset was 12.45pm, having made the same stops en route as the weekday service.

In the up direction on Mondays to Fridays the daily goods departed from the small goods yard adjacent to Wells Tucker Street station at 4.45pm and served Shepton Mallet, Cranmore and Wanstrow, the latter only as required. The arrival time at Witham was 6.46pm. This train then proceeded to Westbury. Note also that it did not serve East Somerset yard. Presumably all work here was carried out by the down train. On Saturdays this service departed from East Somerset yard at 1.30pm and served Shepton Mallet, Cranmore and Wanstrow (as required). The booked arrival time at Witham was at 3.17pm.

There were no trains at all on Sundays. Sunday services had gradually been eroded over the years since the 1920s until, from September 1950, the Sunday service was withdrawn for the duration of the winter timetable. After that, Sunday trains only ran during the summer timetable. During the summer of 1954 there had been one train from Bristol to Witham and return. It left Bristol at 2.10pm arriving at Witham at 4.36pm. The return train left Witham at 5.40pm and arrived back at Bristol at 8.04pm. Both trains stood at Wells for some considerable time, the outbound for 50 minutes and the return for 66! In earlier years, prior to the retiming of the Sunday trains in order to make revised main line connections, the outbound train only waited at Wells for a few minutes but the return service would wait for anything up to 81 minutes! With the introduction of the summer service in 1958 the Sunday service terminated at Wells. Departure time from Bristol was 2.10pm and the return time from Wells was 7.20pm.

This pattern of services remained virtually unchanged apart from minor timing alterations of individual services for the remainder of the branch's existence as a passenger-carrying railway. Diesel multiple units were introduced on the Clevedon branch on 8th August 1960 and Yatton shed closed during the same month. Cheddar Valley line services remained steam-hauled but were now worked from Bristol. Lodge Hill station became partly unstaffed on 2nd October 1961. The overall roof at Cheddar was beginning to show its age. The glass was removed from the gable end at the Axbridge end of the station and the structure was shored up by baulks of timber placed in the ample space between the running lines. It is not known exactly when this work was carried out but photographic evidence narrows it down to the period from 1958 to 1960.

Closure to Passengers; Beginning of the End

In 1962 it was said that school children travelling between Wells and Shepton Mallet accounted for one third of the traffic on the entire line from Yatton to Witham. In view of the timetabling of passenger trains this may come as no surprise. It was alleged that the line was losing over £50,000 a year and there were constant rumours that the line would close, at least to passengers,

Plate 50 - 5700 Class No.8744 on the 55ft turntable at Wells, East Somerset, on 7th May 1959. Like No.5757, opposite, No.8744 was nominally at Westbury during the latter half of the 1950s but probably resided at Frome, Westbury's out-station. East Somerset signal box, guarding the road crossing, is immediately behind the engine, whilst the Somerset & Dorset box is visible just to the left of the engine's bunker. *Rod Blencowe*

long before the publication of the infamous Beeching Report in 1963. Scarcely a week went by without some report in the *Wells Journal* concerning the future of the line. On 5th January 1962 it stated that Wells City Chamber of Commerce would support all efforts to keep the line open. On 26th January it was reported that Cheddar Parish Council were disturbed by the existence of a British Railways booklet on diesel trains services that failed to mention the Yatton to Witham line altogether. It was announced on 9th February that the line was under review, along with many others, and that no decision had been made as to its future. On 2nd March it was reported that the Branch Line Reinvigoration Society had visited the line on the previous Saturday, 24th February, in order to support local efforts to save the line. On 20th April it was reported that a suggestion that local councils should run local rail services had not been well received. Then, on 1st June, it was reported that there would be a meeting of the British Railways Staff Consultative Committee in Bristol within the next few days. On 15th June a report stated that British Railways had no comment following the meeting and that the details of discussions that took place were purely an internal affair.

It was becoming increasingly obvious that the powers-that-be wanted to close the line, along with many others, and would not consider any other means to keep them running, such as the replacement of steam haulage by diesel trains and making other economies such as reducing the number of passing loops and signal boxes. They just wanted the lines to close and be done with it, regardless of the protests from railway users, local councils and other pressure groups. Looking back through nearly fifty years of history, one can only wish that those who made the decision to close so many rural lines, and indeed to destroy the infrastructure, had had more foresight and would see that at the start of the twenty-first century we are no nearer solving the problems of rural transport. In fact, if anything, we are probably further away than we were then.

Meanwhile, there were still plenty of column inches left for the *Wells Journal* to print. On 3rd August the paper printed a more definitive statement of what had been planned for the line. The British Transport Commission stated that the substitution of diesel railcars in place of steam hauled trains would not help. Diesels would cost £24,000 per annum for a projected income of £10,000 per year. The proposals were that all passenger services on the line would be withdrawn. Parcels and general freight at Congresbury, Winscombe, Draycott and Cranmore, coal traffic at Congresbury and Winscombe, bitumen traffic at Cranmore and, during the season, strawberry traffic at Draycott would all be continued. Collection and delivery of freight would also still be available. Goods smalls traffic would continue at Yatton, Sandford and Banwell, Axbridge, Cheddar, Wookey, Wells, Shepton Mallet, Wanstrow and Witham. Also wagon load traffic would be continued. It was estimated that £50,575 per annum would be saved as a result of these measures. The local Member of Parliament did little to support the cause for keeping the line open by stating that rail services should be run economically.

A week later the paper reported on the protest over piecemeal closures prior to the publication of a long term plan for the railways (ie. the Beeching Report). Comments about the formulation of such plans in isolation from other transport considerations, and the inadequacy of the road network to take additional traffic, have a familiar ring in today's transport debate. On 24th August the paper reported that the MP for Weston-super-Mare had warned that if passenger services were withdrawn it would only be a matter of time before freight services would also go and the line would close altogether. No doubt spurred on by the prospect of closure, a three-car DMU charter from Bristol via Radstock worked over the line from Witham to Yatton on Saturday, 15th September 1962.

On 5th October it was reported that a one-day strike by the NUR on the previous Wednesday had caused little inconvenience to the travelling public and the local economy. The effect of such action could only have been bad for the railways at this time. In the 16th November issue there was a report on the meeting of the Western Area Transport Users' Consultative Committee (TUCC) that was held in Wells on the previous Thursday to

Plate 51 - Gradually BR Standard Class 3MT 2-6-2Ts were introduced to the line. No.82009 climbs away from Cranmore towards the summit at Doulting with the 3.17pm Frome-Bristol Temple Meads on 23rd April 1963. *Hugh Ballantyne*

Plate 52 - Two of the larger Prairie designs, 5100 Class 2-6-2T No.4108 and 6100 Class 2-6-2T No.6148, bring the Home Counties Railway Society Mendip tour off the Cheddar Valley branch at Witham on what appears to have been a damp Sunday, 6th October 1963, a month after the branch passenger services were withdrawn.
Ivo Peters

consider objections to the closure proposal. There were many objections to be heard. The general feeling was that alternative road transport was inadequate and that people without cars living in places like Wanstrow would become isolated. The local farming community, in particular strawberry growers, were very much against the closure proposals. During the season five tons of strawberries per day were dispatched by rail, from around 250 local growers. Some economy measures were taken, however. Parcels traffic was concentrated at Frome and delivered from there by road. On 7th December the *Wells Journal* reported that many complaints had been received because of unacceptable delays allegedly caused by the new system.

Heavy snowfalls were experienced after Christmas and rail services were severely affected from the night of Saturday, 29th December. A snowplough was used to clear the line on the following Monday morning, 31st December, and as a consequence the first trains were very late. There were no trains on Tuesday, 1st January 1963 because the early morning goods (that ran as two locomotives only with a snowplough, 0-6-0 No.2277 and 2-6-0 No.46506) had become stuck in a snowdrift near Draycott. The stricken locomotives were eventually rescued later in the week and towed back to Cheddar. The locomotive crew had let the fire go out because they were low on water. A full account is given in chapter fifteen.

On Tuesday, 8th January three locomotives and a snowplough became stuck trying to clear snow in Easton Cutting. This was reported in the *Wells Journal* on 11th January. The locomotives concerned were 0-6-0s Nos.2277, 3218 and a pannier tank. They were rescued the following day by Hymek D7055 and a snowplough. On 18th January the paper reported that services on the line were now almost back to normal except for a 15mph speed limit in Easton Cutting and that delays should be no more than 15 minutes. Meanwhile the TUCC had reported that closure of the line would cause hardship.

The fate of the line was finally sealed on publication of the long-awaited Beeching Report on Monday, 25th March 1963 which recommended that it should close. The entire Somerset & Dorset system was also to close. The Yatton to Witham line was to linger on for a bit longer but in some areas the standard of service deteriorated rapidly and complaints were made. The *Wells Journal* of 28th June reported that local strawberry growers had been angered by delays in getting their produce to market with the consequence that some of the fruit had perished. The local railway staff were exonerated and it was their more distant colleagues who were blamed for the problem.

Finally, the date for the withdrawal of passenger trains was set for Monday, 9th September 1963 but the last trains ran on Saturday, 7th September 1963. The Sunday service, which ran during the summer timetable only, had already been withdrawn after Sunday, 28th July of that year. Through the late summer there was a growing acceptance that the line would close and that there was nothing that anyone could do about it. This tone was reflected by the fact that the papers during August carried reports of the arrangements being made for the replacement bus services rather than reporting, as they had previously, on the campaign to save the railway. Following the passenger closure somewhere between 30 and 40 railway employees were made redundant. On Sunday, 6th October 1963 a Home Counties Railway Society tour worked over the branch hauled by large Prairie 2-6-2Ts Nos.4103 and 6148.

Goods Only

Although the line was still open for goods traffic, it was not without some reduction in service. All of the former Cheddar Valley stations, with the exception of Congresbury, Cheddar and Wells, had already lost their public goods facilities on 10th June 1963. On the East Somerset section only Wanstrow lost its goods facilities before closure to passengers, also on 10th June 1963. However It was not long before the prophecies of the Member of Parliament for Weston came true. Congresbury station closed for goods traffic on 1st July 1964 and the up loop was taken out of use. The entire line between Yatton and Cheddar closed along with the signal boxes at Congresbury and Sandford and Banwell on 1st October 1964. Buffer stops were erected at 30 miles 20 chains, on the Yatton side of the River Yeo bridge near Congresbury, and at 22 miles 12 chains, just east of McAlpine's Siding, west of Cheddar station, that had remained in use for stone traffic up until that time. Congresbury signal box was demolished in April 1965 along with the waiting room on the up platform. The main station building on the down platform survived until October 1968. There is some controversy about the closure date of Axbridge signal box. According to the Signalling Record Society sources, the closure date was 10th June 1963, some three months before the closure to passengers, but the writer has first-hand accounts of the box being open at least until the withdrawal of passenger services. In fact, examination of the last working timetable for the line soon reveals the fact that trains crossed there right up until the last day. The informed view is that Axbridge signal box closed on 1st October 1964, the same date as Congresbury and Sandford and Banwell. There is a photograph in existence taken at Axbridge in August 1964 which shows only the down line in situ but with all the signals still having arms, which would not be the case had the box been closed. The overall roof at Cheddar was removed in 1964, no doubt mainly because of its dangerous condition which has already been alluded to. However the main station building at Cheddar still stands.

Some information is available on the workings after closure to passenger traffic. In the winter timetable for 1963-4 the early goods working from Bristol to Wells departed from West Depot at 6.35am. This was worked by a D6300 diesel hydraulic and was Bristol Bath Road turn 800. Departure times from intermediate stations were Yatton 7.20am, Cheddar 8.15am and arrival at Wells was 8.40am. Wookey was shunted as required. The return trip from Wells departed at 10.15am with intermediate departure times of 11.10am at Cheddar, 11.45am at Sandford and Banwell and Yatton at 12.50pm for West Depot. There was also an afternoon working as far as Cheddar that departed from West Depot at 2.30pm. The time from Yatton was 3.20pm, then Congresbury at 3.38pm, Sandford and Banwell at 4.05pm arriving at Cheddar at 4.38pm where shunting was carried out. The return trip departed at 5.25pm calling only at Sandford and Banwell before departing from Yatton at 7.20pm for Pylle Hill and St. Philip's Marsh.

From the other end of the line a Westbury 5700 0-6-0PT (Bristol turn 945) worked to Wells East Somerset yard and back (Saturdays excepted). The departure time from Westbury was 8.35am. Intermediate departure times were Witham at 8.35am, Cranmore at 10.30am and Shepton Mallet at 11.10am. Arrival at Wells was at 11.38am where the yard was shunted before departing at 1.30pm. Intermediate departure times for the return trip were Shepton Mallet at 2.05pm, Cranmore 2.35pm and Witham at 3.30pm.

In the summer of 1964 both these turns were still running with the addition of a return trip from Westbury to Cranmore for turn 945 (Saturdays only). The departure times were from Westbury at 8.30am and from Witham at 9.40am. The arrival time at Cranmore was 10.15am where shunting was carried out before returning at 11.30am for Witham and Frome, with an arrival time at Westbury of 1.20pm. Strawberry specials were still worked to Draycott as required, which were probably worked by a D6300 although a BR Standard Class 3 2-6-2T was used on at least one occasion.

By the summer of 1965 the line between Cheddar and Yatton

Plate 53 - Picking up the token for the single line section ahead, the footplate crew of Ivatt Class 2MT 2-6-0 No.46525 ease the Cheddar Valley goods off the down main and onto the branch at Yatton with the 9.45am Bristol West Depot-Wells East Somerset goods on 17th February 1962. *Terry Nicholls*

Plate 54 - On 11th May 1963, just a few months before the withdrawal of passenger services, BR Standard Class 3MT 2-6-T No.82035, with a somewhat dirty fire, nears the top of the 1 in 46½ climb up from Dulcote to Three Arch Bridge. *J Spencer Gilks*

had been closed to all traffic so that all access to the line had to be from Witham. Bristol turn 945 from Westbury shed was still running Mondays to Fridays but was now rostered for a Hymek diesel hydraulic. Departure was at 8.25am from Westbury, 9.27am from Witham and 10.42am from Cranmore arriving at Wells at 11.25am. After shunting at Wells, departure from there was at 11.55am arriving at Cheddar at 12.25pm. After shunting at Cheddar the return trip departed at 1.10pm. Intermediate departure times were 2.00pm from Wells, 2.55pm from Cranmore and 3.58pm from Witham, the train terminating back at Westbury. The outward trip also called at Merehead as required. Wookey was served as required by both the outward and return trips.

On Saturday, 16th November 1968 a three-car DMU charter organised by the LCGB Bath Branch ran through to Cheddar from the by then closed Bath Green Park station.

Stone traffic from Cheddar continued until 28th March 1969. This was loaded from an extension of the goods yard headshunt on the down side. The original private siding agreement was made on 27th September 1922 with the Callow Rock Lime Company Limited and was terminated on the closure date with E.C.C Quarries Limited. Public goods facilities at Cheddar were withdrawn on 17th May 1965 with the exception of coal traffic, which continued until 29th November 1965. Goods facilities at Wells, with the exception of the private siding belonging to Sheldon Jones, and at Shepton Mallet were withdrawn on 13th July 1964. Cranmore did not close for public goods traffic until 17th January 1966. The signal boxes at Cheddar, Wells East Somerset and Shepton Mallet were closed on 3rd May 1965, after which the level crossing gates at Draycott and Wells were manually operated by the train crew and secured by a padlock and chain. The signal box at Cranmore remained open until 19th May 1968. During this time there was only one daily working (weekdays only) to Cheddar and return, but an additional train ran on Tuesdays, Thursdays and Saturdays as far as Cranmore. This would have been the reason for the survival of a working signal box at Cranmore because to work the two trains as described it would be necessary to retain Cranmore as a block post. However, the line west of Cranmore would have been worked under one-train regulations and, following the final closure of the signal box, the entire line from Witham to Cheddar was little more than a very long siding!

On 31st May 1969 the RCTS ran a DMU charter from Paddington to Cheddar and return. This was the last revenue earning train to run east of Dulcote. After this, the section from Cheddar to Dulcote was closed and lifted shortly afterwards. In November 1969, after a brief resurrection, the Foster Yeoman company decided to make no further use of the sidings at Dulcote and the line was abandoned west of Cranmore. The track remained in situ for some years after the Dulcote Quarry scheme was abandoned and the line was lifted from there to a point a mile or so east of Shepton Mallet in the mid-1970s. The private siding agreement between Foster Yeoman and British Rail was not formally terminated until 20th August 1975. Bitumen traffic that was used for tarmacadam production at the local road stone quarries was worked into the sidings on the north side of Cranmore station until 1985.

At the other end of the line there was an embryonic plan during the 1970s to move stone from the Sandford and Winscombe area by rail, which would have meant the reinstatement of the line from Yatton to at least as far as the site of Sandford station. It would have been necessary to replace a number of bridges,

Plate 55 - Although carrying an unorthodox headcode, a very smartly turned out 2251 Class 0-6-0 No.3218 calls at Cranmore while working the 6.20pm Witham-Wells (the very last scheduled passenger train) on Saturday, 7th September 1963. Passenger services were officially withdrawn from the following Monday but, in the absence of a Sunday service, the Saturday was the last day of passenger operation. The unsightly pile of S&T equipment in the foreground tells its own story.
Ivo Peters

notably at Sandford and Congresbury, that had already been demolished to make way for road improvements and no doubt this was one reason why nothing ever came of the scheme.

Of the junction stations at either end of the line, Yatton has definitely been the more fortunate in that it remains open for passenger traffic to the present day and is served by both inter-city and local trains. Witham station only served the very small community of Witham Friary and, not being near any main roads, its reason for existence virtually disappeared after the closure of the branch for passenger traffic. It closed for goods traffic on 30th December 1963 and then completely on 3rd October 1966 when passenger services were withdrawn.

Although outside the scope of this work, mention should be made of the present day 'East Somerset Railway'. The two and a half mile long preserved line, started by the well known wildlife painter David Shepherd, is based at Cranmore where a replica Victorian engine shed and maintenance facilities were constructed on the site of the old quarry sidings and wagon repair facilities. From there the line runs over the summit at the site of the former Doulting siding to a terminus at Mendip Vale Halt on the outskirts of Shepton Mallet. Although the bitumen sidings have closed, the line east of Cranmore remains in situ and the occasional through special working from the national railway network into Cranmore has taken place.

It is now over forty-five years since the Yatton to Witham line ceased to be part of the national passenger railway network. The entire Cheddar Valley section and the western part of the East Somerset section have seen no trains in over thirty years although much of the trackbed remains. The bypass at Axbridge and the Wells relief road now follow the former railway route. The main station building at Axbridge still stands as a reminder to the informed motorist that the permanent way once stood where all is now tarmac. The extensive railway facilities at Wells have all disappeared except for the former Bristol & Exeter goods shed near the site of Wells station and a terrace of railway cottages known as 'Cheddar Valley Buildings' that stand at the end of Tucker Street. Only the informed person would recognise the distinctive barge boards on these dwellings as indicating that they are of Bristol & Exeter Railway origin.

Fortunately, a substantial part of the Cheddar Valley section from Yatton to Cheddar is now a public footpath. Some diversions from the trackbed are necessary where the land has been sold for private or agricultural use, where road improvements have necessitated the removal of bridges and along the Axbridge Bypass. For further information the reader should refer to the *Cheddar Valley Railway Walk* by Kidder and Brading.

As for the remaining section still in railway use, the future seems pretty secure, at least for the time being. There have been suggestions of a DMU shuttle service between Cranmore and Westbury for the benefit of people living in the Shepton Mallet area wishing to get to London but whether this will ever happen is another matter. Eventually the massive quarry at Merehead will be worked out and the outward stone traffic will cease. What will become of the railway then? Will the local residents and politicians allow a landfill operation or will the East Somerset take over the rest of the branch and operate steam trains between Witham and Cranmore or even Shepton Mallet? Only time will tell.

Chapter Seven

A DESCRIPTION OF THE LINE

YATTON TO CHEDDAR

Yatton lies on the road, now the B3133, connecting the Victorian resort of Clevedon on the Bristol Channel and the small village of Congresbury which stands on what is now the A370 main road between Bristol and Weston-super-Mare. Although Yatton has grown considerably during the latter part of the twentieth century, it was originally little more than ribbon development along the road to Clevedon. Yatton is now a dormitory for the larger conurbations of Bristol and Weston-super-Mare, the fairly central location of the station ensuring that it enjoys a considerable amount of passenger traffic to this day. The present day station consists of only two platforms (the original through platforms), the footbridge and the Bristol & Exeter Railway buildings, which have been refurbished in recent years, and are still in use. The station is served by First Great Western high-speed trains between Weston-super-Mare and Paddington as well as by local services between Bristol, South Wales, Taunton and the south-west. The booking office is still manned at certain times of the day. Of all the stations between Yatton and Witham this is the only survivor, at least as far as the national railway network is concerned.

When the line from Bristol to Taunton opened in 1841 Clevedon Road, as it was then called, was no more than a small wayside station. The station became a junction with the opening of the Clevedon branch on 28th July 1847, the Clevedon bay platform on the up side being added and the station renamed Yatton at the same time. Its importance increased yet again with the opening of the Cheddar Valley branch on 3rd August 1869 when a bay platform was constructed on the down side for the Cheddar Valley trains. Finally, on 4th December 1901, trains from the Wrington Vale line started running into Yatton. Congresbury was the actual junction for the Wrington line but it was found to be more convenient to continue the service into Yatton. Thus Yatton eventually became an important junction and the largest station on the line between Bristol and Weston-super-Mare. For a full account of the history of Yatton station and the branch to Clevedon, the reader is referred to Colin Maggs' book entitled *The Clevedon Branch*. At Yatton, the station nameboard read:

YATTON
JUNCTION FOR
CHEDDAR VALLEY
AND
CLEVEDON BRANCHES

Plate 56 - It is Whit Monday, 21st May 1956, and engines Nos.6812, 9313 and 5546 stand in the sidings adjacent to the Cheddar Valley bay platform at Yatton. The tender locomotives await their next turn of duty on return Weston-super-Mare excursion trains. *Mark Warburton*

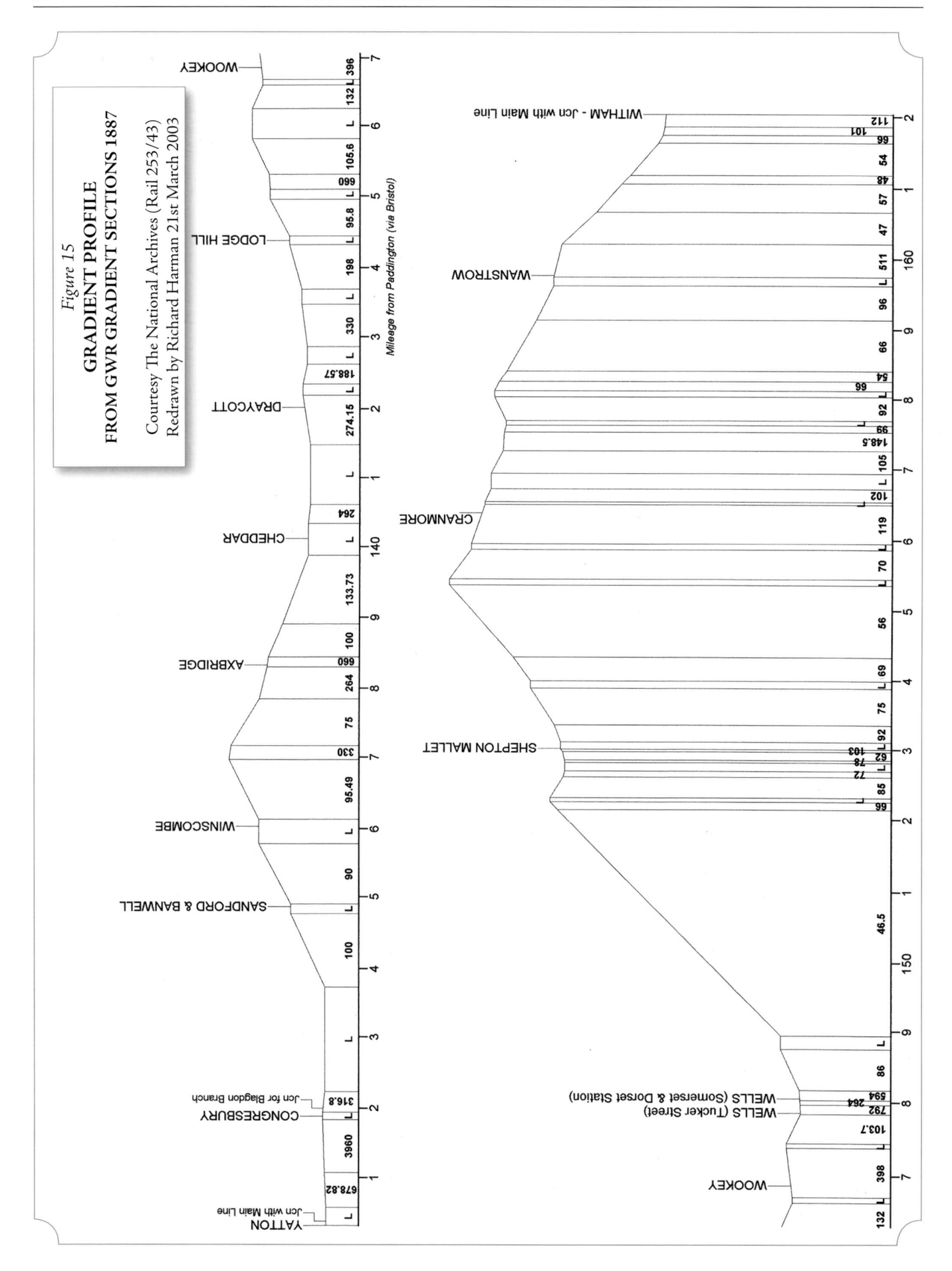

Figure 15
GRADIENT PROFILE
FROM GWR GRADIENT SECTIONS 1887

Courtesy The National Archives (Rail 253/43)
Redrawn by Richard Harman 21st March 2003

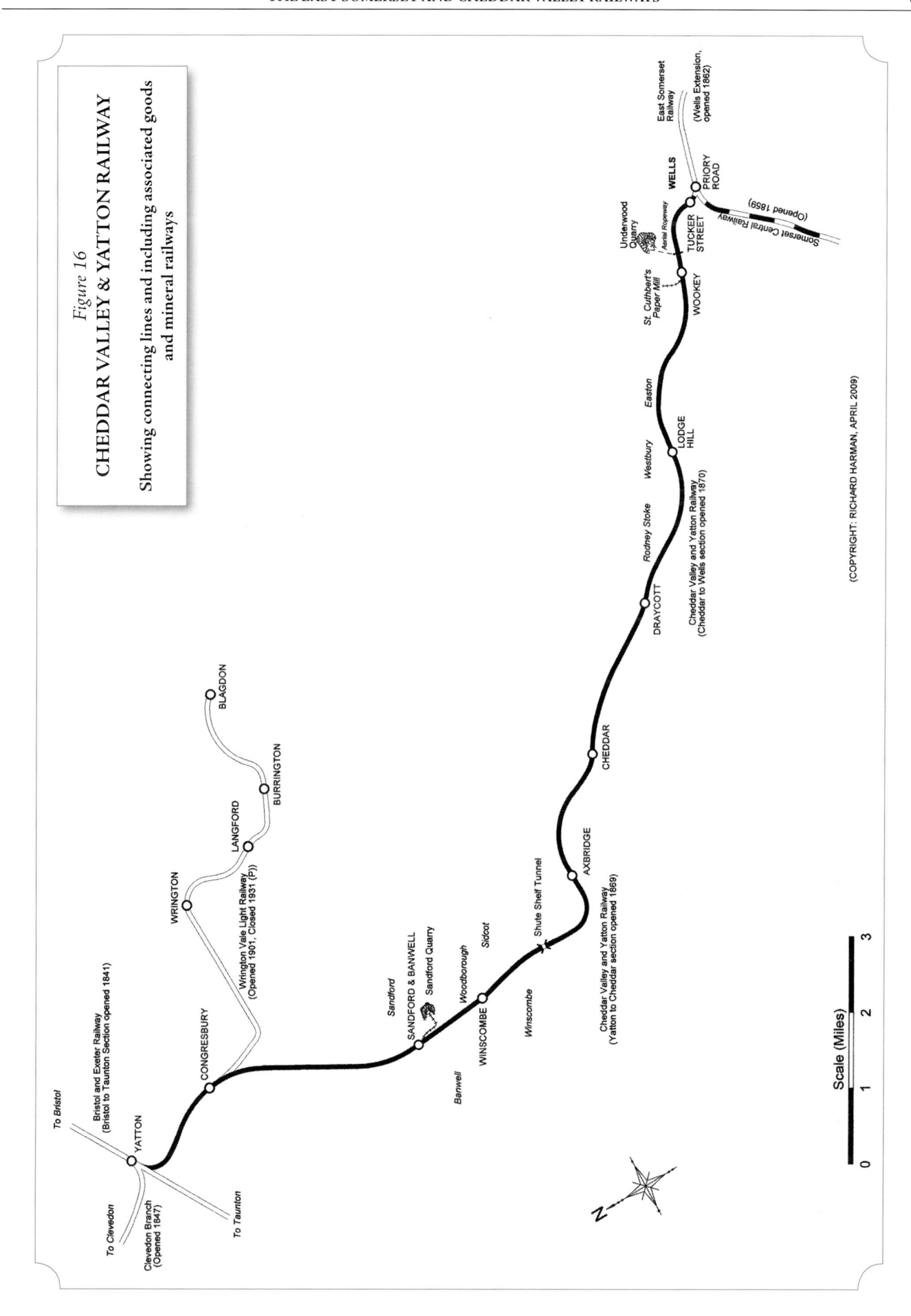

Figure 16
CHEDDAR VALLEY & YATTON RAILWAY
Showing connecting lines and including associated goods and mineral railways

Figure 17
YATTON
circa 1950

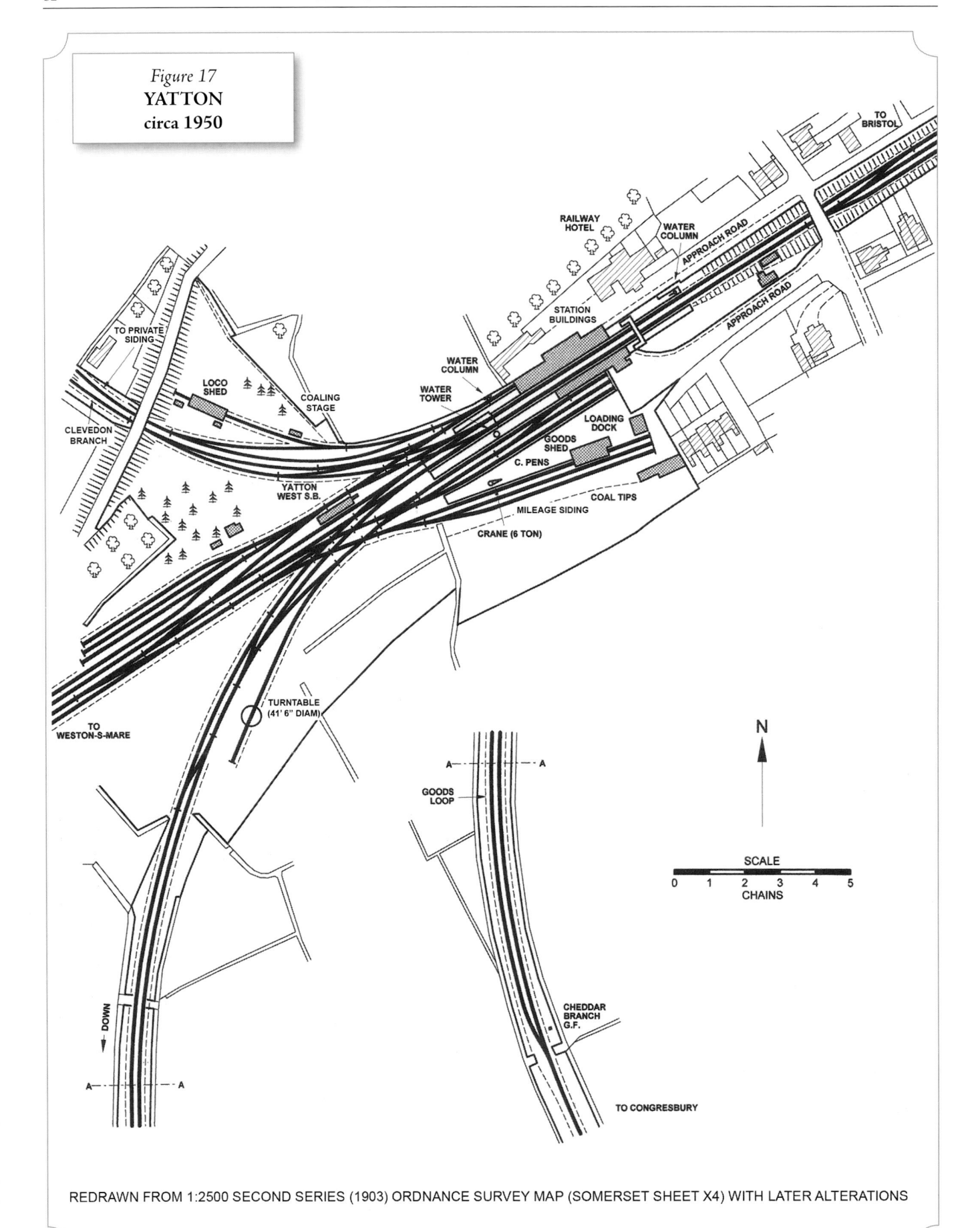

Plate 57 - Yatton West signal box is a prominent feature in this view looking towards Weston-super-Mare from Yatton's down platform on 2nd September 1963. Reference to the plan opposite shows the Cheddar Valley branch curving away to the left, itself being crossed by the connections to the goods yard and those from the down bay platform to the down main line. Sweeping away to the right is the Clevedon branch, showing the connections which enabled branch trains to run to or from the up bay platform or the main lines. *Ian Scrimgeour; Signalling Record Society*

The main line platforms were sandwiched between bay platforms that served the branches. Local transport needs have now changed, however, and the land once occupied by the bay platforms has become car parking space for commuters into Weston-super-Mare and Bristol. Cheddar Valley line trains terminating at or starting from Yatton used the down side bay platform. A crossover was provided to allow the locomotive of an incoming train to be released without shunting the rolling stock out of the platform. The line adjacent to the platform line was designated as a carriage siding as well as being used for running round purposes. Cheddar Valley line trains that either started from or terminated at Bristol Temple Meads would use the main line platforms. At the Weston-super-Mare end of the station both branches formed double line junctions with the main line, the layout being controlled by the magnificent Yatton West signal box of Bristol & Exeter design with 127 levers.

There was a small one-road engine shed on the Clevedon side of the station which was a sub-shed of Bristol Bath Road and normally home to three tank locomotives. Yatton-based locomotives worked certain diagrams on the Yatton to Witham line as well as providing the motive power for the Clevedon branch. An old grounded broad gauge carriage body behind the shed served as the locomotive crew cabin until a more permanent one was built. The line between Yatton West and Huish Crossing, the next signal box towards Weston, had up and down loops to relieve congestion on the main line in the Yatton area.

On the Bristol side of the station the line entered a cutting and passed under a bridge carrying the main road through the village. North of the cutting, 41 chains from the station, stood Yatton East signal box. The line from here to the next box at Claverham also had up and down loops. Both sets of loops were added in 1925, Yatton East box opening at the same time. The ideal situation would have been to have a continuous four-track layout through the station but presumably any potential benefits were far outweighed by the considerable cost of rebuilding the station and widening the cutting out to Yatton East box.

Yatton had a small goods yard on the down side adjacent to the Cheddar Valley bay and the carriage siding. A substantial loading dock was provided with sidings serving both faces and was provided with crane and cattle pens. In the early twentieth century the crane had a maximum capacity of four tons but latterly there was a six-ton crane here. The siding that served the outermost of the two loading dock sidings continued into a stone-built goods shed that contained a three-ton crane. The siding continued through the other side of the goods shed for about three wagon lengths before terminating. The yard also had two other sidings adjacent to that which served the goods shed. The outermost of these served coal tips and other facilities used by local coal merchants. This siding was also designated as a mileage siding. The term 'mileage siding' was generally used by the Great Western Railway to refer to sidings from which wagon-load traffic, excluding coal, could be loaded directly onto or off of road vehicles. The origin of the term probably came from the fact that the railway charged for such traffic by distance rather than by weight.

Before the start of the strawberry season, which brought heavy traffic to the Cheddar Valley line for a few weeks, Fruit C and Siphon G vans would be collected and stored at Yatton.

The length of the branch from the platforms at Yatton to the buffer stops in the bay at Witham was 31 miles and 55 chains. Mileages on the branch were measured from the buffer stops at

Plate 58 - A view of the down side of Yatton taken from a train on the up main c.1948. Two carriages stand in the Cheddar Valley bay platform whilst an unidentified 0-4-2T shunts stock in the adjacent siding. The stone goods shed is visible behind the 0-4-2T. *J Moss; R Carpenter collection*

Plate 59 - BR Standard Class 5MT 4-6-0 No.73011 runs through Yatton with an up express on 30th August 1958. The down platform extended well beyond the bracket signal controlling access to the Clevedon branch from the down main line. *Mark Warburton*

Plate 60 - BR Standard Class 3MT No.82007 runs off the branch onto the up main line at Yatton with a Bristol-bound train on 15th April 1963.
J Moss; Roger Carpenter collection

Witham. Mileages on through lines were always measured from the junction with the more important route. Prior to the opening of the Castle Cary to Cogload Junction cut-off in 1908 the line through Witham was only a secondary route from Westbury to Yeovil and Weymouth. The line through Yatton was, up until then, the more important route. Once the cut-off was opened the line through Witham became the more important and the mileages used in official working documents were recalculated from the Witham end of the line. The official gradient profiles for the line used throughout its existence date from 1882. The Cheddar Valley and East Somerset sections occupy separate pages in the Great Western Railway's gradient diagram book, now held in the National Archives. Mileages are indicated as being from Paddington, via Bristol, thus showing that the line through Yatton was the more important at that date, twenty-four years before the opening of the cut-off.

The double junction for the Cheddar Valley line was immediately adjacent to the Weston-super-Mare end of the down platform. As the West signal box was passed on the right hand side the line curved southwards away from the main line which continued, dead straight, in a south-westerly direction towards Weston-super-Mare. Within a few yards the Cheddar bay platform line connected on the down side and the running line became single track. Shortly before this another track crossed all three running lines at a sharp angle. This was the connection from the goods yard to the down relief line running in the Weston-super-Mare direction. It was not possible for a train to run from the Cheddar Valley line into the goods yard or vice-versa without two reversals. There was a goods loop on the up side of the single line that ran out to a distance of about 600 yards from Yatton West box. On the down side there was a turntable (diameter 41ft 6in) that was only directly accessible from the Cheddar Valley line bay, but it appears to have fallen into disuse before World War II and later photographs show the area to be overgrown. The connection with the single line at the far end of the goods loop was controlled by a ground frame. Because the ground frame was in the single line section rather than within station limits it was released by the Yatton to Congresbury single line token. There was an auxiliary token instrument here which was used when a goods train ran from

Plate 61 - Hall Class 4-6-0 No.6940 *Didlington Hall*, viewed from Yatton station footbridge, working the 11.28am to Bristol on 4th June 1960. It may be that the main line train is awaiting a connection from the Clevedon branch since a train is signalled from the branch into the up bay platform.
Brian Arman collection

Plate 62 - A view towards Yatton from the A370 road bridge at Congresbury and showing the bridge over the Congresbury Yeo River. The original wooden GWR bracket signal has been replaced by one built to a British Railways Western Region tubular steel design.

The approach to Congresbury

Two photographs by Joe Moss from the Roger Carpenter collection

(Below) Plate 63 - The road bridge from which *Plate 62* was taken, giving a track-level view of the bracket signal in the previous plate.

❧

the single line into the loop or vice-versa. This enabled the train crew to either replace or withdraw the single line token without having to go to the signal box. A telephone was provided at the ground frame so that the train crew could talk to the Yatton West signalman. The ground frame was brought into use in 1898 and was originally placed at 31 miles 27 chains, some 22 chains from Yatton West. In 1927 the loop was extended by five chains and the ground frame was repositioned at 31 miles 22 chains. At one time a signal box at approximately 31 miles 38 chains controlled a junction of single lines leading to the Cheddar Valley bay and the up main line. This box opened in 1885 but was closed and replaced by the ground frame in association with alterations to the junction with the main line and the extended goods loop in 1898.

The single line continued across the low-lying wetlands on a left-hand curve towards the south-east. Despite being four miles from the sea, the surrounding land is less than twenty feet above sea level. The formation of the railway across this low-lying land was characterised by drainage ditches on either side and there were culverts under the line at regular intervals connecting the ditches. St. Mary's church is a prominent feature on the left with the wooded slopes of Wrington Hill forming a backdrop. The tower and spire of the church were constructed in 1456 of stone brought from Dundry. The top of the spire was removed in 1595. It is thought that the reason for this was because the spire was too heavy for the underlying marshy ground conditions. Similar problems were faced by railway engineers in the nineteenth century and later by the contractors who built the nearby M5 motorway in the 1970s. Substantial amounts of material were used to build up a firm foundation for the railway and raise the level of formation sufficiently above the surrounding land to reduce the risk of the line being flooded during wet weather.

The line turned towards the south again, crossing Congresbury Moor before reaching the bridge over the Congresbury Yeo River and then almost immediately under the girder bridge carrying the A370 Bristol to Weston-super-Mare road *(Plates 62 and 63)*. Just past this bridge stood Congresbury station at 1 mile 46 chains from Yatton station and 30 miles 9 chains from Witham. The substantial main station building was constructed from local stone. The form of construction employed for the walls is known as 'snecked', in which regular courses of stone are interrupted by large blocks. This was a common form of construction in stone-built station buildings of the Victorian period. The building was situated on the down platform and was a single-winged building built on a 'T'-shaped floor plan with the upright of the 'T' parallel to the running line and the gable end of the wing facing the track. It was single storey with a steeply pitched roof, which gave the impression that the building was of a two storey 'chalet' style construction. It had the ornately carved barge boards and ridge tiles that were to be found at all but the smallest stations on the Cheddar Valley

Plate 64 - A general view of the station buildings at Congresbury on 9th April 1955. Note the most elegant form of the barge boards and a camping coach in the goods shed road. *Mark Warburton*

Plate 65 - This undated view from the down platform is also looking towards Sandford and Banwell and shows the track layout after the 1949 alterations. In the middle distance the Wrington branch curves away to the left whilst the Cheddar Valley line, easing to the right, becomes single by the far bracket signal. The prominent signboard at the end of the far platform states 'PASSENGERS ARE REQUESTED TO CROSS THE LINE AT THE OTHER END OF THE PLATFORM'. So, having walked that far .... *Lens of Sutton Association*

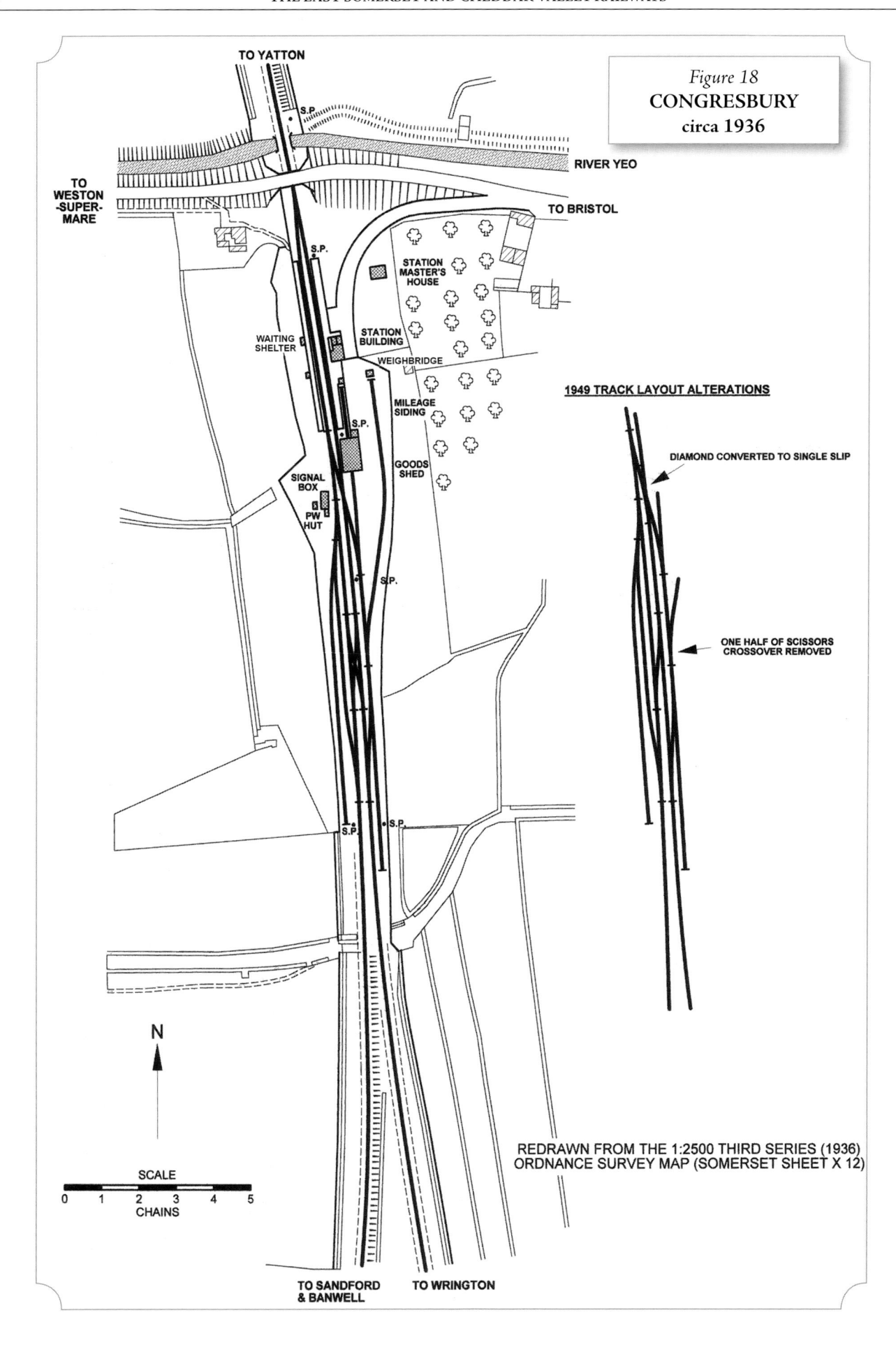

88 THE EAST SOMERSET AND CHEDDAR VALLEY RAILWAYS

Figure 18
CONGRESBURY
circa 1936

TO YATTON

TO WESTON-SUPER-MARE

RIVER YEO

TO BRISTOL

STATION MASTER'S HOUSE

WAITING SHELTER

STATION BUILDING

WEIGHBRIDGE

MILEAGE SIDING

GOODS SHED

SIGNAL BOX

PW HUT

S.P.

1949 TRACK LAYOUT ALTERATIONS

DIAMOND CONVERTED TO SINGLE SLIP

ONE HALF OF SCISSORS CROSSOVER REMOVED

N

SCALE
0 1 2 3 4 5
CHAINS

REDRAWN FROM THE 1:2500 THIRD SERIES (1936)
ORDNANCE SURVEY MAP (SOMERSET SHEET X 12)

TO SANDFORD & BANWELL

TO WRINGTON

Plate 66 - The road side of the station building at Congresbury, probably in 1958 or 1959. *J Moss; Roger Carpenter collection*

line. The roof was tiled with alternate sets of rows consisting of rectangular and curved tiles. The barge boards were typical of Bristol & Exeter Railway design and detailed examination reveals that there were a number of slightly different patterns. All were scalloped with finials at the apex and floral designs at the eaves. Cut-outs in the scalloping added to the intricacy of the design. The most elaborate patterns were used on the station buildings themselves, particularly on the smaller buildings at Congresbury and at Sandford and Banwell. Buildings of lesser importance, such as goods sheds and stationmasters' houses, had a simplified version of the design. There are a number of surviving examples alongside the Bristol & Exeter main line as well as on the Cheddar Valley branch itself.

Looking from the platform, the wing was to the right-hand side and contained the waiting room. The main part of the building contained the entrance hall, booking office and gentlemen's urinal. There was a small awning on the platform side, the outer edge of which was in line with the end wall of the waiting room wing. Towards the Sandford end of the platform stood a waiting shelter, built in stone, in the same style as the main building but much smaller. This was the original Bristol & Exeter Railway 'block hut', as signal boxes were referred to on that railway. It was replaced by a signal box built to a standard Great Western design on the up side in 1901 when the station was enlarged with the opening of the Wrington Vale line on 4th December of that year. Prior to 1901 there was no passing loop on the line between Yatton and Axbridge. On the up platform, also dating from the time that the loop was added, stood a wooden waiting room that was not as ornate as its counterpart on the down platform. It had an unusual design of roof in that the ends were partly hipped and partly gabled. The building also had a bay window. There was also a cast iron gents' toilet on the up platform at one time but it was removed during the 1950s. The platforms were faced in stone in the same manner as the station buildings. Interestingly, the earlier down platform face was vertical but the up platform face was recessed as is usual in those of later construction for the purposes of safety and to provide more space for point rodding and signal wire runs.

The goods yard was at the Sandford end of the station on the down side and had a single road goods shed just off the end of the down platform with a two-ton crane and a loading dock. The goods shed siding ran right through the shed and for about four wagon lengths behind the back of the down platform. A fence ran along the back edge of the platform to prevent access from it to any vehicle standing in the siding. In later years a camping coach was parked here. A short siding terminating at the loading dock also provided an end-loading facility. There was also a mileage siding with capacity for sixteen wagons. On the up side stood the later signal box and there were also two sidings, one of which formed a goods loop the other being designated as a refuge siding. The original junction for the Wrington Vale line was in the form of a scissors crossover between the up and down loops each of which then continued as separate single lines to their respective destinations. The Wrington Vale line lost its passenger service in 1931 but it was not until 1949 that the junction was simplified when the scissors crossover was replaced by a single crossover facing to and from the Sandford direction only. The provision of a single slip point in the intermediate crossover adjacent to the signal box enabled trains to run directly off the Wrington line onto the up loop.

Plate 67 (above) and Plate 68 - Views of the rail access at both ends of Congresbury goods shed, including the end of the resident camping coach. This general Bristol & Exeter Railway style was echoed at other stations along the branch but note the loading gauge suspended from the goods shed wall rather than being mounted on a separate post. The photographs are undated but are obviously BR era.

J Moss; Roger Carpenter collection

Plate 69 - The road access from the office end of the building. The intricate and decorative design of the chimney is similar to that of the main station building. The signal is the down starter.

(Below right) Plate 70 - The interior of the goods shed. The rail line is by the far wall - the end of a wagon is just visible - whilst the floor of the shed is built up to a suitable level to allow for easy transfer of goods from carts or lorries to rail wagons, or vice versa. The main entrance for road vehicles leads directly into the loading bay in the foreground.

CONGRESBURY'S GOODS SHED

Photographs from

J Moss; Roger Carpenter collection

Plate 71 - The Sandford and Banwell end of the shed. Whether the second, but blanked-off, entrance for an additional line of rails was to enable the B&E to open it if traffic so warranted or whether it was purely decorative to provide a measure of symmetry is not known. There would be little space for an 'island' platform between the tracks for unloading or for access, so the perceived need for symmetry is probably the answer.

Plate 72 - The footplate crew of 5700 Class 0-6-0PT No.9626 take delivery of the token to enable them to work the 11.16am onwards to Cheddar on 4th June 1960.

Brian Arman collection

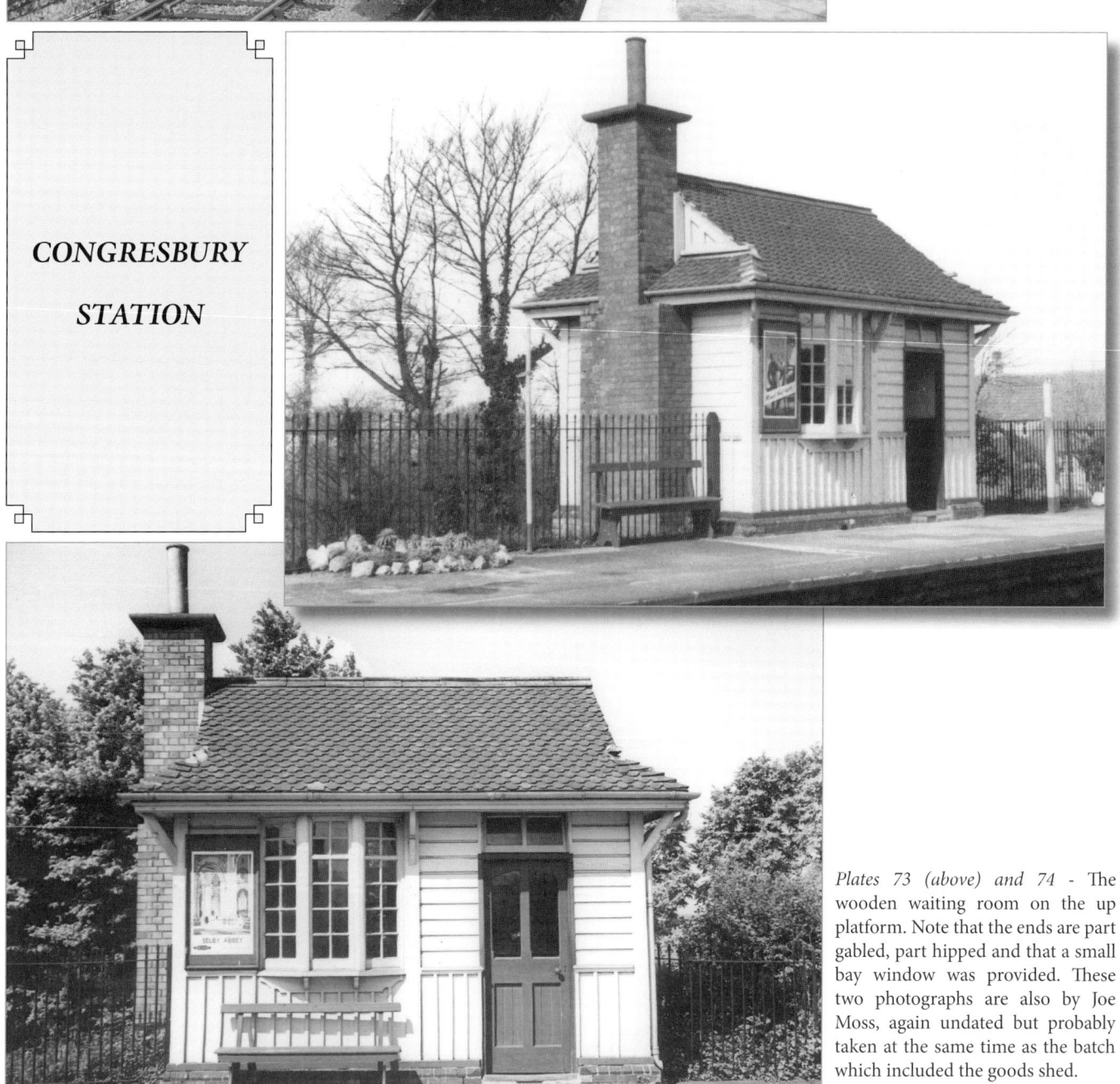

CONGRESBURY STATION

Plates 73 (above) and 74 - The wooden waiting room on the up platform. Note that the ends are part gabled, part hipped and that a small bay window was provided. These two photographs are also by Joe Moss, again undated but probably taken at the same time as the batch which included the goods shed.

J Moss; Roger Carpenter collection

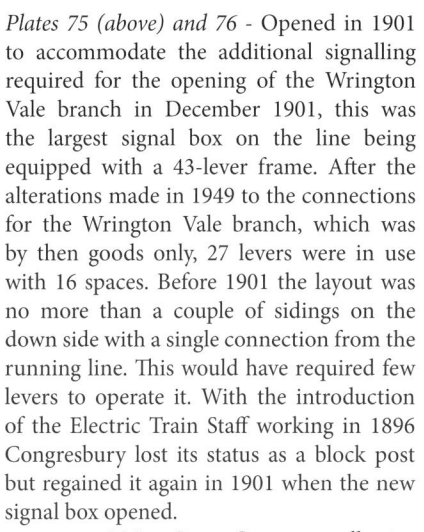

Plates 75 (above) and 76 - Opened in 1901 to accommodate the additional signalling required for the opening of the Wrington Vale branch in December 1901, this was the largest signal box on the line being equipped with a 43-lever frame. After the alterations made in 1949 to the connections for the Wrington Vale branch, which was by then goods only, 27 levers were in use with 16 spaces. Before 1901 the layout was no more than a couple of sidings on the down side with a single connection from the running line. This would have required few levers to operate it. With the introduction of the Electric Train Staff working in 1896 Congresbury lost its status as a block post but regained it again in 1901 when the new signal box opened.

J Moss; Roger Carpenter collection

Plate 77 - A parting shot of Congresbury as a traveller leaves for Sandford and Banwell on 9th April 1955. *Mark Warburton*

Leaving Congresbury, the Cheddar Valley line curved gently towards the south-west with the Wrington Vale line going slightly east of south and then turning sharply east towards Wrington itself. The Cheddar Valley line now ran straight and level across the low-lying moor until about two miles south of Congresbury station, where it started to climb and turned towards the south under Droveway Bridge and past Droveway Farm. Ahead lay the northern rampart of the Mendip Hills with Sandford Hill to the left and Banwell Plain with its Iron Age fort to the right. The railway headed for a gap between the two hills. After a mile or so climbing at 1 in 100 the line crossed the main road from Bath to Weston-super-Mare (now the A368) just to the west of Sandford village.

Sandford and Banwell station, which was 4 miles 40 chains from Yatton and 27 miles 15 chains from Witham, lay a few yards south of the road bridge. It consisted of a single stone-faced platform on the down side upon which stood the station building and the original Bristol & Exeter Railway block hut. Both buildings were of identical design to those at Congresbury and fortunately both survived to become Grade 2 listed on 22nd June 1983. Until recently the site belonged to a local retail company specialising in ornamental brick and stonework but the site is currently out of use. The buildings have been restored and survive in excellent condition. The original track layout at

Plate 78 - The driver's view on 9th April 1955 as he leaves Congresbury for the Cheddar Valley line, which bears to the right past the bracket signal. Curving away to the left is the Wrington Vale branch, which opened on 4th December 1901. *Mark Warburton*

Plate 79 - Apart from the addition of the passing loop and signal box, these two photographs show that there was very little change between the station facilities provided pre- and post installation in December 1905. Taken on 23rd June 1953, this affords a better view of the quarry exchange sidings climbing gently away in the middle distance than the postcard view below. *P J Garland*

Plate 80 - Reproduced from a grainy and slightly grubby postcard, this view predates the installation of the passing loop and signal box. The exchange sidings for the quarry branch are less distinct than in the previous photograph but do have some wagons in them! Note the design similarity of the station building and goods shed to those of Congresbury. *John Alsop collection*

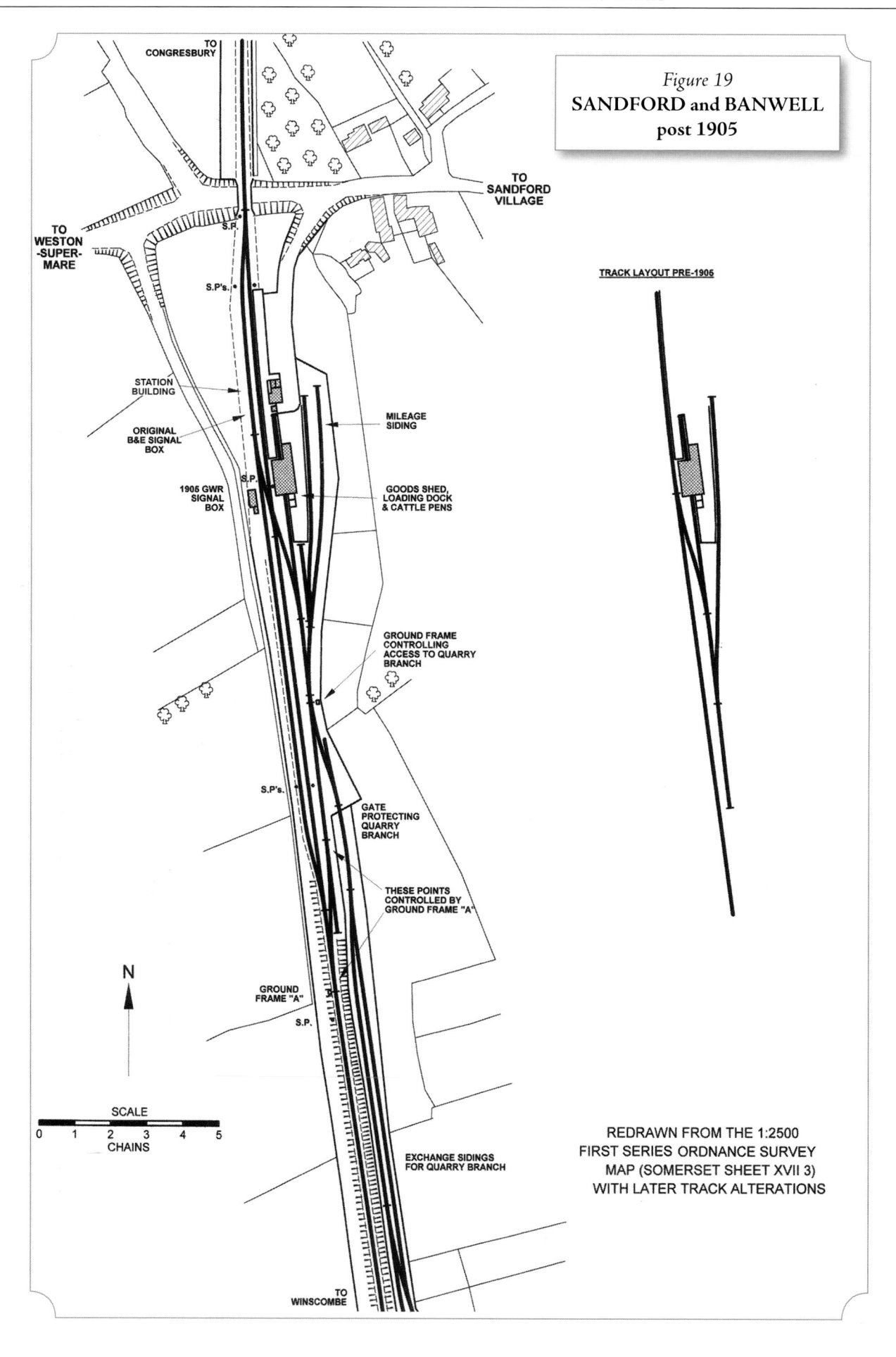

Figure 19
SANDFORD and BANWELL post 1905

Plate 81 - The other end of the station building is partially obscured by BR Standard Class 3MT No.82035 as it departs from Sandford and Banwell with the 2.52pm Yatton-Frome on 1st July 1959. The B&ER block hut is set back on the platform just behind the engine and note the short wooden post of the starter signal.

E T Gill; Rod Blencowe collection

Sandford and Banwell was virtually identical to that which had existed at Congresbury prior to 1901. Sandford and Banwell also had a passing loop constructed in the first decade of the twentieth century. It was brought into use on 12th December 1905 but, unlike Congresbury, there was never a second platform and so the loop could never be used to cross two passenger trains. Two goods trains or a goods and passenger train could cross with the passenger train always using the down side loop (ie. the one with the platform) irrespective of its direction of travel. The goods yard was on the down side at the Winscombe end of the station and had a goods shed, two-ton crane and a loading dock similar to those at Congresbury. The goods yard was enlarged with the addition of two further sidings in 1895, one of which was designated as a mileage siding. The later signal box, commissioned at the same time as the loop, was on the up side of the line opposite the goods yard. A short mineral branch climbed steeply out of the goods yard and paralleled the Cheddar Valley branch on the down side at a higher level for some distance towards Winscombe before turning sharply to the east, running into the nearby Sandford Quarry. The branch was opened in 1903 and is described in more detail in Chapter 8, the section on mineral railways and tramroads.

Plate 82 - BR Standard Class 3MT No.82030 departs from Sandford and Banwell with the 2.45pm Yatton-Frome on 24th March 1960. The signal box dates from 1905.

Brian Arman collection

Plate 83 - Looking along the platform affords a view of the end of the signal box. The goods loading gauge for this station is not fixed to the goods shed but is of the well known free standing variety, and can be seen through the arches of the shed. The signal is the down starter.

(Below) Plate 84 - Roadside view of the goods shed. The style is similar to that at Congresbury although the chimney has been 'modernised'! The only major variation was the addition of the small brick-built office, but the reason for its addition is not known.

SANDFORD and BANWELL GOODS SHED

Photographs c.1949-52 from Joe Moss; Roger Carpenter collection

Plate 85 - The 'country' end of the goods shed, away from station building, and showing the rudimentary cattle dock. Note the second arch, like Congresbury, and the mixture of substantial stone blocks with courses of quite thin material.

Plate 86 - A down passenger train arrives at Sandford and Banwell behind a 4500 Class 2-6-2T No.5511 in August 1958. The starting signal for the loop is ringed to signify that it applies to a good line.

Bob Griffiths

The Summer of '58

Plate 87 - Two months previously on 21st June 1958 the same engine, No.5511, has just left Sandford and Banwell station with a down passenger train and is passing the Sentinel shunter in the quarry branch sidings.

Mark Warburton

After the brief respite at Sandford and Banwell station the line became single again and the climb resumed at 1 in 90 for almost exactly a mile until Winscombe station was reached at 5 miles 53 chains from Yatton and 26 miles 2 chains from Witham. The line ran in a cutting for most of the way to Winscombe except for where Towerhead Brook was crossed. There were two overbridges in this section. Each bridge was built of stone with an arch of sufficient span to accommodate double track, but the formation was never more than single line width. Winscombe station consisted of a single platform on the down side with no passing loop or signal box. When the line was constructed Winscombe (or Woodborough as it was then called) was considered to be only of minor importance. For this reason, combined with the fact that it stood on top of a newly constructed embankment, the station building was smaller than those on the rest of the railway and constructed of wood. According to F. A. Knight in his *History of Sidcot School*, this building was constructed by a builder named Brock who, it is thought, was a local man.

A new station building was opened on 9th January 1905 in response to the growth of high class residential accommodation in the area. By this time the three nearby villages of Winscombe, Woodborough and Sidcot had grown to such an extent that they were now in effect one and the whole was generally known just as Winscombe. The new station building was of brick-built construction to the then current design of the Great Western Railway. This design is typified by the fact that the roof is considerably wider than the building and is cantilevered over the platform to form an integrated awning. Station buildings of similar design were built on all of the Great Western cut-off lines that were constructed during the early years of the twentieth century. The original wooden building was purchased locally; one part became a shop front in the village and another part being incorporated into a residence nearby. The platform was extended at the Axbridge end to a total length of 380 feet in about 1900 in order to accommodate longer sets of passenger stock that were then coming into use on the branch. Since these vehicles were non-corridor it was undesirable that the train should stop with any passenger compartment off the end of the platform! The original part of the platform had a vertical face constructed of stone whereas the extension was faced with engineering brick and recessed.

There was a short loop siding on the down side of the line at the Sandford side of the station, access to which was controlled by ground frames at each end. At the station end of the siding a headshunt gave access to a loading dock behind the platform. As with Congresbury, a camping coach was stationed here in later years.

In the original layout there was only one connection from the siding to the running line. This was at the station end and was controlled by a single ground frame housed in a small hut on the platform. Prior to 1896 this had been a block hut, but when the loop siding was installed a cast plate with the name 'Winscombe South Ground Frame' was attached to it. The hut was notable for its ornate barge boards similar to those on the larger station buildings. There was also a North Ground Frame that controlled the later connection at the Sandford end of the siding. Latterly, both ground frames were positioned at track level and on the up side. There was also a three-ton crane in the goods yard, the plinth of which still exists. The 1903 Railway Clearing House *Handbook* indicates that there was no crane here, so presumably it was added at a later date.

Plate 88 - An early view of Winscombe station from the up side of the line. At this date the ground frame hut stood on the platform and sported a cut-down version of the elaborate Bristol & Exeter barge board design. The adjacent lock-up shed is a more austere affair!

John Alsop collection

Figure 20
WINSCOMBE
post 1905

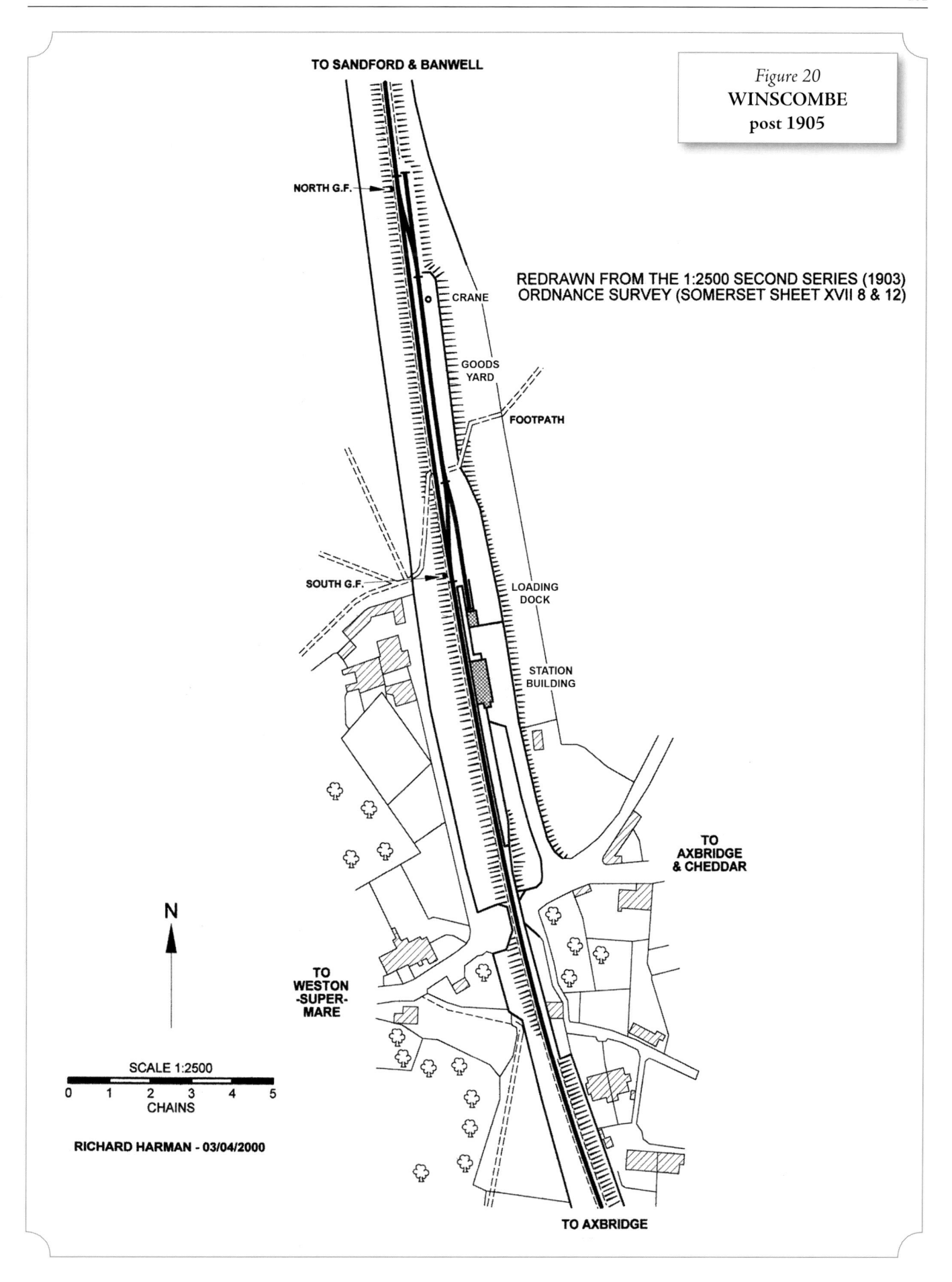

TO SANDFORD & BANWELL

NORTH G.F.

CRANE

REDRAWN FROM THE 1:2500 SECOND SERIES (1903)
ORDNANCE SURVEY (SOMERSET SHEET XVII 8 & 12)

GOODS YARD

FOOTPATH

SOUTH G.F.

LOADING DOCK

STATION BUILDING

TO AXBRIDGE & CHEDDAR

TO WESTON-SUPER-MARE

N

SCALE 1:2500
0 1 2 3 4 5
CHAINS

RICHARD HARMAN - 03/04/2000

TO AXBRIDGE

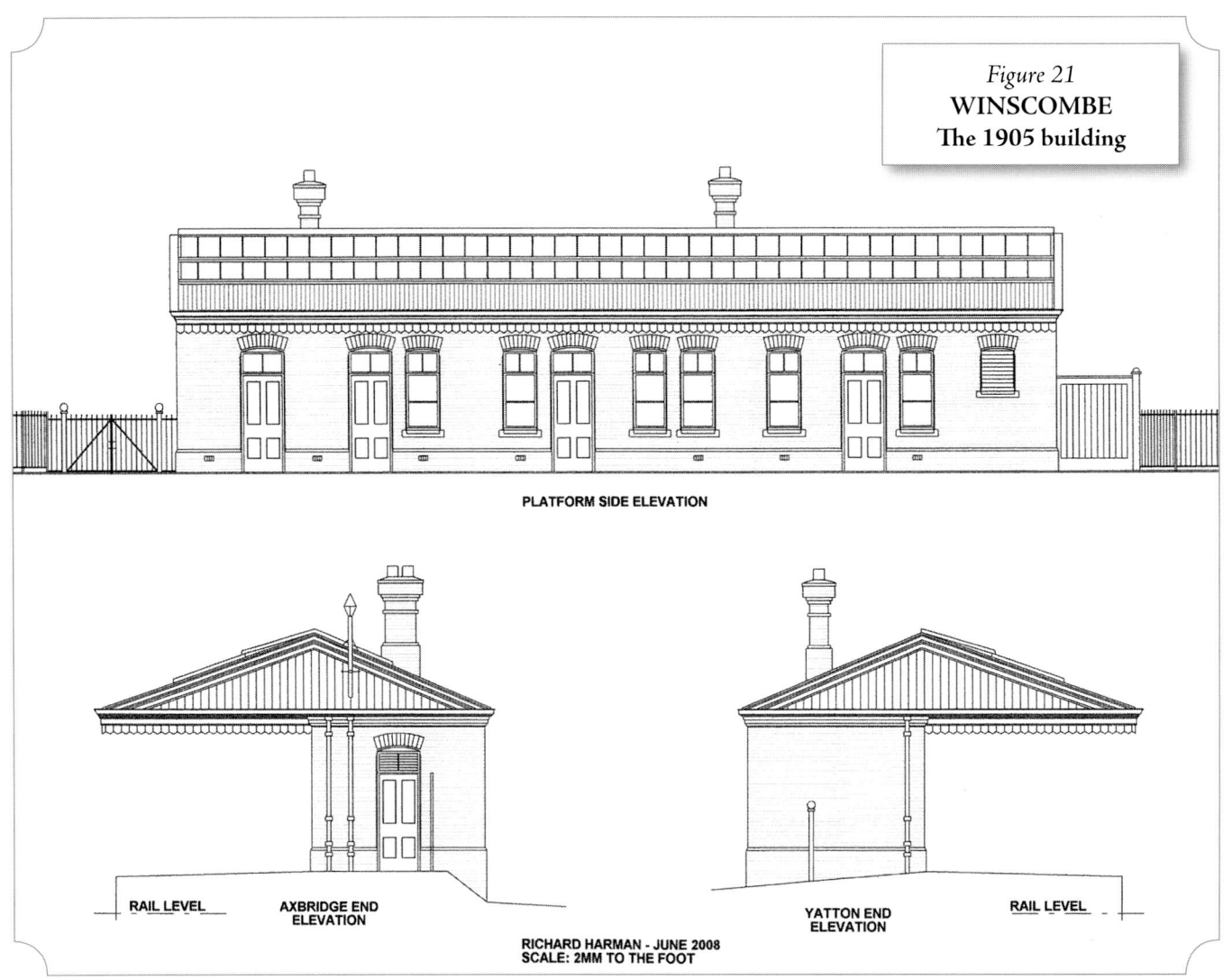

102 THE EAST SOMERSET AND CHEDDAR VALLEY RAILWAYS

Figure 21
WINSCOMBE
The 1905 building

PLATFORM SIDE ELEVATION

RAIL LEVEL — AXBRIDGE END ELEVATION

YATTON END ELEVATION — RAIL LEVEL

RICHARD HARMAN - JUNE 2008
SCALE: 2MM TO THE FOOT

Figure 22
WINSCOMBE
The 1905 building

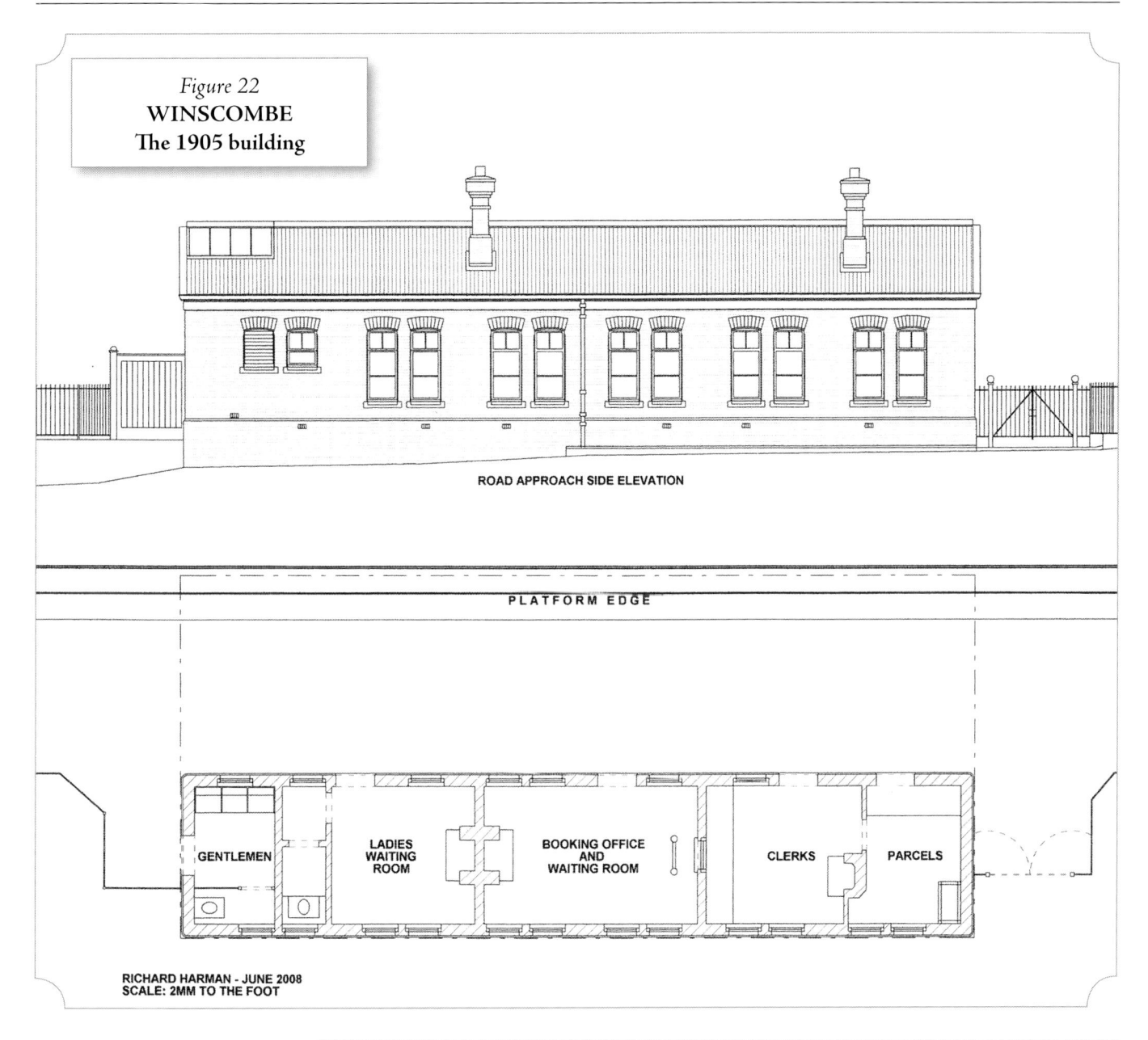

ROAD APPROACH SIDE ELEVATION

PLATFORM EDGE

GENTLEMEN | LADIES WAITING ROOM | BOOKING OFFICE AND WAITING ROOM | CLERKS | PARCELS

RICHARD HARMAN - JUNE 2008
SCALE: 2MM TO THE FOOT

(Left) Plate 89 - BR Standard Class 3MT 2-6-2T No.82006 arrives at Winscombe with the 2.45pm Yatton-Frome on 21st March 1960. This affords a detailed view of the platform side of the building and the construction of the cantilevered canopy. The beginning of the c.1900 platform extension can be seen where the frontage changes from stone to brick and is recessed. Note the camping coach in the siding.
Brian Arman collection

Plate 90 - A view from the platform at Winscombe in about 1930. A solitary figure strolls along the platform, perhaps in anticipation (or hope) of an imminent train. *John Alsop collection*

Besides the railway, the other institution in the Winscombe area was Sidcot School. Charles Clinker, the well-known railway historian and former pupil of the school, wrote about it in his 1950 *Railway Magazine* article:

'. . . *Before entering Winscombe Station, the stately white buildings of Sidcot School are clearly visible to the east. This ancient Quaker establishment, founded in 1808, has several intimate connections with the Cheddar Valley Railway. The Chief Engineer of the Bristol & Exeter, from 1854 to 1876, Francis Fox, M.Inst.C.E., and his assistant, John Hingston Fox, C.E., both old scholars of the school, were destined to lay the railway which passed its door. The opening date of the railway coincided with the reassembly of the school, and its scholars were among the first passengers to use the branch. Since February, 1843, the school had hired a special train to and from Yatton, then the nearest station, whence road conveyances completed the journey.*'

The article also relates an incident that amply demonstrates that youthful pranks are not a purely modern phenomenon:

'*Ten years after the line opened, some venturesome scholars placed a packet of carefully mixed chemicals on the rails in Shute Shelf Tunnel, and the detonation caused a passenger train to pull up abruptly. They were caught, and duly lectured on the enormity of their offence by the railway. Later the Board accepted a letter of apology from the headmaster, and closed the incident. The experiment has, however, been repeated in more recent years, but without the sequel. . . .*'

Plate 91 - A view from the platform at Winscombe looking towards Sandford and Banwell showing the goods yard in about 1950. The ground frame hut on the platform has been replaced by a less elaborate one at track level with a corrugated iron roof.
J Moss; Roger Carpenter collection

WINSCOMBE

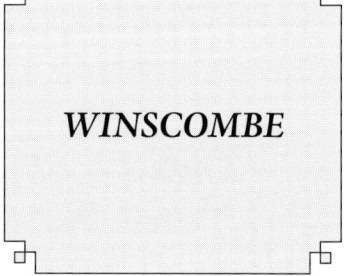

Plate 92 - An early postcard view of the second station building at Winscombe. The square section downpipes are more prominent in this view than in other photographs.
John Alsop collection

THE EAST SOMERSET AND CHEDDAR VALLEY RAILWAYS

Leaving the station at Winscombe the line crossed the main road to Banwell and Weston-super-Mare (now the A371). The line was level through the station but now it began to climb again at 1 in 95 and passed under a stone overbridge that carried Lynch Lane. This bridge was also built with sufficient span to accommodate a second line of rails. The original Winscombe village and the church stood to the west. A mile or so south of Winscombe station the summit was reached and the line plunged into the 198-yard long Shute Shelf Tunnel that ran through a relatively low ridge between Winscombe Hill to the west and Shute Shelve Hill to the east. The northern and central parts of the tunnel were cut through Keuper marl but the southern part was through Carboniferous limestone. The section through the marl was lined for a distance of about 120 yards from the northern portal, using stone for the side walls and brick for the arch. The southern section through limestone was sufficiently secure to be left unlined. There were refuges in the lined portion of the tunnel for the benefit of railway employees. The northern portal of the tunnel consisted of an arch constructed of large stone blocks standing proud of the stone retaining wall which was necessary to prevent the soft bank above the tunnel from slipping onto the track. The northern approach cutting also had a retaining wall for some distance on the down side where there had been evidence of slipping. From the northern portal there was a downward gradient through the tunnel of 1 in 330. About six chains south of the tunnel that steepened to 1 in 75 and the line now ran on an embankment through a broad valley, then continued virtually due south for a third of a mile or so before turning to the east and across a girder bridge over the Bristol to Bridgwater turnpike road (now the A38). It then

Plate 93 - Ivatt Class 2MT 2-6-2T No.41245 enters Shute Shelf Tunnel with a down train. As noted in the text, the geographical feature is named Shute Shelve but the railway named the tunnel Shute Shelf. *Robin Russell*

Plate 94 - Undated view of the bridge over the Bristol to Bridgwater road (now the A38) west of Axbridge. So few road markings ......
Somerset Industrial Archaeology Society

Plate 95 - The railway in the landscape - an aerial view of Axbridge village on 28th June 1929. The hairpin bend in Horne's Lane (modern spelling Horn's Lane) is prominent just before it reached the ungated level crossing this side of Axbridge station. The track layout reflects that shown in *Figure 23* and avoids any facing access to the goods facilities from the platform loop used by up passenger trains. Coal deliveries used the mileage siding, between the level crossing and the station, with the weighbridge evident at the far end of the coal merchants' storage area. There are vehicles in the up platform loop, so some shunting is in progress or use is being made of the strawberry loading bank. *English Heritage/Aerofilms*

THE EAST SOMERSET AND CHEDDAR VALLEY RAILWAYS

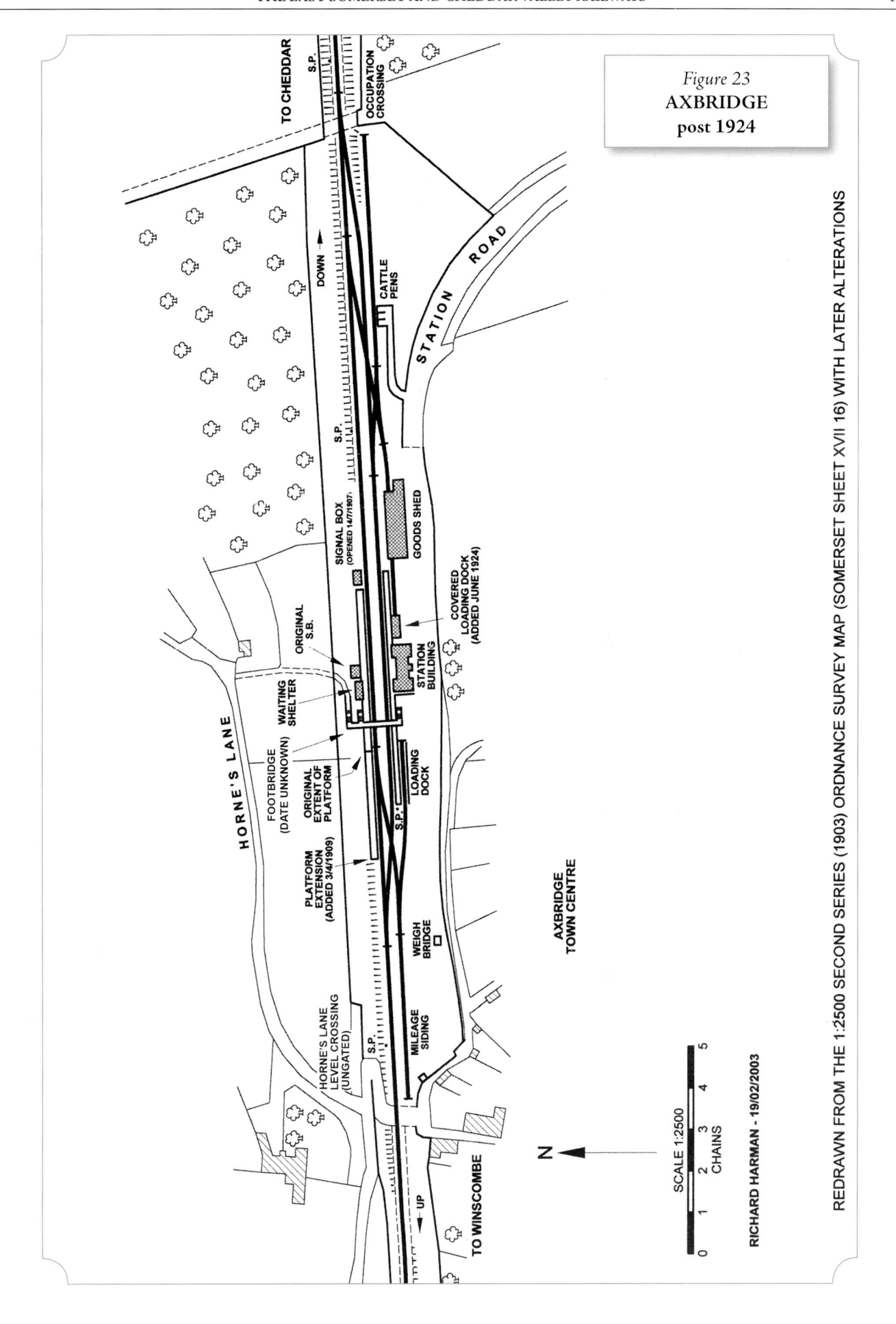

Figure 23
AXBRIDGE
post 1924

Plate 96 - A pregrouping era postcard of Axbridge showing the mileage siding, the hairpin (above the far open wagons) and Horne's Lane crossing. A patient horse waits with cart by the coal storage area, perhaps awaiting Mr Small, whose name can just be made out on the near end of the weighbridge. The postcard is too grainy to allow identification of the private owner and specific GW wagons. *Author's collection*

passed through a cutting and under a bridge that carried a road linking the A38 and Axbridge. Emerging from the cutting the line passed over Horne's Lane level crossing before arriving at Axbridge station, which was 8 miles 1 chain from Yatton and 23 miles 54 chains from Witham. The crossing was ungated and so it was probably classified as an occupation crossing solely for the use of residents and not as a public level crossing. The lane's approach from the northern side was steep and narrow with a hairpin bend in it. Fortunately the lane was a dead end that only served a few houses but users of the crossing must have risked life and limb every time they used it; *see Plate 95*.

Situated as it was on the side of Callow Hill above the ancient town, the view from Axbridge station across the Somerset Levels to the south was superb, from the Quantock Hills in the west to Glastonbury Tor in the east. Axbridge was the most important intermediate station on the original section of the line between Yatton and Cheddar, this being reflected by the fact that it had two platforms and a passing loop from the day it opened. It is interesting to note that the width of the track bed between the platforms at Axbridge was much greater than at Congresbury. This is a reminder that the line was originally built to the broad gauge and also that the second platform at Congresbury was not added until many years after the gauge conversion. The single storey station building stood on the up platform. It was of similar design to those at Congresbury and Sandford and Banwell but, having two wings, it was somewhat larger. It was built to an 'H' shaped floor plan with the gable ends of the wings facing the track; *see Figure 24*. A narrow awning that stretched between the two wings stood in front of the central portion of the building on the platform side. A door in the centre of the building beneath the awning led from the up platform into the booking hall. The entrance to the booking hall from the station approach side was through a porch that was also in the centre of the building. Looking from the platform side, the booking office was to the right of the booking hall which occupied the central portion of the building. The right-hand wing at the Winscombe end of the building contained the gents' toilet with a coal store and the station master's office behind. The gents' and the coal store had external doors whilst the station master's office had an external door and an internal door leading to the booking office. The left-hand wing at the Cheddar end contained the waiting room with the ladies' waiting room and toilets behind. The entrance to the ladies' waiting room was off the booking hall, whereas the entrance to the general waiting room was from the platform under the central awning.

❧

(Opposite) Plate 97 - An early view of Axbridge showing the original Saxby & Farmer signal box on the down platform. This signal box was replaced in 1907 by a new GWR one sited just off the end of this same platform. Note the churns branded 'Axbridge' in the right foreground and the ornate lamps affixed to the station building; a treat indeed. Meanwhile, whilst the station staff and others are content to pose for the photographer, the lady in late Victorian or early Edwardian dress on the up platform and her escort appear to be treating both camera and photographer with disdain. An illicit dalliance, perhaps, so privacy was essential . . . *Lens of Sutton Association*

Figure 24
AXBRIDGE
Floor plan of station building

GLAZED PLATFORM CANOPY

GENTS

WAITING ROOM

COAL STORE

BOOKING OFFICE

BOOKING HALL

LADIES' WAITING ROOM

STATION MASTER'S OFFICE

PORCH

N

SCALE: 2MM TO THE FOOT

APPROACH SIDE

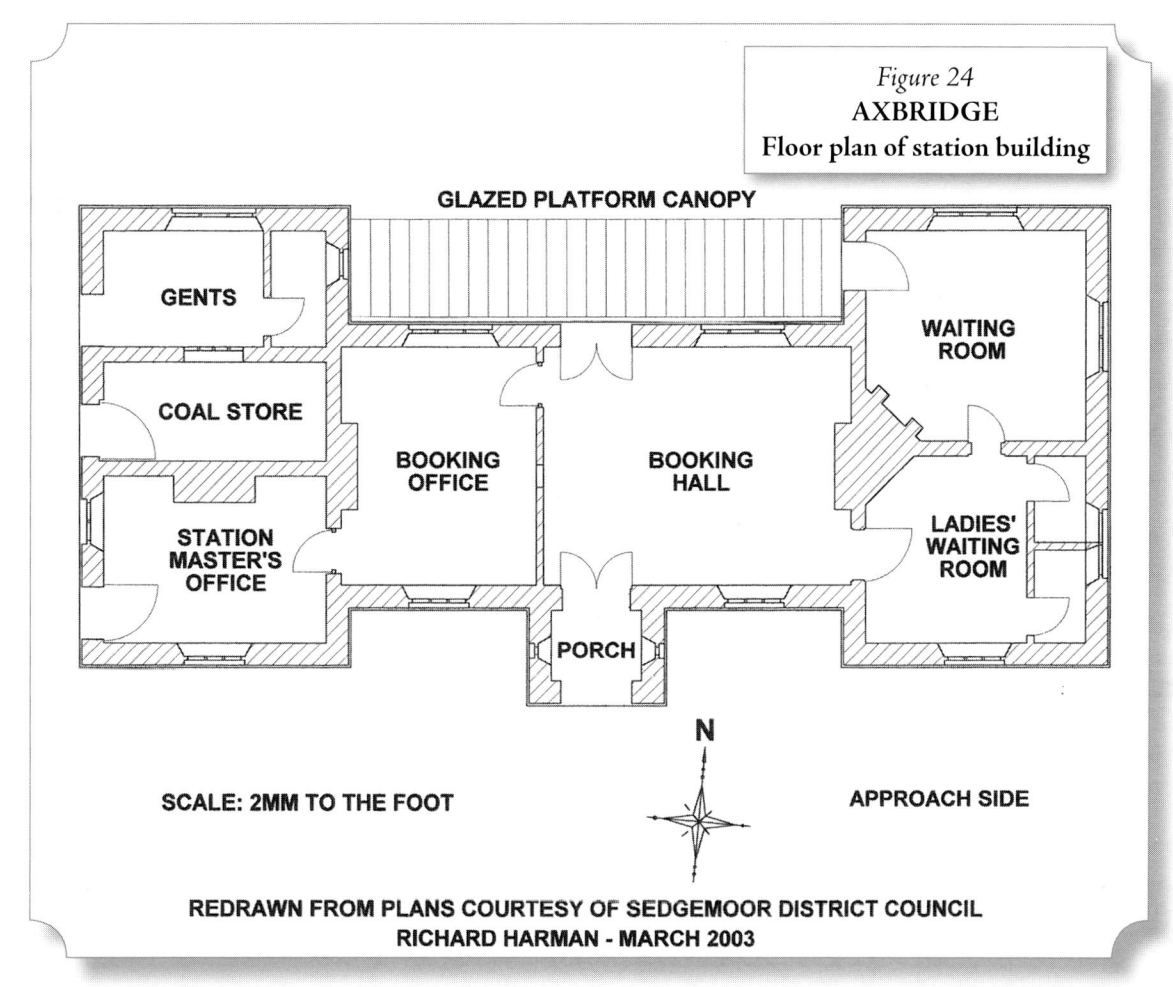

REDRAWN FROM PLANS COURTESY OF SEDGEMOOR DISTRICT COUNCIL
RICHARD HARMAN - MARCH 2003

Figure 25
AXBRIDGE STATION BUILDING

SOUTH ELEVATION (STATION APPROACH SIDE)

NORTH ELEVATION (PLATFORM SIDE)

WEST ELEVATION

EAST ELEVATION

REDRAWN FROM PLANS COURTESY OF SEDGEMOOR DISTRICT COUNCIL
RICHARD HARMAN - JULY 2000
SCALE: 2MM TO THE FOOT

Plate 98 - The undated postcard from which this is taken is actually coloured but is the only illustration to hand that shows nearly all of the platform side of the station building at Axbridge. The widely spaced tracks between the platforms betray the station's broad gauge ancestry. The crest added to the 'sky' depicts Axbridge's sheep-rearing heritage.
John Alsop collection

AXBRIDGE

Figure 26
GABLE END BARGE BOARD DETAIL
(Scale 4mm to 1ft)

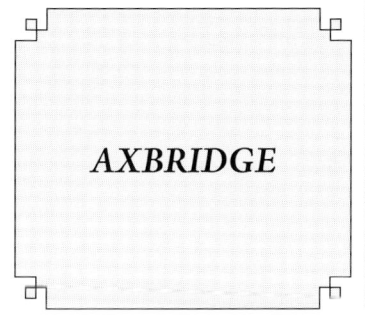

On the down platform stood a wooden waiting room and the original signal box. The replacement signal box opened by the Great Western Railway in 1907 was just off the end of the down platform at the Cheddar end of the station. Connecting the two platforms was an unroofed footbridge, added some years after the line opened. An extension to the Winscombe end of the down platform was brought into use on 3rd April 1909. Goods sidings were provided on the up side at either end of the station, the siding at the Cheddar end having trailing connections to both up and down loops. This siding gave access to a stone-built goods shed with the usual ornate barge boards. A covered loading bank for milk and strawberry traffic was constructed in June 1924 at the Cheddar end of the up platform, between the station building and the goods shed. There was also a three-ton crane here. The siding at the Winscombe end of the station had a trailing connection to the down loop only. The headshunt terminated at the back of the up platform in a carriage shoot. The purpose of this was to allow road vehicles to be loaded onto flat carriage wagons. The other end of this siding was used for mileage traffic.

Plate 99 - A closer, and much more recent, view of the station building as Ivatt Class 2MT 2-6-2T No.41249 stands at Axbridge with 3.17pm Frome-Bristol Temple Meads on 14th March 1961.
Brian Arman collection

Plate 100 - A view c.1955-58 from the footbridge at Axbridge looking towards Winscombe. Note that the siding is connected to the down loop only thus saving the need for a facing point lock. This siding was used for mileage traffic; note the coal storage yard by the boundary fence. The ungated level crossing can be seen crossing the running line at the far end of the yard. *J Moss; Roger Carpenter collection*

Plate 101 - The GWR Type 7B signal box at Axbridge on 19th May 1956. The box was built by the GWR in 1907. *Mark Warburton*

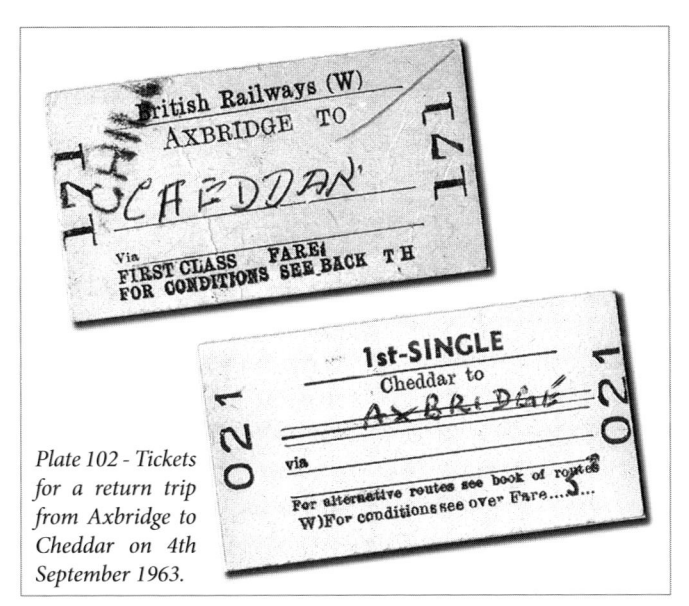

Plate 102 - Tickets for a return trip from Axbridge to Cheddar on 4th September 1963.

Leaving Axbridge, the line resumed its descent towards Cheddar at 1 in 100 and passed under the main road from Cheddar to Axbridge (now the A371). The line curved gently towards the south with the southern slope of the Mendips to the north and the Levels to the south, then passed north of the almost circular Cheddar Reservoir that stands well above the level of the surrounding moorland. The line passed McAlpine's siding on the up side 31 chains before reaching Cheddar station. It was opened under a private siding agreement dated 11th December 1933 and was used for loading locally quarried stone. Access to the siding was controlled by a ground frame. It closed in 1964 at the same time as the line through to Yatton when a stop block was erected 10 chains nearer to Cheddar station. Before passing under Five Ways Bridge, which carried the road to Wedmore, there were further sidings on the up side of the line. These sidings were an extension of the up loop at the station and there was a loading dock for mineral traffic immediately on the Axbridge side of the bridge. Having passed under the bridge the line became level again. On the up side a siding was provided under an agreement of 1st July 1922 for the transport of building materials by rail during the construction of the reservoir. This was known as the Bristol Waterworks Siding and it remained in use until the agreement was terminated in 1961. On the other side of the running line was a stone siding with a loading bank that remained in use until 1969. This siding was an extension of the down side goods yard headshunt.

Cheddar station was reached at 8 miles 64 chains from Yatton and 21 miles 71 chains from Witham. Cheddar was the most important intermediate place on the Cheddar Valley section and the prospect of tourism here must have been an important factor when considering the design of the station. The main building on the down side was similar to that at Axbridge but much larger and it also boasted an overall roof, the only one between Yatton and Witham apart from the Somerset &

Plate 103 - An almost timeless view approaching Cheddar station from Axbridge. This particular view changed little between 1895 and 1940, the only major variation being the extension of the siding to pass behind the signal box in 1898. This picture shows the goods shed, signal box and train shed at Cheddar on 21st June 1958. The crane next to the goods shed had a capacity of six tons. Vans for the impending strawberry traffic stand in the siding behind the goods shed. The vehicle at the end of the row behind the box has no end, just three sides. Mark Warburton

Figure 27
CHEDDAR
circa 1895

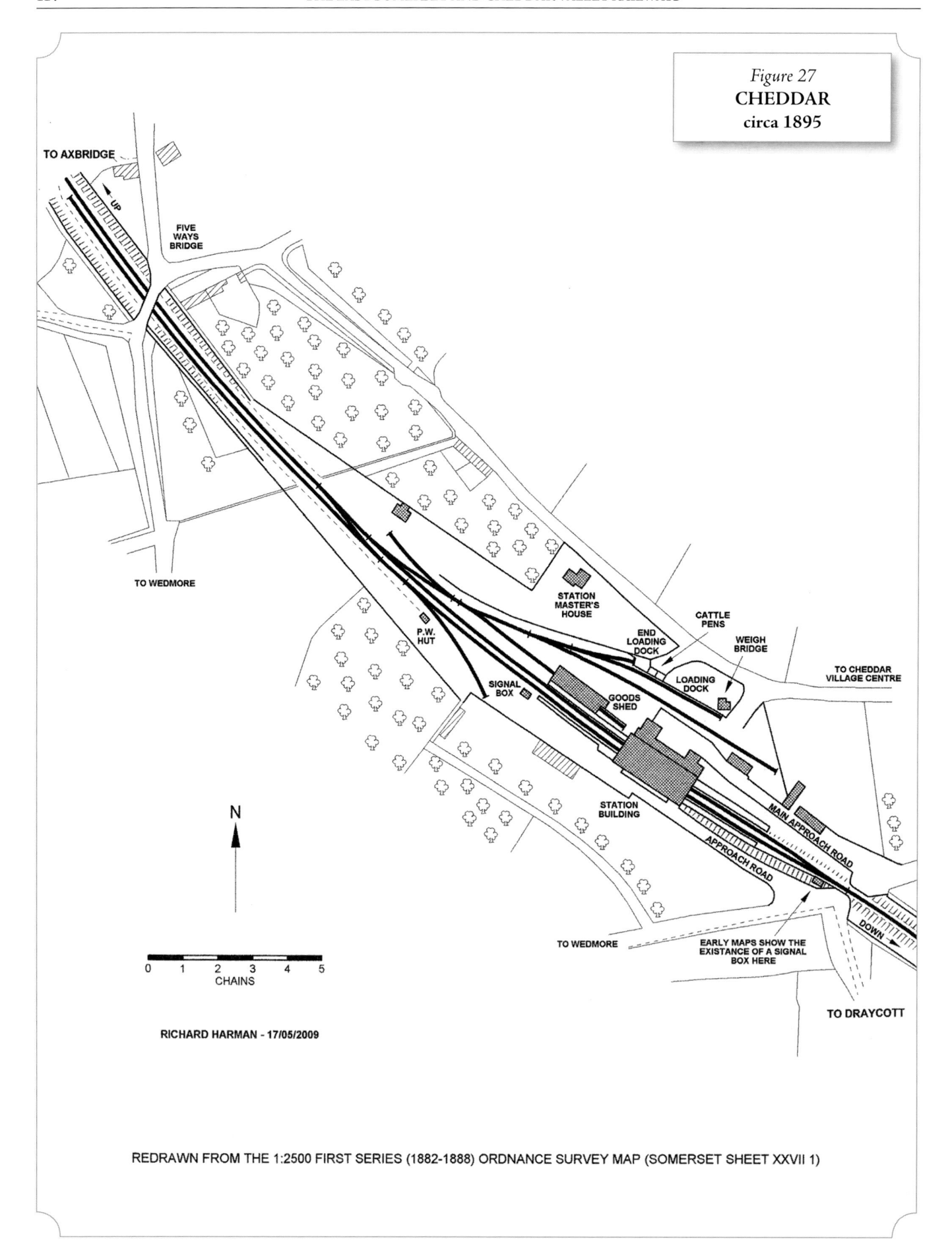

Plate 104 - An undated, but early, view of the Axbridge end of Cheddar station and train shed. The end gable of the train shed looks in pristine condition with few, if any, indications of soot stains. One interesting point is that the angle brackets supporting the roof at this end are mainly solid, whereas those at the other end are a lattice fret. Note there is no 'Shunt Ahead' arm on the starter signal post. *John Alsop collection*

Plate 105 - Under a weary looking facia, BR Class 3MT 2-6-2T No.82009 works a down train; undated. *D Lawrence; Hugh Davies collection*

Figure 28
CHEDDAR GROUND FRAME 1940

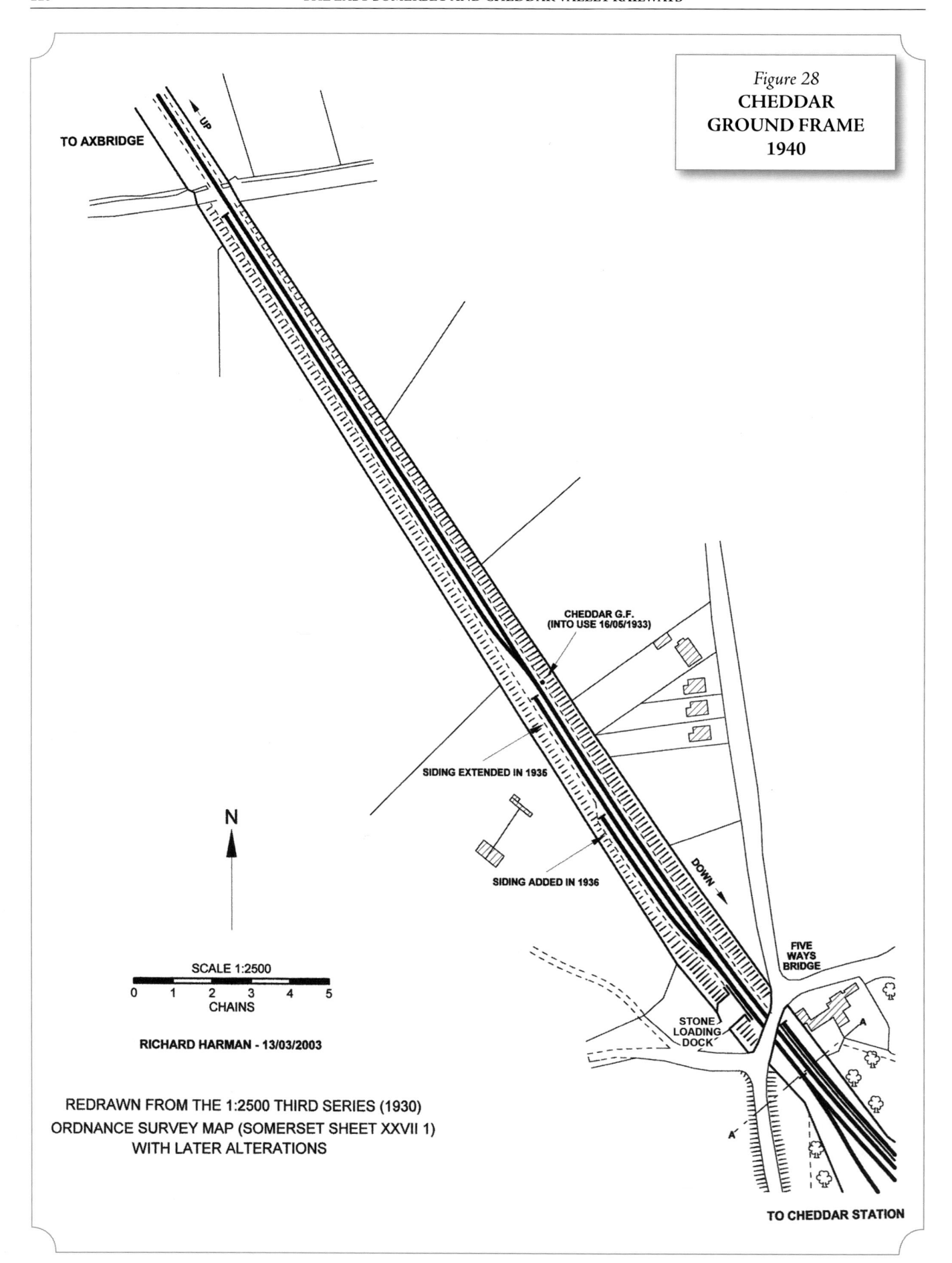

THE EAST SOMERSET AND CHEDDAR VALLEY RAILWAYS

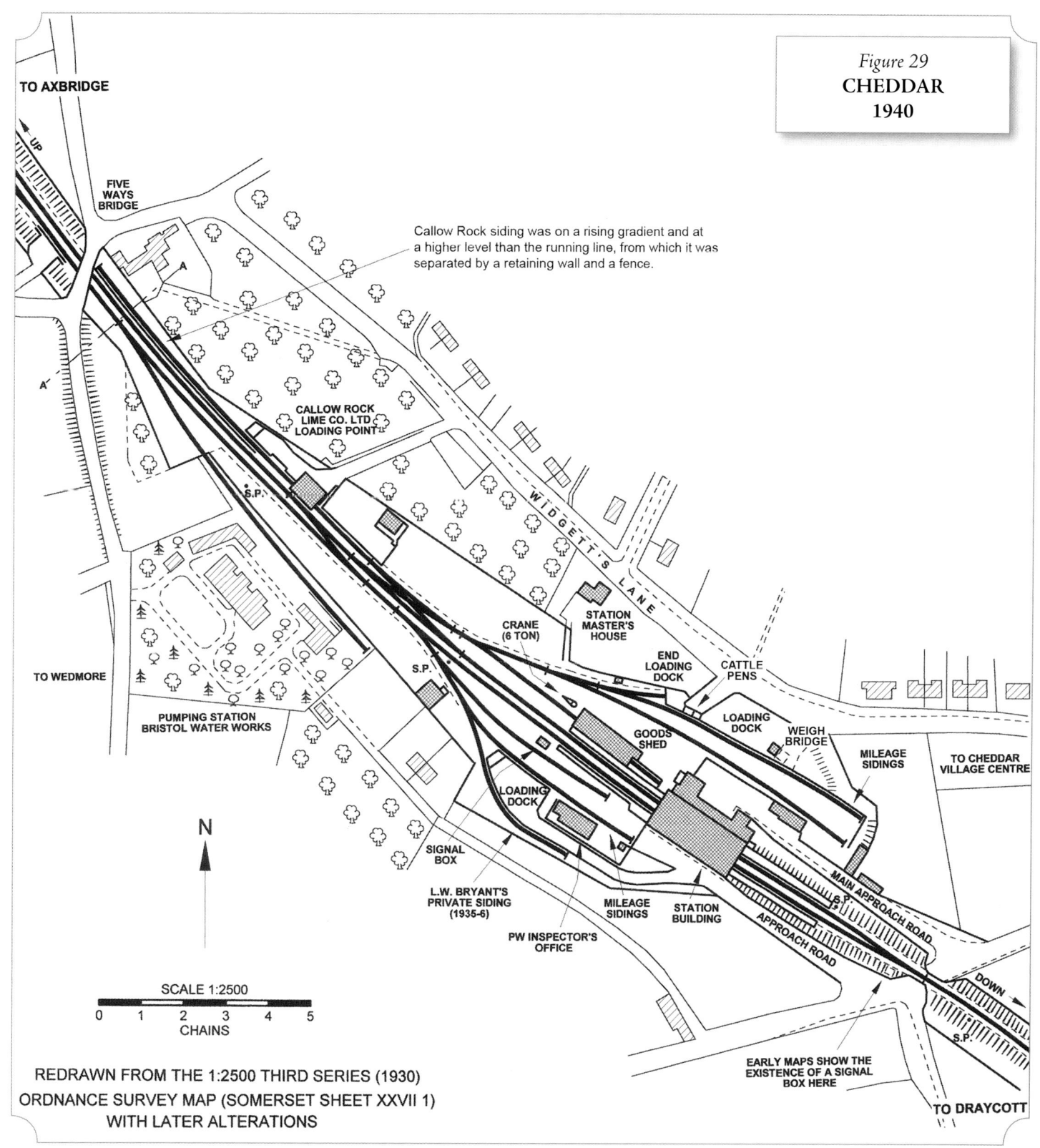

Figure 29
CHEDDAR
1940

Callow Rock siding was on a rising gradient and at a higher level than the running line, from which it was separated by a retaining wall and a fence.

TO AXBRIDGE
FIVE WAYS BRIDGE
CALLOW ROCK LIME CO. LTD LOADING POINT
TO WEDMORE
PUMPING STATION BRISTOL WATER WORKS
SIGNAL BOX
L.W. BRYANT'S PRIVATE SIDING (1935-6)
PW INSPECTOR'S OFFICE
MILEAGE SIDINGS
STATION BUILDING
LOADING DOCK
GOODS SHED
CRANE (6 TON)
STATION MASTER'S HOUSE
END LOADING DOCK
CATTLE PENS
LOADING DOCK
WEIGH BRIDGE
MILEAGE SIDINGS
WIDGETT'S LANE
MAIN APPROACH ROAD
APPROACH ROAD
TO CHEDDAR VILLAGE CENTRE
EARLY MAPS SHOW THE EXISTENCE OF A SIGNAL BOX HERE
TO DRAYCOTT

SCALE 1:2500
0 1 2 3 4 5 CHAINS

REDRAWN FROM THE 1:2500 THIRD SERIES (1930) ORDNANCE SURVEY MAP (SOMERSET SHEET XXVII 1) WITH LATER ALTERATIONS

Figures 28 and *29* - These two plans, joined at the cut-line A-A, show the later arrangements at Cheddar. *Figure 28* shows McAlpine's siding on the up side, access to which was controlled by a ground frame. Some 31 chains from Cheddar station, the ground frame was installed in 1933. The up siding that passed under Five Ways Bridge was extended in 1936 and an additional siding laid. In the station area, the siding behind the signal box was extended in 1898 and another one added. The Bristol Waterworks Siding was laid in 1925 to service the adjacent works and L. W. Bryant Quarries Ltd private siding was added in 1935. No information has come to light regarding the signal box at the Draycott end of the station that is noted on early maps.

Plate 106 - The sweeping approach to Cheddar from the Axbridge direction, taken from Five Ways Bridge. Taken c.1950-55, the photograph shows the gated Bristol Waterworks siding to the right and the Callow Rock Lime Co. siding to the left of the running line. The skeletal building on that siding is the company's loading point. Note the signal post with the station's home signal displaced widely to the right, adjacent to the Waterworks siding. This was necessary for signal sighting purposes. *J Moss; Roger Carpenter collection*

Dorset station at Wells Priory Road and the short-lived one at Wells East Somerset. The gable ends of the overall roof were of an ornate design in wood and glass that would normally be associated with a much grander station serving more than what was then only a small village. At one time the Wells end of the overall roof sported the initials 'G W R'. It is thought that these were removed at the start of World War II. There has been a suggestion that, due to a clerical error, the drawings for Wells and Cheddar stations were mixed up and that it was the eventual terminus at Wells that should have had the larger building and overall roof. However, it is worth remembering that when the grand opening of the line took place Cheddar was the terminus even though the bulk of the celebrations took place at Axbridge. In any case it is an interesting story that has not been corroborated and may well be apocryphal, made up by someone merely to explain an obvious puzzle in rational terms. Cheddar also had a refreshment room but this was closed on 19th September 1925. A footbridge under the overall roof provided access to the up platform.

The goods yard was on the down side at the Axbridge end of the station. A substantial stone-built goods shed stood behind the down platform and there was a six-ton crane in the yard. Behind the goods shed there were two mileage sidings, a cattle dock and a carriage shoot. In latter years a camping coach was stationed here. Originally there was only one short siding on the up side but it was extended behind the signal box and another one added in 1898. The outermost was known as the 'Jubilee Siding' after the Diamond Jubilee of Queen Victoria in 1897. The other siding had the more down to earth name of 'Just behind the box'. Access to these sidings was via a trailing connection off the up loop. A third siding with a loading bank was added in 1935 as the result of a private siding agreement with L. W. Bryant Quarries Ltd. This proved to be a short-lived arrangement as the firm was reported as having gone out of business in October 1936. However, the siding survived until 1969 and was even extended sometime during the 1940s.

Chard Central (also known as Chard Joint) in the south of the county also possessed an overall roof with gable ends. The design was almost identical to that at Cheddar but it was on a smaller scale because, at Chard, the roof only spanned a single line of rails. Chard was, at the time, an important local centre and so the construction of an elaborate station would have been justifiable. Interestingly, the Taunton to Chard line was also built and operated by the Bristol & Exeter so the almost identical design was not just a coincidence.

THE EAST SOMERSET AND CHEDDAR VALLEY RAILWAYS

Plates 107 and 108 - The road frontage of Cheddar's station building in 1961 which, like most of the station buildings on the line, was built from local limestone and embodies the Bristol & Exeter's elegant house style. Note the variation in road level between the carters' access to the mileage siding (*see below*) and the entrance to the building. As highlighted in the text, the perceived status of the station required more extensive facilities than those provided at other stations if, indeed, the plans were not actually intended for Wells! This view shows the juxtaposition of the building and train shed, which looks a little worse for wear when compared with *Plate 104*.   *Ivan Beale*

Plate 109 - The Draycott end of Cheddar station building in 1961 showing the main station approach road. The end of the train shed is just visible at the left hand edge of the picture; comparison with *Plate 108* shows that the shed was just a few feet longer than the main building.
Ivan Beale

CHEDDAR

Passenger and goods facilities

(Above) Plate 110 - The road access to Cheddar goods shed, also in 1961. Whilst the Bristol & Exeter company's house style is perpetuated, Cheddar's goods shed is much longer than the sheds shown earlier in this tour of the line, having two road-side access bays. Unlike the smaller sheds, it has a diamond ventilator in the end rather than a circular one. The shed at Tucker Street is similarly equipped. *Ivan Beale*

Plate 111 - Interior of the goods shed, c.1955-59, viewed from the Axbridge end. The station's train shed is just visible to the right and the shed's position adjacent to the platform can be gleaned from *Plates 103* and *115*. Once again the loading gauge is fixed to the end wall of the shed; the suspension wires can be seen at the top of the picture. The crank handle to lower the 'wings' of the gauge is just in view at bottom left of the photograph.
As with the other B&E sheds, the end without the office was built with two door frames but, as in this view, the stone-work on the inside of the non-rail doorway is hidden from view, so it cannot be determined whether it was a simple plain wall inside. Interestingly, the shape of the rail door frames at Cheddar are of a different shape from those at Congresbury and Sandford and Banwell. *J Moss; Roger Carpenter collection*

Plate 112 - The interior of the train shed at Cheddar from the footbridge steps on the down side, facing Draycott. The spacing between the tracks is evidence of the line's broad gauge origins.

(Below) Plate 113 - A similar view but from the footbridge steps on the up side. These two plates show the metal bracing for the roof trusses, similar to that in the goods shed but obviously with a greater span. The gas lamps, as well as the overhead platform signs, are suspended from the bracing rods. There is a mix of traditional station furniture, the passengers' seats being mainly wooden, not the GWR metal-framed wooden slats variety.
Both from Lens of Sutton Association

CHEDDAR

Inside the train shed

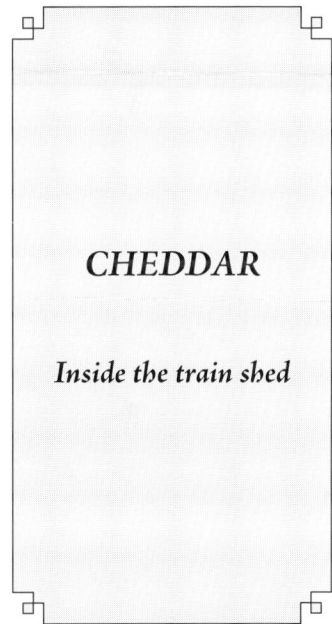

Plate 114 - Viewed from inside the train shed, BR Standard Class 3MT No.82003 arrives at Cheddar with an up passenger train on 21st June 1958. The open lattice-work of the facia support brackets at this end is evident. Note the 'Shunt Ahead' signal arm, not installed at the time of *Plate 104*. *Mark Warburton*

Plate 115 - The view from the footbridge at Cheddar looking towards Axbridge. The positions of the goods shed and signal box are clear. The stone sidings loading shed is in the distance just to the left of the goods shed.

J Moss; Roger Carpenter collection

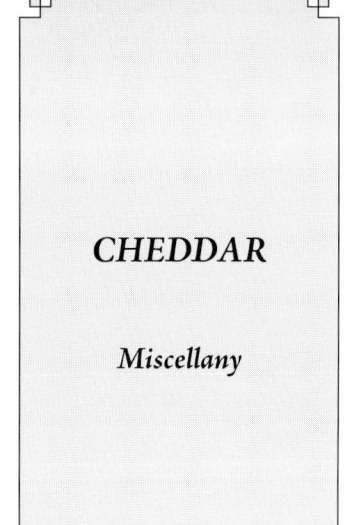

CHEDDAR

Miscellany

(Above) Plate 116 - Cheddar's signal box in 1961. The box and signalling will be covered in more detail in Chapter 12. *Ivan Beale*

Plate 117 - A slightly wider view of the scene that introduced Cheddar in *Plate 103* and taken on the same day, 21st June 1958; the 'end-less' open wagon is still behind the signal box. This departing up train is the same as that in *Plate 114*, hauled by BR Standard Class 3MT No.82003.

Mark Warburton

Cheddar to Wells

Leaving Cheddar the nature of the line changed somewhat. For much of the way to Wells it was constructed along the base of the escarpment of the Mendip Hills but just above the level of the moors in order to provide a firm foundation on the Mendip limestone. Here the line crossed numerous shallow ridges and valleys and was continuously changing from cutting to embankment. There were constant changes in gradient along this stretch, with a number of level sections and a climb of about half a mile at 1 in 95 just past Lodge Hill station. The next station from Cheddar was Draycott at 11 miles 70 chains from Yatton and 19 miles 65 chains from Witham. Approaching the station there was a public level crossing over a minor road leading to the moors. This was the only gated public level crossing between Yatton and Wells. The station consisted of a single platform on the down side, immediately past the level crossing. On the platform stood the station building, the station master's house and a small signal box. The station building was of a similar design to the original at Winscombe although it was constructed in stone rather than wood. The shortness of the platform gave the appearance of being rather crowded. Just past the station was a single siding, access to which was controlled by a ground frame at track level. The siding contained a wagon turntable that led to a short spur and loading dock set at ninety degrees. Both turntable and associated spur were removed some years before the closure of the branch. The far end of the siding, by the stop block, was used for mileage traffic. The station's busiest time was during the strawberry season.

Plate 118 - The small platform-mounted signal box at Draycott, c.1949-50. The box was no longer a block post after 1896 when the ETS was installed, so its only function was to operate the level crossing and signals protecting it. *J Moss; Roger Carpenter collection*

Plate 119 - Draycott station viewed from a stopping train on 30th May 1959. The station master's house was out of picture to the left; it is just visible in the photograph above. The small signal box is the nearest building, followed by the station building and a storage shed. The boxes stacked on the platform have come from, or are destined for, G.G. Portlock of Blackwood, Monmouthshire. *P J Garland*

Plate 120 - The facilities at Draycott, looking towards Cheddar. The date is unknown.
Lens of Sutton Association

DRAYCOTT

Station facilities

(Above) Plate 121 - Draycott station building was of a similar design to the first station at Winscombe, although it was constructed of stone rather than wood. This view, taken from the up side in 1961, indicates that some rationalisation was under way. *Ivan Beale*

Plate 122 - View from the platform at Draycott looking towards Wells. The wagon turntable in the siding, which is mentioned in the text, was probably sited where the sleepers in the siding are unballasted, just to the left of the pole at the end of the platform.

J Moss; Roger Carpenter collection

THE EAST SOMERSET AND CHEDDAR VALLEY RAILWAYS

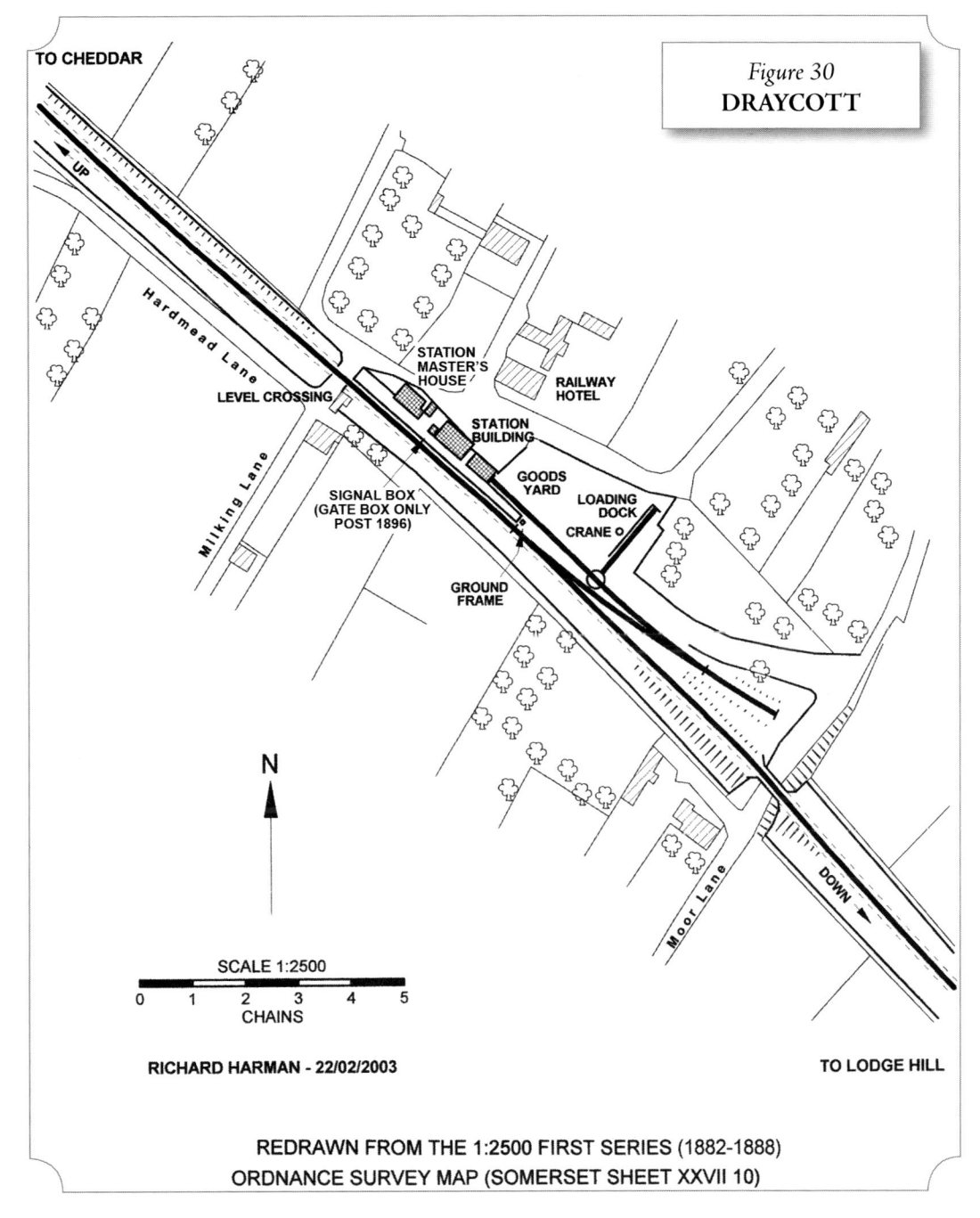

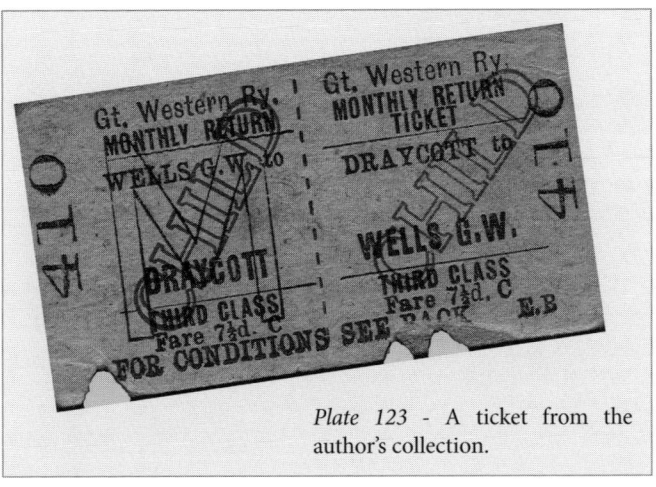

Figure 30
DRAYCOTT

REDRAWN FROM THE 1:2500 FIRST SERIES (1882-1888)
ORDNANCE SURVEY MAP (SOMERSET SHEET XXVII 10)

Plate 123 - A ticket from the author's collection.

After Draycott the next station was Lodge Hill, 14 miles 2 chains from Yatton and 17 miles 53 chains from Witham and again there was only a single platform on the down side. The station building was of the same design as, but the mirror image of, that at Congresbury with the booking hall wing on the left hand side looking from the platform. The goods facilities consisted of a single siding, on the Cheddar side of the station, and a stone built goods shed adjacent to the platform. The siding ran through the shed and for some yards along the back of the platform serving cattle pens. There was also a three-ton crane here. After closure of the line the station canopy was removed and used as a shelter for a light aircraft maintenance facility. It has since been recovered and has been re-erected in the village playing fields.

Figure 31
LODGE HILL
1903

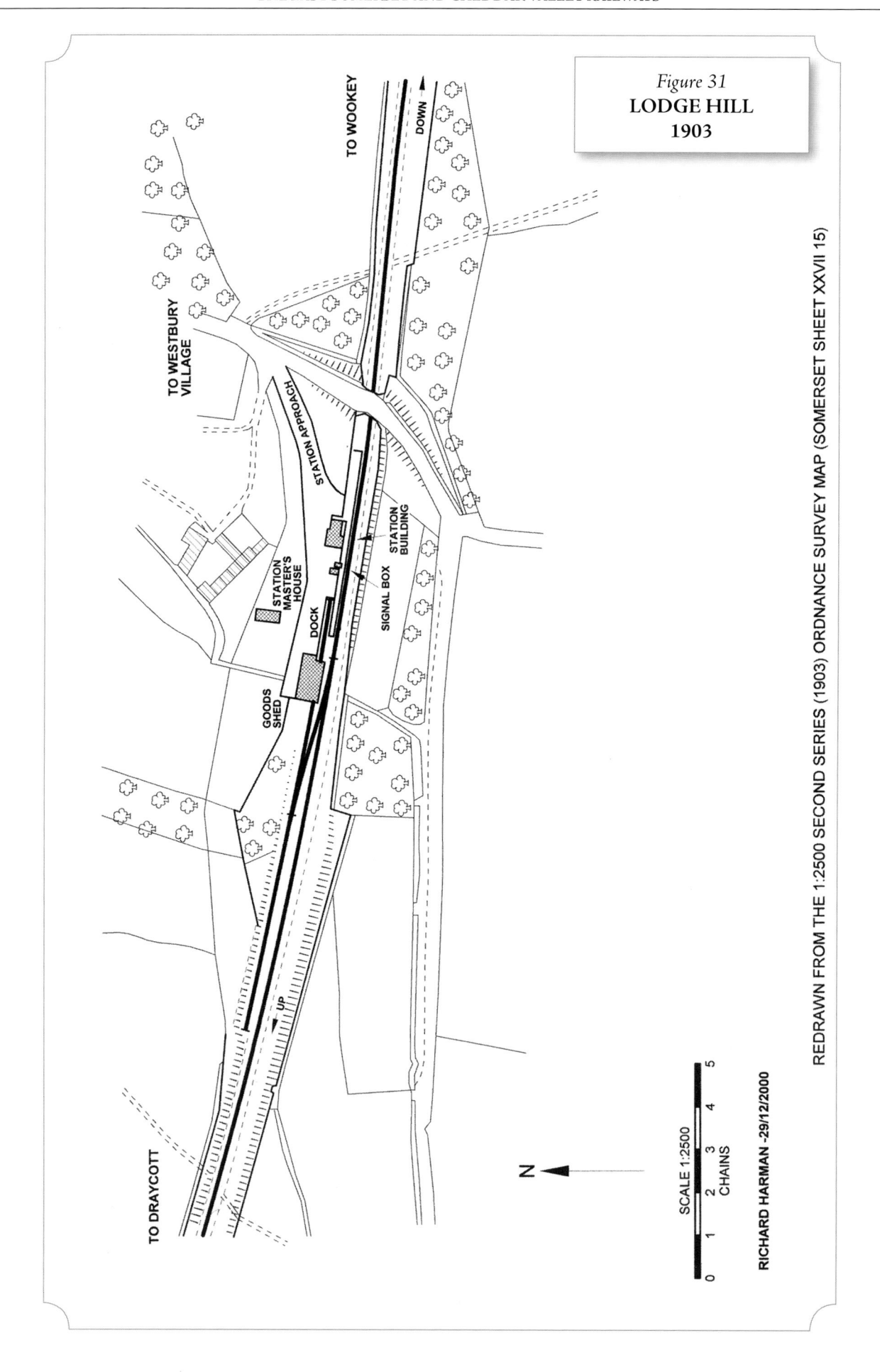

Plate 124 - Lodge Hill station building and goods shed were both built to reflect the Bristol & Exeter's house style.

J Moss; Roger Carpenter collection

Plate 125 - The platform side in 1961 showing the ornate decoration that extended to the former block hut on the platform. Prior to 1952, a small signal box existed on the platform adjacent to the former block hut and the rodding and wires appear to have been routed behind the platform and then across the running line at the end of the platform near the goods shed. After 1952 a ground frame adjacent to the siding points controlled access to the yard.

Ivan Beale

Plate 126 - 5700 Class 0-6-0 pannier tank No.5757 pauses at Lodge Hill station with the 3.17pm Witham-Bristol Temple Meads on 10th June 1959. Note that the overbridge was built to accommodate double track if necessary. *Brian Arman collection*

LODGE HILL

Station facilities

(Above) Plate 127 - Looking from the Draycott end of Lodge Hill platform in 1949 showing the goods shed and the small goods yard.

Two more Joe Moss photographs

Courtesy Roger Carpenter collection

Plate 128 - Lodge Hill station from the road overbridge in late 1950s.

Plate 129 - Wookey looking towards Wells on 8th April 1960 showing the station building, signal box and goods shed. Bags used to bring esparto grass into the nearby paper mill lie on the platform awaiting collection. *Brian Arman collection*

A mile or so past Lodge Hill the moorland was left behind. The line passed under the A371 at a very acute angle just before the village of Easton and ran through a long rock cutting behind the village. The surrounding land from here to Wells was at about 100 feet above sea level and of a more undulating nature than had been experienced since leaving Cheddar. The line continued in a cutting from here for much of the way to Wookey. Snow in this cutting caused the line to be blocked during the bad winter of early 1963.

Wookey was the last station before reaching Wells, at 16 miles 37 chains from Yatton and 15 miles 18 chains from Witham. There was a single platform on the up side upon which stood a

WOOKEY

Station and goods shed

Plate 130 - Ivatt Class 2MT 2-6-2T No.41248 leaves Wookey with the 2.0pm Yatton-Wells on 4th May 1963. This photograph, taken from the road overbridge, is looking towards Lodge Hill and gives a good view of the platform-mounted signal box. The line through the goods shed terminated just below the photographer. *Michael Mensing*

wooden station building and signal box. On the down side was a loop siding that had headshunts at either end. A stone-built goods shed was situated on the headshunt opposite the station platform. Wookey also had a three-ton crane.

A line led off the loop through a gate and into a small network of sidings in the adjacent St. Cuthbert's paper mill. The waters of the nearby River Axe were found to be most suitable for the paper making industry. Prior to 1880 the arrangements here consisted of a wagon turntable in the loop headshunt on which wagons would be turned about ninety degrees in order to gain access to the mill siding. There was a mileage siding with a capacity for twelve wagons which was accessed from the paper mill line and ran more or less parallel to the loop siding. When the line was built the two acres of land required for the station were purchased from the mill company. On the Wells side of the station the line passed under a stone overbridge that carried the road connecting the main Wells to Cheddar road (the A371) at Haybridge with the Wookey Hole road. Between Wookey and Wells the gradients were generally easier than had been experienced after Lodge Hill.

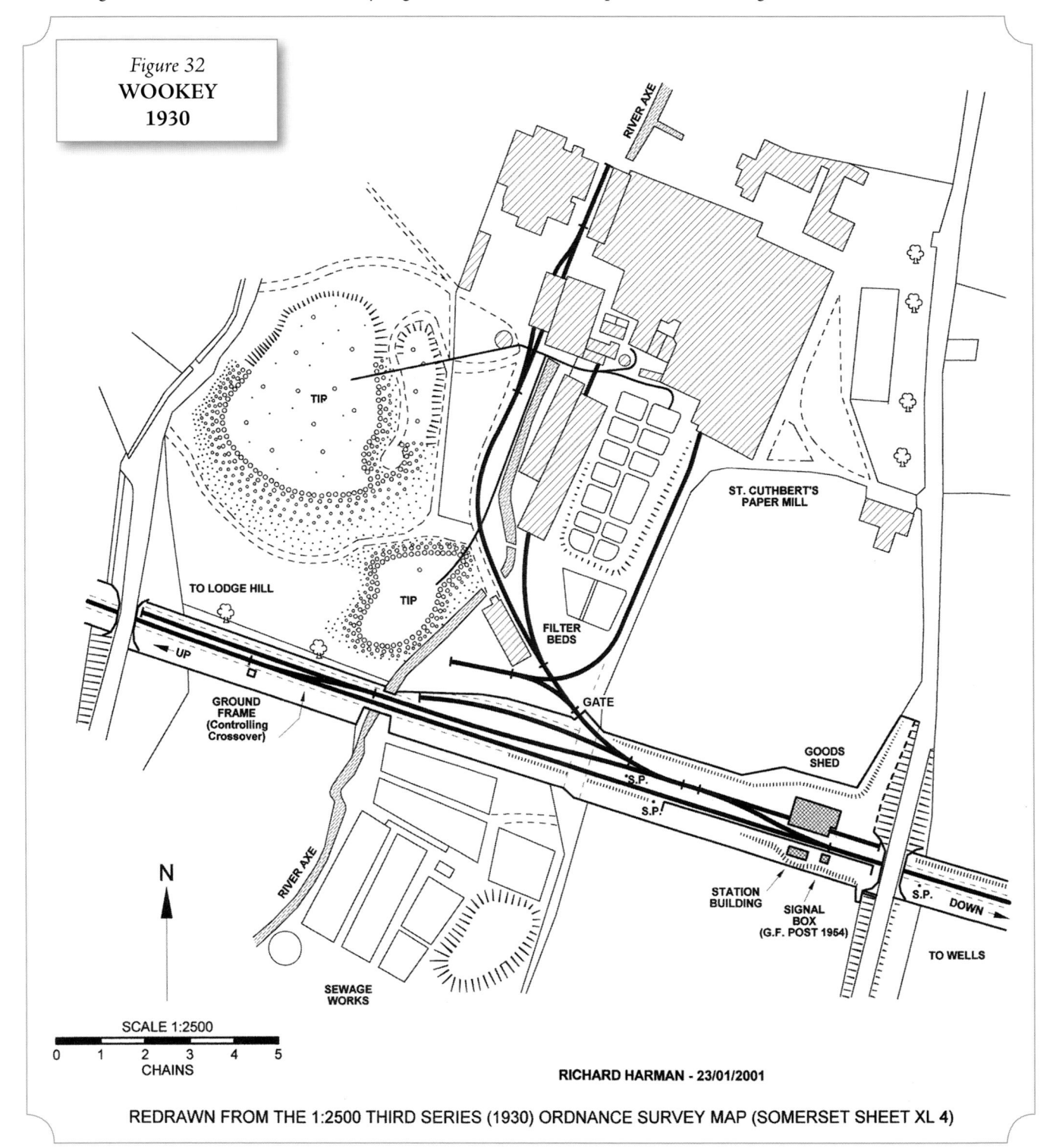

Figure 32
WOOKEY 1930

REDRAWN FROM THE 1:2500 THIRD SERIES (1930) ORDNANCE SURVEY MAP (SOMERSET SHEET XL 4)

Plate 131 - St. Cuthbert's paper mill in 1923 showing the extent of the works, including the waste tip to the left. The rail connection passes through the white-painted gates just beyond the sidings. Both sidings contain wagons from a number of pregrouping companies including Great Central, Great Eastern and London & North Western; the origins of the remaining wagons, apart from a couple of Great Western covered goods, are indecipherable.
English Heritage; Aerofilms collection

WOOKEY

Miscellany

Plate 132 - The Lodge Hill side of Wookey as an unidentified Ivatt Class 2MT 2-6-2T pulls away from Wookey and approaches Hurst Batch overbridge on 4th May 1963. The B-set is obscuring the crossover from the running line to the adjacent headshunt; the ground frame levers are visible to the right of the carriages. *Michael Mensing*

(Above) Plate 133 - The road side of the goods shed which, like others along the line, reveals its Bristol & Exeter Railway ancestry.
F Saunders; Lens of Sutton Association

Plate 134 - The view from the platform at Wookey under the road overbridge towards Wells. This photograph was taken c.1949-52, before the closure of the signal box in 1954.
J Moss; Roger Carpenter collection

Before reaching Wells the line passed Wookey Stone Siding on the down side. Stone was brought here from the Somerset County Council's Underwood Quarry by an aerial ropeway. The stone was loaded into tubs suspended from the ropeway. A safety net to catch any falling stones was positioned beneath the ropeway where it crossed the Wells to Wookey Hole road between the quarry and the siding. After World War I, stone was dispatched by lorry in increasing amounts leading to a general decline in rail-borne traffic from quarry sidings such as this one. In spite of this, the siding remained in use until 1948 and was removed in 1950. The private siding agreement ran from 30th March 1920 until 9th July 1948. The siding could be entered from either direction, the points at each end being controlled by separate ground frames. Interestingly, the ground frames were designated 'No.1' and 'No.2' instead of 'West' and 'East' as was more usual for the Great Western Railway.

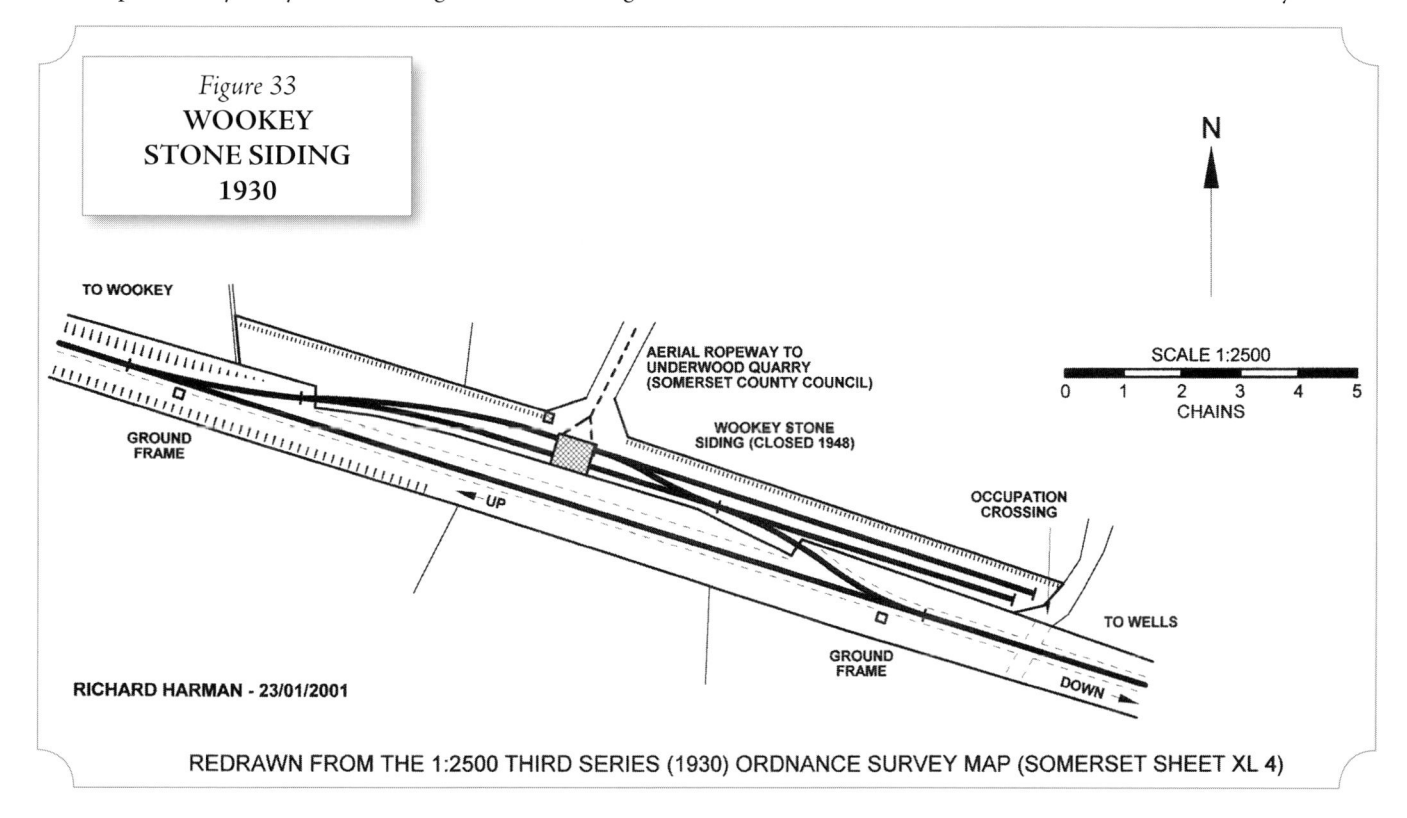

Figure 33 **WOOKEY STONE SIDING 1930**

REDRAWN FROM THE 1:2500 THIRD SERIES (1930) ORDNANCE SURVEY MAP (SOMERSET SHEET XL 4)

The Approach to Wells

Plate 135 - A view taken from Burcott Road bridge looking towards Wookey and showing the cutting on the approach to Wells. BR Standard Class 3MT 2-6-2T No.82035 passes the goods yard with the 2.45pm Yatton-Frome on 3rd July 1963.
Brian Arman collection

Figure 34
WELLS STATIONS 1936

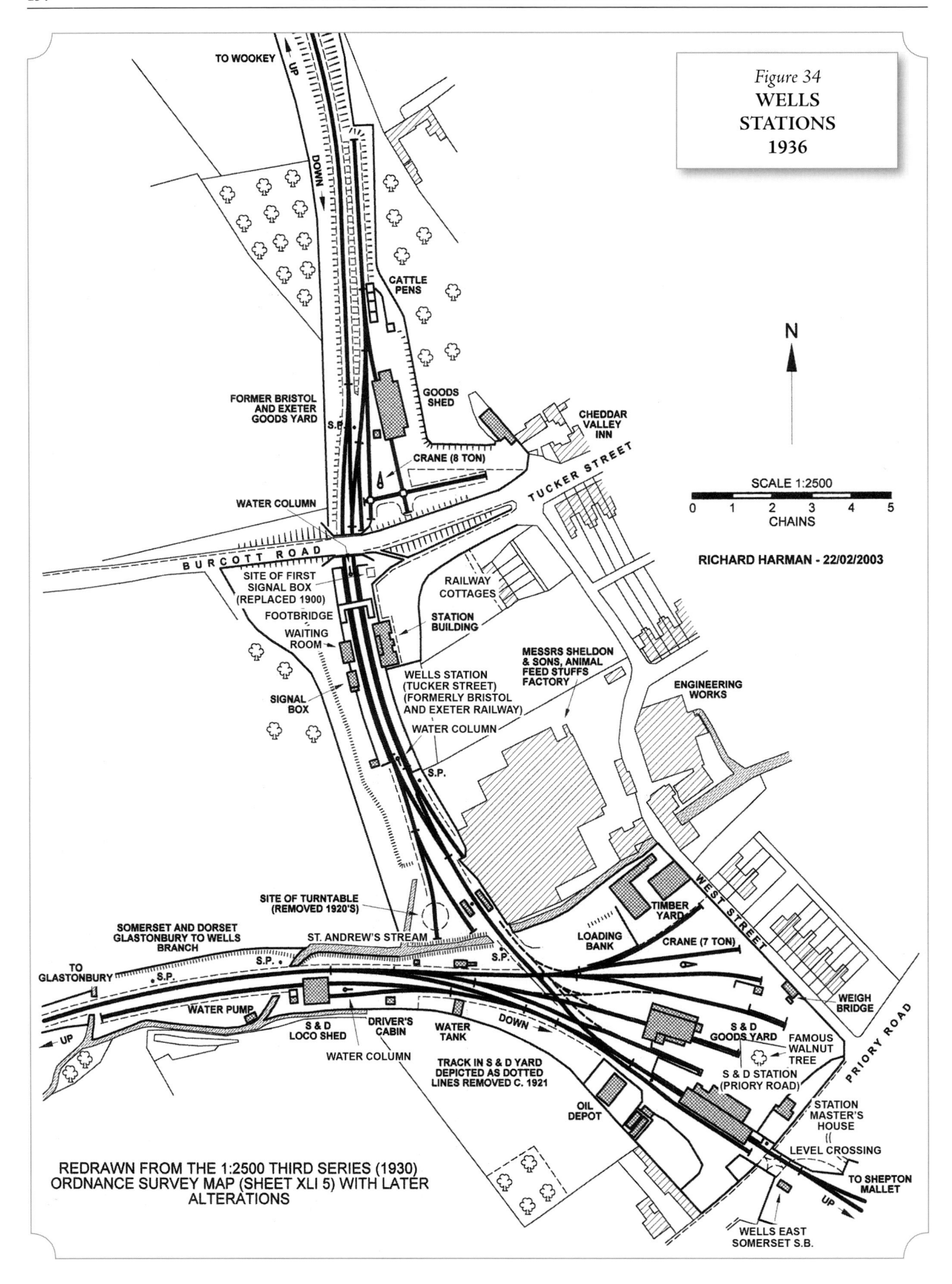

Plate 136 - It is 26th August 1938. Tucker Street station is in the middle distance leading to the junction with the S&D line from Glastonbury which enters the picture from the left, passes the engine shed and continues to Priory Road station, the platform for which is at the right hand edge of the picture. The S&D goods yard is prominent and an S&D train is opposite the signal box. The large tower and workshops between Tucker Street and the junction is the animal feed mill of Sheldon Jones Ltd. *English Heritage; Aerofilms collection*

Plate 137 - Wells Tucker Street goods yard taken from the 3.17pm Frome-Yatton on 30th May 1959. Apart from some former railway workers' cottages, the goods shed, with a diamond ventilator in the end, is the only recognisable railway building left in Wells today. *P J Garland*

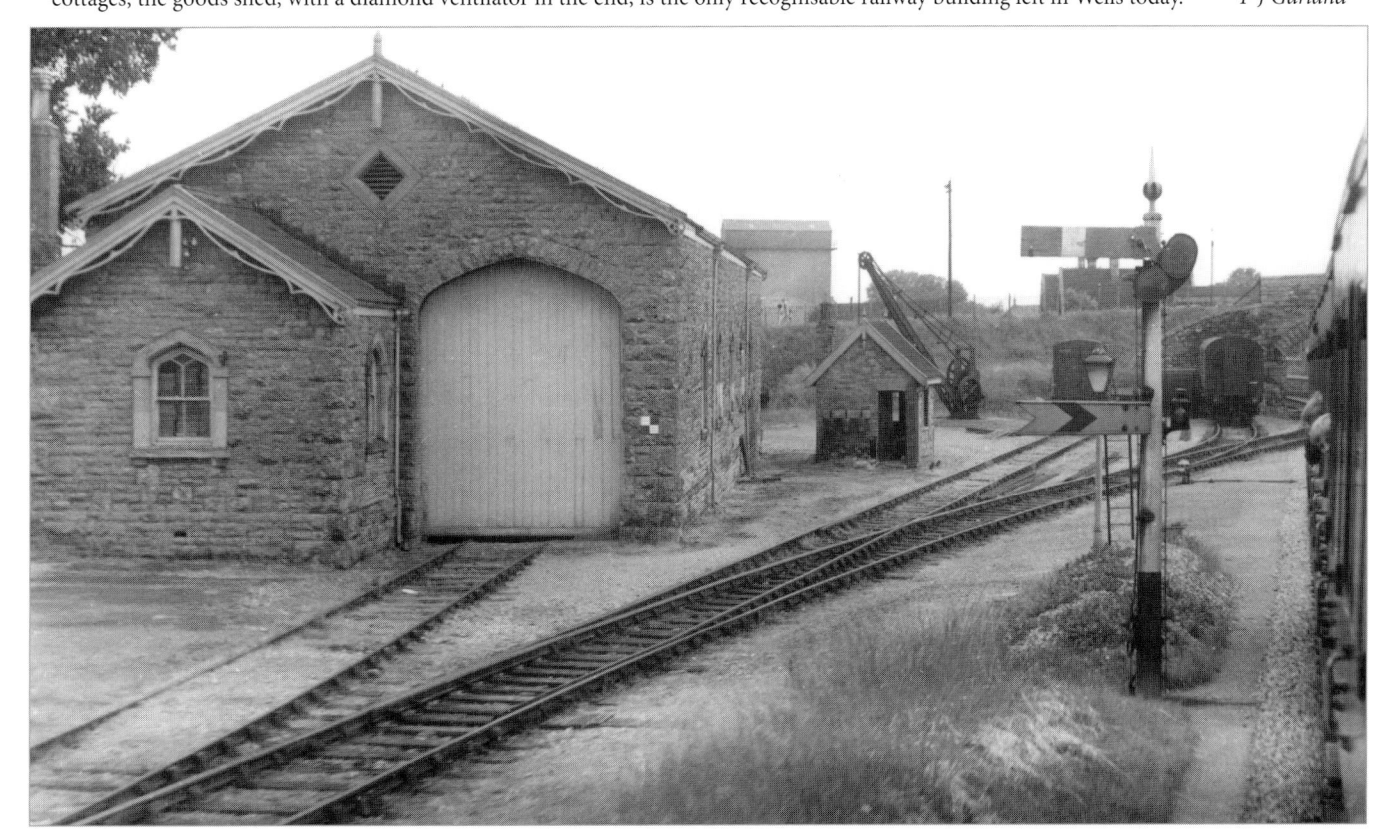

Having passed the stone siding and now approaching Wells, the line entered a cutting and turned sharply right towards the south. It then passed under the stone overbridge carrying the A371 main road. There was a small yard and stone-built goods shed with an eight-ton crane on the down side. In the original track layout two wagon turntables had been provided due to the cramped space available between the two road bridges. The turntables provided access to a siding and loading bank set more or less at right angles to the rest of the layout. The yard was accessed via a trailing connection off the down loop. The headshunt for the goods shed and other sidings served cattle pens and was also used for mileage traffic. Passing under Burcott Road bridge the line reached Wells station, 17 miles 42 chains from Yatton and 14 miles 13 chains from Witham. This was the original Cheddar Valley station and was not officially named Tucker Street until 12th July 1920, although it had been referred to as such in Bradshaw from an early date. It reverted to just 'Wells' on 6th May 1950.

The station stood on a sharp curve. The main building was on the down platform and, having two wings with gable ends facing the track, it was of an identical design to that at Axbridge. On the up side stood the signal box and a waiting shelter. The distance between the platforms was again indicative of the line's broad gauge origins. There was a covered footbridge of typical Great Western design at the Wookey end of the platforms. Early photographs show that the footbridge was a later addition but the writer has not been able to find out when it was put in. Water columns were provided between the running lines at both ends of the station. Interestingly, these were the first water columns since leaving Yatton although there had at one time been plans to provide locomotive watering facilities at Cheddar.

At the Shepton Mallet end of the station a siding off the down loop served the animal feed mill of Messrs Sheldon Jones Ltd, formerly Messrs Alfred Sheldon and Sons, whilst there were two carriage sidings on the up side on the site of the former Bristol & Exeter engine shed that existed prior to 1878. Access to the sidings was via a trailing connection off the up loop. The southernmost siding served a turntable that remained in place until the late 1920s. The private siding to the mill was provided under an agreement dated 15th September 1936 and was brought into use on 7th December that year. The company later amalgamated with Jones of Burton to become Sheldon Jones. The private siding agreement was terminated on 15th February 1967, the siding itself having already been removed during the previous October. Sheldon Jones also had an engineering works on the opposite side of West Street to the feed mill.

Plate 138 - This undated but possibly early 20th century view of Wells station from the down platform features the signal box and waiting room on the up platform, all framed by the roofed footbridge. The relatively wide spacing of the tracks betrays the station's broad gauge origins but the increased spacing allowed water columns to be placed between them at each end of the station. *Neil Parkhouse collection*

THE EAST SOMERSET AND CHEDDAR VALLEY RAILWAYS

Plate 139 - Ivatt Class 2MT 2-6-2T No.41296 arrives at Wells with a down train on 10th October 1960. Note the water column between the tracks and that the parapet of the Burcott Road overbridge bears a striking resemblance to that at Wookey. *J Spencer Gilks*

Plate 140 - The view from an up train as it arrives at Wells from Priory Road hauled by 4500 Class 2-6-2T No.5512. The signal box obscures the waiting room on the up platform and very little can be seen of the main building. *J Moss; Roger Carpenter collection*

Plate 141 - 2-6-2T No.5542 arrives at Wells with the 3.17pm Frome-Bristol Temple Meads on 12th March 1959. There is no record of the happenings in the down platform.
E T Gill; Rod Blencowe collection

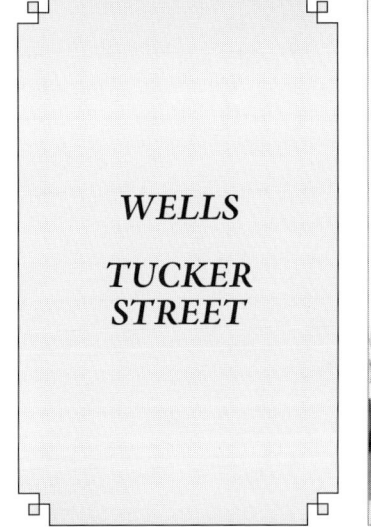

WELLS

TUCKER STREET

(Above) Plate 142 - The road side of the station building at Wells. This was of the double winged design identical to that at Axbridge.
J Moss; Roger Carpenter collection

Plate 143 - A detail view of the station building on 5th November 1952 featuring excursion posters and other details on the platform side. The posters are advertising Chester and New Brighton. *Jack Burrell*

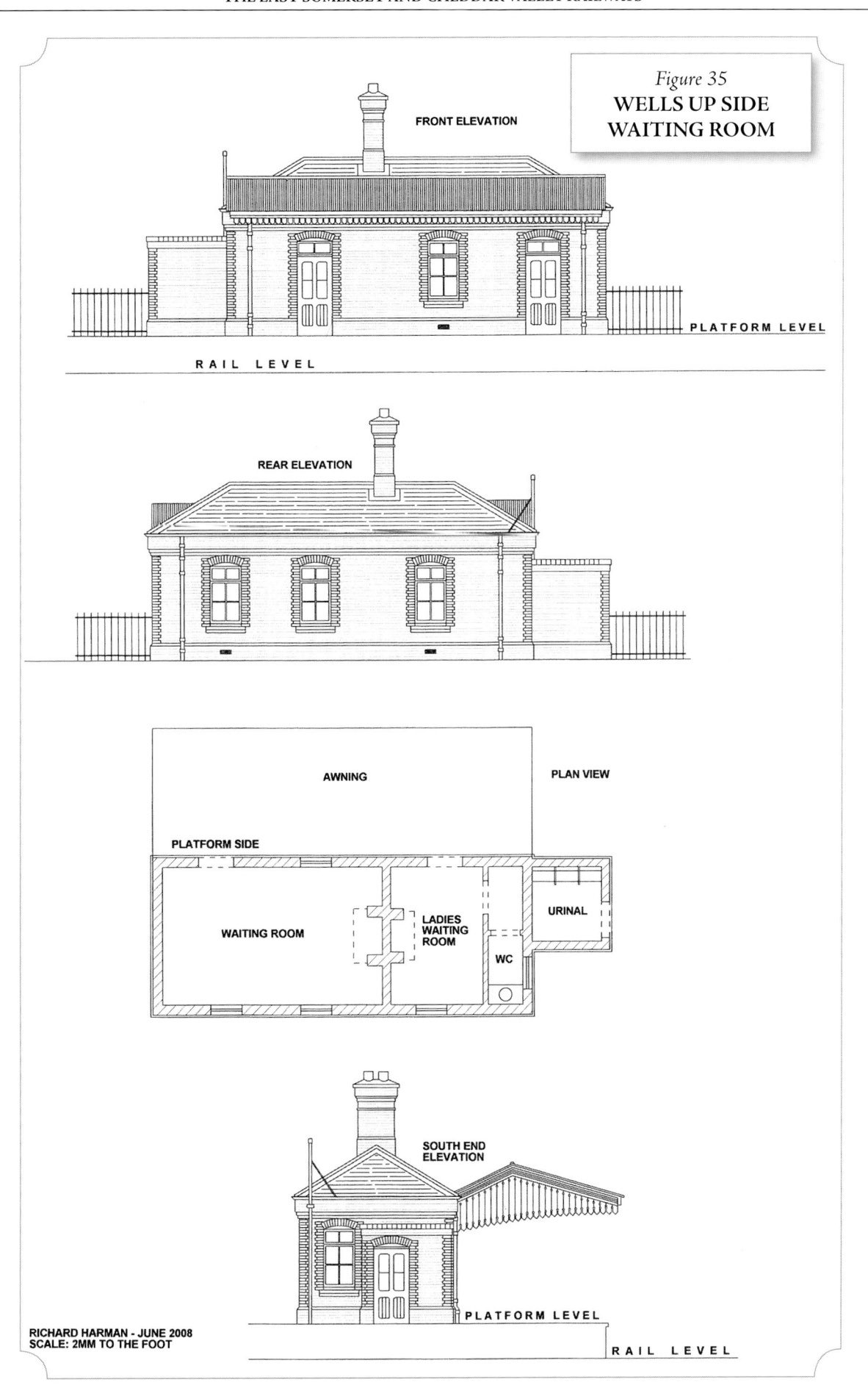

Figure 35
WELLS UP SIDE WAITING ROOM

FRONT ELEVATION

PLATFORM LEVEL

RAIL LEVEL

REAR ELEVATION

AWNING

PLAN VIEW

PLATFORM SIDE

WAITING ROOM

LADIES WAITING ROOM

WC

URINAL

SOUTH END ELEVATION

PLATFORM LEVEL

RAIL LEVEL

RICHARD HARMAN - JUNE 2008
SCALE: 2MM TO THE FOOT

Plate 144 - Wells signal box on 7th May 1959. Note that the name board merely says 'Wells Station' without the 'Signal Box' suffix so common on Great Western lines.
Author's collection

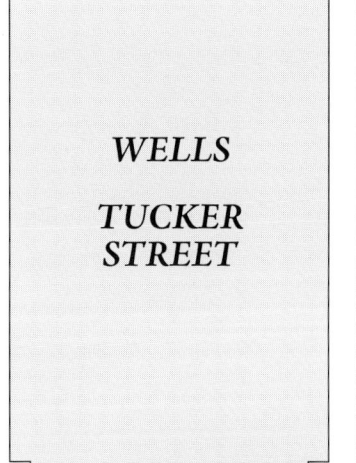

WELLS

TUCKER STREET

(Above) Plate 145 - Once again the frontage of the station building at Tucker Street is obscured, this time by 0-6-0 No.2258 working a goods train on 2nd October 1951.
S Nash courtesy Gerald Nichols

Plate 146 - The date is unknown but 2-6-2T No.5535 is working an unidentified train in the down platform. *Lens of Sutton Association*

Plate 147 - 0-6-0PT No.8744 has set back into the carriage sidings with the stock of the 3.17pm Frome-Bristol Temple Meads on 30th May 1959, possibly to attach or detach vehicles. The tank wagon is standing on the private siding into Sheldon Jones feed mill. *P J Garland*

Plate 148 - The curve past the carriage sidings at Wells looking towards Priory Road. On the extreme left is the Great Western water tower whilst the Somerset & Dorset signal box and water tower are visible on the right. The upper quadrant signals are controlling the access to Priory Road from the Tucker Street direction. *Brian Hillier*

Plate 149 - Looking back towards Tucker Street from Priory Road station c.1959 after closure to passengers. Reference to *Plate 148* will show the close proximity of the two stations; the stop block to the left of the telegraph pole is the end of the Tucker Street carriage sidings and Sheldon Jones feed mill is the industrial complex at the right of the picture. *Rod Blencowe collection*

From Tucker Street the line turned eastward and passed Sheldon Jones' mill with its distinctive grain silo on the down side. Alongside the mill was a 6,875 gallon water tower on a substantial stone-built plinth that fed the water columns at the station. Within a few yards the line crossed the throat of the S&D goods yard on the level. It was this feature that caused so many problems with establishing a connecting link between the three stations in the years leading up to 1878. Immediately before arriving at the S&D station at Priory Road the line from Glastonbury trailed in from the south. For nine chains the Cheddar Valley and East Somerset trains ran on S&D metals through Priory Road, which was 17 miles 56 chains from Yatton and 13 miles 79 chains from Witham. The S&D station did not officially receive the title 'Priory Road' until 1883. Leaving the junction, the Glastonbury line turned sharply to the south between the S&D's signal box (known as Wells 'A') and the two-road engine shed. The station consisted of a single platform and station building with an overall roof on the north side of the running line; up and down are confusing terms here! South of the running line stood a single carriage siding which also used to serve an adjacent oil depot. Following closure of the station to passengers, the overall roof was removed during 1955 when 0-6-0 No.2253 brought the crane used to do the job. The station building itself was not demolished until many years later.

Plate 150 - The view through Priory Road towards Tucker Street after closure to passengers. The S&D line to Glastonbury curves to the left past the S&D signal box. The line curving to the right leads to Tucker Street after crossing the access to the S&D goods yard. Priory Road's station building is on the platform and shows the layout of the building now that the overall roof has been removed. The photograph was taken from East Somerset signal box on 7th May 1959.

Rex Conway collection

Priory Road

Plate 151 - When photographed on 2nd October 1951 the overall roof was still in place and the bracket signal still had an arm controlling departures for the Glastonbury line. After closure to passengers this arm was removed. *S Nash courtesy Gerald Nichols*

Plate 152 - The S&D two-road engine shed. MR 1P 0-4-4T No.58086 rests awhile on 19th August 1951. *F A Wycherley*

Plate 153 - East Somerset signal box and the 55ft turntable installed in 1948. The photographer is standing on what remained of the original East Somerset passenger station, which closed on 1st January 1878. *Rex Conway collection*

Leaving Priory Road station the line immediately crossed the main road to Glastonbury (Priory Road) by a level crossing, just visible in *Plates 150 and 153*. It was here that a down train from Yatton became an up train to Witham and likewise a down train from Witham became an up train to Yatton. Wells East Somerset signal box stood on the down side and controlled the level crossing as well as connections to sidings on both sides of the line. The level crossing here was the cause of much complaint from road users throughout its existence. There were calls for its replacement by a bridge from the very earliest days but the railways resisted, no doubt on the grounds of the considerable cost that would incur. To make matters worse, the gates would be closed across the road when a Somerset & Dorset train was approaching from Glastonbury and before it passed the Wells 'A' home signal. Once the train had stopped at Priory Road the gates would be opened to road traffic again without any railway vehicle having passed them. The reason for this action was to make allowances for the driver misjudging his braking distance and overrunning the station but to road users and City councillors, who understood little about railway operation, this was merely a further irritation. As well as the timetabled passenger and freight trains running over the level crossing, there were other movements during the day such as short freight workings between East Somerset yard and the various sidings to the west of the level crossing. In addition, there were light engine movements between the passenger station at Tucker Street and the locomotive shed at East Somerset yard.

Continuing towards Shepton Mallet, the line passed the site where the former East Somerset passenger station had once stood. In later years all that could be seen of this was the platform face and a steep grassy bank on the up side adjacent to the running line between the level crossing and the goods yard. On the down side a connection near the signal box led to two sidings that were set back some yards from the running line,

Plate 154 - Part of the East Somerset installations taken from the top of the water tower at Wells locomotive depot. The receding passenger train is passing the site of the East Somerset station en route to Priory Road and Tucker Street. Wells East Somerset Box, to give its official title, is visible just ahead of the train and some road traffic is waiting to cross the line. *Harry Viles*

WELLS EAST SOMERSET YARD, AUGUST 1938

Plate 155 - An aerial view of Wells showing the facilities at East Somerset yard and the engine shed on 26th August 1938. The platform facing of the original East Somerset Railway station is evident at the left hand side whilst just above it is the gas works building with its siding. This side of the gasholder there is an oil or petroleum storage depot and a siding with five tank wagons on it. It will be another four years or so, after the outbreak of war, before the large cold store is built. The turntable at the engine shed is destined to remain for another ten years since it will be 1948 before the turntable adjacent to East Somerset signal box is installed.

English Heritage; Aerofilms collection

146 THE EAST SOMERSET AND CHEDDAR VALLEY RAILWAYS

LOCO SHED OPENED IN 1879 TO REPLACE THE FORMER EAST SOMERSET AND BRISTOL AND EXETER SHEDS.

EAST SOMERSET STATION WAS CLOSED IN 1878 WHEN GWR PASSENGER TRAFFIC WAS CONCENTRATED AT THE FORMER BRISTOL AND EXETER STATION. THE BUILDING WAS SUBSEQUENTLY USED AS A CHEESE STORE UNTIL DESTROYED BY FIRE IN 1929

THE FORMER ROUTES OF SOUTHOVER AND GATE LANE ARE SHOWN BY FAINT CHAIN LINES. SOUTHOVER WAS DIVERTED AT 90 DEGREES OPPOSITE THE GASWORKS TO MEET PRIORY ROAD WHEN THE LEVEL CROSSING WAS INSTALLED. THE LEVEL CROSSING AT GATE LANE WAS DISCONTINUED IN 1900 AND A ROAD CONNECTION TO THE SOUTHERN PART OF THE LANE WAS MADE BY AN EASTERN EXTENSION OF ROWDENS ROAD 1.36 CHAINS IN LENGTH

REDRAWN FROM THE 1:2500 SECOND SERIES (1908) ORDNANCE SURVEY MAP (SOMERSET SHEET XLI 5) WITH LATER ADDITIONS

DRAWN BY RICHARD HARMAN - 19/05/2009

Figure 36
**WELLS
EAST SOMERSET YARD
1929**

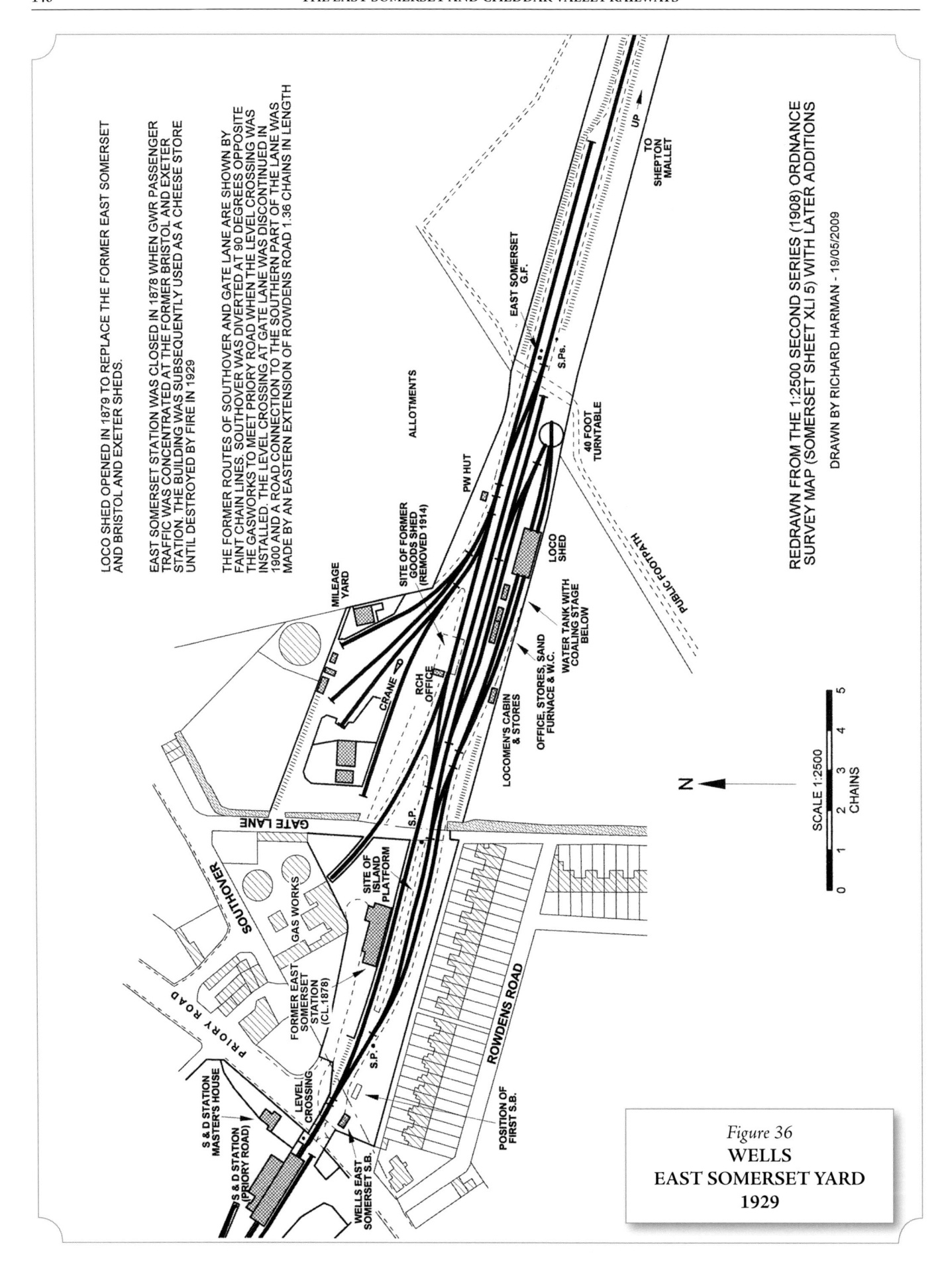

the intervening gap being the location of the former exchange platform mentioned in Colonel Yolland's report of 1875. A plan dated May 1879, interestingly after the closure of the station to passenger traffic, shows that this platform extended as far as the then existing Gate Lane level crossing, after which the sidings moved closer to the running line again. There was little, if any, alteration to the position of the sidings right up until the 1960s. The same plan also shows that the station had an overall roof covering part of the single running line between the main and exchange platforms. The line serving the outer, or southernmost, face of the exchange platform being more or less in the same position as the northernmost of the two sidings mentioned above. Other than the main station building itself, there appears to be little information as to what happened to the overall roof and exchange platform. Presumably they were demolished shortly after the closure of the station in 1878.

East Somerset yard stood on the up side of the running line and had a goods loop, loading banks, gas works siding and mileage sidings. At one time there had been a goods shed here but it was removed in 1914. The yard was primarily for the reception, marshalling and dispatch of goods trains. The loading and unloading of goods under cover was carried out in the former Bristol & Exeter goods shed at Tucker Street. There was another building adjacent to where the East Somerset goods shed had stood. This had been the Railway Clearing House number taker's office but it was latterly used as a shunters' and guards' cabin. It was known as Long John's Cabin after a shunter at East Somerset yard called John Gould. The two-road locomotive shed stood at the Shepton Mallet end of the layout on the down side. Originally there was a turntable at the Shepton Mallet end of the shed but this was later replaced by a larger one near the signal box.

WELLS

EAST SOMERSET

The former East Somerset Railway station platform

and

The engine shed in 1960

(Above) Plate 156 - BR Class 3MT No.82033 passes the site of the East Somerset passenger station with a train for Witham on 7th May 1959. The platform face is still visible over eighty years after closure. *Rod Blencowe*

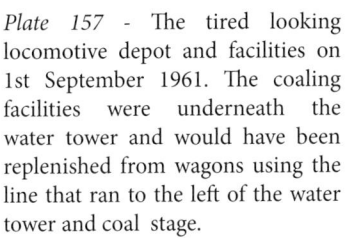

Plate 157 - The tired looking locomotive depot and facilities on 1st September 1961. The coaling facilities were underneath the water tower and would have been replenished from wagons using the line that ran to the left of the water tower and coal stage.

Roger Carpenter collection

Plate 158 - A general view of East Somerset yard and locomotive depot. The building on the left of the running line and goods loop was, at one time, the office of the Railway Clearing House number taker. This was required because of the amount of exchange traffic between the Great Western and the Somerset & Dorset. It was also known as Long John's Cabin named after John Gould, a shunter at East Somerset. Note the lock bar which would work in conjunction with the facing points leading to the loop and, on the right, the government cold store opened in 1942. The resulting revision to the track layout is shown opposite.
Wells Railway Fraternity collection

Plate 159 - The locomotive depot, minus most of the shed roof, on 1st September 1961.
Roger Carpenter collection

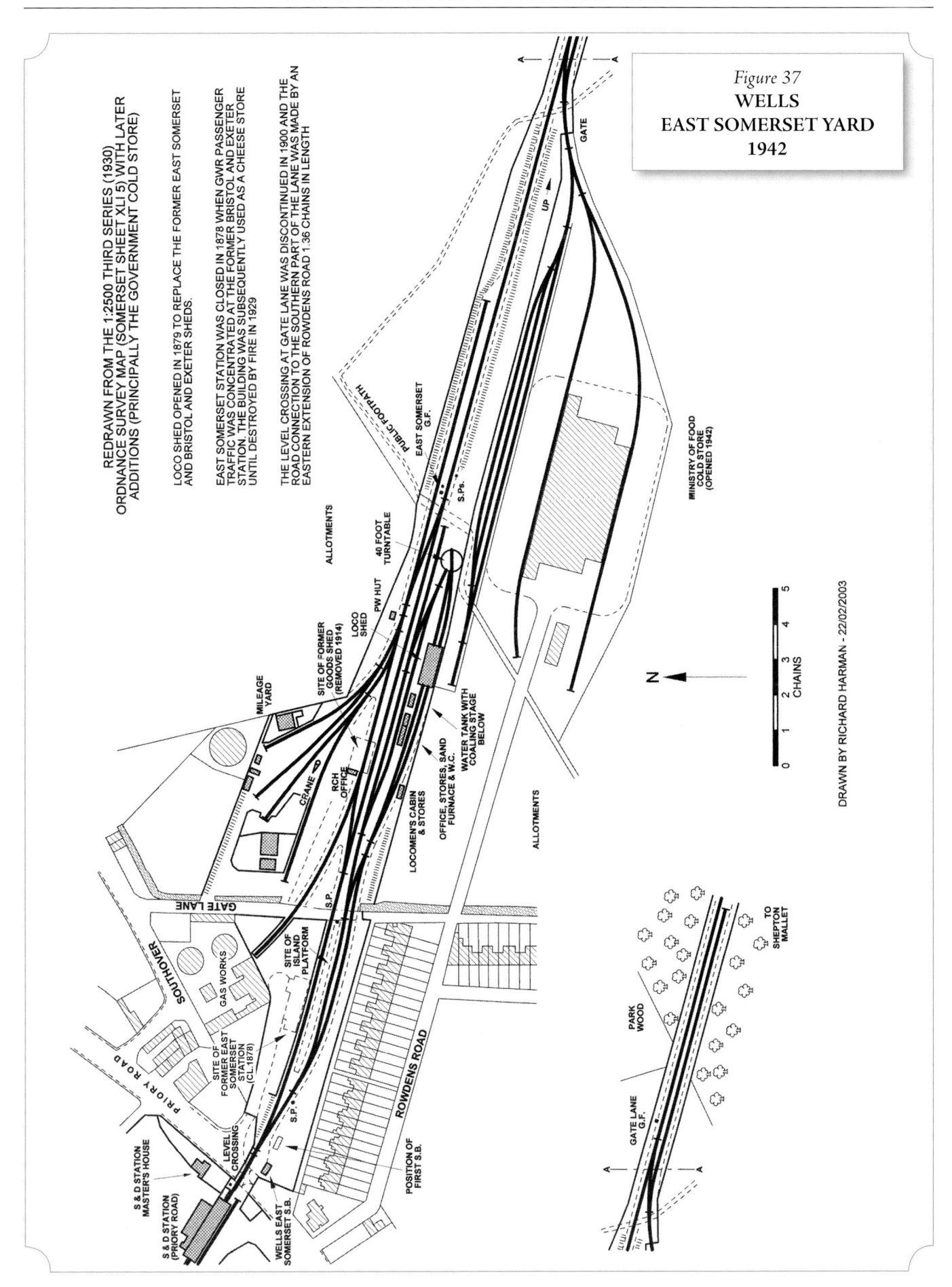

Figure 37
WELLS
EAST SOMERSET YARD
1942

Plate 160 - Dean 0-6-0 No.2578 shunting in East Somerset yard.
R Told; Wells Railway Fraternity

WELLS EAST SOMERSET

and on past DULCOTE

(Above) Plate 161 - Wells engine shed on 19th May 1959. A pannier tank and an Ivatt Class 2MT 2-6-0 await their next turn of duty. *P J Garland*

Plate 162 - 2251 Class 0-6-0 No.2268 is climbing the bank near Dulcote Quarry on 4th May 1963 heading towards Shepton Mallet with the 6.15pm Yatton-Witham. *Michael Mensing*

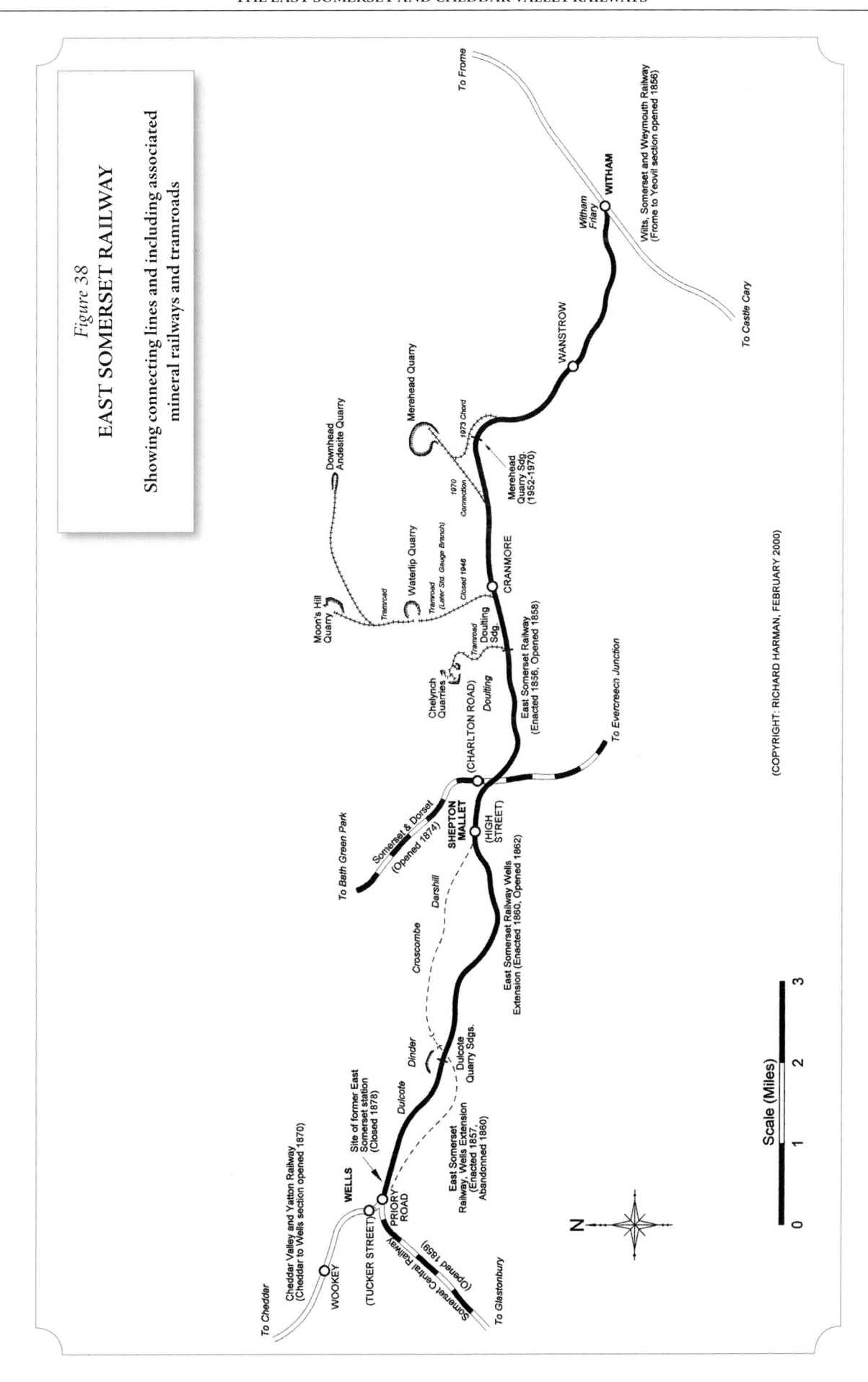

Figure 38
EAST SOMERSET RAILWAY

Showing connecting lines and including associated mineral railways and tramroads

(COPYRIGHT: RICHARD HARMAN, FEBRUARY 2000)

Wells to Shepton Mallet

The topography between Wells and Shepton Mallet is quite different from that further west. The steep escarpment of the Mendip Hills gives way to broken hilly country that rises gradually out of the levels up to the eastern Mendip plateau at around 700 feet above sea level. The valley of the River Sheppey runs west from Shepton Mallet towards Wells through the villages of Croscombe, Dinder and Dulcote. The main road from Shepton Mallet to Wells runs down this valley as did the original planned route of the railway for much of its length. When built, however, the railway ran a mile or so further south in order to avoid tunnelling through Church Hill and at the insistence of one of the major shareholders but at the expense of severe gradients and heavy earthworks.

Once past the locomotive shed and the Wells Cold Store on the down side the line started to climb at 1 in 86 towards Dulcote Hill. A glance back out of the carriage window on the up side would afford the traveller a fine view of the Cathedral and the walls of the Bishop's Palace before entering a cutting at Park Wood. Once out of the cutting the line levelled out over the high embankment that took it across the valley of the River Sheppey past the small village of Dulcote on the up side. On the approach to Dulcote Hill the climb was resumed but now at an awesome 1 in 46 which was maintained for the next 3 miles and 16 chains towards Shepton Mallet. The line ran to the south of Dulcote Hill and passed Dulcote Quarry with its siding connections on the up side. Due to the proximity of the railway to the quarry, special arrangements had to be made for the conduct of blasting operations here. Blasting could not commence until an appointed railwayman had arrived from Wells carrying the 'blasting disc' and an electric train staff (or electric key token in later years) for the Wells East Somerset to Shepton Mallet section, thus ensuring that the line was closed for the passage of trains. It was during the construction of the railway that engineers discovered the suitability of stone from Dulcote Hill for track ballast. It was this that led to the development of the quarry there although later development of the quarry by Foster Yeoman was to support the increasing demand for stone for other construction work and roads.

In about 1880 the layout consisted of two sidings linked by a single crossover. Access to and from the main line was via a single crossover facing from the Wells direction. Because of the severe gradient on the running line, the Board of Trade had not been satisfied with the layout of the sidings as built. Once alterations had been made, the arrangement was perfectly safe provided that the recommendations of the Board of Trade were adhered to with regard to shunting operations. By about 1900 a second crossover between the two sidings was added in order to provide a run-round facility.

It is worth mentioning that there were alternative spellings for Dulcote. As far as the local authorities, the Ordnance Survey and the local population were concerned it was Dulcote. In all official railway publications, such as working timetables and appendices, it was always Dulcot right up until closure. More detail about Dulcote Quarry is contained in Chapter 9.

The steep ascent continued almost as far as West Shepton, the gradient easing to 1 in 66 for the last 6 chains approaching the summit. There were considerable earthworks on this section as a result of the undulating nature of the land with the formation alternating between cutting and embankment. Here the surrounding landscape was a far cry from that experienced between Axbridge and Wells. To the south of the line lay steep-sided outlying hills of the Mendips whilst the line itself climbed along the southern slope of Dulcote Hill and then Church Hill south of Dinder. In several places ridges of land connected the outlying hills through which the line had to cut. At one moment when on an embankment the passenger would obtain a brief glimpse of Glastonbury Tor and the surrounding levels through a gap in the hills before plunging into the deep cutting

Plate 163 - BR Standard Class 3MT 2-6-2T No.82039 drifts downhill with the 6.20pm Witham-Wells on 4th May 1963. The train has just passed Dulcote Quarry.
Michael Mensing

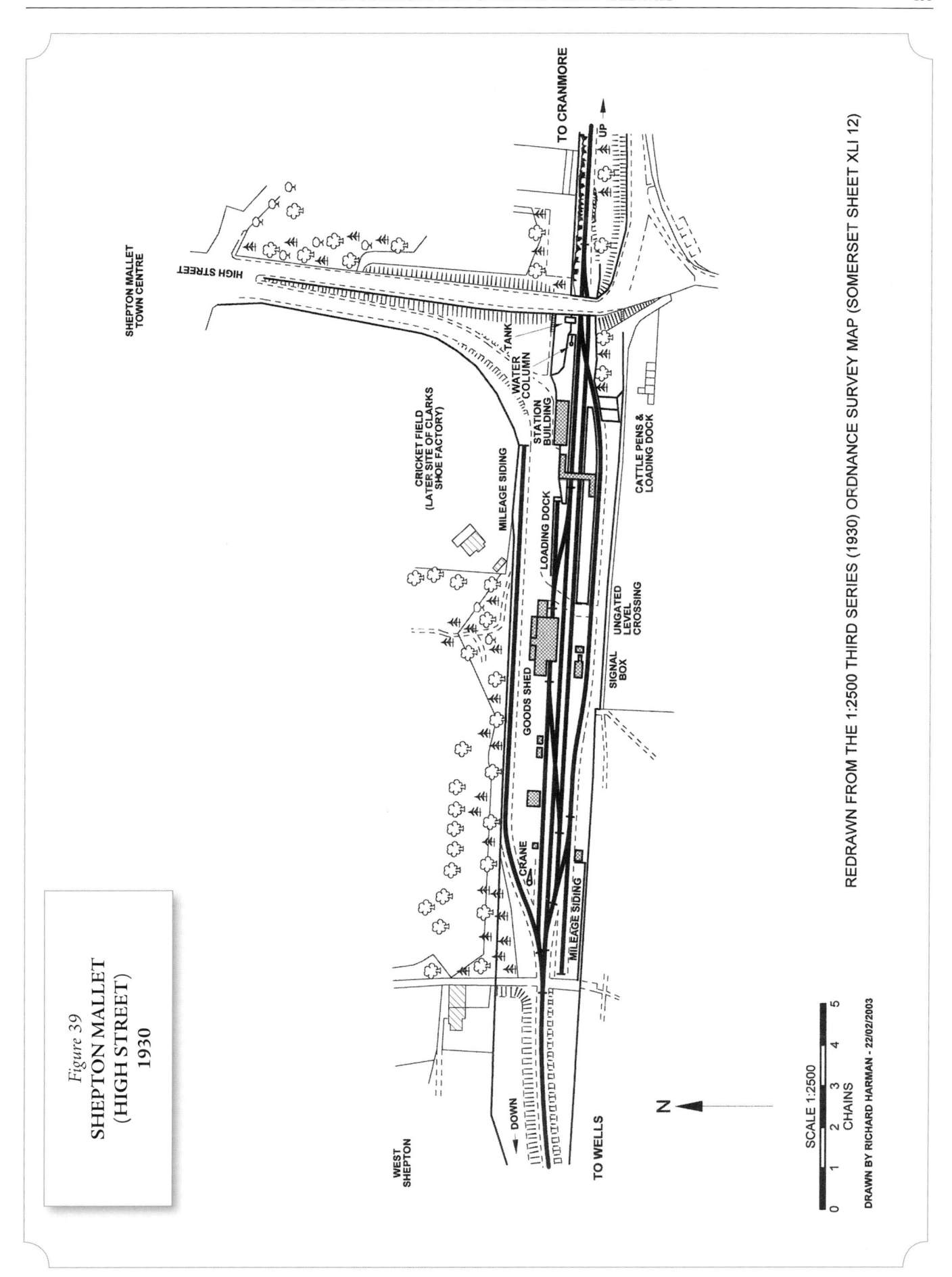

Figure 39
SHEPTON MALLET
(HIGH STREET)
1930

Plate 164 - Actually taken from a down train heading away from Shepton Mallet, this August 1948 view shows the station as trains arrive from Wells. The up mileage siding is at the extreme left, whilst the loop adjacent to the running lines continues through the goods shed to the loading dock depicted in *Plate 165* opposite. Note the catch point in the up line to derail any vehicles running away down the 1 in 103 gradient and the spur to ensure runaways are turned clear. There is an engine at work in the down loop behind the platform. *J Moss; Roger Carpenter collection*

on the approach to the summit. At the summit itself the line was crossed by a minor road that ran along the ridge of Church Hill from Dinder to Cannard's Grave, south of Shepton Mallet. A stop board for the benefit of down unfitted goods trains was provided at the summit. For the last three-quarters of a mile or so into Shepton Mallet the line descended at 1 in 85 and 1 in 72 before a brief level section at West Shepton where the line crossed over the main road to Glastonbury (A361). There was a brief climb again at 1 in 78, 1 in 62 and finally at 1 in 103 on the approach to Shepton Mallet station at 22 miles and 52 chains from Yatton and 9 miles and 3 chains from Witham. The station name acquired the suffix 'High Street' on 26th September 1949 to avoid confusion with the station on the Somerset & Dorset's Bath Extension, which itself had the suffix 'Charlton Road' added to its name.

The Yatton to Witham line's entry to Shepton Mallet passed almost unnoticed which was in sharp contrast to that of the Somerset & Dorset line from Bath which swept around the north and the east of the town over two impressive viaducts. Shepton Mallet itself is of a rather different character from Wells and Cheddar, which are typical West Country market towns on the edge of the Somerset levels. Shepton Mallet, on the other hand, is a hill town with an industrial past although it is of about the same size as the other two. Its woollen mills had declined during the 1830s. The remaining industries, including brewing,

had also declined during the early twentieth century and the town was rather down at heel by the 1950s but fortunately there has been much improvement since.

Returning to High Street station, which was equipped with two platforms and a passing loop, the main building was on the up platform and was of an entirely different design from those on the Cheddar Valley section. It was a single storey building constructed with rectangular blocks of dressed stone and lacked the ornate roof and barge boards that we had become accustomed to between Yatton and Wells. There was an awning on the platform side for the full length of the building and a covered footbridge of Great Western design linking the platforms. At the Cranmore end of the station there was a bridge over which ran the road linking the top end of the High Street to Cannard's Grave. On the down side a siding ran behind the platform which was staggered slightly to make room for the connection with the up loop. Past the platform and the signal box on the down side, the siding made a connection with the down loop. The main goods facilities were on the up side at the Wells end of the station and included a mileage siding, a stone-built goods shed that had been the engine shed prior to the opening of the Wells extension, a three-ton crane and a loading dock. An ungated crossing between the platforms and the signal box provided access for road vehicles to a mileage siding on the down side of the line. Special instructions were issued

Shepton Mallet

(Above) Plate 165 - This photograph, also August 1948 and slightly closer to the station than *Plate 164*, gives a good view of the loading dock and entrance to it from the station's link with High Street. The ungated crossing, lit by an absolute gem of a lamp, enabled road vehicles to reach the down mileage siding behind the down platform. The signalman warned station staff of an approaching train by ringing a hand bell.
J Moss; Roger Carpenter collection

Plate 166 - The down side of the station showing the down loop behind the platform and, at the far end past the covered wagon, the fence of the cattle pens. Ivatt Class 2MT 2-6-2T No.41249 waits with the 3.17pm Frome-Bristol Temple Meads on 1st April 1960. The ungated level crossing is clearly visible.
Brian Arman collection

to protect the crossing when a train was approaching. A water column was provided on the up platform and was no doubt needed on occasions when a heavy train had been hauled up the bank from Wells. The water column was fed from a tank set into the road embankment adjacent to the High Street road bridge. The water was supplied from the town mains and was metered.

Consequently locomotive crews were discouraged from taking water here unless absolutely necessary. The water column was close to the up starting signal and an instruction was issued stating that drivers were not to draw past the up starting signal at danger in order to take water unless permission was given by the person in charge.

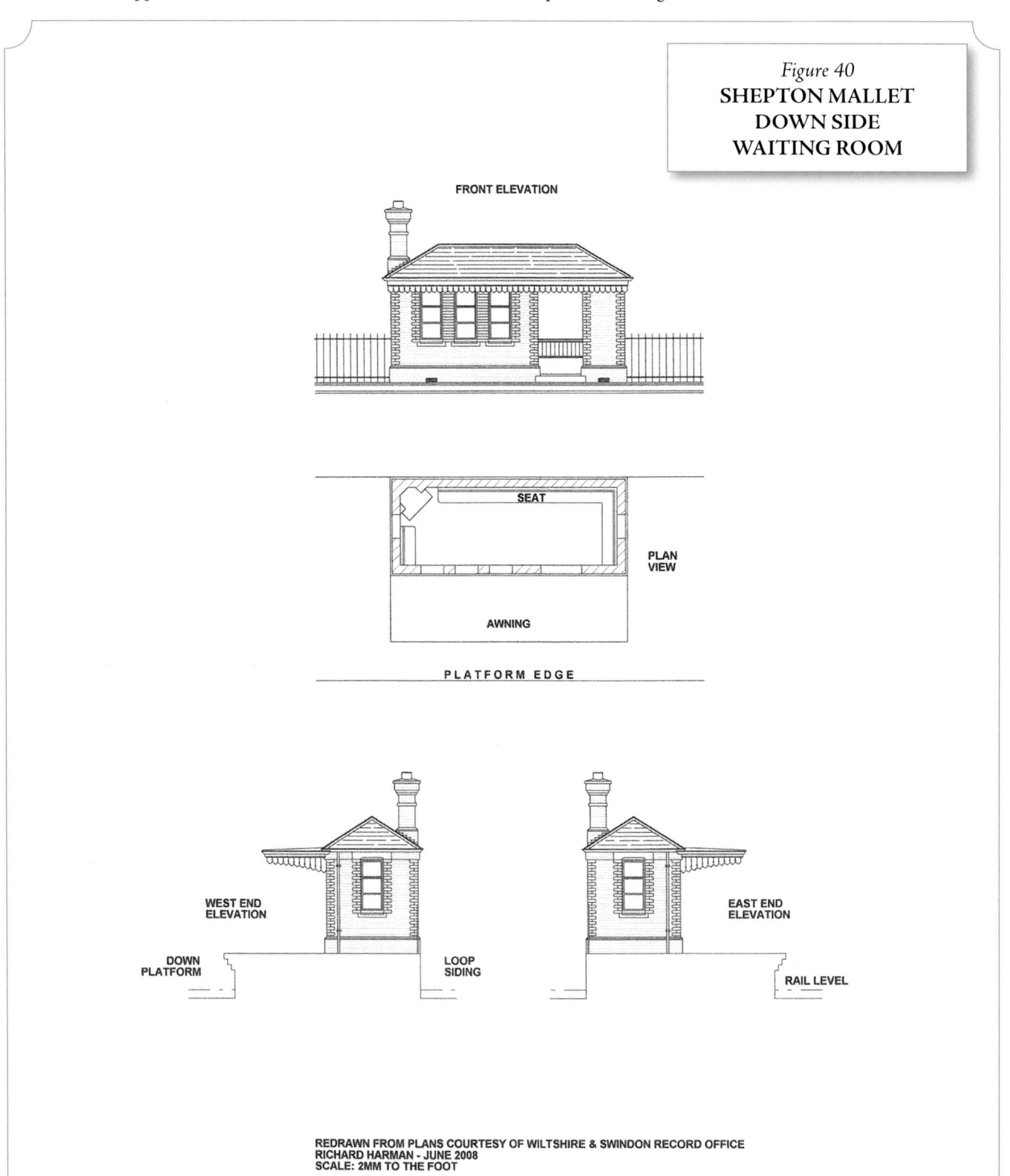

Figure 40
SHEPTON MALLET DOWN SIDE WAITING ROOM

REDRAWN FROM PLANS COURTESY OF WILTSHIRE & SWINDON RECORD OFFICE
RICHARD HARMAN - JUNE 2008
SCALE: 2MM TO THE FOOT

THE EAST SOMERSET AND CHEDDAR VALLEY RAILWAYS

Plate 167 - General but undated view of Shepton Mallet taken from the up platform. The activity opposite the signal box and lack of passengers on the platforms indicate shunting operations may be in progress. The residential development by the down loop has yet to be built, the old lamps are still in situ and 'High Street' has yet to be added to the running-in boards. *John Alsop collection*

Plate 168 - The station approach road, again an undated view. The significant change from the earlier view in *Plate 7* is the addition of fencing and gates to restrict access to the goods yard area. *Neil Parkhouse collection*

Plate 169 - The access to the down loop and the location of the cattle pens. The picture is undated but as yet there is no housing development adjacent to the loop line. On the up platform, both wooden buildings are still in place.
Lens of Sutton Association

(Right) Plate 170 - 0-6-0PT No.4647 pauses at Shepton Mallet High Street on 28th August 1958 with the 6.13pm Yatton-Frome. This train returned to Bristol via Radstock and the North Somerset branch. By now what appears to be a row of garages has been built adjacent to the down loop and one of the wooden buildings on the up platform has been replaced by a brick one. *Michael Hale*

(Below) Plate 171 - 4500 2-6-2T No.5561 arrives at Shepton Mallet High Street from Wells with a passenger train whilst pannier tank No.8744 waits for the road on 30th May 1959. *P J Garland*

Opposite page

(Upper) Plate 172 - 0-6-0PT No.4607 stands in the up loop at Shepton Mallet with a goods train from Wells whilst sister locomotive No.9668 awaits to depart with the 1.10pm (SO) Witham-Yatton on 17th February 1962. This affords a good view of the end of the goods shed, originally the engine shed until completion of the Wells extension. *Terry Nicholls*

(Lower) Plate 173 - 0-6-0 No.3218 at Shepton Mallet with the 2.45pm Yatton-Frome on 7th September 1963, the last day of passenger working. The tail end of the 3.17pm Frome-Bristol Temple Meads is visible at the bottom left of the photograph. *Ivo Peters*

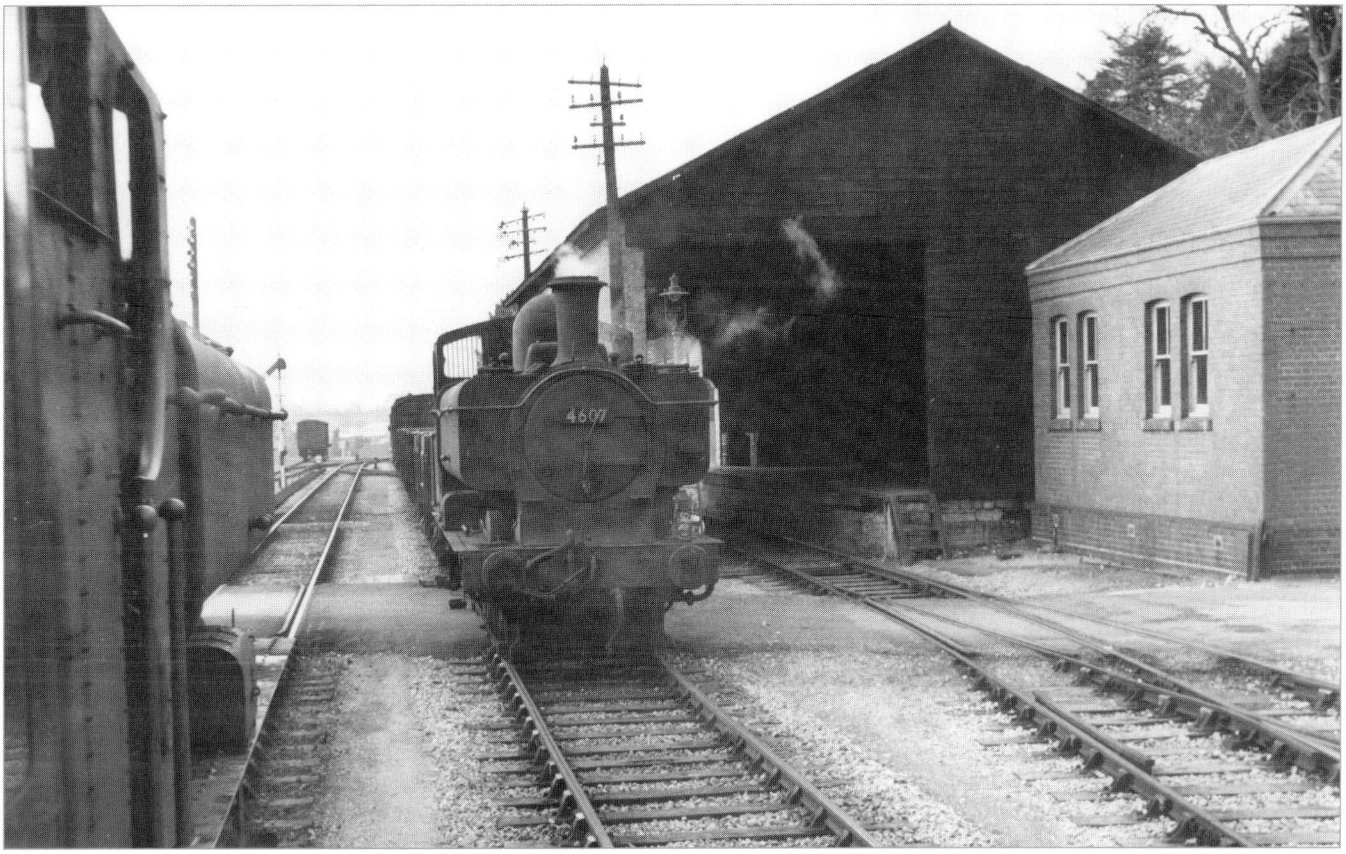
4607

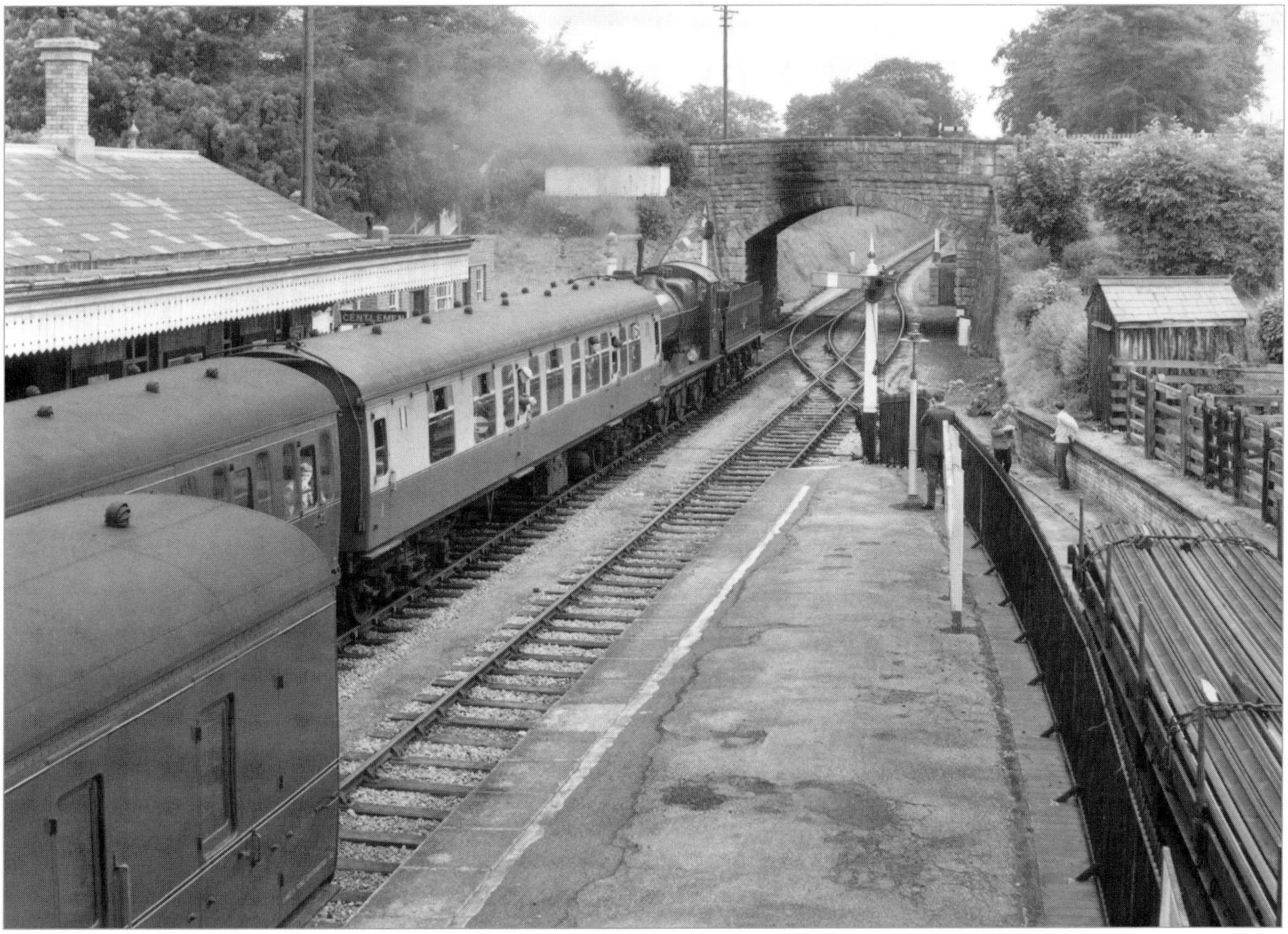

SHEPTON MALLET to DOULTING

Plate 174 - Kilver Street level crossing in 1960 where the railway crosses the A37 on the east side of Shepton Mallet. BR Standard Class 3 2-6-2T No.82009 passes with the 3.17pm Frome-Bristol Temple Meads on 21st March 1960.
Brian Arman collection

(Above) Plate 175 - The East Somerset Railway crossed the Somerset & Dorset main line just east of Shepton Mallet. A train from Witham passes over the bridge whilst No.53802, one of the well known Somerset & Dorset 7F 2-8-0s, runs into Charlton Road station tender first with an up goods train on 10th October 1960.
S Nash courtesy Gerald Nichols

Plate 176 - Ivatt Class 2 2-6-2T No.41202 climbs away from Shepton Mallet towards the summit at Doulting with the 2.45pm Yatton-Witham on 23rd April 1960.
Hugh Ballantyne

ELEVATION

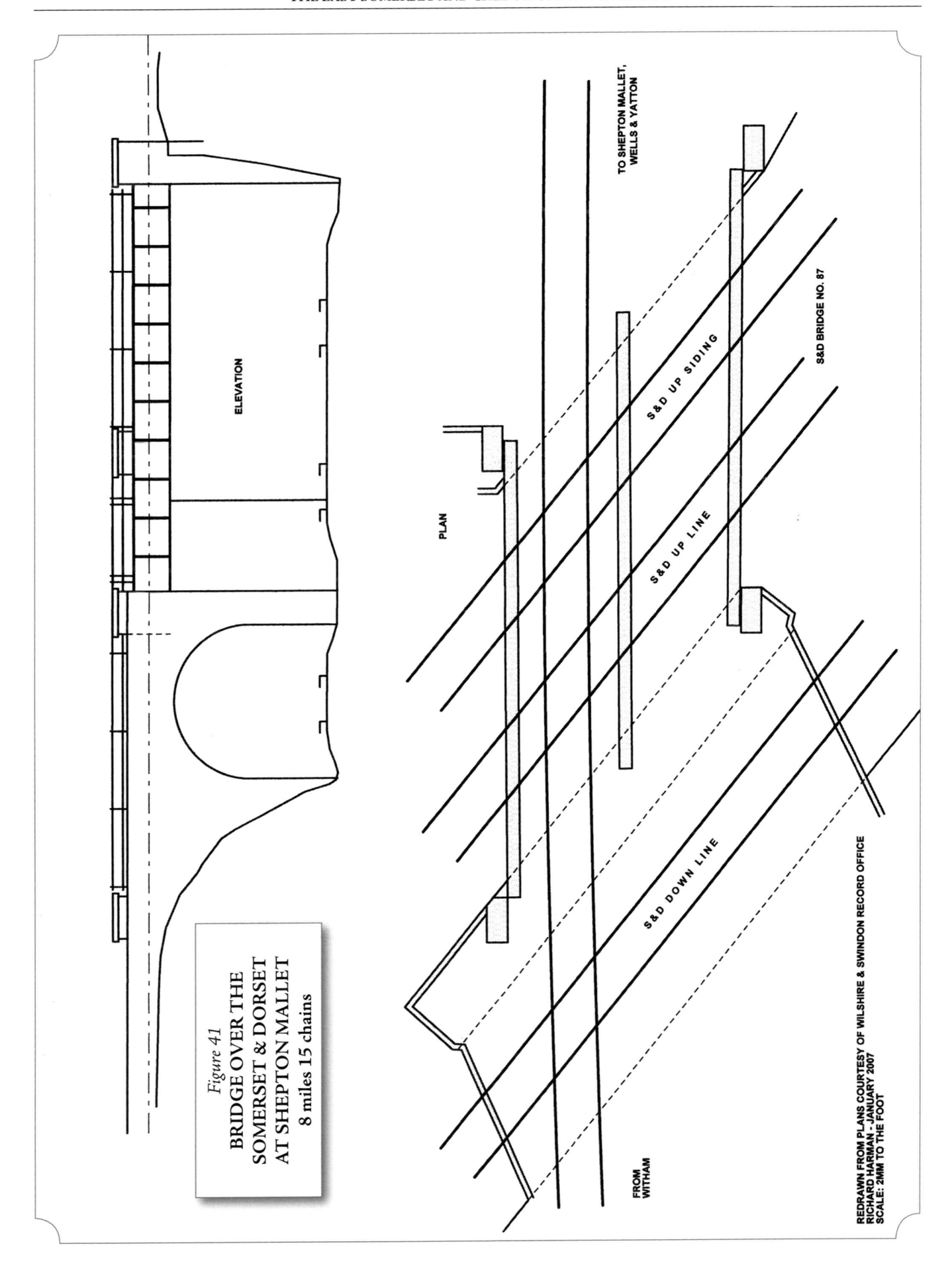

PLAN

TO SHEPTON MALLET, WELLS & YATTON

S&D UP SIDING

S&D UP LINE

S&D BRIDGE NO. 87

S&D DOWN LINE

FROM WITHAM

Figure 41
BRIDGE OVER THE SOMERSET & DORSET AT SHEPTON MALLET
8 miles 15 chains

REDRAWN FROM PLANS COURTESY OF WILSHIRE & SWINDON RECORD OFFICE
RICHARD HARMAN - JANUARY 2007
SCALE: 2MM TO THE FOOT

Shepton Mallet to Witham

After Shepton Mallet the line started to climb again at 1 in 92 steepening to 1 in 75 after 18 chains. At Kilver Street Crossing the main A37 road was crossed on the level. This has been an increasingly busy road since the private car became commonplace, affording as it does a route to the south coast from Bristol, Bath and the south Midlands. The level crossing gates were worked by hand but there was a three-lever ground frame to lock the gates and to operate the up and down distant signals. Shortly after the level crossing the line passed over the Somerset & Dorset Bath Extension just south of Charlton Road station. The bridge here was in two sections. When constructed the Somerset & Dorset line was only single track, on the alignment of what became the down line when it was doubled. Thus the East Somerset crossed the Somerset & Dorset down line over the original bridge, an arch constructed of engineering brick. This section dated back to the construction of the Somerset & Dorset line between 1872 and 1874. The up line and the extended up siding were crossed by a single span girder bridge on brick abutments that was erected when the Somerset & Dorset line south of Shepton Mallet was upgraded for double line working on 5th February 1888.

Crossing a minor road on the alignment of the 'Fosse Way' Roman road, Shepton Mallet was left behind and the line climbed steeply at 1 in 56 towards the summit near Doulting. Nearing the summit the line entered a deep cutting and passed under a bridge that carried a minor road between Doulting and Evercreech. At the summit of the line on the up side stood Doulting Siding which, at around 700 feet above sea level, could be a bleak place in winter.

After the short level section at the summit adjacent to the siding, the line descended at 1 in 70 and 1 in 119 to Cranmore at 25 miles and 78 chains from Yatton and 5 miles and 57 chains from Witham. It was always known to local railwaymen as 'Siberia' because of the weather conditions that could be experienced there. Its position on a plateau at around 650 feet above sea level gave it little shelter from strong winds from any direction. The station had two platforms with the main building on the up side and of similar design to that at Shepton Mallet but rather smaller. The signal box stood on the down side, off the platform at the Shepton Mallet end. A small wooden shelter was the only building on the down platform. No doubt passengers wished for something better on many an occasion!

As recounted in earlier chapters, when the line opened Cranmore station consisted of little more than a single platform but it gradually grew over the years. The passenger accommodation was improved by the addition of a second platform in 1880 and both platforms were extended on 2nd February 1912. Eventually there was extensive siding accommodation on the up side of the line at the Shepton Mallet end of the station. There was also a two-ton crane here. The

Plate 177 - Taken from a down train as it regains the single line, this picture affords a driver's view if he were approaching Cranmore from Wells in August 1948. The stone sidings and remains of the stone crushing and loading facilities are on the left, whilst the spur leading to the station's mileage sidings and loading bank swings away to the left from the turnout just behind the train. *J Moss; Roger Carpenter collection*

Figure 42
CRANMORE
circa 1910 and 1927

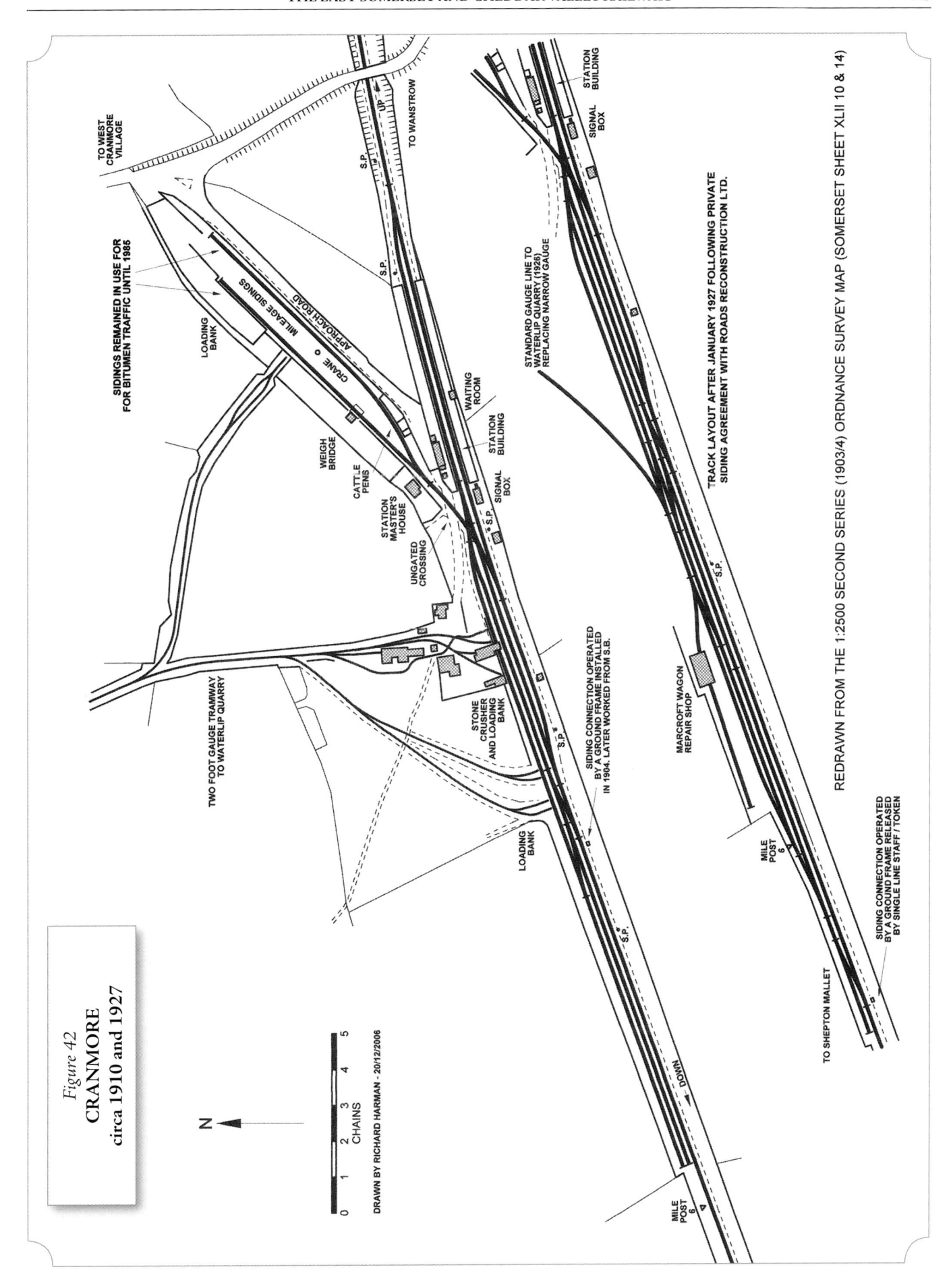

sidings served the local quarrying industry and at one time up to one hundred wagons of stone would be handled here every day. Marcroft Wagons also had a repair depot here that was opened sometime during the 1930s.

Two sidings were laid behind the up platform about 1904 serving cattle pens and a loading bank and were also used for mileage traffic. Facilities here also included a weighbridge and a two-ton crane. These sidings remained in regular use for bitumen traffic for many years after all other traffic had ceased, finally closing in 1985. A short mineral branch ran northwards from the station yard, under the A361 by the crossroads near West Cranmore to a quarry at Waterlip. The history of this branch and its origins as a tramway are described in the section on mineral lines and tramways. The sidings on the up side at Cranmore were extended further in association with the conversion of the quarry branch from two foot to standard gauge in 1927.

After Cranmore the line passed under a bridge carrying a minor road and continued in a more or less easterly direction past East Cranmore before turning towards the south. Merehead Quarry Siding was passed on the up side. This was in use between 14th March 1948 and 30th April 1970 and the main traffic was bitumen brought in by tank wagons for use in a nearby factory that produced building materials such as tiles. Unfortunately, none of the output of the factory seems to have been taken out by rail.

(Left) Plate 178 - A view from the up platform showing the station building on the right, the signal box on the down side and the now little-used stone sidings.
Lens of Sutton Association

(Below) Plate 179 - Looking towards Shepton Mallet from the end of the up platform in about 1950 with the stone sidings on the right of the running line. The siding at middle right of the photograph leads behind the station building into the mileage sidings and loading bank.
J Moss; Roger Carpenter collection

Plate 180 - The main station building on the up platform which also sports a classic cast-iron gentlemen's urinal. *Jack Burrell*

Plate 181 - Cranmore signal box taken from the rear of a train bound for Witham in August 1948. *J Moss; Roger Carpenter collection*

Plate 182 - 0-6-0PT No.8744 arrives at Cranmore with the 3.17pm Frome-Bristol Temple Meads on 28th August 1958. Nothing complex about the layout at the Wanstrow end of Cranmore station, but note the sighting board on the down home signal. *Hugh Ballantyne*

The line descended on gradients as steep as 1 in 66 and 1 in 54 for a mile and a half to Wanstrow station, 29 miles and 29 chains from Yatton and 2 miles and 26 chains from Witham. Passenger provision was a single platform on the down side with a wooden station building and there was a single siding on the down side at the Cranmore end of the station. Basic though this station was, it represented a considerable enlargement over the original which, prior to 1909, was no more than a single platform the length of two six-wheel coaches. The driver was called upon to take great care to ensure that the train was brought to a stand with the guard's compartment at the platform. Passengers for Wanstrow would be seated in compartments adjacent to the guard who would ensure that no one would alight or board the train other than onto or from the platform.

Plate 183 - Ivatt 2-6-2T No.41202 on a passenger train between Cranmore and Wanstrow on 15th April 1961. *Ivo Peters*

Figure 43
WANSTROW
circa 1930

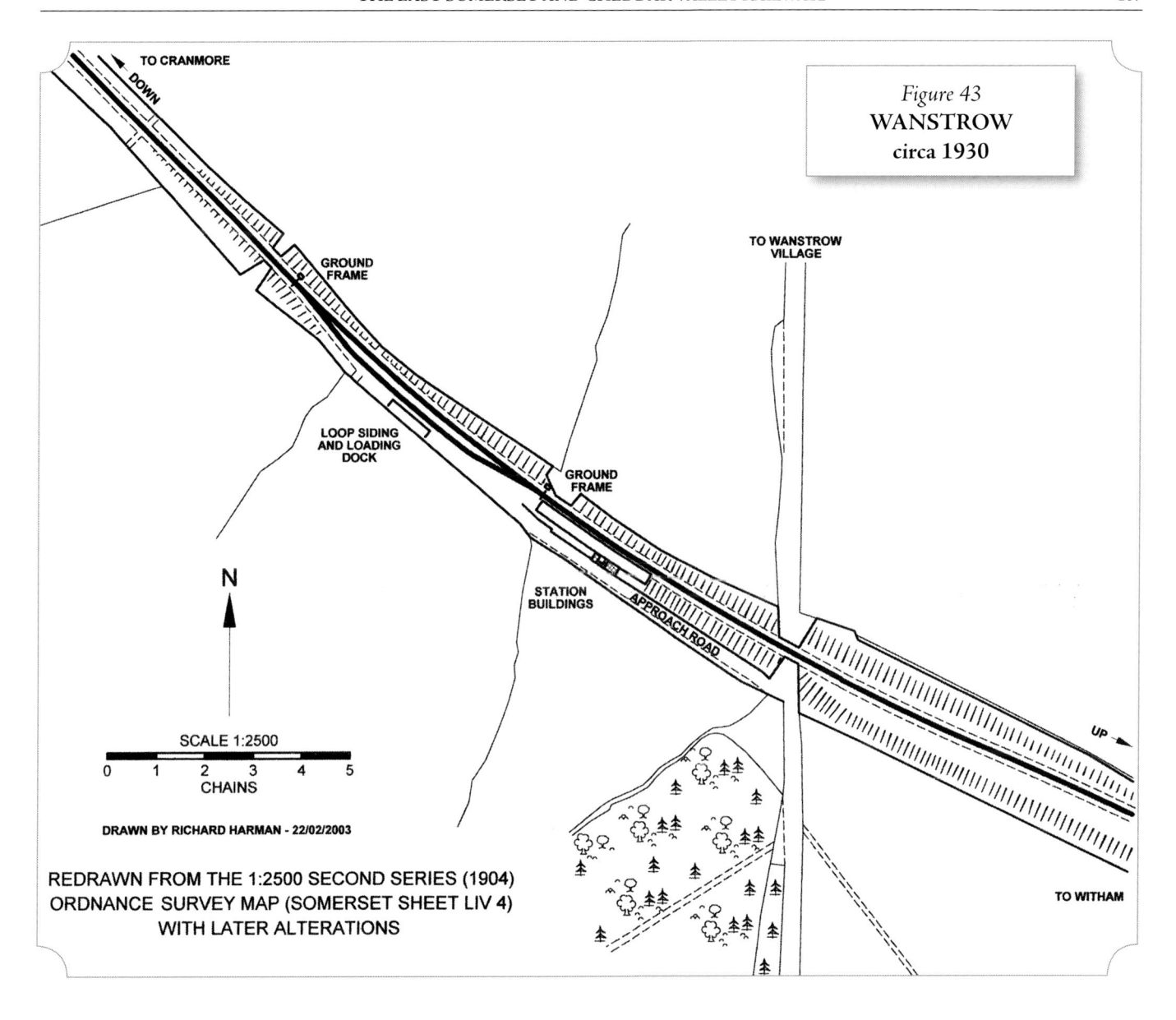

Plate 184 - The minimal facilities at Wanstrow on 4th August 1933 with the single siding occupied by a wagon.
Brunel University, Mowat collection

THE EAST SOMERSET AND CHEDDAR VALLEY RAILWAYS

Plate 185 - Wanstrow station looking towards Witham on 22nd October 1959. The points in the foreground provided access to the single siding and were controlled by a ground frame, just out of picture to the left.

Brian Arman collection

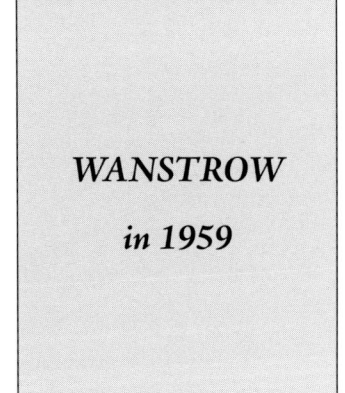

WANSTROW

in 1959

(Above) Plate 186 - Few passengers in view as 0-6-0PT No.9628 stands at Wanstrow with the 3.17pm Frome-Bristol Temple Meads on 22nd October 1959. Note the ground frame controlling access to the siding and the sheer drop at the end of the platform.

Brian Arman collection

Plate 187 - The minimal station buildings at Wanstrow, looking towards Witham from a passing train on 20th June 1959. *R.E. Toop*

From Wanstrow the line descended again on varying gradients that took it down from the eastern Mendip plateau and into the valley of the River Brue. The steepest stretch here was 1 in 47 which lasted for 38 chains. Approaching Witham the gradients eased as the main line came into view to the south. Although the station itself was generally known by the name of Witham, the name of adjacent small village of Witham Friary is a reminder that the first Carthusian monastery to be founded in England once stood here. All that remains of that establishment is the small parish church of St. Mary distinguished by its massive bell-cote containing three bells. The bell-cote was a relatively recent addition, being constructed in the 1870s to replace a tower that had become unsafe.

The official name of the station was changed to Witham (Somerset) on 9th June 1958. This was to avoid confusion with the other Witham on the Eastern Region that itself became Witham (Essex). The station nameboard read:

**WITHAM
JUNCTION FOR
SHEPTON MALLET & WELLS**

The suffix 'Somerset' was added in smaller letters to the right of the station name on the top line. One wonders why this renaming took place over ten years after nationalisation when other station renamings in similar circumstances took place before 1950. Perhaps the level of confusion reduces as the distance between the stations concerned increases.

The station at Witham had two through main line platforms and a bay platform for branch trains on the up side. The stone-built main station building stood at the Frome end of the up platform. This was a single storey building similar to that at Shepton Mallet. The signal box and goods yard stood at the Castle Cary end of the station on the down side. There was a small waiting room on the down platform constructed in a similar style to the main station building. The main line platforms were linked by an unroofed footbridge. The bay platform had an overall roof that was added in 1870 but it was removed sometime between 1958 and 1961. There was no engine release road at Witham so when all of the passengers had disembarked, the stock would be propelled back onto the branch until the locomotive was clear of the points. The locomotive would be uncoupled and run out of the way so that the stock could be run back towards the platform under gravity, assisted by the favourable gradient of the branch. The locomotive would then run back into the bay and be coupled up ready for the return working. A turntable had been installed at the insistence of the inspecting officer when the branch was opened through to Wells but it had fallen into disuse by 1936. It had a diameter of 34 feet 6 inches.

The former Wilts, Somerset & Weymouth line was doubled in the late 1870s but retained secondary line status until 2nd July 1906 when the cut off line from Castle Cary to Cogload Junction, a few miles east of Taunton, was opened for all traffic. From that date the line through Witham became the London to West of England main line serving the important holiday areas of Devon and Cornwall, a status that it still enjoys today. Now First Great Western inter-city trains pass the site although all trace of the station has long since disappeared.

Plate 188 - A view from Witham's up platform showing the overall roof over the bay and a train on the down main. The overall roof to the up bay had been erected in 1870 and lasted until 1958-61, during which time it was dismantled. *Michael Hale*

Plate 189 - Looking west from the up platform at Witham showing the station buildings on both sides and the footbridge. The very ornate chimney serving the down waiting room is prominent. *Lens of Sutton Association*

Plate 190 - A similar view but from the western end of the up platform in May 1948. The line to the bay platform passes behind the water column and the layout is such that trains for the Cheddar Valley can enter or leave the bay without fouling the main lines. The branch turns away to the right just past the signal box. *J Moss; Roger Carpenter collection*

THE EAST SOMERSET AND CHEDDAR VALLEY RAILWAYS

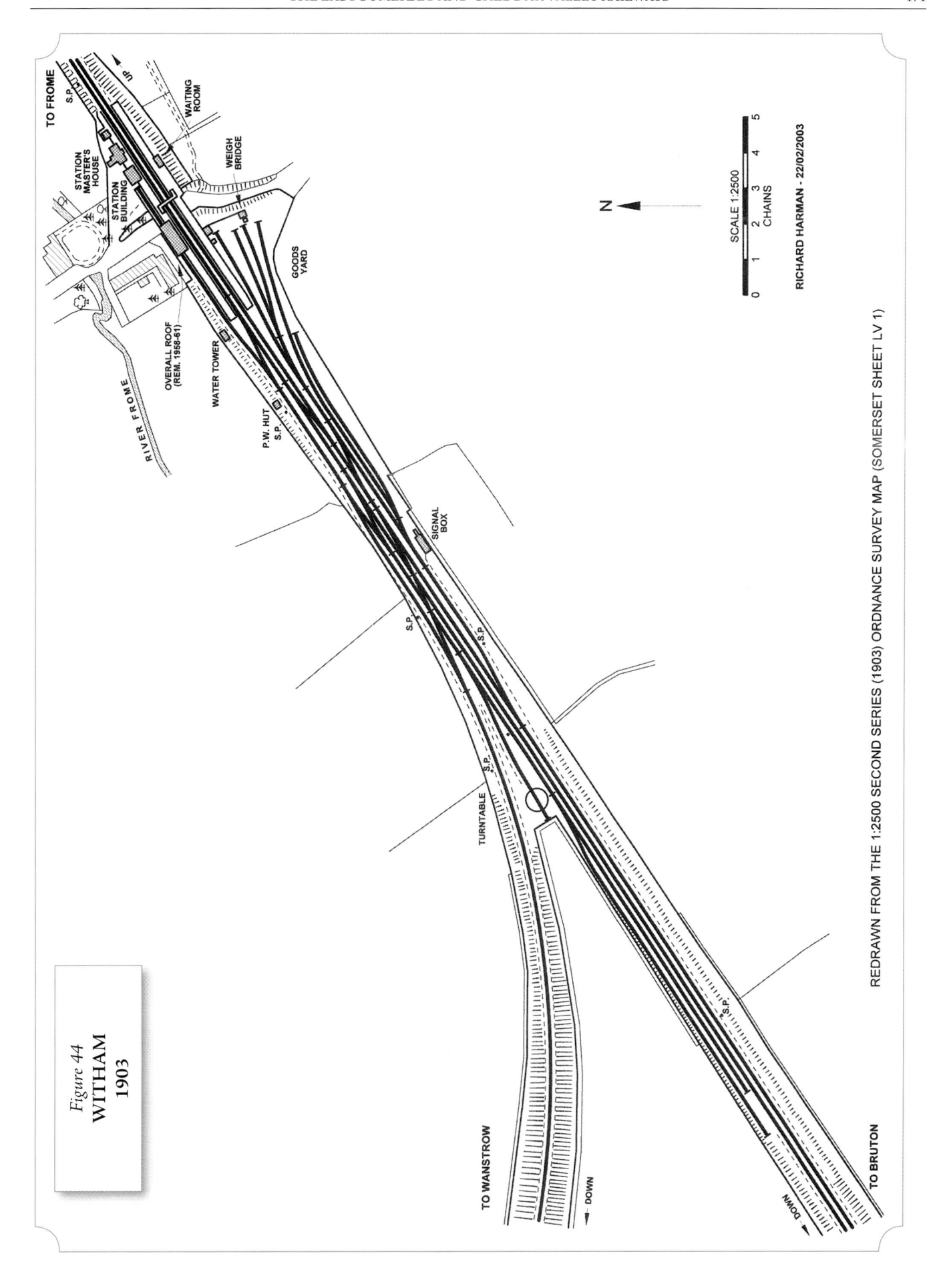

Figure 44
WITHAM
1903

Plate 191 - 4500 Class 2-6-2T No.5512 in the bay platform at Witham and ready to work a Bristol Temple Meads train via the Cheddar Valley, probably in May 1948. Note the LMS carriage next to the engine. *J Moss; Roger Carpenter collection*

Witham - the end of the line

Plate 192 - Ivatt Class 2MT 2-6-2T No.41203 stands in the down main platform before running onto the Cheddar Valley branch with the 3.17pm Frome-Bristol Temple Meads on 21st June 1961. By now the bay's overall roof has been dismantled. *Brian Arman collection*

Chapter Eight

MINERAL BRANCHES AND TRAMWAYS

Running as it did through an area in which quarrying was one of the main industries, the Yatton to Witham branch was served by a number of mineral lines and tramways that were constructed to provide an outlet for the products of these quarries. For the most part, these lines were concentrated on the East Somerset section between Witham and Shepton Mallet but there was one on the Cheddar Valley section at Sandford and Banwell.

The Sandford Quarry Branch

Sandford Quarry was opened in the early 1900s although old maps do show evidence of smaller scale quarrying on the same site in the middle of the nineteenth century. So this was more of an expansion of existing activity and the reason behind it was to provide stone for the construction of the Royal Edward Dock at Avonmouth. A standard gauge mineral branch from the goods yard at Sandford and Banwell station was constructed into the quarry but the various sources disagree as to when it was opened for traffic. According to some it opened in about 1903, at about the same time as the quarry, whereas others put it as late as 1915. However, it was definitely in place when the Great Western Railway put forward plans to install a goods loop and additional sidings in 1905. These alterations came about as a result of a private siding agreement between the railway company and John Aird & Co. dated 25th September 1903.

Two sidings were constructed on the down side of the line south of the station goods yard. A single line connection from the goods yard headshunt was via a crossover controlled by a hand lever. The connection led though a gate where almost immediately it split into the two sidings that were at a higher level than the running line. In order to achieve this level, the sidings were on a gradient of 1 in 35 at the station end. The sidings converged into a headshunt at the far end. A standard gauge incline ran from a loading dock on the easternmost siding into the quarry. Wagon loads of stone were worked down to the sidings by gravity and the empties were horse-drawn back to the quarry. The incline seems to have terminated on the loading dock at very nearly ninety degrees to the sidings which would suggest that gravity working must have been a most dangerous escapade! There was also a stone crushing plant situated at the bottom of the incline.

Sir John Aird's company had been awarded the contract to extend the dock facilities at Avonmouth and it was presumably quarrying its own stone at Sandford. The construction of the Royal Edward Dock was approved by Act of Parliament that received Royal Assent on 17th August 1901. The cutting of the first sod was on Wednesday, 5th March 1902 by the Prince of Wales and Sir John Aird's company was instructed to start work on 3rd April 1902. The fact that over a year elapsed between the commencement of work on the dock and the implementation of the private siding agreement comes as no surprise. A considerable amount of excavation work would have to have taken place before any stone would be required for the construction of the dock walls. The dock was completed in 1907 and opened by the King on Thursday, 9th July 1908. The private siding agreement was terminated on 9th April 1908 and the incline fell into disuse. It seems, therefore, that all of the stone taken by rail from Sandford Quarry during this period was for the Royal Edward Dock construction project. Whether

Plate 193 - Sandford Quarry's resident Sentinel shunter, works No.9391 of 1949, arrives at Sandford and Banwell goods yard with a loaded train from the quarry; 21st June 1958. *Bob Griffiths*

Sandford stone was taken by road for other purposes during this period is another matter but, as we shall see, later developments would imply that other markets had been opened up.

On 17th July 1915 a new agreement was made between the railway and the then quarry owner, Sir John Jackson Ltd. Whether the sidings saw any use in the intervening seven years is not known. It is likely that the extension into the quarry was completed at this time. South of the loading dock the easternmost siding was extended by turning sharply at nearly ninety degrees to run steeply into the quarry complex. The gradient on the curve was 1 in 40 but this steepened to 1 in 20 on the straight section leading up to the quarry. After a further ten chains or so the gradient eased and the line crossed the road from Sandford to Winscombe immediately before entering the quarry. A siding with a small engine shed was situated to the north of the branch just west of the road crossing. A crossover provided a facing connection from the quarry branch to the westernmost of the two 1903 sidings. This siding terminated at a headshunt.

From that date the two sidings were used for the exchange of traffic between the quarry company's locomotives and those of the Great Western and latterly British Railways. Something like 95% of all goods traffic at Sandford and Banwell was stone from the quarry. In view of the gradients special operating instructions were issued for the exchange of traffic, described in more detail in the section on goods traffic operation. The quarry had an extensive two-foot gauge network employing locomotives as well as the standard gauge sidings connected to the branch. Stone from the quarry was used for road construction, as aggregates for the building industry and track ballast for the Great Western Railway and later British Railways.

The quarry branch finally closed on 30th September 1964 providing the last traffic on the section between Yatton and Cheddar. The narrow gauge network was closed in 1931, only to reopen again in 1935 but finally closed for good in 1940. From 1935 the quarry was owned by Roads Reconstruction Limited and it finally closed in 1970.

Latterly the standard gauge network between the quarry

SANDFORD QUARRY

Photographs from Mark Warburton

21st June 1958

(Above) Plate 194 - The Sentinel shunter with a train of mineral wagons at the entrance to Sandford Quarry where the branch crosses the Sandford to Winscombe road. The registration of the car in the wooden garage is PAE 410.

Plate 195 - Shunter No.1700 derelict in the quarry where it had been laid up for several years. Originally built as a Manning Wardle petrol-mechanical shunter, works No.1954 of 1918, it was rebuilt as a vertical-boilered steam locomotive by Sentinel in about 1927.

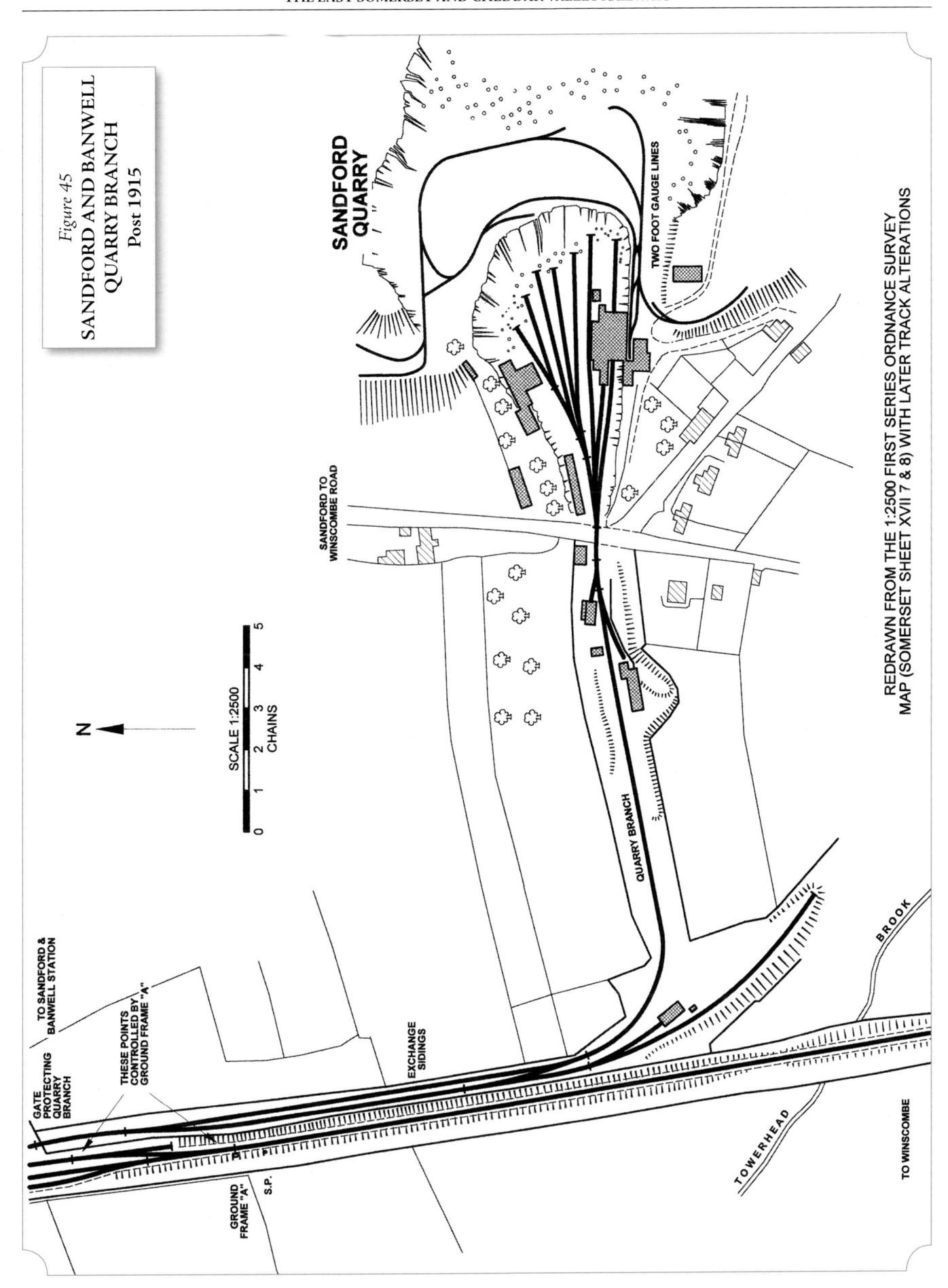

Figure 45
SANDFORD AND BANWELL
QUARRY BRANCH
Post 1915

Figure 46
DOULTING STONE SIDING
1903

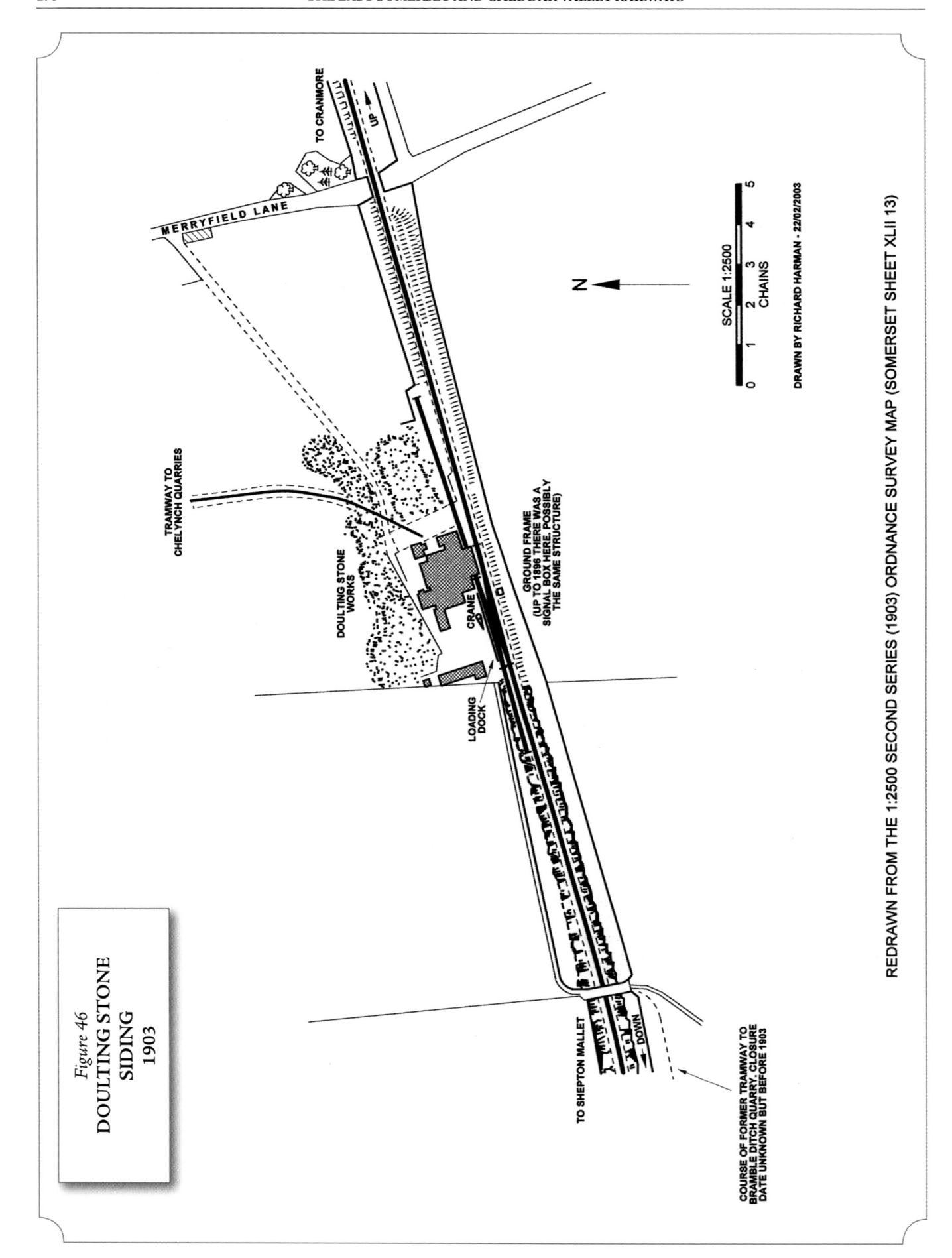

and the exchange sidings was worked by a Sentinel steam locomotive, works number 9391 of 1949. An outside cylinder 0-4-0 saddle tank built by Avonside, works number 1565 of 1911 and named *Finetta*, also worked the quarry branch at one time but was transferred to Conygar Quarries at an unknown date. A third locomotive known to have worked on the quarry branch had a most unusual history. This locomotive was numbered 1700. It was originally built as a Manning Wardle 0-4-0 petrol-mechanical locomotive, works number 1954 of 1918, but was rebuilt as a vertical-boilered steam locomotive by the Sentinel Wagon Works in about 1927. It is recorded as being derelict in 1949, presumably superseded by the later and more conventional Sentinel. It was still in a derelict condition in the quarry in the late 1950s. Nothing else is known about its eventual disposal.

Doulting Stone Siding, Stone Works and the Chelynch Tramway

The history and location of Doulting stone siding have already been described. Quarrying at Chelynch had been conducted for centuries and the freestone from there was used in the construction of Glastonbury Abbey and Wells Cathedral. At the same time as the siding and the adjacent stone works opened in 1868, a two-foot gauge horse drawn tramway was constructed from there into the quarries. It was about one and a half miles in length. From the stone works the tramway ran northwards over the fields with minimal earthworks and across the main Shepton Mallet to Frome (A361) road just to the east of Doulting village before curving to the east and into the quarries at Chelynch. The tramway and siding dated from 1868 and they fell out of use about 1948. Little or nothing of this tramway is still visible today.

Another tramway ran westwards from the stone works to a quarry located at Bramble Ditch about a quarter of a mile to the west. It ran north of the railway cutting for about half of its length, crossed over the railway via a bridge and then continued along the south side of the railway. The quarry was situated just south of Maesdown Bridge, which was the first bridge over the railway on the steep ascent from Shepton Mallet. The bridge carried an unclassified road from the A361 at Doulting south towards Evercreech. The tramway was in existence in 1882 but had gone by 1903. It seems that there was once a siding off the East Somerset Railway on the Shepton Mallet side of Maesdown Bridge but little is known of its history and it appears to have become disused by the 1880s. It is possible that its purpose was to serve the quarry at Bramble Ditch but working a siding on a 1 in 56 gradient would definitely have its limitations.

Waterlip Quarry and Branches

The Waterlip Quarry branch from the East Somerset Railway at Cranmore also originated in the 1860s and started life as a two-foot gauge horse drawn tramway. Quarrying on a fairly large scale seems to have begun in the Waterlip area at about this time. The original proposal to construct the tramway was made by Captain Strode, the owner of Waterlip Quarry, in November 1865. He reached an agreement with the East Somerset Railway to obtain a 20% rebate on the carriage of all tonnage in excess of 10,000 per annum brought down by the tramway. Quite why the tramway was not constructed there and then is a mystery but the tenant of the quarry, Edward Haynes, became insolvent just over a year later and Captain Strode again negotiated with the East Somerset Railway and obtained a 10% rebate on all tramway traffic in order to revitalise the trade. In March 1870 the new tenant, a Mr. W. B. Beauchamp (or Beachim in some sources), promised to lay the tramway and carry 20,000 tons annually.

The tramway was operational by 1871 and over the next three years the average tonnage carried was in excess of that promised. Additional siding accommodation was provided at Cranmore station in 1880 under an agreement between the railway and the quarry company, which was then trading under the name of the Mendip Black Rock Stone Company. By 1889 it

Plate 196 - Narrow gauge outside cylinder locomotive at Waterlip Quarry, possibly Kerr Stuart KS3065. The corrugated iron used as a weather-board for the rear of the cab of the adjacent engine is noteworthy!
Industrial Locomotive Society, Frank Jones Collection

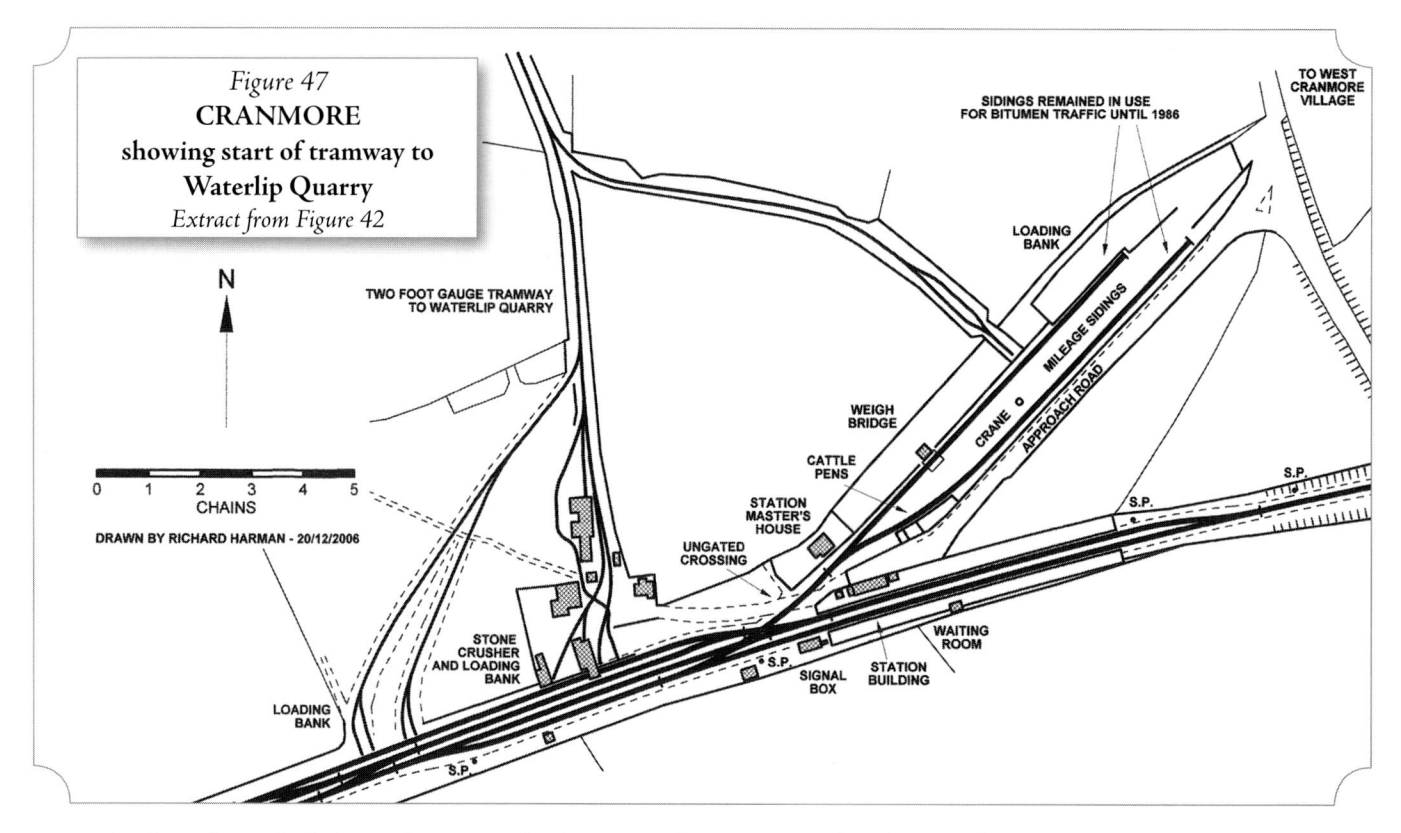

Figure 47
CRANMORE
showing start of tramway to Waterlip Quarry
Extract from Figure 42

seems that Beauchamp had obtained a partner by the name of John Hamblin. Beauchamp died in 1894 and the quarry passed to the Mendip Granite and Asphalte Company Ltd (Hamblin and Frederick Spencer). Later Mendip Mountain Quarries Ltd took a lease on the quarry, probably on 2nd July 1923. Not long after that, possibly in 1924, the quarry was taken over by Roads Reconstruction Ltd.

From Cranmore station the tramway turned northwards and passed under the A361 by means of a tunnel with very limited clearance. From there it ran along the eastern side of the minor road from West Cranmore to Waterlip. Loaded wagons were worked down from the quarry by gravity and were returned by horse power. A locomotive would be employed at the quarry to start the loaded wagons rolling. Once started they would be accompanied by a brakesman whose sole means of control was an iron bar that he could wedge between the spokes of the wagon wheels in order to effect a stop. Health and safety was not a consideration in those days!

From Waterlip an extension of the tramway was built in about 1907. It ran alongside the road to Longcross where the line split. The branch continued over the ridge to the basalt quarry at Moon's Hill that opened in 1897 and is still open although not rail connected. The main line turned to the east and, following the contours around the hill, crossed the Old Frome Road again at Waltyning Plantation before descending down a half mile incline to the andesite quarry at Downhead. The incline itself was worked by a stationary engine but locomotives were used on the line between the top of the incline and Waterlip.

At least four locomotives are known to have worked this line. They were named *Gamecock*, *Tattoo*, *Keighley* and *Horwich*. The first of these is known to have been a Peckett, No.1030 which was built in 1904, delivered new to the quarry and scrapped in 1927.

Assuming that the date of 1907 is correct for the construction of the Downhead line, it is not clear to what use *Gamecock* was put during the intervening period. A photograph of the locomotive with its driver, Bob Baker, and fireman, Joe Bryant, shows it to have been an 0-4-0 saddle tank with outside cylinders. The following extract from the *Industrial Railway Record* No.82 gives us some more insight into the history of the locomotive:

'Mendip Granite and Asphalte's managing director, John Hamblin, wrote to Peckett's on 31st December 1903 seeking a quote for a locomotive to haul 15 tons (18 tons gross) over a maximum gradient of 1 in 25-30. Peckett's quoted £750, with an extra £15 for a steam brake.'

The latter would appear to be an essential item in view of the specified gradient! The extract continues:

'Another director, Frederick Spencer, already had experience of narrow gauge locomotives, being a director of the Oakhill Brewery Co. Ltd., which company had just acquired a locomotive (Bagnall 1701 of 1903) for its 2ft 6in gauge brewery tramway a few miles away. Perhaps Spencer did not like Peckett's original quotation, for he wrote on 2nd February 1904 specifically seeking a quote for a 'Gamecock' class locomotive. The price dropped dramatically, to £545 with a seven week delivery time. The duties of the locomotive were given as hauling stone at Cranmore. The firm's notepaper of this period does not mention Downhead Quarries, which were being opened up at the time. An order must have been placed quickly, for by 23rd April 1904 Spencer was ready to take delivery within a fortnight. Then negotiations degenerated into an argument as to the method of delivery and 'Gamecock' does

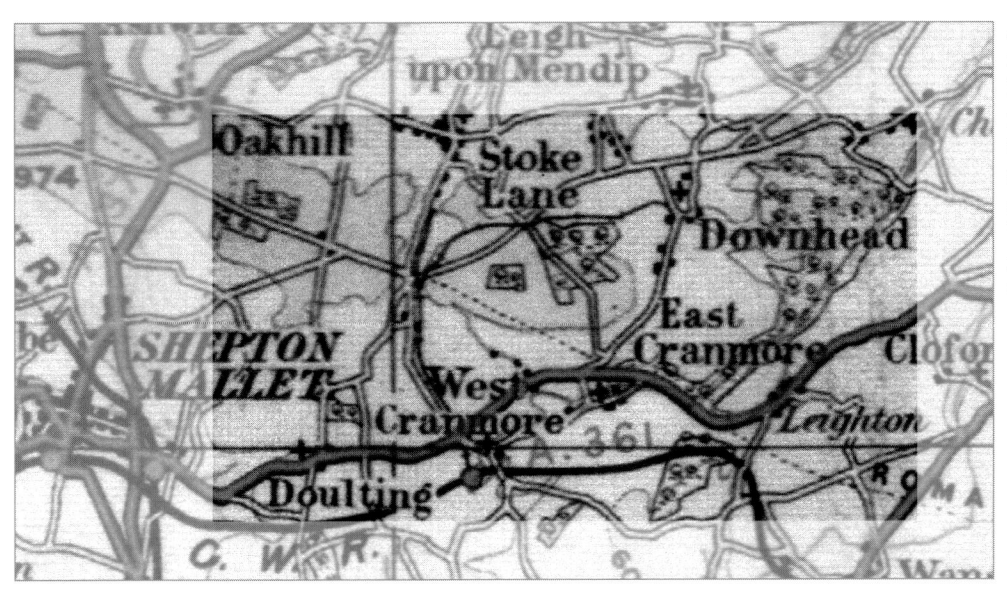

Figure 48 - An extract from the Ordnance Survey Map, Quarter Inch Series, Sheet 11, of 1919 (with minor corrections to 1928) showing the extent of the tramways from Cranmore station to the quarries at Moon's Hill and Downhead.
The tramways can just be traced northwards from the station before turning east to reach Downhead.
Crown Copyright

not seem to have arrived [by road] until June. One immediate complaint was that the locomotive bore the wrong name; Hamblin had wanted 'Cranmore', not 'Gamecock', but thought that this could easily be altered. Presumably it never was, for photographs of the locomotive show the original name, which is also mentioned in subsequent correspondence with Peckett's. In December 1907 Hamblin asked for a quote for a second locomotive, similar to 'Gamecock' but with a larger firebox to assist in maintaining steam. Peckett's seem to have quoted £479 but, if the matter went any further, it was with another builder.'

There is also a photograph of *Horwich* in existence which shows it was possibly an 0-4-0 well tank, also with outside cylinders, which suggests it was Andrew Barclay, Sons & Co. Ltd No.1855 built in 1931. What does lend some uncertainty to this supposition is that the records show that *Horwich* was not transferred to Waterlip until 1949 and it would appear that the photograph was taken some years before this. Little is known of the other two locomotives but the records do show that Kerr, Stuart 0-4-2 saddle tanks, Nos.856 of 1904 and 3065 of 1918, as well as Avonside 0-4-0 side tanks Nos.2072 and 2073 of 1933, worked in the quarry. They were all disposed of in 1951, the Avonside locomotives going to India and the earlier Kerr, Stuart being scrapped. The fate of the other Kerr, Stuart is unknown. As well as steam there were also a number of diesel and petrol driven locomotives working in the quarry.

Andesite was used as a 'binding agent' in road construction but the widespread adoption of tarmacadam for road surfaces made it redundant. As a consequence, Downhead Quarry closed in about 1925 and the tramway was abandoned back to Waterlip along with the branch to Moon's Hill. Unfortunately the short life of these lines meant that they never appeared on any large-scale maps so there is some uncertainty as to the exact route they took. The writer has seen part of an old tithe map which shows a section of the line near to Downhead and it is also depicted on the Ordnance Survey Quarter Inch map of 1919. Some earthworks are also visible, in particular in the Long Cross and Waltyning Plantation areas.

In about 1926 the tramway was converted to a standard gauge locomotive line, mostly on a new alignment. Following a private siding agreement between the railway and Roads Reconstruction Limited, facilities for handling quarry traffic at Cranmore were expanded. The agreement was dated 19th January 1927 and the new sidings were completed on 16th June. On the branch itself, a new tunnel under the A361 was constructed some yards to the east of the old one and the line was carried northwards on an embankment. The new alignment was set back from the road to Waterlip running behind the dwellings just north of the A361 crossroads. There is a photograph in existence that shows dual gauge track running through the steep cutting near the A361 tunnel. The two-foot gauge rails can be seen running in the centre of the standard gauge track. It is not known how long the branch operated with the two gauges but one can only assume that it was an interim situation that only existed until the standard gauge was fully commissioned.

As a standard gauge line it was worked by a variety of motive power that included a Sentinel steam locomotive (No.6090 of 1925) and allegedly a Barclay 0-4-0ST named *Medway* (No.969 of 1903). The latter is known to have worked at quarries in the area but it is not known for definite that it worked at Waterlip. An 0-4-0 petrol engined locomotive, Manning Wardle No.1954 of 1918, worked on the branch for a short time but it went to Vobster in about 1927. A Fowler 0-6-0 diesel, No.19645 of 1932 also worked on the branch after being transferred from Vobster Quarries. Traffic on the branch ceased on closure of the quarry in 1946. The Fowler diesel went to ICI, Winnington Works in January 1946 via Abelson's of Sheldon, Birmingham. The remains of the quarry branch have now largely disappeared. The embankment that carried the branch north of the A361 was still plainly visible in the 1960s but has now fallen victim to the needs of modern agriculture and the steep sided cutting near the village of West Cranmore is now filled in, although its course is still visible in places.

A third two-foot gauge tramway served the original Merehead quarry but all trace of this seems to have disappeared under the modern railway yard.

Plate 197 - Unidentified GWR railcar and makeshift trailer approaching Cranmore c.1949/50. This view is the only one of Cranmore to show, albeit distantly, the shed built on the bank for loading stone from the Waterlip Quarry tramroad.
J Moss; Roger Carpenter collection

CRANMORE
and
WATERLIP QUARRY

(Above) Plate 198 - Narrow gauge locomotives at Waterlip Quarry. The engine in the foreground is possibly *Horwich*, Andrew Barclay No.1855 built in 1931.

From the Industrial Locomotive Society, Frank Jones collection

Plate 199 - Avonside 0-4-0 side tank No.2072 of 1933.

Chapter Nine

DULCOTE AND MEREHEAD: THE FOSTER YEOMAN QUARRIES

The early development of Dulcote Quarry, and its later development by the Foster Yeoman Company into the present day enterprise at Merehead, are of great importance to any history of the Yatton to Witham line. Consequently the writer has decided to dedicate a chapter to this subject.

The suitability of the limestone at Dulcote Hill for track ballast was discovered when the railway was being constructed and the Great Western Railway first took out a fourteen year lease on the site on 25th March 1873. At that time, whilst the Great Western was running the train services, the line itself was still the property of the East Somerset Railway Company since the Great Western take-over of the East Somerset did not take place until June 1874. The Great Western's original lease on the quarry expired in 1887 at which time it was extended for a further fourteen years.

The Great Western constructed a siding and contacted the Board of Trade in November 1873 to request an inspection. Colonel Rich R.E., reporting for the Board of Trade, expressed some concern about the arrangements in view of the steep gradient on the running line. The following extract from his report highlights these concerns:

'The siding has been constructed for the purpose of loading and carrying away stone. A home signal, locked with points, has been erected, and is controlled by a catch siding which is also interlocked with the home signal, but a second home signal and distant signals in each direction are required.

The position of the siding is very dangerous, as moving to the steep incline and vehicles that are left standing on the main line while the wagons are being got out of the siding will be liable to break away, and if so they will probably attain a speed of 30-40 miles per hour by the time they reach Wells Station and the public level crossing beyond it. I submit that in order to guard against this danger a catch should be taken off the junction between the siding and the passenger line, and that this catch should be long enough to hold such portion of a train and the brake van that may be left whilst wagons are got out of, or put into, the siding. The catch siding may be laid close to the passenger line but the points which lead to it should not be on the passenger line.

Any train when stopped at the new siding should be placed into the catch siding before the engine is detached from it.

The company have already obtained the Board's sanction to use the siding at Dulcot [sic] Hill, but I submit that it is very desirable that the catch siding and additional signals should be put up before any further use is made of the siding. The completion of these works should be reported so that they may be inspected if thought desirable.'

The report was sent to the Great Western Railway in December 1873 along with a reminder that a layout drawing had been requested but not yet received. It seems that the railway company eventually sent in the drawing and that it contained a proposed layout somewhat different from that suggested by Colonel Rich in his December 1873 report. Unfortunately this drawing has not survived. Colonel Rich replied on the matter of the railway company's proposal on 28th February 1874 as follows:

'I do not see any objection to the arrangements proposed by

Plate 200 - Foster Yeoman 5-plank open wagon built for the company by the Gloucester Railway Carriage and Wagon Company in September 1923. As the text will reveal, Foster Yeoman Ltd was formed in 1923 and obviously lost no time before expanding the business. There is an interesting comparison between the height of this vehicle, a 5-plank wagon, and that of the 4-plank wagon in *Plate 202*.

GRC&W Co.
Gloucestershire Archives

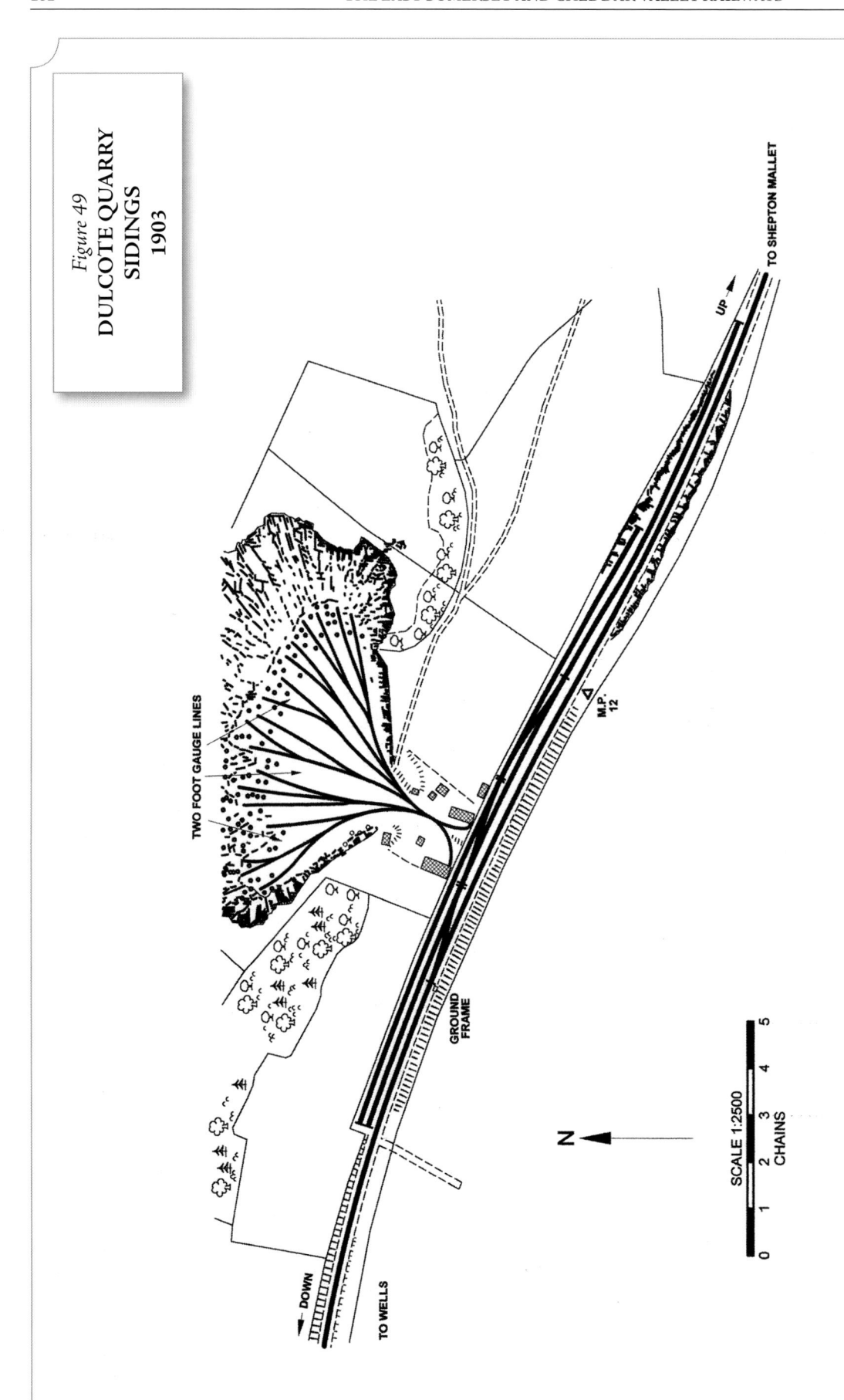

Figure 49
DULCOTE QUARRY SIDINGS
1903

the enclosed sketch so long as it is intended to place the train in the siding and not leave it on the main line without an engine attached to it. This is to say the engine must not be detached from the train while the train, or any part of it, is on the main line.'

The Board of Trade was happy that the siding could be brought into use when ready and it was agreed that Colonel Rich would inspect the layout when next in the area.

Colonel Rich returned to Dulcote Quarry in April 1875 to inspect the alterations. He commented on the fact that the down distant signal could not be seen by the signalman and asked for a repeater to be provided. The Great Western felt that this was not a valid request since the siding would only be worked with the shunting engine driver having possession of the train staff and thus all signals here could be dispensed with. The Board of Trade then pointed out that shunting at intermediate sidings was often carried out by men or horses without the use of a locomotive and so another train could legitimately occupy the section whilst such shunting was in progress. It was also necessary to prove that the signal had actually returned to danger when the lever was returned to the normal position. (Note that at that time the restrictive aspect of a distant signal was referred to as 'Danger' rather than 'Caution'). Unfortunately, any documents indicating the eventual outcome have not survived. In any case, all signals at Dulcote were removed in 1896 when it was abolished as a block post in conjunction with the introduction of the electric train staff.

James Grierson's letter of 31st May 1875 in which he rejects the Board of Trade's request for a repeater for the down distant signal is rather interesting in that it contradicts other documents in relation to the working of the line between Wells and Witham. Grierson plainly states that the line was worked in two sections, Witham to Shepton Mallet and Shepton Mallet to Wells. The writer can only assume that Grierson was somehow misled in making this statement as the undertaking made by the East Somerset Railway on 4th November 1858 to work the line between Wells and Witham on the one engine in steam principle was still in force. This remained the case until a further undertaking was issued by the Great Western Railway on 19th August 1880 to work the line on the staff and ticket system as a consequence of Cranmore being made a crossing place. As far as is known Shepton Mallet did not become a block post until the passing loop and second platform were added in 1895.

At one time the quarry was not worked directly by the railway but by a contractor. The foreman's name was William Bailey (inevitably known as 'Bill') with the consequence that the quarry became known as Bailey's Quarry. It is not known exactly when this was but it was definitely before World War I and possibly before 1900. The quarry provided work for up to seventy men and much of the work was carried out by hand although the rock crusher and a rock drill were both steam driven. The rock drill was used to drill holes in the rock face to take explosive charges for blasting operations. There was a narrow gauge system within the quarry itself. The likely gauge was two feet and it was probably worked by manpower alone.

Foster Yeoman, the son of a ship owner from West Hartlepool, arrived in the area in the early 1920s and started a business whose name has been synonymous with the quarrying industry and the haulage of stone by rail ever since. After returning from military service at the end of World War I he was concerned about the widespread problem of unemployment amongst ex-servicemen like himself and was determined to do something about it. After some involvement in the iron and steel industries he decided to move into quarrying. He acquired the lease for Dulcote Hill from the local land-owner, Charles Clement Tudway, in February 1923 and within a short time he had a workforce of at least one hundred, so realising his objective of doing something towards reducing unemployment.

Foster Yeoman Limited was formed in April 1923 and an agreement was reached with the Great Western Railway in 1924 for the transportation of quarry products by rail. Quarrying operations had been started at a second site on Dulcote Hill some years before, probably in the 1890s, and it was this site that Foster Yeoman had plans to develop further. This quarry was known as 'Dulcote New Quarry' in order to distinguish it from the original 1873 quarry. It was also known locally as 'Ball's Quarry'. It was situated to the west of, but was separate from, the original quarry. When the lease for the original quarry was due for renewal in 1901, Charles Clement Tudway had asked the Great Western Railway for an extension to the existing quarry sidings in order to serve the new quarry but the railway was not willing to oblige. Foster Yeoman met with more success as a new junction and sidings were provided to the west of the existing sidings. The two existing quarry sidings had to be slewed away from the running line at their western end in order to accommodate the new junction. The cost of this work was estimated to have been £4,075 which was funded by the quarry company who also carried out the necessary earthworks and laid the sidings within its own boundary. The quarry company also provided a rock crushing plant and a weighbridge. The Great Western agreed to pay a 5% rebate based upon the first five years' receipts in order to encourage traffic onto the railway. The agreement also allowed for the early termination of the rebate if the £4,075 cost was repaid within five years. Maintenance of the junction and sidings was provided by the Great Western at the expense of the quarry company and a rental of five pounds per annum was paid for the actual junction itself.

The new quarrying eventually led to the removal of much of the south-western side of Dulcote Hill. A fleet of 150 private owner wagons was purchased, starting in 1923, from the Gloucester Railway Carriage and Wagon Company at a cost of £14,445. The wagons were of two slightly different designs, some being five plank and some four plank. Both designs had a capacity of twelve tons and were painted black with white lettering. They also carried the company name, 'Foster Yeoman Ltd'. The quarry company was responsible for marshalling loaded wagons before they were handed over to the Great Western Railway. A locomotive was hired from the railway at a cost of one pound per hour in order to carry out shunting duties in the quarry sidings. Due to growth in traffic the loading sidings were extended by 325 yards in 1927. Output from the quarry in the first year was 24,018 tons. This had risen to 75,457 for the year ending in 1927, whilst during the 1930s the output

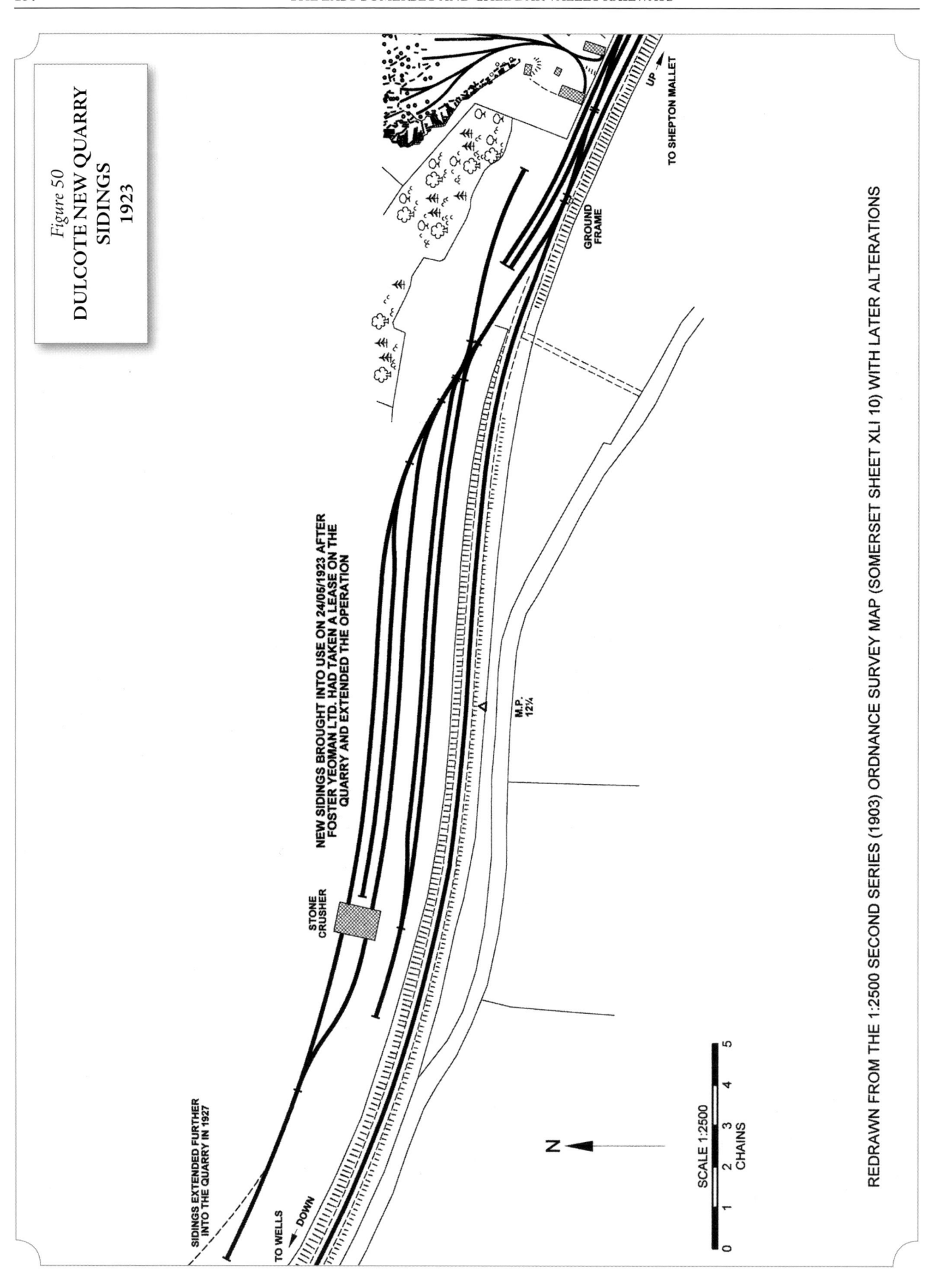

Figure 50
DULCOTE NEW QUARRY SIDINGS
1923

TO SHEPTON MALLET

GROUND FRAME

NEW SIDINGS BROUGHT INTO USE ON 24/05/1923 AFTER FOSTER YEOMAN LTD. HAD TAKEN A LEASE ON THE QUARRY AND EXTENDED THE OPERATION

M.P. 12¼

STONE CRUSHER

SIDINGS EXTENDED FURTHER INTO THE QUARRY IN 1927

TO WELLS

DOWN

UP

N

SCALE 1:2500
0 1 2 3 4 5 CHAINS

REDRAWN FROM THE 1:2500 SECOND SERIES (1903) ORDNANCE SURVEY MAP (SOMERSET SHEET XLI 10) WITH LATER ALTERATIONS

Plate 201 - This is possibly a commercial photograph taken by Frank Colville, Shepton Mallet, maybe specially commissioned to illustrate the work in progress at Dulcote Quarry. This work may have been carried out in conjunction with the Foster Yeoman extensions to the quarrying at Dulcote and the associated railway alterations in 1923. The roof and walls of the building containing the crushing machine have been removed but the front upright is still in place. The railway crane is removing the top spindle of the stone crushing machine and it may be that the rest of it is in the wagon nearest the crane.
GWR 1076 Class 0-6-0PT No.1626 waits while the work is undertaken. Pannier tanks replaced the locomotive's saddle tank in 1912, whilst the latest date of the photograph is the summer of 1928 since No.1626 was withdrawn in August of that year. The engine was allocated to Yeovil in 1922 and was withdrawn from St. Philip's Marsh. The goods wagons are no help with dating since they are both in the 811xx series, the nearer one being 81109. These are to Diagram O9, built between 1906 and 1911.
Neil Parkhouse collection

varied between 30,000 and 78,000 tons annually. Over the years up to the start of the Second World War rail-borne traffic from the quarry remained steady, but following the death of Foster Yeoman in 1949 the shift to road haulage began and rail traffic had ceased altogether by 1955. Output from the quarry in 1949 was 32,449 tons which was considerably down on the good years of the 1930s.

Like the Great Western quarry, Dulcote New Quarry also had an internal narrow gauge network. This was constructed to a gauge of two feet and it remained in use until the mid-1950s. It was worked latterly, at least, by a four-wheeled Ruston and Hornsby diesel locomotive which was scrapped in 1962. Unfortunately, there are no known maps that show the extent of the narrow gauge network in this quarry but at least the network in the Great Western quarry is shown on the 1:2500 Second Series Ordnance Survey map of 1903 (Somerset Sheet XLI 10).

In the meantime the original quarry and sidings continued to be worked by the Great Western Railway for ballast but working had ceased by the mid-1930s. The sidings remained but became overgrown and had been lifted by 1938.

The Foster Yeoman sidings remained in situ after 1955 but saw no further use until 1969. Quarry traffic from Cheddar had ceased on 28th March of that year. The line closed altogether west of Dulcote on 19th April 1969 and the track was lifted soon afterwards. At that time Foster Yeoman was developing a new quarry at Merehead near East Cranmore. A number of stone trains were worked out of Dulcote in the autumn of 1969 in order to ease the pressures on Merehead and develop rail traffic flows pending the completion of a new line from a junction with the East Somerset branch between Cranmore and Wanstrow into the new quarry. The resurrection of the sidings at Dulcote was only ever seen as a temporary measure. The Dulcote trains were formed of 13-ton 'Hyfit' vacuum braked wagons and were hauled by Western Region Hymek diesel hydraulic locomotives. The maximum permitted load was 13 wagons out of Dulcote largely because of the gradients. The trains were worked to Westbury (Wiltshire) where they were made up into 39 wagon trains with a payload of just over 500 tons prior to onward dispatch to West Drayton or Taplow.

Following the brief resurrection Dulcote Quarry sidings were finally abandoned. The ground frame was taken out of use in November 1969 but the track remained in situ until the mid-1970s. It was realised that the severe gradients between Shepton Mallet and Dulcote were incompatible with the railway economics of the late 20th century. Foster Yeoman's new Torr Works quarry at Merehead was now open and being developed into a large scale operation, the like of which had not previously been seen in the North Somerset quarrying industry. The new line constructed from the former East Somerset branch into the quarry has already been mentioned. It was three quarters of a mile in length and was brought into use on 1st June 1970. The junction with the East Somerset branch was facing from the Cranmore direction which meant that trains running to and from the quarry had to reverse. As traffic developed a chord facing towards Witham was added to form a triangle of lines. The running line between Merehead and Witham was also upgraded to permit heavier and more powerful locomotives. Additional sidings, a shed and maintenance facilities were added at Merehead. Now stone trains of 3,000 tons or more work out of Merehead hauled by the Class 59 locomotives built by General Motors. They were the first class of 'private owner' locomotives to operate on what was the then nationalised railway network and further examples were built for a couple of other private heavy freight operators. The Class 59 has created such an impression that an almost identical locomotive known as the Class 66 was introduced by EWS in 1998. The class now numbers nearly four hundred locomotives and is in use by several UK rail freight operators. They will be the mainstay of freight train motive power for many years to come. There are also a number working on several other European railways.

In 2006 Foster Yeoman was acquired by Aggregate Industries Ltd.

Plate 202 - A later wagon built for the Foster Yeoman concern by the Gloucester Railway Carriage and Wagon Company, this time January 1925. It was one of a batch of 50 wagons numbered 101-150. Comparison with *Plate 200* reveals that the builder's placard records the height of the sides of this 4-plank vehicle to be but an inch less than the 5-plank wagon No.36.
GRC&W Co. Gloucestershire Archives
(Right) Plate 203 - An introduction to 'Operation'; notice of a 7.50pm excursion to be run on 17th and 18th May 1875 from Wells to Yatton. Note that the stock for this excursion will return empty to Wells at 9pm.
Neil Parkhouse collection

(184a.)

BRISTOL & EXETER RAILWAY.

NOTICE OF SPECIAL TRAIN.

On Tuesday 17 & 18 of May 1875 a Special _Excursion_ Train will run as under, and _____

DOWN LINE.			UP LINE.	
Leaving.		Remarks.	Leaving.	Remarks.
	H. M.			H. M.
Yatton	9 . 0 pm	Empty Carr's	Wells	7 . 50 pm
Wells	9 . 50		Wookey	7 . 55
			Lodge Hill	8 . 4
			Draycott	8 . 11
			Cheddar	8 . 18
			Axbridge	8 . 25
			Winscombe	8 . 32
			Sandford	8 . 37
			Congresbury	8 . 45
			Yatton	8 . 50

This train must pull up at all intermediate Stations

Tickets on the _____ journey must be examined at _____ and on the _____ journey collected at _Guard Jeffs_ _____ to take charge of this Train.

The attention of persons in charge of Stations, Guards, Signalmen, and others, is particularly directed to the safe and regular working of the Special Trains, as set forth in this Notice, and to the necessity for keeping other Trains clear of them. As Goods and Mineral Trains are passing over the Line at or about the same hours at which the Special Trains will be running, care must be taken to shunt those Trains in sufficient time to leave the Line clear for the Special Train to pass; and the person in charge of Stations are requested to acquaint all persons concerned at their respective Stations that these Trains may be expected, and at what time. No excuse of want of knowledge of these special arrangements can be admitted for any failure, or neglect of duty. No Excursion, or Special Passenger Train must be permitted to run more than twenty miles without stopping, unless the Cord Apparatus is fixed on the Train, and in good working order. The Guard in charge of each Train will be held responsible for seeing that this instruction is carried out. There must be Two Guards for a Passenger Train not exceeding ten Carriages and an additional Guard for every additional five Carriages. The last Vehicle must invariably have a break with a Guard in charge.

J. C. WALL,

Per _J. Wall_

General Manager.

Please acknowledge receipt per First Train.

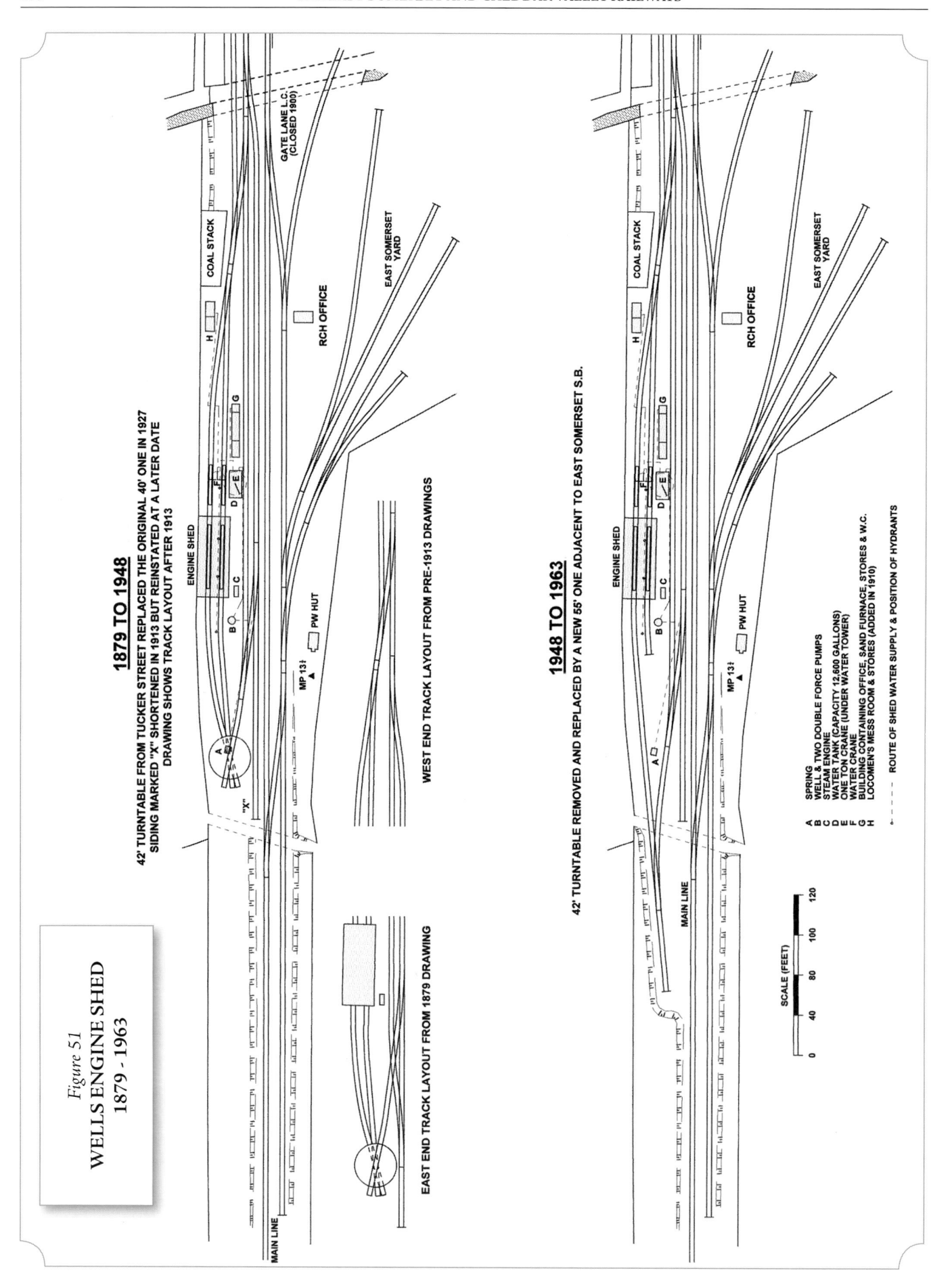

Figure 51
WELLS ENGINE SHED
1879 - 1963

Chapter Ten

OPERATION OF THE LINE

WELLS ENGINE SHED

Following the completion of the Yatton to Witham line as a through route, the only remaining locomotive shed was at Wells. It was a two-road shed situated at the Shepton Mallet end of East Somerset yard on the down side of the running line and opened in 1879. It was built to replace the former East Somerset shed that had existed on more or less the same site which had been opened in 1862 when the line was extended from Shepton Mallet. The new shed was 75ft in length and was complete with a turntable, shed offices, a water tower and coaling stage. The previous shed was 50ft by 20ft and was only a single road affair. The original turntable at the far side of the engine shed was 40ft in diameter and it is thought that this was retained although site plans suggest that it may have been moved some yards in the Shepton Mallet direction in order to accommodate the enlarged facilities of the new shed. The construction of a new, larger shed may be seen as an indication that, although the two branches were now connected, they still retained much of their separate identities with many trains still starting from or terminating at Wells. The shed closed after 7th September 1963, when the passenger service ceased, and not at the end of 1963 as some sources have suggested. The three firemen and two drivers stayed on for one week following the closure and driver Harry Viles and fireman David Sheppard stayed on for another week after that. Their main task was to load sand into a wagon and various other items into a van. The last item loaded was the shed's Great Western Railway scales on Sunday, 22nd September. The two roads through the shed were removed in 1964 but a short spur from the turntable towards the shed was retained until 1965. The shed itself was demolished in April 1965 but most of the roof had already been removed in 1960. The turntable was taken out of use on 12th October 1964. Prior to that it was used by the Westbury pannier tank that worked the daily goods from that end of the line.

In July 1926 there were seven sets of footplate men plus four cleaners and two shedmen, one of whom worked days and the other nights. By 1941 this had been reduced to six sets of footplate men and two cleaners but there were still two shedmen. In 1963 there were three sets of footplate crew and one night shedman. Driver Griffiths went to Old Oak Common in July 1963 and the shedman left as well. After that, for the last couple of months before the shed closed, two of the firemen took turns at doing the shedman's work and the remaining two drivers covered all of the driving.

For much of its existence Wells was a sub-shed of Bristol Bath Road, which was the principal passenger locomotive shed of the Great Western and later of British Railways Western Region for the Bristol area (shed code 82A). There were two other sheds in Bristol. St. Philip's Marsh was the Great Western's goods locomotive shed and Barrow Road was the LMS (formerly Midland Railway) shed. Bath Road was closed to steam in September 1960 and was redeveloped as a diesel depot. Bath Road's remaining steam locomotives were reallocated to the

Plate 204 - Undated photograph of Collett 2251 Class 0-6-0 No.2213 on shed at Wells East Somerset.
Rex Conway collection

Plate 205 - Collett 2251 Class 0-6-0s Nos.3218 and 2251 on shed on 4th September 1963 during the last week of passenger services. Unlike its sister, No.3218 had been spruced up for the occasion since Driver Harry Viles had asked for it to be Wells' overnight engine that week. *Ivo Peters*

other two sheds in that month and Wells became a sub-shed of Barrow Road in January 1961 (shed code 82E).

The coal stage at Wells was situated under the water tank at the western end of the shed and to the north of the shed roads. A crane was used to load coal directly from a wagon into the locomotive tender or bunker. Some of the coal wagons did not have doors which meant that the shedmen had to dig down through the coal before they got to a level base to shovel from. The bunkers of the Ivatt 2-6-2 tanks and the British Railways Standard Class 3s were too high for the crane, so coal had to be tipped onto the stage and shovelled into the bunker by hand. This was probably not helped by the fact that both classes had cutouts on either side of the bunker in order to give the crew a better view of the road when running backwards. This resulted in the opening at the top of the bunker being much narrower than that on Great Western tank engines. A single storey brick building with a pitched roof adjacent to the coal stage contained the shed office, toilet, sand store, sand drying furnace and the fire lighter store. Another building on the opposite side of the shed roads contained the shed staff cabin and the oil store.

Although the former Bristol & Exeter shed probably closed as long ago as 1876, the turntable at Wells station remained until the late 1920s. It seems likely that it had been out of use for many years as locomotives were taken from there to the turntable at East Somerset for turning. Apparently this prompted some concern from the road authorities and more than likely some frustration from road users in response to the closing of the level crossing gates for road traffic whilst this operation was taking place. A Great Western Locomotive Committee minute dated 31st March 1927 authorised the replacement of the turntable near the locomotive shed with the one at Wells station at a cost of £480. It seems that work on the railway was short at this time and apparently the quicker a driver booked off duty then the better chance he had of work next day. One driver raced to get onto the old turntable at the shed and it was damaged as a consequence, hence the need for the replacement. What has not been told is whether the driver in question did get any work the next day! Also during 1927, plans were drawn up to install a 55 foot turntable at East Somerset in the same place as the existing one but nothing came of it.

In the event, a new turntable was erected adjacent to East Somerset signal box in 1948. Manor Class locomotive No.7811 *Dunley Manor* was brought down from Westbury on 30th September 1948 in order to test it, although pannier tank No.5784 was actually the first locomotive to be turned two days previously. The new turntable was 55 feet in diameter and so a Manor Class with a wheelbase of a couple of inches over 52 feet would have been a fairly tight fit. Larger locomotives have visited Wells. In 1949 West Country Class No.34092 *Wells* (to give it its original name, it was eventually renamed *City of Wells*) ran into the Somerset & Dorset station for an official naming ceremony. The Bulleid Light Pacific's wheelbase of 57 feet 6 inches meant that it could not have been turned there. Photographs taken at the time show No.34092 in the loading dock at Priory Road and indicate that it ran tender first into Wells. (Please see *Railways into Wells* by Paul Fry for more detailed account of the event). There is an unconfirmed report that a Stanier Class 5 4-6-0 ran into Wells before No.34092 in order to test the track. Another larger locomotive that did use the new turntable was ex-LMS 2P No.40697. It worked tender first from Glastonbury in order to work a special to Bournemouth the following day. It was turned and spent the night on the shed at East Somerset.

The old turntable near the shed was only 42 feet in diameter and so was not able to turn anything larger than a 2251 0-6-0. It may be that it was this restriction that prompted its replacement. As things turned out there was never a day-to-day need to turn anything very much larger. At 44 feet 1 inch the ex-LMS Class 2MT 2-6-0s probably had the longest wheelbase of any class to be turned regularly on the new turntable.

The water tower had a capacity of 13,650 gallons and was replenished by a pump that was operated by steam drawn from the steam heating connection on the shed's resident 4500 Class tank locomotive. In 1926 an average of 90,875 gallons was pumped each month. From the 1940s and into British Railways days the shed's resident goods locomotive carried out the pumping since the resident passenger locomotive would have been out all day and so probably never carried out any pumping except in an emergency. After the rationalisation of services in 1958 with the consequent reduction of locomotive diagrams, pumping was carried out by the locomotive that had worked the first Bristol to Wells goods that day. This locomotive was diagrammed to stay at Wells until the following day prior to working the first up goods back to Bristol and presumably the main reason for this was to provide a locomotive for pumping. Full details are given later in this chapter. The steam engine that drove the pump was located in a wooden hut alongside the engine shed, the locomotive supplying the steam would stand inside the shed whilst the operation was taking place.

As a result of the severe weather experienced during January 1963 the water feed pipe up to the tank burst and consequently pumping ceased and was never resumed. The pipe had been boxed in with wood and lagged with straw but this was not enough to withstand the unusually severe conditions experienced during that winter. Interestingly, the water for the tower at Wells station was also originally pumped by steam but was later modified to use an electric pump. A shedman used to look after the pump when it was steam operated. Alfred Augustus West was employed on this task but was killed in an accident at East Somerset in 1916. The tower fed water columns in the six foot way at either end of the station. The Somerset & Dorset could boast an 'environmentally friendly' means for raising water, its pump being powered by a water wheel in the nearby St. Andrew's stream. During World War II a 4-inch main was laid to connect the water tank at the Somerset & Dorset locomotive shed with that at Wells station.

LOCOMOTIVE CLASSES AND ROLLING STOCK NOTES

During the broad gauge era until 1875 the East Somerset and Cheddar Valley sections were unconnected. The two sections were worked by various broad gauge classes during this period. By the time that the connecting link was opened for passenger traffic in 1878 both sections had been converted to the standard gauge and were now owned and operated by the Great Western. From this time standard Great Western classes began to appear on the line. The 2301 Class 'Dean Goods' 0-6-0, 0-6-0T classes

Plate 206 - Dean Goods 2301 Class 0-6-0 No.2340 on the 1948 turntable at East Somerset. The chimney of the nearby milk factory displays an advertisement for Diploma cheese. *R Told courtesy Wells Railway Fraternity*

Plate 207 - An early 20th century postcard of Congresbury taken from the road overbridge at the Yatton end of the station. The saddle tank is in the up platform, bound for Yatton and perhaps beyond, whilst the down platform line is harbouring what appears to be a 388 Class 'Standard Goods' engine. One covered vehicle appears to be behind the tender but any vehicles beyond that are uncertain. *Author's collection*

of the saddle or pannier tank variety and the 2-4-0T 'Metro' tanks were typical of the motive power used. In the early years of the twentieth century the GWR developed the 2-6-2T for use on branch lines and the 4500 Class soon became a familiar sight on the branch. This class with its 4ft 7½in driving wheel diameter was ideally suited for use on steeply graded branch lines. The 4575 variant of the class that had sloping top tanks, and consequently a greater water capacity of 1,300 gallons as opposed to 1,000 gallons of the 4500, were also to be seen working on the branch. Further building necessitated the number series being extended into the 55xx range.

Because of the length of the Yatton to Witham line, tender locomotives were frequently to be seen on it, particularly on goods trains. Former GWR 'Bulldog' 3300 Class 4-4-0s frequently worked the first passenger train from Witham to Yatton until the 1950s. Until the mid-1940s it was usually a Bulldog turn. Westbury allocated Bulldogs Nos.3363 and 3364 (named *Alfred Baldwin* and *Frank Bibby* respectively) were seen on this working which had originated at Trowbridge and continued through to Bristol. In later years this train was worked by a Westbury based 4300 Class 2-6-0. Another Bulldog, No.3455 *Starling* was seen working the 7.55am Wells-Bristol West Depot goods on 24th June 1944.

During the 1930s, goods traffic on the line was largely dealt with by the 2301 Class 0-6-0s supplemented by former Midland & South Western Junction Railway 10xx 0-6-0 tender locomotives. This class was originally constructed by Beyer Peacock but were 'Swindonised' by the Great Western after the Grouping and became similar in appearance to the Collett 2251 Class. Three of the class, Nos.1006, 1011 and 1013 were transferred to the Bristol area in 1936 but were withdrawn not long afterwards. Over a period of time the more modern 2251 Class 0-6-0s that were known as the 'Collett Goods' took over these workings. The ubiquitous pannier tanks were also used on goods trains and by nationalisation the Deans were a rarity on the line. From the 1930s there were two locomotives stabled overnight at Wells, one passenger and one goods, but because of the way in which the diagrams worked, the goods locomotive was different from day to day.

The Wells overnight passenger locomotive was generally changed weekly. In later days during the winter timetable it was normally changed on Saturdays at Barrow Road after working the 1.30pm Saturdays only (SO) Witham-Bristol passenger train. If the locomotive was a good one, Wells shed might keep it for up to four weeks. Occasionally it would be changed during the week with the locomotive that had worked the second Bristol goods if they had been given a 'rough one' on the previous Saturday. During the summer timetable the Wells locomotive worked the 8.15pm (SO) Wells-Yatton that crossed the 8.20pm (SO) Yatton-Wells at Axbridge (times are for summer 1963). Here the crews changed footplates and the Wells men would return with a different locomotive that became the Wells passenger locomotive for the following week.

The 4500 Class 2-6-2Ts dominated the Wells passenger locomotive diagrams until the 1950s when pannier tanks started to appear. Also in the 1950s a few non-Great Western locomotive classes began to make their presence felt, appearing alongside the familiar 45/55xx 2-6-2Ts, the 2251 0-6-0s and

Plate 208 - Collett 0-4-2T No.5813 in the up platform at Wells awaiting departure to Yatton with a passenger train in 1949. This was a Saturdays only working as this locomotive would be diagrammed to work the Wrington goods Monday to Friday. The B-set was a common site working the branch trains.

(Below) Plate 209 - GWR 4500 Class 2-6-2T No.5512 at Cheddar in May 1948, too soon after nationalisation to have had the GWR markings painted out. The GWR developed the 2-6-2T genre for branch line working and, in latter days, ex-LMS and BR 2-6-2Ts worked the branch as well as ex-GWR examples.

BRANCH LOCOMOTIVE TYPES

Photographs by J Moss

from Roger Carpenter collection

the 0-6-0PTs. These included the LMS designed Ivatt 2MTs in both the 2-6-0 tender and 2-6-2 tank varieties as well as the BR Standard Class 3MT 2-6-2Ts. All of these classes put in regular appearances right up until closure, but withdrawal of the ex-Great Western 2-6-2Ts meant that the former LMS and BR Standard classes were seen in increasing numbers. The BR Standard Class 3MT locomotives appeared in 1958 when a number were allocated to Bath Road. They had previously worked in the South Wales valleys but had been displaced by the dieselisation of those services. After the closure of Bristol Bath Road shed in 1960, the 4500 Class were no longer to be seen stabled overnight at Wells although they did still appear on workings from Westbury and Frome.

The line was classified as 'Dotted Blue' which meant that, although the line was normally limited to Class 3 locomotives with a maximum axle loading of 17 tons 12 cwt, larger ones could be used subject to certain restrictions. The British Railways Western Region Engine Loads document dated 17th June 1963 lists maximum loads over the whole line for Class 4 locomotives, including the BR Standard Class 4 4-6-0s and 2-6-0s, and former Great Western 7800 (Manor Class), 4300, 5100 and 5600 but it is not known whether any members of these classes ran on the line apart from the specific instances mentioned in this chapter. Although the 0-6-0PT 9400 Class was not officially permitted on the line because it was classified as 'Red', No.8492 was noted during the 1950s working the 9.30am Bristol West Depot-Wells goods; *see Plate 228*.

The 2251s and the panniers were capable of hauling similar loads on the easier sections of the line where they were limited to 242 tons. On the East Somerset section with its much stiffer

G. W. R.
Excursion to the South Coast.

On SATURDAY, July 25,

A DAY-TRIP EXCURSION will run to

BOURNEMOUTH
(WEST)

BY THE DIRECT ROUTE VIA SALISBURY.

LEAVING	AT	Return Fare, 3rd Class.
	A.M.	
Cheddar	5 52	
Axbridge	6 0	
Winscombe	6 8	4/3
Sandford and Banwell	6 12	
Congresbury	6 20	
Yatton	6 25	

The Return Train will leave Bournemouth (West) at 8.55 p.m. the same day.

Children under Twelve Years of age, Half-price.
No Luggage Allowed.

The Tickets are not transferable. Should an Excursion or Cheap Ticket be used for any other Station than those named upon it, or by any other Train than those specified, it will be rendered void, and therefore the fare paid will be liable to forfeiture, and the full Ordinary Fare will become chargeable.

The Issuing of Through Tickets is subject to the conditions and regulations set out in the Bill, Books, Bills, and Notices of the respective Companies and Proprietors on whose Railways, Coaches, or Steamboats they are available, and the holder, by accepting a Through Ticket, agrees that the respective Companies and Proprietors are not to be held liable for any loss, damage, injury, delay, or detention, caused or arising out of their respective Railways, Coaches, or Steamboats. The contract and liability of each Company and Proprietor is limited to their or his own Railways, Coaches, or Steamboats.

For any further information respecting the arrangements shewn in this Bill, application should be made at any of the Company's offices or agencies, to Mr. C. KISLINGBURY, Divisional Superintendent, G.W.R. Temple Meads Station, Bristol, or to Mr. J. MORRIS, Superintendent of the Line, Paddington Station, W.

Paddington, July, 1908.   JAMES C. INGLIS, General Manager.
(Bristol—1,000 R. 8vo, 2 pp.)   Arrowsmith, Printer, Quay Street, Bristol. (B 531)

Plate 210 - Great Western handbill advertising an excursion from stations between Cheddar and Yatton to Bournemouth on Saturday, 25th July 1908. *Author's collection*

and the crews had to either risk stalling on the bank or split the load by making two journeys between Axbridge and Sandford with a consequently late arrival back in Bristol.

There is a story that an ROD 2-8-0 entered one of the sidings in East Somerset yard that was laid with concrete pots in place of sleepers and that it spread the track and sat down between the rails. However, the truth of this story has never been substantiated. Concrete pots were introduced during World War II as a result of a shortage of new timber for railway sleepers. The pots were made of reinforced concrete and were rectangular in plan with dimensions of approximately two feet by one foot six inches. They were five and one quarter inches in depth and had chamfered edges. Standard bullhead chairs were bolted to each pot and lengths of track would be made up using tie bars of two and a half inch angle iron bolted to every third pot in order to tie the two rails together and to keep them to gauge. At some locations tie bars would be bolted to alternate pots where they were adjacent to rail joints. The use of concrete pot track was restricted to sidings and goods loops and the only known locations where it was used on the Yatton to Witham line was in East Somerset yard and at Gate Lane Sidings although there is evidence that it may have been used on the Wrington Vale line.

There was no shunting turn at Wells shed and consequently all shunting was carried out by train engines, for which allowances were made in the working timetable. There were transfer trips between the three goods yards at Wells that were worked, for the most part, by Somerset & Dorset locomotives and crews.

During the 1940s and 1950s prior to the incursion of non-GWR locomotive types, one could see classes other than the 4500 2-6-2Ts and 0-6-0PTs on passenger trains. For example the early morning working from Yatton to Wells departing at 7.00am (6.55am from summer 1948 until closure) and its balancing working, the 8.00am Wells-Yatton, were worked by the Yatton shed No.2 pilot, a 1400 0-4-2T. On Saturdays the 1.05pm Yatton-Wells and the return working from Wells at 2.40pm were worked by the Yatton No.1 pilot, which was either a 1400 0-4-2T or a 4500 2-6-2T. There were no watering facilities in the seventeen and a half miles between Yatton and Wells, which would not have been far short of the limit for the 1400 with its relatively small tank capacity of 800 gallons. A 1400 would certainly need its tank replenished before setting off on the return journey to Yatton! This class was designed primarily for use on short branches and those allocated to Yatton were normally used for the Clevedon branch auto trains. A Yatton-based 0-4-2T was also used to work the Wrington Vale line, heavier locomotives being prohibited before the arrival of the ex-LMS designed Ivatt Class 2s. Both the 2-6-2T and the tender version 2-6-0 were of a sufficiently low axle loading to be used on the Wrington line. One notable occasion was on 28th April 1957 when Ivatt Class 2MT 2-6-2Ts Nos.41202 and 41203 worked an eight coach RCTS special through to Wrington. The Ivatt locomotives of both tank and tender variety were well liked

gradients the limit was 140 tons and it was frequently necessary for trains to be divided and worked up the bank in two portions. What this did for timekeeping may only be guessed at! As luck would have it, it was this section of the line that generated much of the mineral traffic.

During World War II many of the Dean Goods were loaned to the War Department and were replaced in the Bristol area by ex-Midland Railway Johnson designed 2F 0-6-0s on loan from the LMS. They had a reputation for being a bit rough. These locomotives would work the second goods down from Bristol to Wells which was crewed by Wells Turn Four men (see later) from Axbridge to Wells. Individual members of the class noted on this duty included Nos.3071, 3078, 3094, 3103 and 3603. They were not used on the first down goods because this turn included working the last passenger train back from Witham and this class was not vacuum fitted. At times the loadings were beyond the capability of the class on the climb to Shute Shelve

THE EAST SOMERSET AND CHEDDAR VALLEY RAILWAYS

Plate 211 - The capabilities of 4300 Class No.4377 are barely stretched by the two coach B-set as it runs into Wells station with an up train.
Robin Russell

(Below) Plate 212 - 0-6-0PT No.9771 at Lodge Hill with the 11.35am (SX) Yatton-Witham passenger train on 20th April 1960. The station building was of the same design but a mirror image of those at Congresbury and Sandford and Banwell. The station master's house can also be seen.
Brian Arman collection

WORKING THE BRANCH

by footplate crews as they were of a modern design and could be used on any train from a through Bristol to Frome passenger to the Wrington goods.

During 1953 the last three Ivatt Class 2MT 2-6-0 tender locomotives Nos.46525, 46526 and 46527 were allocated to St. Philip's Marsh from new and appeared at Wells on a regular basis. The latter two were reallocated before closure of the line but were replaced by Nos.46506 and 46507. Another of the class, No.46517, also appeared on the line. These locomotives were equipped with tender cabs and cut-out tender sides that made them ideal for tender-first working such as on the 4.45pm Cheddar-Witham goods. In reality, virtually any class that worked on the line could be seen on goods trains during the final years.

Most trains were steam worked right up to the withdrawal of the passenger service but the line had seen a certain amount of diesel operation. The former GWR diesel railcars had been diagrammed to work over the line for many years. Their operation was not without incident. On 18th February 1947 No.37, one half of a twin-car set, was badly damaged by fire near Draycott. The vehicle is believed to have been towed to Axbridge where it was stored for a while. Strangely, it was not until October 1949 that a decision was made about the future of this vehicle when it was officially condemned. Meanwhile the surviving vehicle, No.38, was paired with single car unit No.22. Later No.22 was replaced by No.33, another single car unit that had been rebuilt as a twin-car vehicle. Several other members of the class were also destroyed by fire. Both vehicles of another twin-car set, Nos.35 and 36, were burned out in an incident in Fox's Wood Tunnel on the main line between Bristol and Bath on 10th April 1956. This set had been noted on a down Cheddar Valley line service at Sandford and Banwell station on 31st March, just a few days before the fire. Shortly before the closure of the line to passenger trains in 1963, diesel-hydraulic

Ex-LMS INTERLOPERS

Plate 213 - Ivatt Class 2MT 2-6-0 No.46525 has its chimney pointing towards Tucker Street on the ex-GWR line between that station and Priory Road as it straddles the two level crossings that lead from the Glastonbury line into the ex-S&D goods yard.

R Holmes; Hugh Davies collection

(Above) Plate 214 - The 1.20pm Wells Priory Road-Glastonbury eases away from Wells on 2nd October 1951. The engine is ex-Midland Railway 1P 0-4-4T No.58046, formerly LMS No.1298.

S Nash courtesy Gerald Nichols

Plate 215 - Ivatt Class 2MT 2-6-2T No.41207 stands in the platform at Wells Tucker Street with a down train in the early 1960s.

A W V Mace collection

Plate 216 - A Bristol Division B-set stands in one of the sidings adjacent to the Cheddar Valley bay platform at Yatton awaiting its next duty. The set consists of vehicles Nos.6188 and 6191 built in the early 1930s as part of Lot 1479 to diagram E145 for service in the Bristol Division.
J Moss; Roger Carpenter collection

locomotives could be seen at work on the line. D6357 made a debut for this class over the line when it worked the 9.55am (SO) Westbury-Yatton on Saturday, 8th December 1962. This train continued to be worked by the class up until the end of passenger services.

Some information has come to light concerning the locomotive workings during the goods only period. In the winter of 1963-4 Bristol Turn 800 worked two return trips, Saturdays excepted (SX), from West Depot with a D6300 diesel hydraulic. The first ran through to Wells and returned to Pylle Hill, whereas the second only worked as far as Cheddar and returned to St. Philip's Marsh. From the other end of the line Turn 945 with a Westbury 5700 pannier tank worked one return trip to Wells East Somerset yard. Both of these turns were still working during the summer of 1964 with an SO working from Westbury with a 5700 pannier tank. In the summer of 1964 strawberry specials worked to Draycott as required. Their method of working in the down direction was to run round at Cheddar and propel to Draycott. D6300 diesel-hydraulics have been noted on this working and Harry Viles recalls working one with a BR Standard Class 3MT 2-6-2T. After the total closure of the line west of Cheddar in 1964 all workings were from the Witham end of the line. In the summer of 1965 Turn 945 from Westbury was booked for a D7000 'Hymek' diesel hydraulic. This class worked the remaining traffic up until the closure west of Cranmore in 1969.

The Great Western Railway introduced the two-coach 'B-sets' during the 1920s. They were made up from two identical non-corridor vehicles that were close-coupled and with guards and luggage compartments at the outer ends. They were constructed to a number of different diagrams with detail differences up until the mid-1930s and their main purpose was for branch passenger services. They were in use on the Yatton to Witham line right up until closure. The B-sets provided sufficient passenger accommodation for most services but additional vehicles could always be added if traffic demanded it. Certainly between March and June 1962 the 9.57am (SO) Westbury-Bristol Temple Meads, the 7.05am Wells-Yatton and 8.00am Wells-Yatton were four-coach trains. In the 1960s corridor coaches were used at times and there is at least one photograph showing an ex-Great Western Centenary coach on the line. On the last day, No.3218 was seen hauling a British Railways Mk.1 coach in 'Blood and Custard' livery.

Locomotive and Footplate Crew Diagrams

Locomotive and footplate crew diagrams on the Yatton to Witham line were more complex than one would have expected for a branch. This was due in part to the fact that many of the services running on the line started from or terminated at important railway centres such as Bristol and Westbury (Wilts) that were some miles from the main line junctions at either end of the branch. Another factor was that, even into British Railways days, the two sections of the line were largely treated as separate branches with many services either starting from or terminating at Wells.

Even into the 1950s locomotives and crews would be supplied by a number of different sheds including Bristol Bath Road, Yatton, Wells, Frome and Westbury (Wilts). It has already been noted that Bath Road shed closed to steam in 1960 and its allocation of locomotives which would have been seen on the branch was transferred to Barrow Road and St. Philip's Marsh.

There is very little information available on locomotive and crew diagrams in the early days and to date the writer has not even been able to obtain a full picture of the situation in the 1950s. From nationalisation and through the early 1950s, diagrams remained much the same with minor alterations caused by changes in the working timetable. Major changes came after the end of the 1958 summer timetable when services were reduced dramatically. These changes have already been described in some detail. Other major changes to workings came about as a result of the closure of the Bristol and North Somerset line to passenger traffic in 1959 and the dieselisation of the Clevedon branch in 1960.

Plate 217 - Great Western diesel railcar No.28 and a conventional carriage at Wells Tucker Street down platform. *John Alsop collection*

Wells Shed Workings

In 1944 there were still six turns at Wells shed. They are referred to as Turns One to Six in this work purely for the sake of clarity. The footplate men had their own names for these turns (in brackets) but the writer does not know what they were actually designated by the railway authorities.

Turn One (The 7.05)

Book on duty at 6.00am and work the first Cheddar Valley up passenger train of the day, the 7.10am Wells-Bristol Temple Meads. The footplatemen's name of 7.05 probably arose after the date sometime in the early 1950s when the train was retimed to start from Wells at 7.05am, a start time retained until closure. On arrival at Bristol the locomotive (at that time a 4500 Class 2-6-2T) ran onto Bristol Bath Road shed. The crew returned to Yatton 'on the cushions' (ie. in a passenger compartment) and then worked the 10.20am Yatton-Witham passenger with a Yatton based 45xx or 55xx. They then worked the 1.30pm Witham-Yatton train (with the same locomotive and stock) as far as Wells Priory Road where they were relieved by the Wells Turn Two men. Priory Road would have been used due to the fact that it was nearer the shed than the Great Western station. The Turn One men returned to the shed on foot and booked off duty.

Turn Two (The 2.02 or the Afternoon Passenger)

Book on duty at 1.37pm and walk to Priory Road station to relieve the Turn One men on the 1.30pm from Witham. This train departed from Wells station at 2.02pm, hence the name given by the footplatemen for the turn. After arrival at Yatton they worked the 4.05pm passenger to Clevedon (with the same locomotive and stock), returning to Yatton with a mixed train having carried out any necessary shunting and attaching of wagons at Clevedon. Meanwhile, the Clevedon auto train would be serviced at Yatton shed. Having arrived back at Yatton the crew would leave the locomotive at Yatton shed and relieve the crew of the 2.35pm Paddington-Weston-super-Mare at 5.15pm and work that train into Weston. The locomotive on this train was generally the same 4500 that was left at Bath Road earlier the same day by the Turn One men. The locomotive would have spent much of the day on Bristol area local workings. The 2.35pm Paddington was in itself quite an interesting working as it ran down the Berks & Hants and via Devizes. The locomotive and crew would return light engine to Yatton but would sometimes pick up milk tanks at Puxton that would be dropped off at Yatton. The men would then be relieved by the Wells Turn Five crew and return to Wells by the 8.47pm from Yatton on the cushions.

Turn Three (The 8.40 Goods)

Book on duty at 8.40am and relieve a Westbury crew on the first down goods over the East Somerset section. The Westbury men returned home on 7.58am Yatton-Frome that was due off Wells station at 9.05am. The locomotive provided for this turn could be a Pannier tank, a 4500 or a Mogul. The locomotive would go on shed at Wells to be coaled and watered. It would then carry out any necessary shunting in the yard before working the 10.30am goods to Cranmore that worked through to Witham as required. They would return on the 2.25pm goods from Cranmore (1.45pm from Witham if they had worked through), shunt again at Wells as required, and go on shed again to see to the fire and take water. They would then run the locomotive up to the catch point on the locomotive road by East Somerset signal box where they were relieved by another Westbury crew who would have come down on the 3.17pm Frome-Bristol on the cushions. Turn Three would then book off duty at 4.25pm.

Turn Four (The 7.55 Goods)

Book on duty at 7.00am and work the 7.55am Bristol goods ex-East Somerset yard. The locomotive would be a 2251 or a Dean Goods that would have spent the night on Wells shed. Much time was spent shunting at the intermediate stations and the train was booked to cross the 9.30am goods from Bristol West Depot at Axbridge at 12.27pm. That train would be hauled by a Dean Goods, 2251 or an LMS 2F with a Bristol crew. The crews would change over and the Turn Four men would work back to Wells with a booked arrival time at East Somerset yard of 2.40pm. The locomotive would go on shed for servicing prior to the men booking off.

Turn Five (The 5.10 Goods)

Book on duty at 3.55pm and work the 5.10pm goods to Bristol St. Philip's Marsh as far as Yatton. The locomotive would have been used on the 9.30am goods from Bristol. On arrival at Yatton at 8.37pm they would be relieved by Bristol men and would in turn relieve the Wells Turn Two men and work the 8.47pm passenger train from Yatton to Wells. On arrival at Wells station the stock would be uncoupled and the locomotive would run light to East Somerset and be turned and put on shed overnight ready to start the same diagram next day starting with the 7.10am passenger train to Yatton.

Turn Six (The Witham)

Book on at 1.45pm and shunt the yard with the same locomotive that had worked the first goods in from Bristol (3.55am from West Depot). This was either a 2251 or a Dean Goods. During the morning this locomotive would have been used for pumping water at the shed. They would then attach a brake van and work to Wookey at 5.00pm and attach the paper van that had been left just inside the gate of the Mill siding. This train would form the 5.20pm (SX) Wookey-Witham goods with the locomotive running tender first. Having arrived at Witham the locomotive and crew would return with the 9.17pm Witham-Wells passenger train. The stock would be stabled in the carriage sidings at Wells station for the night and the locomotive would go onto shed and be ready to work the 7.55am goods to Bristol the next day.

During the ensuing years there were various alterations to the above pattern. After nationalisation the Dean Goods were disappearing and the Collett 2251 0-6-0s shared freight duties with the ex-LMS Ivatt 2-6-0 tender locomotives. In the summer 1946 timetable the last Yatton to Wells passenger train had been retimed to 8.10pm. This train was now worked by the Wells Turn Two men as the Turn Five men on the 4.45pm Wells to Bristol goods could not get to Yatton in time. The Turn Five men were relieved at Axbridge or Sandford by a Bristol crew and then came home by the 6.10pm Yatton-Wells on the cushions. In the winter of 1947-48 the Wells Turn One men worked the 7.10am passenger departure from Wells only as far as Yatton. They then worked the 10.50am Yatton-Wells followed by 12.07pm Wells-Frome. This was, in fact, the same train that stood at Wells station for over half an hour. Next they worked the 1.20pm Witham-Bristol back as far as Wells where they were relieved by the Wells Turn Two men who took the train through to Bristol. Turn Two then worked the 6.05pm Bristol-Weston-super-Mare and then light engine back to Yatton before working the 8.08pm Yatton-Wells. It seems that the mixed train working to Clevedon in the afternoon had finished by then.

From the summer of 1948 the Turn Six working of engine and van to Wookey was extended to Cheddar, leaving Wells at the earlier time of 2.45pm. The yard would be shunted, a task that on average took more than ninety minutes, and a stone train was made up to form the 4.45pm (SX) to Witham. On Saturdays this was just a trip working from Wells to Wookey and back leaving Wells at 5.00pm as in the 1944 timetable. Turn Three was still worked by Wells men in the winter 1954-55 timetable although actual times had changed. By the summer timetable of 1956 Westbury men had taken over the turn. By the summer of 1955, after working the first passenger train to Yatton the Wells Turn One men now worked the 9.35am (SX) Yatton-Wells and the return working, the 10.30am (SX) Wells-Yatton. This working remained in the winter timetable for a couple of years and in the summer timetable until closure. In the summer of 1956 Turn Three was no longer worked by Wells men and Turn Five became Monday to Friday only. It seems likely that in the summer of 1957 the Wells Turn Two men changed footplates (SO) when working the 1.10pm Witham-Bristol at Yatton and worked the 2.52pm Yatton-Frome, then the 9.20pm Witham-Wells as the locomotive for this train would normally be the Turn Six one but this did not run on a Saturday. Also this would leave a passenger locomotive on shed at Wells, along with the locomotive off the first down goods from Bristol that morning, ready for the workings on Monday morning as the locomotive off the 8.08pm Yatton-Wells ran on to Frome light engine on Saturdays.

As a result of the changes introduced when the winter 1958 timetable came into force Turn Two disappeared except on Saturdays. Turn Six disappeared altogether and Turn Three had finished previously. Turn Four remained as it was until closure. Turn Five was back in the working timetable on Saturdays. It is not known if it had been in the previous two winter working timetables. After working the 11.35am Yatton-Witham with Turn One men, the locomotive returned light engine to Wells but this was not in the working timetable. In summers up to closure this was a timetabled ECS working. It seems that Turn Two men were working the 8.08pm (SO) Yatton-Wells again, which they did until closure during the winter only. Wells driver Les Parsons was made redundant and transferred to Old Oak Common. It seems likely that Wells was short of firemen at the time so none lost his job. Bristol firemen worked the Wells turns on a regular basis and would often work the 8.08pm (SO) Yatton-Wells and would have to catch the bus back to Bristol!

Another Wells turn from the late 1950s until 1960 was to work the 1.11pm (SO) Yatton-Wells and return. A Wells driver would travel to Yatton on the cushions by the 9.57am Westbury-Bristol Temple Meads that left Wells at 10.55am. On arrival at Yatton he would prepare the locomotive at Yatton shed and work the train with a Bristol fireman. This was normally an Ivatt 2-6-2T duty. One Wells man who worked this diagram regularly when a passed fireman tells the story of the time he got to Yatton and found that the fire in the rostered locomotive had virtually gone out. He used most of the shed's supply of firelighters to get some sort of fire going. Apparently the train was worked as far as Congresbury with insufficient steam pressure to operate the vacuum brake. The train was worked with the locomotive

Plate 218 - 4500 2-6-2T No.4573 was the penultimate member of the class with flat top tanks. It is seen at Cranmore on a train from Witham in 1949.

J Moss; Roger Carpenter collection

brake only, presumably the strings having been pulled to release the brakes on the rolling stock. Of course, this was all strictly illegal, unfitted passenger trains having been outlawed by the Regulation of Railways Act of 1889.

By the summer of 1959 the second Bristol goods, worked by Turn Five, was again suspended on Saturdays. The Saturday Westbury goods was also suspended but both were reinstated in the following winter timetable. This pattern of suspension of these services on Saturdays in summer and their reinstatement in winter continued until closure. In the winter 1961-62 working timetable no return working of the second Bristol goods is shown. Presumably it returned to Bristol light engine (with or without van) or else the locomotive workings would have been unbalanced. In the summer of 1962 the Westbury goods became Tuesdays and Thursdays only. In the summer 1960 working timetable the 1.00pm (SO) passenger train worked by Turn Two men terminated at Yatton instead of Bristol. They then worked the 2.52pm (SO) Yatton-Frome.

By the time the last working timetable, that of summer 1963, came into effect there were only three turns left at Wells. In order to demonstrate how they relate to the turns going back to 1944, they are referred to as Turns One, Four and Five.

Turn One

Book on at 5.00am and off shed at 6.35am working light engine to Wells station. Pick up two sets of coaches (ie. four vehicles) from the carriage sidings and work the 7.05am passenger train from Wells to Yatton returning on the 9.38am (SX) Yatton-Wells with just two coaches. Next work the 10.35am (SX) Wells-Yatton and the 11.35am (SX) Yatton-Witham returning to Wells at 1.30pm ECS. Interestingly, during the previous working timetable, that for the winter of 1962-3, the ECS was worked to Frome, leaving Witham at 1.04pm with the locomotive and crew returning to Wells light engine. The coaches would be stabled in the carriage sidings at Wells station and the locomotive would go on shed ready for the same duty next day. The men would book off duty at 2.50pm. On Saturdays the crew would book on and work the 7.05am to Yatton as during the rest of the week. They would then work the 11.12am (SO) Yatton-Witham passenger and return with the 1.10pm (SO) Witham-Yatton as far as Wells where they were relieved by the Turn Five men at 1.47pm. They would book off at 3.30pm. After Driver Griffiths left for Old Oak Common in July 1963, Turn One worked the 1.10pm Witham-Yatton through to Yatton and returned to Wells on the cushions by the 2.45pm Yatton-Frome.

Turn Four

Book on at 7.00am and off shed at 8.40am with the locomotive that had worked in on the 3.30am Bristol West Depot-Wells goods. After any necessary shunting they would work the 10.00am Wells-Bristol West Depot goods as far as Axbridge and change footplates with the Bristol crew on the 9.45am Bristol West Depot-Wells goods. After working this train back to Wells they would run onto shed and book off at 3.25pm. On Saturdays the up goods to West Depot was timed to leave Wells at 9.45am. Turn Four men would work this train right through to Yatton where they would be relieved by a Bristol crew. They returned to Wells by the 2.45pm Yatton-Frome on the cushions and booked off at 3.30pm. After Driver Griffiths' departure, as noted above, the Turn Four men actually worked the 2.45pm Yatton-Frome train followed by the rest of the turns for the day. This meant a very long day! During 1963 Wells men worked most of their rest days.

Tune Five

Book on at 11.00am and carry out shedman's duties then shunt the yard with the locomotive off the 9.45am Bristol West Depot-Wells goods. Then make up the 3.35pm Wells-Bristol West Depot goods and take it as far as Wells station and be relieved by Bristol men. Return to the shed on foot, resume shedman's duties and book off at 7.00pm. On Saturdays book on at 1.47pm and relieve Turn One men

Plate 219 - Cheddar station on 20th June 1960. BR Standard Class 3MT 2-6-2T No.82007 arrives with the 3.17pm Frome-Bristol Temple Meads passenger train, whilst sister locomotive No.82044 prepares to propel vans to Draycott.
Brian Arman collection

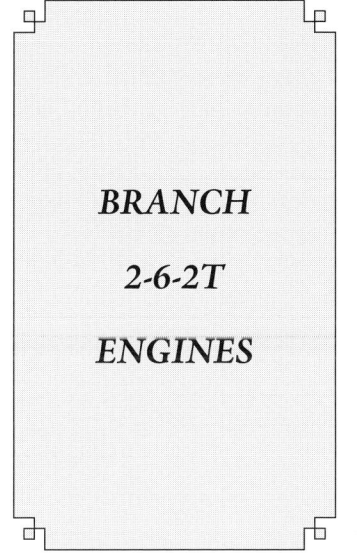

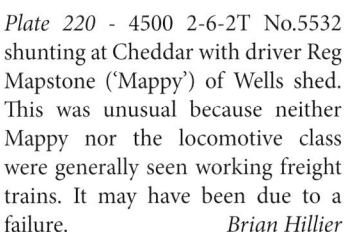

Plate 220 - 4500 2-6-2T No.5532 shunting at Cheddar with driver Reg Mapstone ('Mappy') of Wells shed. This was unusual because neither Mappy nor the locomotive class were generally seen working freight trains. It may have been due to a failure. *Brian Hillier*

BRANCH 2-6-2T ENGINES

on the 1.10pm (SO) Witham-Yatton passenger and work the train through to Yatton. They would then work the 2.45pm Yatton-Frome passenger. Next they would return to Witham with the 4.50pm empty carriage stock and work the 6.20pm Witham-Wells passenger with a wait at Wells station before working the 8.15pm Wells-Yatton as far as Axbridge. There they would change footplates with the Bristol men on the 8.20pm (SO) Yatton-Wells. On arrival at Wells, they would leave the stock in the carriage sidings and turn the locomotive before going on shed and booking off duty at 10.00pm. During the previous winter timetable they would have relieved Turn One at 2.02pm on the 1.30pm (SO) train from Witham, which they would have then worked through to Bristol Temple Meads. Following this they would have gone onto Barrow Road shed, changing locomotives and taking on coal as required before running light to Yatton and then would have worked as per the summer timetable on the 8.20pm (SO) Yatton-Wells and booked off duty at 10.00pm.

Bristol Bath Road Shed Workings

Bristol Bath Road had three passenger turns that involved working over the Yatton to Witham line. The exact timings varied a little over the years and those quoted here are taken from the working timetable for the summer of 1954. At this time there was still one train in each direction on Sundays for the duration of the summer timetable. This was worked by a Bristol Bath Road locomotive and crew as Wells shed was closed on Sundays. No other details of the Sunday turn have as yet come to light.

Turn 101

This turn involved two sets of men and the rostered locomotive was a 4500 2-6-2T. This diagram included working the 7.25am Bristol Temple Meads-Frome. This train stood at Wells station for 21 minutes from 8.44am to 9.05am and was due to arrive at Frome at 9.54am. The stock then formed the 10.50am Frome-Bristol via Radstock and the Bristol and North Somerset line. Other services worked by this diagram included local passenger trains to Bath, Avonmouth, Severn Beach and Portishead.

Turn 115

This turn also involved two sets of men and a 4500 Class 2-6-2T. After booking off shed and collecting the stock from Malago Vale Sidings, the train formed the 6.47am Bristol Temple Meads-Bruton via Radstock and Frome. Arrival at Bruton was at 8.35am and the stock then formed the 8.35am to Westbury arriving at 9.05am. Next was the 9.57am (9.47am (SO)) from Westbury to Bristol Temple Meads via Wells arriving at Bristol at 12.13pm with a 15 minute stop at Wells from 10.55am to 11.10am. Later in the day the same locomotive would work the 5.20pm Bristol Temple Meads-Frome via Radstock with the second set of men. This train then formed the 6.36pm Frome-Yatton that stood at Wells for 49 minutes from 7.26pm to 8.15pm. On arrival at Yatton the locomotive went on shed at 9.05pm and the crew returned to Bristol on the cushions by the 6.07pm from Plymouth that left Yatton at 10.03pm. The locomotive remained at Yatton and became Yatton's early turn 4500 for the next day (see below for Yatton workings). Thus Yatton's 4500 locomotive was changed on a daily basis.

Turn 132

This turn was listed in the working timetable as an AEC diesel railcar diagram but could also be steam worked by a 4500 with a B-set. Three drivers were required to cover the full diagram. In the morning, services worked included locals to Portishead, Bath (Green Park) and Yatton. The 2.00pm Yatton-Clevedon and the return working that departed from Clevedon at 2.17pm were worked as part of this turn, whilst the locomotive on the auto was coaled and had its fire attended to on Yatton shed. The auto coach would remain coupled to the locomotive whilst this was done. Turn 132 continued with the 2.52pm Yatton-Frome (SX) with a 13 minute stop at Wells. Arrival at Frome was at 4.53pm. The stock then formed the 6.06pm Frome-Bristol via Radstock.

The two goods workings over the Cheddar Valley section from Bristol to Wells and return were worked by Bristol locomotives and crews but Wells men did play a part in the diagrams. Again there were some variations in the timings of these over the years. In later years the second goods train did not run on Saturdays for the duration of the summer timetable. The times quoted here come from the summer timetable of 1963 but they had changed little since the drastic service reductions of 1958. Of course, by 1963 Bristol Bath Road was a diesel shed and steam workings were from Barrow Road.

Turn 801

This turn was booked for a 2251 0-6-0 locomotive and was the down working of the first Wells goods train of the day. The crew booked on at Barrow Road at 1.40am and prepared the locomotive. Time off shed was 3.05am and they ran coupled light engines to West Depot, arriving at 3.30am. There they coupled up to the waiting train and departed at 3.40am. Departure from Yatton was at 4.50am and arrival at East Somerset yard was at 6.59am. The locomotive would work a trip to the Wells Cold Store as required. The train they brought in would be shunted by the locomotive which had worked the Westbury goods. Work for Turn 801 was due to finish at 8.45am and the locomotive booked on shed at 8.50am. Prior to January 1963 the crew would have returned to Bristol on the cushions by the 9.08am (9.15am SO) from Wells station (8.12am from Frome) and book off at 10.39am (SX) or 10.42am (SO). Certain Bristol crews liked to catch the 8.00am Wells-Yatton train and so get away early but would put on their ticket that they travelled home by the 9.08am train. They would book the locomotive on shed without having turned it first, much to the annoyance of the Wells men. The locomotive remained at Wells shed that day

Plate 221 - Another 4500 2-6-2T, No.5553, pauses at Congresbury with a down passenger train on 9th April 1955. *Mark Warburton*

Plate 222 - 2251 Class 0-6-0 No.2244 arrives at Cheddar with a down goods train; date unknown. *R.E. Toop*

to pump water and worked the Bristol 802 diagram (first up goods to Bristol) on the following day. When the feed pipe to the water tank fractured during the severe weather in January 1963 pumping ceased and consequently there was no longer any need to keep the goods locomotive at Wells overnight. Locomotives requiring water at Wells after that would have had to use the water columns situated in the six-foot at the passenger station. From January 1963 the locomotive and crew on Turn 801 worked back to Bristol with the first up goods, thus carrying out the duties of Turn 802 as well. This alteration must have been somewhat unofficial as the working timetable for the summer of 1963 does not indicate this change. Although only having one locomotive on shed overnight meant one less to prepare, the enginemen wanted the shed to look more important in an effort to avoid closure. Apparently the pipe was repaired but they could not get the pump working again.

Turn 802

Prior to January 1963 this turn was booked for the same locomotive which had worked the Bristol 801 diagram the previous day but with a Wells crew who booked on at 3.55am. This turn was for the first up Wells goods of the day. Locomotive and crew ran off shed at 8.40am and shunted East Somerset yard. Next they departed from Wells East Somerset with the first up goods at 10.00am (SX). At Axbridge the crew of this train changed footplates with the Bristol crew on the second down Bristol to Wells goods (10.00am off West Depot, see Bristol Turn 800). Sometimes the Bristol men on the down goods would hang back at Sandford and Banwell so the crews would change footplates there. The up goods arrived at Yatton at 1.28pm and departed again at 1.40pm (SX). Calling at Nailsea and Backwell on the way, arrival at West Depot was at 2.57pm (SX). They then ran light engine back to Barrow Road shed, departing from West Depot at 3.02pm and arriving at 3.32pm (SX). The Bristol crew booked off at 4.22pm having originally booked on at 7.55am (SX).

On Saturdays there were some differences in this diagram. The departure time from Wells East Somerset was 9.45am and arrival at Yatton was 2.13pm, the Wells crew working the train right through to Yatton where they were relieved by the Bristol crew who had booked on at 12.49pm. The Wells crew returned to Wells on the cushions whilst the up goods with the Bristol crew in charge left Yatton at 2.35pm and arrived at West Depot at 3.40pm, having again called at Nailsea and Backwell. They then ran light engine to Barrow Road arriving at 4.15pm. The Bristol crew booked off at 8.49pm. From January 1963 this turn was worked by the same locomotive as the first down goods (Turn 801) although it seems that the crew rosters were unchanged, at least until the shortage of men at Wells later in the year made itself felt. During the last two months of the passenger service, the Wells men worked the 2.45pm Yatton-Frome passenger train back to Wells rather than travelling back on the cushions.

Turn 800

This turn was booked for a 2251 0-6-0 locomotive in order to work the second Wells goods train of the day. Unlike the first goods, the second used the same locomotive for both up and down workings although the turn was shared between Bristol and Wells crews. The Bristol crew booked on at Barrow Road at 7.05am (SX), were off shed at 9.20am and ran light engine to West Depot. There they coupled up to the waiting train and departed at 10.00am. Departure from Yatton was at 10.40am. At Axbridge they crossed the first Wells to Bristol goods (10.00am off Wells East Somerset, Bristol Turn 802) and changed footplates with the Wells crew on the up train. Arrival at East Somerset yard was at 2.50pm. The locomotive was booked on shed at 3.00pm for servicing but twenty minutes later, at 3.20pm, it was off shed again with a new Wells crew who had booked on duty at 11.00am. The first Wells crew would book off at 3.55pm. Turn 800 would continue with the second up goods that departed from East Somerset yard 3.35pm and ran to St. Philip's Marsh arriving

Plate 223 - BR Standard Class 3MT 2-6-2T No.82009 passes the former Somerset & Dorset station at Wells Priory Road with the 3.17pm Frome-Bristol Temple Meads on 8th April 1960. *Brian Arman collection*

at 8.40pm. The locomotive would then run to Barrow Road departing from St. Philip's Marsh at 8.45pm and arriving at 9.05pm. The turn was finished by a Bristol crew who had booked on at 2.00pm and would book off at 10.00pm. It seems likely that this crew worked the 5.20pm (SX) passenger train from Bristol Temple Meads to Wells that crossed the up goods at Sandford and Banwell just before 6.00pm. They would have changed footplates with the Wells crew who worked the passenger train on to Wells arriving at 6.28pm. The Wells crew would book off at 7.00pm.

Turn 806

This turn was booked for an Ivatt Class 2 2-6-2T locomotive and, according to the working timetable, involved one set of Bristol men and one set of Weston-super-Mare men but no Wells men. Weston-super-Mare and Yatton sheds had closed by this time but were still used as signing-on points. It is probable that the so-called Weston-super-Mare men actually booked on at Yatton. The Bristol crew booked on at 1.40am and ran off shed at 3.05am coupled light engines to West Depot where it was uncoupled and ran light to Yatton arriving at 4.00am. It would shunt at Yatton before departing with the Clevedon goods at 5.10am and arriving at 5.21am. By this time this was the only steam working to Clevedon and this did not last long as goods traffic here was withdrawn in June 1963. The return goods departed from Clevedon at 6.06am and arrived at Yatton at 6.17am. The turn continued with the 6.55am Yatton-Wells passenger train and the 8.00am Wells-Yatton. Arrival back at Yatton was at 8.39am. The 'Weston' men booked on at 8.15am (SX) or 9.04am (SO). They probably booked on at Yatton, as stated above, and there they would have taken over the footplate from the Bristol men who would travel back to Bristol on the cushions. The Bristol crew booked off duty at 10.11am (SX) or 10.13am (SO). The turn continued with the Wrington goods that left Yatton at 9.10am and arrived at Wrington at 10.55am having run via Sandford and Banwell. The return trip from Wrington departed at 11.25am and arrived at 12.01pm. The Wrington goods did not run on Saturdays and consequently the Weston men did not book on until 9.04am. Back at Yatton the turn continued with some shunting before returning to Barrow Road shed light engine at 1.00pm. The turn for the locomotive continued later in the day with a passenger train from Bristol Temple Meads to Portishead and back. This would have been worked by a Bristol crew as the Weston men booked off at 4.15pm (SX) or 6.06pm (SO). Unfortunately the working timetable does not give details.

Yatton Shed and Workings

In British Railways days the allocation at Yatton was three locomotives. As with Wells, Yatton was a sub-shed of Bristol Bath Road and any locomotives at Yatton were effectively outstationed from the parent shed. There were two 14xx/58xx 0-4-2Ts that worked the Clevedon auto trains and the Wrington Vale line goods as well as other general shunting and pilot duties. The third locomotive was a 4500 2-6-2T which was principally used for Cheddar Valley line services. On 1st January 1948 the three locomotives allocated to Yatton were Nos.1415, 1463 and 4563. There had been a turntable at Yatton at one time but it seems to have fallen into disuse before World War II. It could only be accessed directly from the Cheddar Valley bay or the adjacent sidings.

Yatton Early Turn

The Yatton early turn booked on at 3.15am and prepared two locomotives for the day's work ahead. The Wrington engine might be a non-auto fitted engine (58xx) but an auto-fitted one was preferred as it could be substituted for the Clevedon engine in the event of a failure. The 4500 would work to Clevedon with a B-set (empty stock) and the goods. On arrival at Clevedon it would shunt as necessary and sort vehicles for the up mixed train later in the day. The 4500 with the B-set then worked the first up passenger train of the day at 6.40am, which arrived at the up main platform at Yatton. Having unloaded, it would shunt to the Cheddar Valley bay on the down side and work the first down passenger train of the day from Yatton to Wells. The departure time from Yatton was 6.55am throughout the 1950s. This service crossed the first up passenger train from Wells to Bristol at Cheddar, the latter having a Wells crew with the Wells overnight passenger locomotive. On arrival at Wells the locomotive would run round and the train formed the second up passenger train of the day from Wells to Yatton. The departure time from Wells was 8.00am and the train arrived in the Cheddar Valley bay at Yatton station. After shunting at Yatton as required they worked down to Weston-super-Mare and shunted there before returning to Yatton. Another reason for running down to Weston was to turn the locomotive as the Yatton turntable had gone by this time. On arrival back at Yatton the 4500 would go back onto Yatton shed and the crew booked off at 11.00am. Over the years this diagram remained essentially the same but there were many detail alterations.

Yatton Afternoon Turn

The afternoon turn booked on and worked to Clevedon and back using the same 4500 as the early turn. This train arrived back at Yatton at 4.25pm, ran round behind Yatton West signal box and shunted the stock to the Cheddar Valley bay. Following that the 4500 would shunt as required before working the 6.10pm Yatton-Frome, which included an eight minute stay at Wells station. In the late 1950s the departure time was 6.13pm from Yatton with a correspondingly shorter wait at Wells. The stock next formed the 9.25pm Frome-Bristol via Radstock. The crew were relieved at Bristol and returned to Yatton on the cushions. The train continued its diagram as the 11.00pm to Portishead. Returning to the East Somerset section, the 6.10pm Yatton-Frome crossed the 5.20pm Bristol Temple Meads-Yatton via Radstock, Frome and Wells at Shepton Mallet. On reaching Yatton the locomotive from this train was put on shed for the night in readiness for working the Cheddar Valley services next day. Thus the Cheddar Valley line locomotive shedded at Yatton was rotated on a daily basis. The Bristol Turn 115 crew who had worked the train to Yatton returned to Bristol on the cushions. After 1958 the 5.20pm from Bristol only worked to Yatton on Saturdays. Monday to Friday it terminated at Wells and the locomotive ran to Yatton light engine. Prior to the closure of Yatton shed and the dieselisation of the Clevedon passenger services, the 5.20pm from Bristol was taken over by a Yatton crew who worked the train forward to Yatton. That crew then relieved the crew on the Clevedon auto and worked the last four return trips from Yatton to Clevedon.

In the summer timetable for 1954 the Wrington goods departed from Yatton at 7.10am and ran through to Sandford and Banwell calling at Congresbury as required. Once shunting at Sandford and Banwell was complete it retuned to Congresbury at 8.10am and then onwards to Wrington at 8.45am. The return working left Wrington at 9.25am and was booked to arrive at Yatton at 10.01am having called at Congresbury on the way.

The locomotive would then shunt at Yatton as required. The Wrington goods ran SX and consequently on Saturdays the Wrington locomotive worked a passenger train from Yatton to Wells and back. The departure time of each varied a little over the years but was about 1.10pm from Yatton and the return at about 2.40pm. The writer has already mentioned that running a 14xx to Wells was probably a bit of an endurance test because of the lack of intermediate watering facilities. The introduction of the Ivatt Class 2 2-6-2Ts in the mid-1950s was something of a godsend as here was a locomotive with a sufficiently low axle loading to work to Wrington yet with sufficient power and water capacity for working passenger traffic all the way to Witham. Thus the class gave the locomotive department greater flexibility in drawing up working diagrams.

With the introduction of diesel multiple units on the Clevedon services in 1960, Yatton shed became redundant and was consequently closed on 8th August of that year. Weston-super-Mare shed also closed at the same time as Yatton but both were retained as signing on points for locomotive crews. Locomen Colin Forse, Dusty Miller and Charlie Warburton transferred to Bristol Bath Road and signed on there whilst Fred Flower, George Stockham and Sid Sledge continued to sign on at Yatton. Fred Flower worked the Wrington goods and retired when it was withdrawn. Although what were Yatton turns had now become Bristol turns, men who signed on at Yatton still continued to work over the line.

Westbury and Frome Shed Workings

In the years between the end of World War II (or possibly earlier) up until closure, the first passenger train of the day to work through from Witham to Yatton was a Westbury turn. Up until the mid-1950s it started from Trowbridge at 7.53am. The locomotive was a 4300 2-6-0 and was prepared by the shedmen. In the summer of 1953 the crew booked on at 6.40am, ran off shed at 7.00am and worked light engine to Trowbridge. This crew worked the 7.53am right through to Bristol. This diagram only involved a single trip over the Yatton to Witham line, the rest of the day being spent on various workings between Bristol, Westbury and Warminster. By the summer of 1955 the train no longer started from Trowbridge but had become the 8.14am from Frome, and by 1958 it had been retimed to start from Frome at 8.12am. By 1962 the driver and fireman on this working changed footplates at Wells station with the Bristol men working the 7.35am Bristol-Frome. During the afternoon the locomotive ran light engine back to Yatton and shunted there before working the 6.15pm Yatton-Frome passenger train. During 1963 Collett 0-6-0 No.2268 could frequently be seen on this diagram. In 1962 the 3.17pm Frome-Bristol was a Frome turn. The locomotive on this working had previously worked the 7.58am Yatton-Westbury.

In earlier times the locomotive on this working had a Bristol crew (see Bristol Turn 101) and would have returned to Bristol on a service via Radstock; but of course the North Somerset line was closed to passenger traffic by this time. In 1948 the same Frome to Bristol train that was then timed to depart from Frome at 3.27pm was worked by a Westbury pannier tank subshedded at Frome. This train later returned home as the 6.15pm Bristol Temple Meads-Frome via Radstock.

By the summer of 1963 there was just one return goods train on Mondays to Fridays over the East Somerset section between Witham and Wells East Somerset yard. This was booked for a 5700 0-6-0PT locomotive and a set of Westbury men (Bristol Turn 945). The men booked on duty at 8.00am and ran off shed at 8.15am. Departure time from Westbury with the down goods was at 8.35am and arrival at Wells was at 11.38am. The locomotive would then shunt the yard, which would include dealing with wagons from the early down goods over the Cheddar Valley section from Bristol West Depot. The return working to Westbury would depart from East Somerset at 1.30pm and arrive at Westbury at 4.20pm. The locomotive would uncouple and go back on shed at 4.35pm, allowing the crew to book off duty at 4.50pm.

The summer timetable for 1962 shows different timings for the down working, these being departure from Westbury 9.35am with an arrival time at Wells East Somerset of 12.55pm. The timetable also shows this working as being Tuesdays and Thursdays only. There would not have been enough time for the locomotive and crew on this turn to carry out shunting at Wells. Presumably this would have been carried out by one of the Cheddar Valley section goods locomotives with either a Bristol or Wells crew.

Locomotive Workings during the Final Days

Latterly there was only one locomotive stabled at Wells overnight. In 1963 it worked the first up passenger train to Yatton each morning, departing from Wells at 7.05am. The duty continued with the 11.35am passenger service from Yatton to Witham and then back to Wells with the 1.30pm ECS. On Saturdays the latter was a through passenger train to Yatton.

During 1963 the following classes and individual locomotives were noted on this duty:

Ex-GWR 0-6-0PT
Nos.3643, 3675, 3677, 3702, 3735 and 9623.

Ex-GWR 0-6-0 (Collett Goods)
Nos.2217, 2251, 2277 and 3218.

Ex-GWR 2-6-2T (Large Prairie)
4103.

Ex-LMS 2-6-2T
Nos.41207, 41208, 41245, 41249 and 41304.

BR Standard Class 3MT 2-6-2T
Nos.82007, 82009, 82035, 82039, 82040 and 82041.

The locomotive that worked the first down goods from Bristol in the morning would work straight back on the first up goods from Wells to Bristol as there was no longer a goods locomotive stabled at Wells overnight.

During the first week of January 1963 when the branch was subject to much disruption due to heavy snowfall, No.82007 was the overnight locomotive at Wells. On Monday, 31st December 1962 diesel hydraulic (Hymek) No.D7003 worked the 3.17pm Frome-Bristol train (via Wells) after working a snow plough along the branch. On the morning of Tuesday, 1st January 1963 Nos.46506 and 2277 became stuck in a snowdrift between Draycott and Lodge Hill. No.D7046 was sent to the rescue but it became derailed between Cheddar and Draycott. On Friday, 4th January No.2217 worked a breakdown train to retrieve No.D7046. The problems with the weather continued into the following week such that on Tuesday, 8th January a snowplough was worked from the Yatton direction by three locomotives and became stuck in Easton cutting. The locomotives concerned, Collett 0-6-0s Nos.2277 and 3218 along with an unidentified 37xx pannier tank, were left there overnight. They were rescued the next day by Hymek No.D7055. The events of early 1963 are

Plate 224 - Ivatt 2-6-2T No.41207 arrives at Shepton Mallet with the 2.52pm Yatton-Witham on 7th August 1962. It is crossing another train hauled by an unidentified member of the same class. The first coach is interesting in that it is of a former LMS design allocated to the Scottish Region. *D P Leckonby*

Plate 225 - 5700 0-6-0PT No.5757 arrives at Wells Tucker Street on 10th June 1959 with the 3.17pm Frome-Bristol Temple Meads. In the other platform No.8744 waits with a handful of covered vehicles; being high summer, it is quite likely to be involved with strawberry traffic.
The writer has not yet been able to recognise any of his old school friends on the platform!

Brian Arman collection

recalled by former Yatton driver Colin Forse in Chapter 15.

There are a few recorded instances of 'Large Prairies' working on the line during 1963. On 21st January 1963 No.4103 was noted on the 7.05am Wells-Yatton passenger train. On at least two occasions during August 1963 No.8102 worked the 9.30am Bristol West Depot-Wells goods. Another unusual visitor on Monday, 8th July 1963 was ex-LMS 4F 0-6-0 No.44226 of Saltley shed that worked a strawberry special to Draycott.

During the last week of passenger services starting on Monday, 2nd September 1963, Collett 0-6-0 No.3218 was the overnight locomotive at Wells. It was especially asked for by Harry Viles of Wells shed because of its generally clean condition and was given an additional clean during its stay. It was also in reasonable condition mechanically as it had recently been in works for repairs following a collision with Ivatt 2-6-2T No.41208 at Congresbury. The two goods turns were worked by Collett 0-6-0s Nos.2217, 2277 and 2251 variously throughout the week. These were Barrow Road locomotives and were worked by Bristol crews. On the penultimate day, Friday, 6th September, the passenger locomotive workings were:-

6.55am Yatton-Wells	82037
7.58am Yatton-Westbury	41208
9.38am Yatton-Wells	3218
11.35am Yatton-Witham	3218
2.45pm Yatton-Frome	82040
5.20pm Bristol TM-Wells	82037
6.15pm Yatton-Frome	2268
7.05am Wells-Yatton	3218
8.00am Wells-Yatton	82037
8.12am Frome-Bristol TM	2268
10.35am Wells-Yatton	3218
1.30pm Witham-Wells (ECS)	3218
3.17pm Frome-Bristol TM	41208
7.00pm Wells-Bristol TM	82037
6.20pm Witham-Wells	82040 then LE to Bristol

On that day the first down goods did not run. Collett 0-6-0 No.2251 ran down to Wells light engine, crossing the 8.00am Wells-Yatton passenger train at Cheddar. On the previous day, Thursday, 5th September, there was no locomotive available for the first down goods but No.2251 ran down to Wells later in the morning. It was attached to the 9.38am Yatton-Wells passenger train which was double headed with sister locomotive No.3218. They were coupled tender to tender with No.2251 leading.

On the last day, Saturday, 7th September, the passenger locomotive workings were as follows:-

6.55am Yatton-Wells	Not known
8.03am Yatton-Frome	82037
11.12am Yatton-Witham	3218
1.45am Yatton-Wells	41245
2.45pm Yatton-Frome	3218
6.15pm Yatton-Frome	2268
7.05am Wells-Yatton	3218
8.00am Wells-Yatton	Not known
8.12am Frome-Bristol TM	2268
8.20pm Yatton-Wells	3696
10.28am Westbury-Bristol TM	D6353
1.10pm Witham-Yatton	3218
2.52pm Wells-Yatton	41245
3.17pm Frome-Bristol TM	82037
6.20pm Witham-Wells	3218
8.15pm Wells-Yatton	3218

The former Great Western 0-6-0PT worked the 8.20pm from Yatton which was the last passenger train to Wells. The footplate crew were driver Harry Viles and fireman David Sheppard, both of Wells shed. A Bristol locomotive crew rode down on the cushions to take the train back to Bristol ECS. The locomotive was taken to East Somerset for turning prior to the return trip at the insistence of the Bristol fireman.

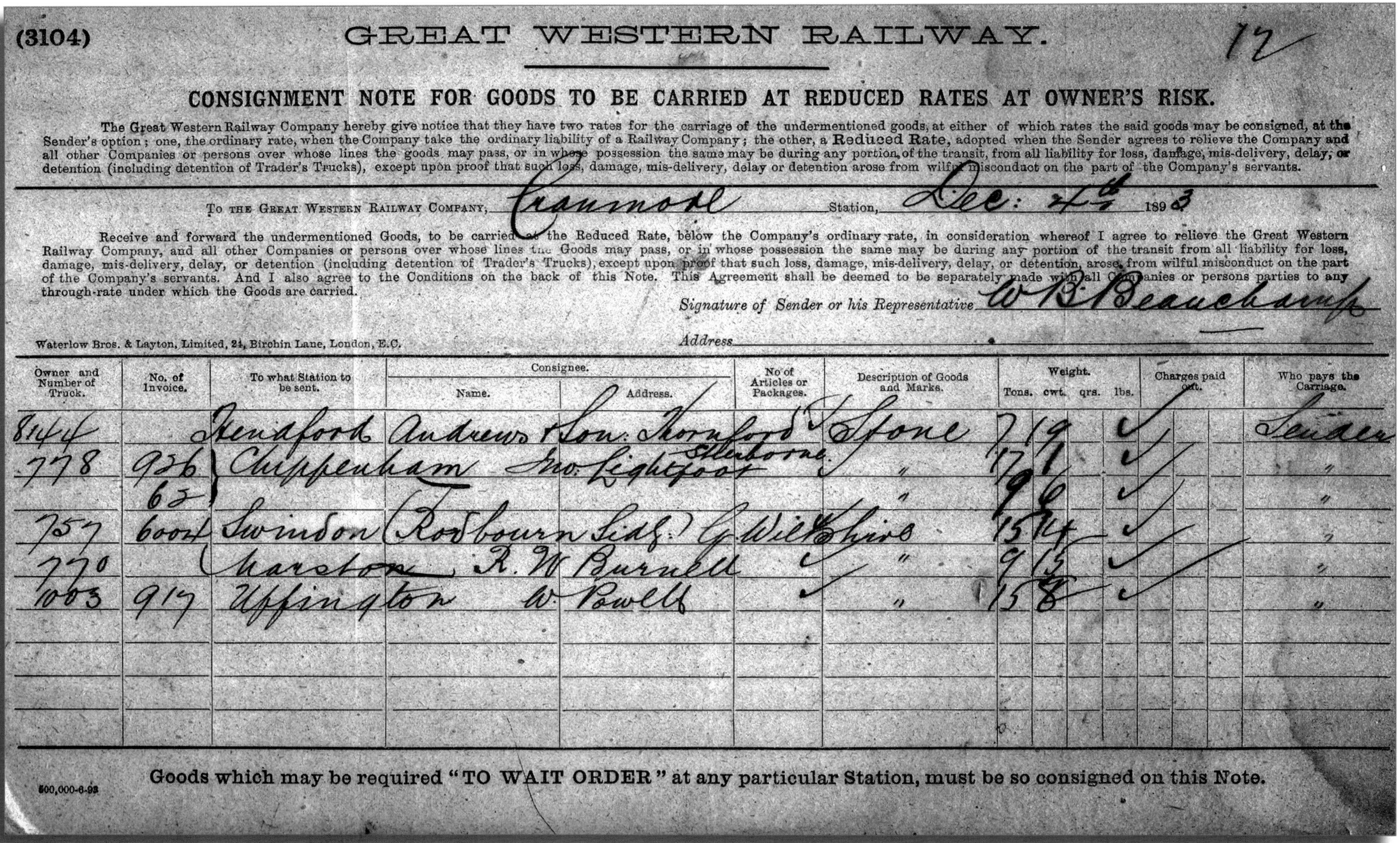

(3104) GREAT WESTERN RAILWAY. 12

CONSIGNMENT NOTE FOR GOODS TO BE CARRIED AT REDUCED RATES AT OWNER'S RISK.

The Great Western Railway Company hereby give notice that they have two rates for the carriage of the undermentioned goods, at either of which rates the said goods may be consigned, at the Sender's option; one, the ordinary rate, when the Company take the ordinary liability of a Railway Company; the other, a Reduced Rate, adopted when the Sender agrees to relieve the Company and all other Companies or persons over whose lines the goods may pass, or in whose possession the same may be during any portion of the transit, from all liability for loss, damage, mis-delivery, delay, or detention (including detention of Trader's Trucks), except upon proof that such loss, damage, mis-delivery, delay or detention arose from wilful misconduct on the part of the Company's servants.

TO THE GREAT WESTERN RAILWAY COMPANY, Cranmore Station, Dec: 4th 1893

Receive and forward the undermentioned Goods, to be carried at the Reduced Rate, below the Company's ordinary rate, in consideration whereof I agree to relieve the Great Western Railway Company, and all other Companies or persons over whose lines the Goods may pass, or in whose possession the same may be during any portion of the transit from all liability for loss, damage, mis-delivery, delay, or detention (including detention of Trader's Trucks), except upon proof that such loss, damage, mis-delivery, delay, or detention, arose from wilful misconduct on the part of the Company's servants. And I also agree to the Conditions on the back of this Note. This Agreement shall be deemed to be separately made with all Companies or persons parties to any through-rate under which the Goods are carried.

Signature of Sender or his Representative W B Beauchamp

Waterlow Bros. & Layton, Limited, 24, Birchin Lane, London, E.C.

Address

Owner and Number of Truck.	No. of Invoice.	To what Station to be sent.	Consignee. Name.	Consignee. Address.	No of Articles or Packages.	Description of Goods and Marks.	Weight. Tons.	Weight. cwt.	Weight. qrs.	Weight. lbs.	Charges paid on.	Who pays the Carriage.
8144		Hendford	Andrews & Son	Thornford		Stone	7	19			✓	Sender
778	936	Chippenham	Jno. Lightfoot	Sherborne		"	7	1			✓	"
	63					"	9	6			✓	"
757	6007	Swindon	Rodbourn Sidg.	G. Wiltshire			15	14			✓	"
770		Marston	R. W. Burnell		✓	"	9	15			✓	"
1003	917	Uffington	W. Powell		✓	"	15	8			✓	"

500,000-6-93 Goods which may be required "TO WAIT ORDER" at any particular Station, must be so consigned on this Note.

Plate 226 - A consignment note for goods despatched from Cranmore by W. B. Beauchamp on 4th December 1893. All six vehicles were loaded with stone and were labelled for a variety of destinations; wagon No.8144 to Hendford (goods station at Yeovil), No.778 and the unspecified one to Chippenham, No.757 to Rodbourne Sidings at Swindon, No.770 to Marston and No.1003 to Uffington. There are several possible 'Marston' destinations but, given the lack of any additional information in the name, it is likely that the wagon would remain in Somerset and travel as far as Marston Magna, to the north of Yeovil. Uffington, of course, is on the Great Western main line between Swindon and Didcot. *A Miller collection*

Chapter Eleven

GOODS AND MINERAL TRAFFIC OPERATION

The southern slopes of the Mendip hills to the west of Wells provide ideal conditions for strawberry growing and it was the seasonal strawberry traffic for which the Cheddar Valley section of the line is probably best remembered. Most of this traffic was concentrated at Draycott, Axbridge and Cheddar. 'Strawberry Specials' as they were called were worked to Bristol, Birmingham Moor Street and the North of England. The line also had its share of the area's equivalent of the Kentish hop-picking traffic, although this was on a much smaller scale than its well known counterpart. This was at a time before the Great War when the only way that many town and city dwellers could afford a holiday in the country was to combine it with work, picking fruit.

In latter days the vehicles used for the strawberry traffic were Siphon Gs marked 'Return to Yatton'. These vehicles had replaced bogie parcels vans that were used up until the 1950s and were stabled at Cheddar all year round in spite of the fact that they were only actually in use for the all too brief strawberry season. In British Railways days the vehicles were attached to the rear of the 7.25am passenger service from Bristol to Frome and were detached at stations from Axbridge to Wookey on the way. What this operation did for timekeeping does not bear thinking about. The growers would bring their produce to the stations by whatever means were at their disposal and loading would take place through the day. Later in the afternoon a locomotive and passenger train full brake would depart from Bristol to pick up the loaded vans. The train worked through to Wells before running round for the return trip to Bristol. In the summer of 1954 the Birmingham Moor Street working originated from Frome at 8.20pm with the locomotive and van running through to Axbridge before departing again at 9.50pm, also stopping at Cheddar and Draycott to attach additional vehicles. The train arrived at Witham at 11.17pm before running to Birmingham Moor Street. It ran as a Class C express freight.

As well as other agricultural traffic that was typical of any West Country branch, the line also carried substantial amounts of mineral traffic in the form of limestone for the construction and road building industries as well as for track ballast. During the mid-1920s, stone traffic represented about 75% of the total goods traffic carried on the branch. It was during that decade that the facilities on the branch for transporting stone developed rapidly and by 1930 over 300,000 tons of stone from Mendip quarries were being taken out by rail each year. It is worth noting here that stone traffic from Foster Yeoman's Merehead Quarry is the sole reason for the survival of the eastern section of the line which remains open for goods traffic to this day.

St. Cuthbert's Paper Mill at Wookey also provided traffic for the branch. A private siding into the works from the adjacent Wookey station became operational in about 1880. Inbound traffic consisted of esparto grass for the manufacturing process. The railway was also used to distribute the finished products. Interestingly, the goods shed at Wookey was the only one on the line to be lit by electricity, courtesy of the paper mill.

The position of the quarry sidings at Dulcote on the severe gradient between Wells and Shepton Mallet meant that special working instructions were always in force. In fact, as discussed in Chapter 9, the railway company had some problem getting the Board of Trade to sanction the sidings here in the first place. During the 1930s both the Great Western ballast quarry sidings and the adjacent Foster Yeoman quarry sidings were still in use.

Plate 227 - 2251 Class 0-6-0 No.2277 arrives with a goods brake van from the East Somerset direction on 26th June 1963, possibly a transfer trip to clear Tucker Street goods yard. Meanwhile, BR Standard Class 3MT 2-6-2T No.82036, hauling the 2.45pm Yatton-Frome, takes water at the down platform.

Brian Arman collection

Plate 228 - 9400 Class 0-6-0PT No.8492 shunting at East Somerset yard. This class of engine, with its 'Red' axle load classification, was prohibited from working anywhere on the Cheddar Valley or East Somerset sections, both being classified 'Dotted Blue'. The story behind this particular working on the 9.30am Bristol West Depot-Wells is not clear! *R Told courtesy Wells Railway Fraternity*

The fact that the two connections with the running line, one into each of the two quarries, faced in opposite directions did nothing to help the situation. Shunting to and from the running line was only permitted with a locomotive at the Wells end of the train. Propelling from Wells to Dulcote was permitted with the brake van leading. The instructions also made allowance for two trains to work together from Wells up to Dulcote Quarry. In the event of a loaded train leaving Dulcote Quarry heading up the bank an assisting engine could be sent from Wells if the load demanded.

The working of heavy mineral trains over a single line with fearsome gradients was no easy matter and the Sectional Appendix to the Working Time Table (Bristol District) dated October 1960 gives some insight into how this was achieved. By this date some intermediate sidings had fallen into disuse but there were several that outlasted the passenger service.

By this time electric token working was in force along the entire line from Yatton to Witham having superseded the earlier electric train staff. The electric tokens were able to unlock the ground frame controlling access to sidings in the single line sections. Intermediate electric token instruments were installed at a number of places to enable a mineral train to be 'locked in' the siding and the section cleared for another train to pass. This was a useful feature that must have greatly assisted in compiling the working timetable. As far as is known there were no intermediate instruments installed in single line sections worked by electric train staff on the line. The signalman's general instructions publication does make reference to the operation of intermediate electric token instruments but does not mention intermediate electric train staff instruments. Because of this the writer is of the opinion that they did not exist. So it seems that at the time when the electric train staff was in use no other train would be able to pass through a single line section occupied by a goods train until that train had completed all shunting at intermediate ground frames and had travelled through to the far end of the section. The only alternative would have been to find a way to return the train staff to one of the signal boxes at either end of the section, with the assurance that the goods train had been shunted clear of the running line and the points had been set and locked to enable another train to pass safely. No doubt this limitation of electric train staff working contributed to its replacement on a line such as this with a fair number of intermediate sidings.

Once shunting was complete and the train was ready to resume its journey, the man in charge would, with the sanction of the signalmen at both ends of the section, withdraw a token from the intermediate instrument. He would then unlock the ground frame and set the points for the train to run out onto the running line. After setting the points back again he would lock the ground frame and hand the token to the driver advising him at the same time that the line was only clear to the home signal of whichever signal box he was returning to. This was known as 'warning acceptance' and was only ever applied to goods trains under normal circumstances. Thus if a passenger train had passed the home signal but not the clearing point (normally 440 yards in advance of the home signal) then the goods train could not be accepted under the warning arrangement.

By 1960 the only sidings with intermediate token instruments were at Gate Lane, which was quite close to Wells East Somerset yard, and at Dulcote Stone Quarry Sidings. Both these sidings were on gradients falling towards Wells that meant that special instructions were issued to control their operation so as to prevent runaways. In fact, the gradient at Dulcote was 1 in 46. Unless the train was fully fitted with the vacuum brake operative on all vehicles it could not be drawn from Wells East Somerset to Gate Lane without having a brake van attached in the rear. During daylight or in clear weather a train of not more than five wagons could be propelled to Gate Lane without a brake van at a speed not exceeding ten miles per hour. At Dulcote, vehicles were not permitted to stand on, or be shunted onto, the running line unless there was a locomotive at the Wells end. The Great Western ballast quarry sidings had been lifted many years before but the Foster Yeoman quarry sidings were still in situ although they had not been used since 1955. Because they had not been officially closed, the instructions for shunting them were still in force.

There was a ground frame 573 yards on the Shepton Mallet side of Cranmore station to provide access to a siding belonging to Mendip Mountain Quarries. At this point the running line was on a gradient of 1 in 119, falling towards Cranmore. Although not as steep as at Gate Lane and Dulcote, it was still steep enough to require special instructions to avoid a runaway. Wagons could be left on the running line during shunting operations provided great care was taken to ensure that sufficient brakes were applied. Wagons could be propelled from the siding towards Cranmore provided there was a brake van leading with a man in it able to operate the hand brake if required.

A ground frame 31 chains from Cheddar on the single line section towards Axbridge provided access to McAlpine's siding. At this point both the main line and sidings were situated on a 1 in 100 gradient falling towards Cheddar so, again, special instructions were needed to ensure safe operation. The sidings came under the responsibility of the Cheddar station master. To work the siding a locomotive could propel not more than 25 wagons without a brake van from Cheddar. On the return trip a locomotive could draw no more than 25 wagons back to Cheddar without a brake van, but with a tail lamp attached. On the return journey the guard or shunter had to ride on the rearmost vehicle. These movements were restricted to daylight hours and during clear weather only.

There were sidings on the down side at Sandford and Banwell station for the exchange of traffic to and from the short mineral branch into Sandford Quarry. Empty wagons were shunted into one of two loop sidings by main line locomotives. The quarry company had its own locomotives including a Sentinel steam locomotive. A notice board was provided, past which only the quarry company's locomotives could work. Loaded wagons were brought down from the quarry by one of its own locomotives and shunted into one or other of the loop sidings ready for collection. The branch was steeply graded so that all loaded trains had to be brought down from the quarry with the locomotive leading and trainloads of empty wagons had to be propelled back to the quarry. There was a gradient of 1 in 35 at the station end of the loop sidings and it was the quarry company's responsibility to ensure that the brakes were applied to all wagons left on the gradient once shunting had been completed. The quarry branch was also protected by catch points and a gate on the station side of the loop sidings. When not in use the lever operating the catch points was locked with the points in the open position. The gate was to be kept shut and padlocked. The keys were kept in Sandford and Banwell signal box and could only be used by a 'responsible member of the station staff'.

The yard and sidings at the Wells end of Shepton Mallet station stood on a gradient falling towards Wells. Because of this, all shunting operations had to take place with the locomotive at the Wells end of the wagons. Unattended wagons were not allowed to stand on the down loop but could stand on the up line provided that the catch point at the Wells end was open. Wagons could not be propelled out of the Wells end of the loop sidings onto the main line on either the up or the down side.

Traffic at Doulting Stone Siding ceased around 1948 and unfortunately no record has yet been found of any special instructions, although it is certain there must have been some in view of the position of the siding at a summit with severe gradients on either side. There were two connections between the siding and the running line. These faced in opposite directions in order to facilitate the working of trains into the

Plate 229 - A touch of modernity; Class 37 No.37290 has brought a train of loaded bitumen tank wagons from Ellesmere Port by a trip working from Westbury to Cranmore on 2nd February 1983. It is 1.45pm; empty tank wagons have been assembled during shunting and the locomotive will shortly draw clear of the siding, run round its train and return to Westbury with the empties. The driver was Chris Fell. Modellers seeking a prototype for some dodgy track-laying need only look at the siding in front of No.37290 for inspiration. The sidings remained in use until 1985. *Michael Mensing*

Plate 230 - 0-6-0PT No.5757 stands at Axbridge with the 3.17pm Frome-Bristol Temple Meads on 10th June 1959 whilst Collett 2251 Class 0-6-0 No.2213 stands in the down platform with a train of stone. *Brian Arman collection*

Passengers and stone at Cheddar and Axbridge

Plate 231 - Taken from an up passenger train on 23rd August 1960, this view shows Ivatt Class 2MT 2-6-0 No.46517 shunting the sidings on the up side at Cheddar. Hoppers containing stone are at the rear of the wagons being shunted. *Kidderminster Railway Museum*

Plate 232 - A 6-plank wagon with an additional narrow top board for W. Counsell & Co. of Yatton. As is evident, the firm advertised themselves as coal and builders' merchants and were also at Congresbury and Wrington. Built by Gloucester Carriage & Wagon Co., this vehicle was completed in September 1914; company records show that Counsell ordered this vehicle on deferred purchase terms for three years. It was Counsell's responsibility to arrange for repairs, which they did with the GRC&WCo. for seven years. According to the placard, the wagon was painted black, lettered white, shaded red.
GRC&W Co.
Gloucestershire Archives

PRIVATE TRADERS' VEHICLES RESIDENT ON THE BRANCH

Plate 233 - Alfred G. Weeks & Sons, of Winscombe, also had premises at Sandford and Banwell. This 7-plank wagon, rated to carry 10 tons, was built in 1913 by Ince Waggon & Ironworks Co. of Wigan; paint colour unknown. In the 1938 Colliery Year Book the firm's office was listed as the Garage, Winscombe.
HMRS collection

siding from either Shepton Mallet or Cranmore. Ground frames controlling the crossovers were locked by an Annett's key on the Shepton Mallet to Cranmore train staff (later electric key token). Shunting operations at the siding were the responsibility of the porter at Cranmore.

Other goods traffic workings that deserve mention include the transfer trips between the three goods yards in Wells at Tucker Street, Priory Road and East Somerset. As well as being another good reason to hold up road traffic at the level crossing, one of the interesting facts about these was the use of special shunting discs in place of head and tail lamps. Many of the discs soon disappeared, possibly because the shunter forgot to remove them and they ended up going elsewhere. In the absence of a disc other suitable objects would be pressed into service, which might be a tin can, a bundle of rags or a bit of wood. It did not matter provided that the signalman understood its purpose. This was not exactly complying with the rules but no-one seemed to care and at the end of the day the job had been done.

According to the working timetable for winter 1933-4, the first transfer trip departed from Priory Road at 12.10pm bound for East Somerset. A Somerset & Dorset locomotive was rostered for this duty and it would return to Priory Road either light or with brake van attached at 12.17pm. Next was a trip from Tucker Street to Priory Road, departing from the former at

Plate 234 - 5700 0-6-0PT No.7723 stands in Park Siding at Shepton Mallet High Street with driver Wilf Taylor in charge.

J Moss; Roger Carpenter collection

12.50pm. This was a Great Western locomotive which then ran light to East Somerset at 12.57pm. The rest of the day's transfer trips were carried out by Somerset & Dorset locomotives. Next was a transfer from Priory Road to Tucker Street at 1.45pm, with the locomotive returning light to Priory Road at 1.50pm. Meanwhile, a light engine left Priory Road at 1.50pm in order to work the 2.08pm transfer from East Somerset back to Priory Road. The last two of the day were from Priory Road to East Somerset at 4.20pm and from East Somerset to Priory Road at 5.32pm. The corresponding light engine workings were 4.27pm from East Somerset back to Priory Road and 5.25pm from Priory Road to East Somerset.

The working timetable also made provision for trips in addition to those in the working timetable to be arranged as desired for livestock, meat and urgent traffic.

Table of Trip Workings between Great Western and Somerset & Dorset yards, winter 1933-34

		S&D	S&D Engine	S&D	S&D Engine	S&D
		p.m.	p.m.	p.m.	p.m.	p.m.
East Somerset	dep.	12‖17	…	2.08	4‖27	5.32
S & D	arr.	12‖19	…	2.10	4‖29	5.34
S & D	dep.	…	1.45	…	…	…
Tucker Street	arr.	…	1.47	…	…	…

		S&D	GW	S&D Engine	S&D Engine	S&D	S&D Engine
		p.m.	p.m.	p.m.	p.m.	p.m.	p.m.
Tucker Street	dep	…	12.50	1‖50	…	…	…
S & D	arr.	…	12.52	1‖52	…	…	…
S & D	dep.	12.10	12‖57	…	1‖50	4.20	5‖25
East Somerset	arr.	12.13	12‖59	…	1‖52	4.23	5‖28

‖ Light engine or light engine and brake van.

Chapter Twelve

SIGNALLING

When the Cheddar Valley Railway opened, signal boxes (known as block huts by the Bristol & Exeter) were constructed at Congresbury, Sandford and Banwell, Winscombe, Axbridge, Cheddar, Draycott, Lodge Hill and Wells station. The smaller block huts were of Bristol & Exeter design but Axbridge, Cheddar and Wells, all of which required larger installations, were equipped with Saxby & Farmer designed signal boxes. The Bristol & Exeter would have still referred to these as block huts even though they were of a more substantial construction than the name would imply. At that time Axbridge and Cheddar were the only intermediate stations equipped with passing loops.

Yatton West signal box controlled the junction of the Bristol to Taunton main line with both the Cheddar Valley and Clevedon branches and was of Bristol & Exeter design. In its final form, brought into use with track alterations in 1898, it contained a 135-lever frame, although the highest number in use on the diagram was 129. There was also another isolated lever which operated the up main detonator placer. It seems that some later alterations took place as some remarks in the inspecting officer's report at the time are at odds with the later lever numbering. Unfortunately the writer has not as yet obtained any details of these alterations. The box survived until 31st January 1972 when it was superseded by the Bristol MAS scheme. It is worth noting that the Bristol & Exeter made use of Saxby & Farmer signal boxes on other parts of its system. Examples include Nailsea East on the main line between Yatton and Bristol and Stoke Canon Crossing a few miles north of Exeter. The former survived until 6th December 1971, also making way for the westward advance of the MAS, but the latter still stands although it is no longer in use by the railway. Interestingly, a report in the *East Somerset Advertiser* of the opening of the Cheddar Valley line mentions the

> 'Saxby and Farmer's patent locking apparatus installed at Yatton Junction by which 27 points can be working without moving out of the signal box.'

Of the original Cheddar Valley line boxes and block huts, most were eventually replaced or superseded by boxes of Great Western design. Many of the replacements were in conjunction with alterations to the layout requiring the installation of larger frames that would not fit in the older boxes. Other replacements do not seem to be associated with any alterations, so it is assumed that they were replaced because their condition became unsound or because the equipment they contained needed to be brought up to date. The line was fully signalled from the day it opened and trains were regulated by block telegraph in conjunction with a wooden train staff for each single line section. The Bristol & Exeter had committed itself to block working some years prior to the opening of the Cheddar

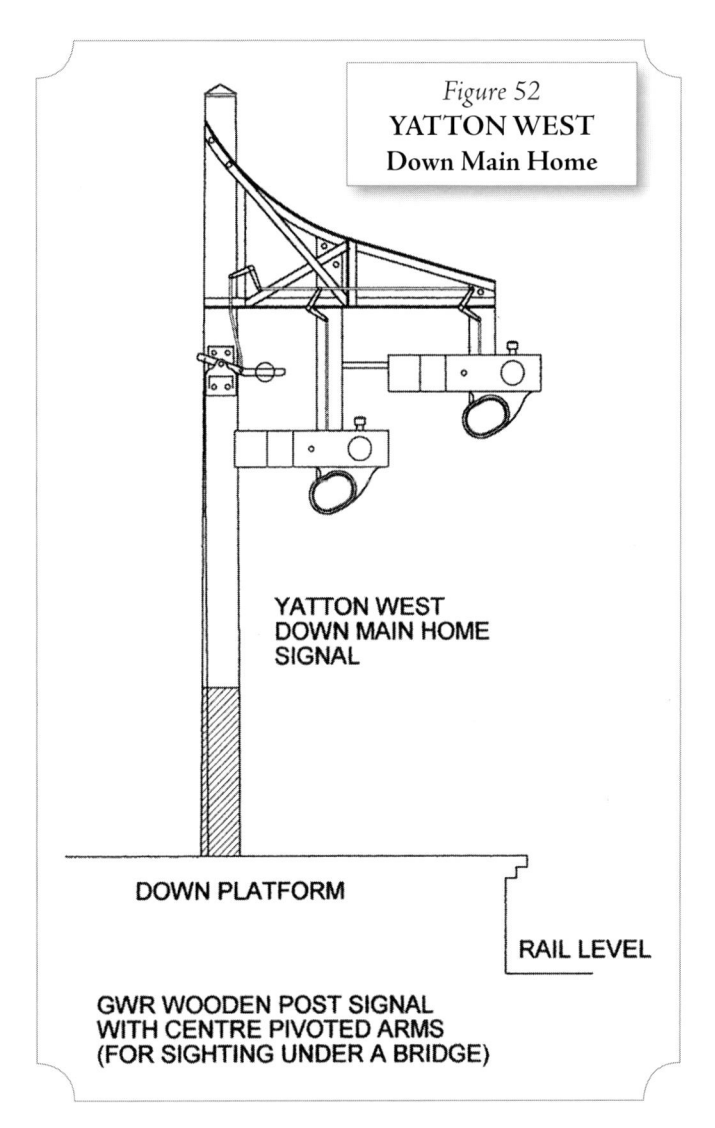

Figure 52
YATTON WEST
Down Main Home

YATTON WEST DOWN MAIN HOME SIGNAL

DOWN PLATFORM

RAIL LEVEL

GWR WOODEN POST SIGNAL WITH CENTRE PIVOTED ARMS (FOR SIGHTING UNDER A BRIDGE)

Valley line. The signals were an adaptation of Brunel's disc and crossbar signals used by the Great Western Railway. C. H. Gregory, who was at one time Engineer to the Bristol & Exeter, is credited with the invention of the railway semaphore signal but it is thought that they did not appear on that line until 1877, which was after the takeover by the Great Western.

The original block hut at Congresbury was replaced by a signal box on 14th April 1901 in conjunction with the opening of the Wrington Vale Light Railway to Blagdon. A passing loop and second platform were added at the same time. It seems that Congresbury lost its status as a block post between 1896, when the Electric Train Staff was installed, and 1901 when the new expanded layout came into use. The old block hut stood at the Cheddar end of the original (subsequently the down) platform between the station building and the goods shed. The replacement box was a Great Western type 5 (gable-end roof)

216 — THE EAST SOMERSET AND CHEDDAR VALLEY RAILWAYS

Plate 235 - Yatton West on 28th April 1957. Of Bristol & Exeter Railway design, this imposing signal box contained a 135-lever frame. *Mark Warburton*

YATTON & CONGRESBURY SIGNALLING

(Above) Plate 236 - The interior of Yatton West box on 2nd September 1963. *Ian Scrimgeour; Signalling Record Society*

Plate 237 - A prototype for everything? Prefabricated switch and crossing work nestling between the up platform and the signal box at Congresbury. No doubt part of the work undertaken during the remodelling of the track layout in August and September 1949, the time this photograph was taken.
J Moss; Roger Carpenter collection

Plate 238 - Looking towards Winscombe from Sandford and Banwell station on 31st March 1956. Note the lamp by the board crossing to aid token exchanges aftert dark.
Mark Warburton

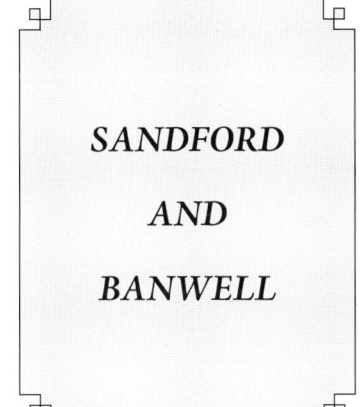

SANDFORD AND BANWELL

with a double twist frame with the levers at 5¼in centres. Later, in 1949, the layout was simplified and almost completely re-laid. The existing double twist frame in the box was relocked with 5-bar locking. Two track circuits were also installed to protect the facing points in place of the original fouling bars. This was the first such installation on the branch. The Blagdon branch was never equipped with signal boxes or any signalling and was worked under 'one train' regulations with a wooden train staff. Ground frames were provided to control siding connections.

The levers of the ground frames were locked into position to prevent movement of the points by unauthorised persons. An Annett's key attached to the train staff was provided to enable the train crew to release the levers so that points could be changed to allow shunting movements to be carried out into and out of the sidings. Before operating the ground frame, the end of the train staff with the key on it would be inserted into the lock on the ground frame and turned through ninety degrees. This action would release the levers and the ground frame become operative. It would also cause the Annett's key to be locked into the ground frame so that the points would have to be set back to their normal position and the ground frame locked again before the Annett's key could be withdrawn and the train proceed on its way. This procedure was necessary to ensure that sidings not worked from a manned signal box were left in a state so that passenger trains could operate on the running line in complete safety. Sidings were always equipped with a catch point or point that was also operated by the ground frame so that any vehicles running away in the siding would either be derailed or diverted into a headshunt and not foul the running line, which could possibly result in a collision with any passing train.

Sandford and Banwell received a new signal box to replace the old block hut on 12th December 1905 when a crossing loop was installed. The expansion of the layout became necessary after the opening of Sandford Quarry and the sidings that were later extended into the quarry itself. The new box was a Great Western type 7B (hip roof) with a 5¼in stud frame. The station retained its single platform which meant the loop could not be used for crossing two passenger trains. The goods loop was on the up side whilst the goods shed and goods yard were on the down side at the Cheddar end of the passenger station. The quarry branch led from the goods yard on the down side. Access to the quarry branch was controlled by a crossover operated by a separate lever, which was kept padlocked when not in use. Access to the goods yard from the running line was via two crossovers. The one at the north end was operated directly from the signal box whilst the one at the south end was operated by a ground frame released by lever 22 in the signal box.

Winscombe had a block hut towards the Sandford end of the platform. After 1896 the starting signals were removed and it was reduced to ground frame status, only controlling access to the siding and goods yard. The ground frame was unlocked by an Annett's key on the electric train staff. In about 1902 the original siding was realigned and made into a loop siding. The points giving access to either end of the siding were controlled by separate ground frames on the up side of the line and set ten chains apart. The original block hut on the platform was later demolished and the lead-away in the platform face blocked up. The new ground frames were known as Winscombe North and Winscombe South. The South ground frame was originally housed in a hut that was later removed. Whether the North ground frame ever received such a luxury is not known.

Axbridge received a new signal box on 14th July 1907. The new box was a Great Western type 7B (hip roof) with a 5¼in stud frame and was situated just off the Cheddar end of the down platform. The original Saxby & Farmer signal box was situated on the down platform opposite the station building and survived until sometime in the 1950s. The layout was designed in such a way that all the connections from the sidings to both the up and down loops were made by the means of trailing points, thus obviating the need for facing point locks. In his April 1950 *Railway Magazine* article entitled 'The Cheddar Valley Railway', C.R. Clinker states that the original box was still in existence. According to some sources the signal box and loop at Axbridge were taken out of use on 10th June 1963, some months before

Plate 239 - Cheddar signal box and the station with an unidentified train in the up platform on 5th May 1956.
Bob Griffiths

CHEDDAR

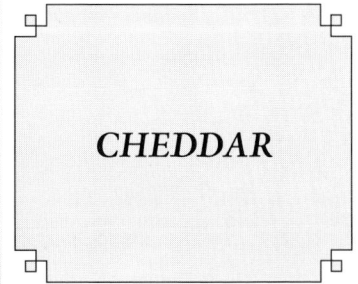

Plate 240 - The down starting signal at Cheddar. Note the 'shunt ahead' arm under the main arm. The up home signal is 'off' for a train approaching from Wells.
P J Garland

the passenger closure. The writer has a first hand account of the box being in use at least until the end of the passenger services; in fact, examination of the working timetable reveals that there was a crossing movement there right up until the closure date.

Cheddar retained its Saxby & Farmer box until the line closed. Quite why it did survive when those at Axbridge and Wells station were replaced is not known. There are no records of major alterations at Cheddar and it could just be that the box remained in a sound condition and any alterations that were made could be accommodated within the existing structure. Certainly most of the documented layout alterations were confined to sidings, so there were probably no radical changes necessary to the equipment in the box. As well as a passing loop there were sidings on the up and the down side. Early maps, including the Great Western Survey of the line carried out in about 1895 (TNA RAIL/274/73), show the presence of a second signal box adjacent to the loop points at the Wells end of the station. This was in addition to the box already described but no information has as yet come to light about this signal box, its purpose or its dates of construction and removal.

Draycott was equipped with a small non-standard platform-level box that was not a block post, although it would have been prior to the installation of Electric Train Staff in 1896. It was similar in design to the block hut at Winscombe but may have been a little larger in order to accommodate the gate wheel. It also lacked the ornate barge boards carried by the Winscombe block hut. It may have been that the barge boards were replaced at some time when aesthetic considerations were not so important. After 1896 the sole purpose of this box was to control the level crossing at the Cheddar end of the platform. The 7-lever frame included up and down distant signals. The level crossing gates were worked by a wheel in the signal box that was situated about half way down the platform, so the signalman would have no view of approaching road traffic. Presumably the fact that this was only a minor road meant that this was rarely a problem. Instructions were issued stating that the level crossing gates were to be closed across the public road immediately that

the 'train entering section' signal was sent from the signal box on either side. There was a single siding at Draycott and the points controlling access to this were operated by a ground frame which was released by a key on the electric train staff and later by the electric key token. Vehicles for Draycott on down passenger trains were marshalled next to the engine, whilst those on up passenger trains were marshalled at the rear of the

Plate 241 - Cheddar signal box viewed from the down platform on 5th May 1956. The former private owner wagon behind the box is 7-plank No.P122983, carrying capacity 13T. *Mark Warburton*

Plate 242 - Cheddar signal box interior showing lever frame and one of the token instruments. *Brian Hillier*

Plate 243 - The apparently sylvan setting of Wells Tucker Street station viewed from the vantage point of Sheldon Jones' grain silo gives no hint of the junctions just out of picture to the left and behind the photographer. The platform-mounted signal box dates from 1901 and the bracket carrying the starter signal features in more detail on the opposite page. *Gordon Scammell*

train. After closure of the line to passengers the gates became hand worked and the distant signals were fixed.

Lodge Hill also had a non-standard platform-level box which was equipped with an 8-lever Saxby & Farmer frame. Although it was a block post there was no passing loop. However, a passenger train would have been able to cross a goods train by shunting the goods into the siding. The box was closed in 1952 and all signals were removed. After that, access to the siding was controlled by a 2-lever ground frame released by the Cheddar to Wells electric key token. Vehicles for Lodge Hill on up and down passenger trains were marshalled next to the engine.

Wookey was equipped with a Great Western type 28B platform-level box containing a Saxby & Farmer frame with 4in centres. It was a block post but, in view of the fact that there was only a single platform, passenger trains could not be crossed there. There was a loop siding on the down side with a goods shed and a private siding that served St. Cuthbert's paper mill. Shunting of these sidings was supervised by the paper mill's foreman. The crossover at the station end of the loop siding was controlled by the signal box but the crossover at the Cheddar end was controlled by a ground frame. Because this crossover was not in station limits but actually in the Wookey to Cheddar single line section, it was unlocked by a key on the Wookey to Cheddar electric train staff. The box was abolished as a block post on 29th August 1954 and all running signals were removed. It was retained as a ground frame until 21st September 1965 and was known as Wookey East Ground Frame. The existing ground frame at the Cheddar end of the loop siding became Wookey West Ground Frame. The single line section became Wells Station to Cheddar.

Wookey had an intermediate key token instrument that allowed a goods train to be 'locked in' the loop siding and the line cleared for another train to proceed through the section from Wells or Cheddar. However, it was the responsibility of the signalman at Wells or Cheddar to ensure that there was sufficient room in the sidings at Wookey before the goods train to be shunted was dispatched. When the goods train was ready to proceed, it would be subject to 'warning acceptance' in which the train crew were advised that the line was only guaranteed to be clear to the home signal at the next block post in advance. This meant that trains which spent a long time in the section because of the need to shunt at intermediate sidings would not restrict shunting movements within station limits at the block post in advance. It is worth noting that the warning arrangement (as it was known) could not be applied to passenger trains under normal cirumstances.

Wells station originally had a Saxby & Farmer signal box on the down platform adjacent to Burcott Road overbridge. Positioned as it was between the bridge and the station building on the inside of the curve through the station, it must have meant that the signalman had a very restricted view of the layout. In the early days there was no footbridge between the platforms and had it been there whilst the original signal box was in use, the signalman's view would have been even more restricted. Unfortunately no photographs of the original signal box have yet come to light. A replacement box of Great Western type 7B design was constructed on the up platform and brought into use on 15th September 1901. It was equipped with a double twist frame with levers at 5¼in centres. As well as the passing loop, the signal box controlled access to the goods yard on the Wookey side of the overbridge, carriage sidings on the up side and a private siding into Sheldon Jones' engineering works. It seems that the erection of a new signal box was newsworthy in those days as the *Wells Journal* dated Thursday, 5th October 1901 contained the following report:

'*New G.W.R. signal cabin.*

A new signal cabin has been erected at the Great Western station to replace the one nearer the bridge. It has been provided with 27 levers and is connected with the cabin at Wookey on the West side and with the Somerset and Dorset Junction cabin on the East for ordinary working purposes and with the East Somerset cabin near the level crossings by telephone and telegraph which would be utilised on special occasions.

A reliable system of Bell and disc signals [sic] has been adopted, and the action of the signal nearer Wookey is ascertained by means of electrical instruments which indicate the position of the semaphore and also whether the light is

Plate 244 - A view from the down platform at Wells featuring the down starting signal and water column on 3rd October 1958. The imposing stone building in the background is the Priory Hospital, formerly the Wells Union Workhouse.
Roger Carpenter collection

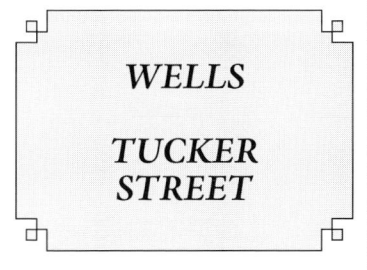

WELLS TUCKER STREET

(Below right) Plate 245 - Restriction notice for Sheldon's private siding.
Gordon Scammell

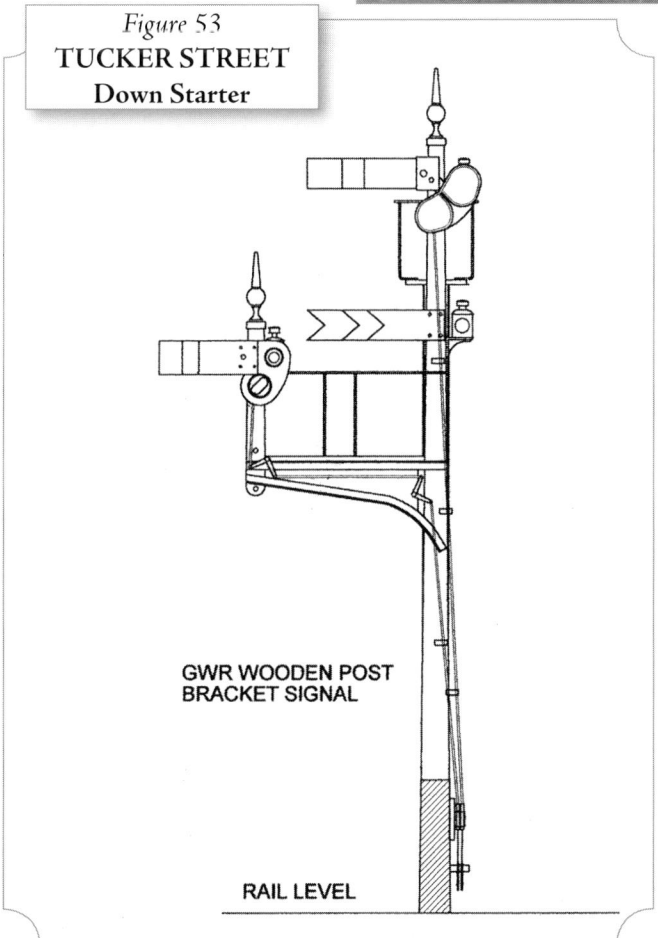

Figure 53
TUCKER STREET
Down Starter

GWR WOODEN POST BRACKET SIGNAL

RAIL LEVEL

burning at night. If the light becomes extinguished, a thermo-electrical apparatus raises the alarm in the cabin where a bell rings to warn the signalman.'

It seems that the ability of journalists to report on the technical aspects of railways was no better in the early twentieth century than it is today!

The Somerset & Dorset station at Priory Road was controlled by Wells 'A' box. Ironically this box was of a Bristol & Exeter design and may be compared with the box at Williton on the West Somerset Railway, which is, of course, still in use. It may be that the Bristol & Exeter built the box at the expense of the Somerset & Dorset but, given that the two companies were generally hostile to one another, there must be more to this story than meets the eye. Unfortunately it seems now that we shall never know. The signalman at Wells 'A' was responsible for regulating the Great Western trains that passed through Priory Road station as well as those of the Somerset & Dorset. The two block sections between the three boxes were extremely short, the distance from East Somerset box to Wells Station box being 367 yards. The distance from East Somerset box to Wells 'A' box was a little over 200 yards. As a consequence of this, the down main inner home and the down siding starter at East Somerset were electrically released by lever 28 at Wells 'A'. A detailed account of the method of working between the three boxes is given below.

Plate 246 - Wells East Somerset signal box viewed from Priory Road. This box, opened in July 1912, replaced an earlier box that may have been further from the crossing.
Rod Blencowe

WELLS EAST SOMERSET

Wells 'A' box was switched out after the last Somerset & Dorset train on Saturday until 6.30am on Monday. It would also be switched out at other times as demanded by Great Western traffic running outside of normal working hours. It is interesting to note that no other box between Yatton and Witham was capable of being switched out. The junction boxes at Yatton West and Witham were open continuously but all of the intermediate branch boxes would close after the last train at night and open before the first train in the morning, except as already noted.

Details of early signalling on the East Somerset section are rather sketchy. There is no record of any signal box prior to the first at Wells East Somerset installed in the mid-1870s. This would have been in preparation for the connection of the East Somerset and the Cheddar Valley branches via the Somerset & Dorset station and the concentration of all Great Western passenger traffic at the former Bristol & Exeter station. There was also an early box at Cranmore installed in 1880. Other than that, all of the signalling information on the East Somerset section relates to the post-1893 era.

Wells East Somerset signal box controlled access to East Somerset goods yard and the locomotive shed as well as the level crossing on the busy Wells to Glastonbury main road. The Great Western type 27C box was opened on 3rd July 1912 to replace the original box of unknown design. It was situated adjacent to the level crossing in order to give the signalman good visibility of approaching road traffic. Old maps suggest that the previous box was further away from the level crossing and the replacement was presumably positioned nearer the crossing in order to give the signalman a better view of the road. The original box contained 28 levers and may have been constructed at the same time as the link between the three stations was completed in 1875. The original frame installed in the second box was a 21-lever 5¼in stud but this was replaced on 2nd December 1955 by a 27-lever 5-bar vertical tappet frame with the levers at 4in centres.

The new frame was installed in conjunction with the closure of the Somerset & Dorset Wells 'A' box. The former junction of the Cheddar Valley and Glastonbury lines at Priory Road was retained to provide access to the ex-Somerset & Dorset goods yard that still remained open even though the rest of the branch had closed. Control of the running line points was transferred to East Somerset signal box and a short length of the single line towards Glastonbury was retained as a headshunt. The running signals for the Glastonbury line were removed and replaced by ground discs. Control of the running signals to and from the Cheddar Valley line, one of which was a Southern Region design upper quadrant, was transferred to East Somerset. In addition the entire layout at East Somerset was renumbered. Movements in and out of the Somerset & Dorset yard still crossed the Cheddar Valley running line so a 2-lever ground frame was installed near the site of Wells 'A' box to control the catch points that protected the running line. The ground frame was released by the East Somerset to Wells Station electric key token. Following this alteration the working of Priory Road goods yard had to be carried out in accordance with Electric Token Block Regulation 7 (this Regulation covers the occupation of a single line block section for shunting purposes).

The loop at East Somerset could only be used by goods trains, so it was never possible to pass two passenger trains there. The proximity of Wells station, where two passenger trains could be crossed, meant that this was never a problem. Before accepting a passenger train in either direction the signalman had to be sure that he had not already accepted another passenger train in the opposite direction. In 1949 the signal box steps at East Somerset were moved from the east to the west end of the box. The level crossing on this side restricted the space available so the steps were re-positioned at right angles to the running line. This was unusual for a Great Western signal box but the reason for moving the steps was because a new turntable had been installed adjacent to the box in late 1948 to replace the one on the Shepton Mallet side of the locomotive shed. Presumably the

Two interior views of Wells East Somerset signal box. *Plate 247*, left, shows the block instrument used for regulating traffic on the single line to Wells 'A' (Somerset & Dorset) and Wells Station signal boxes. When Wells 'A' was closed in 1955, electric token working was introduced between East Somerset and Wells Station box. *Plate 248*, right, shows the Electric Train Staff instrument for the single line section to Shepton Mallet. Notes about signalling on single lines are contained in Appendix A. *Ian Scrimgeour; Signalling Record Society*

signal box steps were in the way, although it does seem that they were not moved until some months after the commissioning of the new turntable.

The original method of single line working used between Wells East Somerset, Wells 'A' and Wells Station signal boxes is worthy of detailed attention. Originally there was no form of train staff or token in use and the block arrangements consisted solely of a block bell and a single deck pegging block instrument of the type normally used for one line of a double line. The same dial was used for up and down trains, the only indication of a train's direction being shown by whichever signalman's keys were depressed. It was even possible for one signalman to cancel whatever the other had pegged up by depressing the 'opposite' key. It is doubtful whether such arrangements would be allowed in these safety conscious days but it appeared to work without any problems.

It seems that the local instructions required the Somerset & Dorset signalman to get 'Line Clear' from East Somerset before returning 'Line Clear' to Wells Station signal box, and vice versa, although in practice he would acknowledge 'Line Clear' when it was asked and then immediately ask for 'Line Clear' to the box in advance. When the Somerset & Dorset box was switched out, East Somerset would work directly with Wells Station box on the same block instruments used when the Somerset & Dorset box was switched in. When the S&D box was abolished in 1955, electric key token working was introduced between East Somerset and Wells Station signal boxes. The regulations also permitted vehicles to be drawn or propelled between East Somerset and Wells Station with or without a brake van. If being propelled then the guard or shunter would ride in the leading vehicle or walk alongside it in a position to be able to signal to the driver. He would also be responsible for seeing that the level crossing gates were opened and that the appropriate signals were cleared.

Another interesting operational feature that lasted until closure of the line was the fact that up and down directions were reversed at Wells. This was yet another manifestation of the fact that the line originated as two separate entities. Thus a train from Yatton to Witham would travel in the down direction as far as Wells but would then become an up train to complete its journey to Witham. Likewise a train from Witham to Yatton would also change from down to up at Wells. The exact point where the transformation from down to up took place is not clear but the signal box diagrams would suggest that it was in the few yards between the east end of Priory Road station and the level crossing. Here stood both the East Somerset up home and the Wells 'A' (Somerset & Dorset) up home on opposite sides of the single line and reading in opposite directions! Note that the up direction on the Somerset & Dorset line was from Wells to Glastonbury. The Railway Clearing House junction diagram for Wells indicates that this point also coincides with the boundary between the Great Western and the Somerset &

Plate 249 - View from a train at Shepton Mallet High Street station heading towards Witham, possibly in August 1948. The signal was the release from the down platform line for an up train departing from that platform. The ground disc would be the release from the down siding to the up platform line.
J Moss; Roger Carpenter collection

Dorset railways. Great Western trains therefore traversed S&D metals from this point for a distance of 9 chains to a point 4 chains on the Cheddar side of the junction with the line to Glastonbury.

Shepton Mallet was equipped with a Great Western type 5 signal box in 1894 when the passing loop was installed. A second platform on the down side was brought into use on 8th January 1895. It is not known what prior signalling arrangements existed, particularly during the period from 1858 to 1862 when it was a terminus, although it seems that there may have been an earlier signal box. As well as the passing loop there were up and down loop sidings. Also on the up side were a goods shed, loading dock and additional siding accommodation. Spring points were installed at the Wells end of the up loop to ensure that any runaway vehicles were derailed well before reaching the 1 in 46 descending gradient to Wells.

Kilver Street Crossing stood on the outskirts of Shepton Mallet where what is now the A37 main road crossed the line on the level. The gates were worked by hand and a 3-lever ground frame was provided to lock the gates and work the up and down distant signals that protected the crossing. After the closure of the line to passenger trains the ground frame was disconnected and the distants were fixed. During the goods-only period the gates would have been worked by the train crew.

Doulting Siding did have a signal box dating from before 1880 but it was abolished and replaced by a ground frame when Electric Train Staff working was introduced in 1896. The Great Western Survey of the line carried out in 1878-9 (TNA RAIL/274/41) shows the presence of a signal box adjacent to the scissors crossover that provided the connection to the siding. It was positioned on the down side of the line whilst the siding itself was on the up side. The same survey also shows that there were signals on either side of the signal box, each at a distance of about three chains. No other information has come to light on this signal box.

Cranmore was equipped with a Great Western type 7B signal box which was opened on 11th September 1904 to replace the original of unknown design which stood on the up platform and originally opened in 1880. The 1904 signal box contained a double twist frame with the levers at 5¼in centres. The new signal box was opened in conjunction with additional siding accommodation and alterations to the passing loop. There was a loop siding on the up side and extensive siding accommodation for traffic from local stone quarries. The crossover at the Shepton Mallet end of the loop siding was controlled by a ground frame, but that was in the Cranmore to Shepton Mallet single line section so it was released by the electric train staff and, in later years, by the electric key token. The ground frame was abolished on 30th April 1963.

The orginal signal box at Witham was opened in about 1880 and was a Great Western type 2. It was equipped with a 30-lever frame but was rebuilt in about 1896 as a type 5 with a 47-lever frame. In 1942 the frame was replaced with a 67-lever 5-bar vertical tappet frame with the levers at 4in centres. This frame remained in use until the signal box was closed on 24th November 1984 when control of the junction was transferred to the new Westbury panel signal box. The box was situated on the down side of the line opposite the junction, giving the signalman a good view of trains on the branch as well as the main line.

In addition to those already described there were other in-section ground frames at McAlpine's Siding between Cheddar and Axbridge, at Gate Lane Siding and Dulcote Stone Quarry Sidings between Wells and Shepton Mallet, Doulting Stone Siding between Shepton Mallet and Cranmore and at Merehead Quarry Siding between Cranmore and Wanstrow. Special instructions were issued for the working of the sidings controlled by these ground frames. These instructions are dealt with elsewhere.

The East Somerset section was worked 'one engine in steam' when first opened but this soon proved to be too restrictive. The line was eventually equipped with disc block telegraph and

Plate 250 - The signalling notice issued in May 1896 to herald the introduction of Electric Train Staff operation of the single line sections. Prior to that the mode of operation was Train Staff and Ticket. The implementation of the new system is discussed on the next page. It seems, however, that it was some while before the operating staff were at ease with the new equipment as the letter from the Bristol Inspector's office (*overleaf*) was to reveal some seven years later.

Author's collection

Notice No. 175.

GREAT WESTERN RAILWAY.

(For the use of the Company's Servants only.)

Notice to Station Masters, Engine Drivers, Guards and Signalmen.

Introduction of Electric Train Staff System between Yatton, Wells, and Witham.

The Single Line between these Points (except between Tucker Street and East Somerset Stations at Wells), which at present is worked on the Block Telegraph system in addition to the Train Staff, will, on and from **Monday, May 11th**, be worked by the Electric Train Staff system, which is a combination of the Train Staff and Block Telegraph systems, under Rules 384 to 411. The Line between the Tucker Street and East Somerset Stations will continue to be worked under Yard Instructions.

The Train Staff Sections and the persons who alone must exchange the Staffs at the Stations are as under :—

Staff Sections.		Persons Authorised to Exchange the Staffs.
Between Yatton and Sandford	Yatton	Foreman or Acting Foreman
„ Sandford and Axbridge	Sandford	Person in charge of Block and Staff Instrument
„ Axbridge and Cheddar	Axbridge	Signalman
„ Cheddar and Lodge Hill	Cheddar	Signalman
„ Lodge Hill and Wookey	Lodge Hill	Person in charge of Block and Staff Instrument
„ Wookey and Wells (Tucker Street)	Wookey	Person in charge of Block and Staff Instrument
„ Wells (East Somerset) & Shepton Mallet	Wells (Tucker Street)	Signalman
	„ (East Somerset)	Signalman
„ Shepton Mallet and Cranmore	Shepton Mallet	Signalman
„ Cranmore and Witham	Cranmore	Signalman
	Witham	Signalman

The Points at Congresbury, Winscombe, Draycott, Dulcot, and Doulting will be locked by Annett's Key attached to each Staff. The Driver of any Train which has to call at those places to put off or pick up trucks, must hand the Staff to the Guard, and must take care that he does not resume his journey until it has been returned to him.

worked with train staff and ticket. The adoption of this system of working coincided with the opening of the first signal box at Cranmore in 1880. According to the 1886 working timetable the Witham to Cranmore section had a red square staff and the Cranmore to Wells section had a white round staff. The Cheddar Valley section was worked by block telegraph in conjunction with train staff and ticket from the outset. The 1886 working timetable shows that the Wells to Cheddar section had a green square staff and the Cheddar to Yatton section had a red round staff. This begs the question as to why Axbridge was not a staff station at this time in view of the fact that it was equipped with a passing loop and signalling.

The staff and ticket method of operation was superseded by the introduction of Electric Train Staff working on Monday, 11th May 1896 with the exception of the two sections from Wells East Somerset to Wells 'A' and Wells Station boxes as was noted previously. At this time Congresbury, Winscombe, Draycott, Dulcote Siding and Doulting Siding did not have loops to enable trains to be crossed. In order to save the expense of installing electric train staff instruments at these places, they were abolished as block posts and their signals were removed on Sunday, 10th May 1896. Details of the alterations were circulated in GWR Operating Notice No.178 dated 5th May 1896. Distant signals were retained at Draycott to protect the level crossing and targets and lamps were placed on the gates in lieu of home signals. At Winscombe, Dulcote and Doulting the siding points were operated by ground frames that were released by an Annett's key attached to the electric train staff. Interestingly, the signal boxes at Lodge Hill and Wookey escaped this fate despite not having passing loops. It was possible to cross two trains at either location by shunting a goods train into the siding but two passenger trains could not be crossed. Perhaps it was deemed necessary to break up what would otherwise be an unacceptably long section of eight and three-quarter miles between Cheddar and Wells.

Some days prior to the change over, Notice No.175 bearing the date 6th May 1896 (*Plate 250*) was circulated to station masters, locomotive crews, guards and signalmen. It described the method of signalling using the electric train staff and emphasised that care was to be taken in the handling of the staffs themselves. This instruction appears to have been ignored by some as may be concluded from the content of a letter from the Inspector's Office in Bristol dated 4th December 1903. The letter was addressed to the signalmen at Cheddar and reads as follows:

'Electric Train Staffs

Attention is called to the fact that a very large number of these staffs are sent to Reading for repairs and in many cases it has been found that if a little care had been exercised the damage would not have occurred. It is important that all concerned who deal with these staffs should use them very carefully. Please give this matter your special attention and acknowledge receipt.

Yours . . . . '

Distant signals on the branch were altered to yellow arms and lights between 2nd and 20th April 1928. Signal notice No.S 1330 was issued in order to inform staff of this change. Long before that, as notified in the signalling notice No.S 381 of November 1904, the red lights in ground discs, siding and backing signals of the Cheddar Valley section were to be replaced by white ones. The work was to be carried out over three days, November 22nd to 24th, as listed in the notice, reproduced opposite.

During the 1940s and 1950s the electric train staff itself was replaced by the more modern and less cumbersome electric key token and every single line section between Yatton and Witham had been converted by the mid-1950s. In 1948 electric key token working was in use on the Yatton West to Congresbury and the Sandford and Banwell to Axbridge sections, the other sections on the Cheddar Valley line still being operated by electric train staff. By 1950 the Congresbury to Sandford and Banwell and the Axbridge to Cheddar sections had been similarly treated. When the signal box at Wookey was closed in 1954, electric key token working was instituted between Wells Station and Cheddar.

According to information obtained from an ex-Great Western Railway employee some years ago and passed on to the writer, electric key token working was in use on the Shepton Mallet to Wells East Somerset section by 1948. The change to electric key token may have been associated with the installation of Gate Lane Ground Frame during the Second World War. The introduction of electric key token working between Wells East Somerset and Wells Station has already been described and the date of its introduction on the Shepton Mallet to Cranmore and the Cranmore to Witham sections is not known. Each section was equipped with 40 electric key tokens but token transfers had to be carried out because of unbalanced train workings. On the Cheddar Valley section in particular, where there was one more up train per day than down, tokens tended to accumulate at the Yatton end of the section and token transfers were carried out monthly. The in-section ground frames were released by the electric train staff or electric key token as appropriate.

Information with regard to the actual token configurations in use on the line is rather sketchy. It is known that the section from Yatton West to Congresbury used an 'A' pattern that was red in colour, the section from Witham to Cranmore used a 'B' pattern and the section from Shepton Mallet to Wells East Somerset used a 'D' pattern. It seems that the latter section was originally equipped with the old style steel tokens and that these were later replaced by aluminium ones. This ties in with the earlier suggestion that token working was introduced on this section during World War II as aluminium was then in short supply. After 1954 following the closure of Wookey signal box, the Cheddar to Wells Station section used an 'A' pattern token. The token for the Congresbury to Sandford and Banwell section was yellow in colour but of unknown pattern.

After the line closed for passenger trains all of the branch signal boxes except for Cranmore had closed by the summer of 1965. The electric key token systems were removed and working by train staff was found to be sufficient for the level of traffic now using the line. After the closure of the signal box at Cranmore the entire line was worked under one train regulations with a single train staff.

Plate 251 - Signal notice S 381 dealing with replacement of red lights by white in some signals. As is typical of such notices, other work scheduled at more than one location is frequently listed in the same notice.

Author's collection

[PRIVATE AND NOT FOR PUBLICATION.]   Notice No. S 381.

GREAT WESTERN RAILWAY.

(For the use of the Company's Servants only.)

Alteration of Signals at Swindon "D" Box.

SUNDAY, NOVEMBER 20th, 1904.

Commencing at 6.0 a.m., the Signal Engineer will move the Down Platform Line to Main Starting, and Down Platform Line to Branch Starting Signals (on same post) 35 yards farther from the Box, and the Down Main Starting Signal 47 yards farther from the Box.

These Signals are all slotted from "E" Box.

During the time the work is being carried out, Distant Signals Nos. 1 in "D" Box and 2 in "E" Box will be disconnected and placed at danger.

WHITE LIGHTS IN GROUND DISCS, SIDING AND BACKING SIGNALS IN PLACE OF RED LIGHTS.

This alteration will be made as under:—

November 22nd.—Clevedon, Congresbury, Sandford and Banwell and Winscombe.

November 23rd.—Cheddar and Draycott.

November 24th.—Wookey ground frame and station, Wells (Tucker Street), East Somerset and ground frame.

The work will be commenced at 10 a.m. each day.

District Inspectors to make the necessary arrangements in accordance with Rule 71.

Advise all concerned, and acknowledge receipt to Head of Department.

C. KISLINGBURY,
Divisional Superintendent.

TEMPLE MEADS STATION,
BRISTOL, November, 1904.

(2500)   J. W. Arrowsmith, Printer, Quay Street, Bristol.

Chapter Thirteen

ACCIDENTS

There were a number of accidents on the Yatton to Witham line during its existence but fortunately all of those involving passenger trains were of a minor nature and no passenger ever received serious injuries as a result.

The first accident occurred at Wookey not long after the Cheddar Valley section was opened and whilst it was still broad gauge. The date was Thursday, 18th December 1873, a day of dense fog that certainly contributed to the accident. The 3.20pm luggage train (as it was referred to by the *Wells Journal*) stopped at Wookey for the purpose of setting down and picking up wagons. At this time there was only a single connection between the running line and the siding on the down side of the line. The siding did not achieve its final length and become a loop until 1900. The connection to the running line faced towards Cheddar, so in order to shunt the siding the train would have had to set back into it. Having completed its work it would have run straight back onto the running line and departed for Bristol. Once the train had cleared the points, they should have been set back to the normal position (ie. to the running line) ready for the 5.20pm passenger train from Bristol. Unfortunately, this was not done and the passenger train ran into the loop siding. The combination of the dense fog, and the fact that it seems that the signal lamps were not lit, meant that the train crew were not immediately aware of their unplanned deviation and the train struck two wagons that were standing some distance apart on the siding, scattering them either side of the line in the process. It seems that there was some considerable damage to the locomotive and it was unable to continue its journey. The wagons were no doubt written off! Fortunately the train was slowing down as it was due to stop at Wookey and no passenger received serious injury although they were somewhat shaken by the event. A telegraph message was sent to Wells and road transport was arranged to convey the passengers to their destination. A message was also sent to Bristol from where Inspector Rudd dispatched a special train to Cheddar. Meanwhile, the driver of the stricken train had made sufficient repairs to enable it to reach Wells and return to Cheddar, enabling passengers to connect with the special train and continue their journey, although somewhat delayed.

It seems that the points were connected to some form of indicator referred to in the newspaper report as an 'auxiliary signal'. The indicator was designed to show a red light when the points were open to the siding but it appears that the light was not lit. The pointsman was on the platform waving a white light to show all clear. Had the rule book of the Bristol & Exeter Railway been sufficiently rigorous then this accident would have been avoided. Of course, this all happened some years before the Regulation of Railways Act of 1889 which enforced the interlocking of points and signals with the additional requirement that signals had to give a definite indication of both clear or danger aspects by day and by night.

The Bristol & Exeter Railway never lost the life of any passenger during its independent existence. Unfortunately the same could not be said of its employees. In spite of the fact that the rule books, even at that time, made an emphasis on personal safety, accidents did happen. The cause was frequently due to non-observance of the rules, and one such incident that led to the death of an employee happened on the Cheddar Valley line in June 1875.

A gang of four men had been working somewhere between Sandford and Yatton. Sandford was in fact the limit of their particular length. They were returning towards Yatton with their trolley, which was a four wheeled vehicle without suspension or brakes. Such trolleys were intended only to be pushed by the gang who were to remain on foot. They were not designed to be ridden on, especially at any speed above walking pace! The main purpose of the trolley was for the transport of heavy tools and it was intended to be removed from the line when a train was due. In fact they pushed the trolley into Congresbury station to allow a down train from Yatton to pass. Presumably they ran it into the siding, as Congresbury at that time did not possess a passing loop.

In order to speed up their return journey they hitched the trolley to the rear of the train and climbed aboard. This was a practice that was expressly forbidden by the rule book. It is difficult to conceive how they actually performed this feat because the siding access from the running line was at the Sandford end of the station, so the train must have already been moving before they ran out of the siding and hitched a rope to the coupling of the rearmost vehicle. The train accelerated away from Congresbury with the crew oblivious to their illegal tail traffic. A mile or so outside Congresbury the trolley became derailed at speed. No doubt the occupants had been subjected to a very rough ride already due to the lack of springing and weight on the trolley and were probably considering the wisdom of their actions. Of the four, Frank Hemmans was killed, George Radford and Sam Gardner suffered fracture injuries and Edward Marks remarkably escaped unscathed. There is no record of the disciplinary measures the survivors were subjected to as a result of this misdemeanour.

The East Somerset section witnessed the derailment of a passenger train on 8th May 1889 between Cranmore and Witham but fortunately there were no injuries. The 9.40am from Wells, hauled by a 1016 Class 0-6-0ST and consisting of five 4-wheeled coaches, was running down a gradient of 1 in 47 about one and a half miles short of Witham at a speed approaching 30mph. The wheels of the leading axle of the leading vehicle became derailed and ran like this as far as an occupation crossing a couple of hundred yards further on. Here the wheels of the other axle of the vehicle also became derailed

Plate 252 - Obviously reproduced from a postcard, this view of Congresbury station was taken from the road bridge. The picture is undated but is after the construction of the Wrington Vale Light Railway since the signals are installed for the diverging line.

It was near Congresbury that an accident occurred in June 1875 when non-observance of the rules and regulations contributed to the death of one employee, Frank Hemmans, and serious injuries to two others.

John Alsop collection

along with the wheels of the leading axle of three of the other vehicles in the train. The driver and guard became aware of this almost immediately and between them brought the train to a halt within 100 yards (the locomotive was equipped with a steam brake and the train fitted with Fay's continuous brake under control of the guard). A couple of days before the accident a number of longitudinal and transom timbers (although now standard gauge, the permanent way was still of Brunel's 'baulk road' construction) had been replaced but the ballasting had not been completed. Colonel Rich, the inspecting officer, recommended the introduction of a speed restriction where ballasting had not been completed following permanent way work. He also had some comments to make about the method of coupling the locomotive to the leading vehicle and remarked that had the train been fitted with a good automatic continuous braking system no damage would have been done. As it was, the damage was largely confined to the permanent way, which required the replacement of a further 20 transoms.

January 1894 saw the death of another railway employee, although this time on the face of it there was no infringement of the rules. This was at Draycott where the small goods yard contained a wagon turntable in order to access a siding that was at right angles to the running line. A goods train was shunting a coal wagon from the running line into the yard when, at the same time, the station master, William Hallet, was moving another vehicle from the right angle siding onto the wagon turntable. The coal wagon struck the other vehicle causing the unfortunate station master to fall underneath and, although he was pulled out alive, he died on his way to hospital.

In 1904 there were two fatalities on the line in the Dulcote area. The first was on 14th March 1904 when a man carrying a sack of coal across the line was killed instantly when he was struck by the 1.30pm from Shepton Mallet. He was at the time returning from the quarry engine house and failed to react to a warning shouted at him by two other men who were unloading a wagon at the quarry. During the following month a 12 year old boy was killed by a train nearby.

On Tuesday, 19th September 1911 there was a collision at Congresbury in which, fortunately, no one was injured. The 5.10pm Wells-Bristol goods train ran into the up loop at 9.35pm where it was booked to cross the 9.42pm Yatton-Wells passenger train. The passenger train arrived at 9.58pm and when its work was complete it started off at 10.00pm. The locomotive of the passenger train struck the brake van at the rear the goods train. The brake van was derailed and there was some damage to the locomotive and the first three vehicles of the passenger train, which was mainly confined to the door handles, foot boards and one window was broken. There were forty passengers on the train at the time. A breakdown train was sent down from Bristol at 11.30pm. Signalman Hartnell at Congresbury stated that the guard of the goods train had assured him that his train was clear of the down line. The station master was off duty and relief porter Treasure was in charge. The goods train was later dispatched to Bristol with the Blagdon branch brake van. The passengers finally got away from Congresbury at 12.09am, a relief train having come up from Wells for that purpose. The guard of the goods train admitted that the collision was his fault and he was suspended.

A man named Wood who had been employed on odd days at Wells station for 12 to 14 years was killed during shunting on 29th November 1911. Whilst he seemed to have some knowledge of shunting, he was under strict instruction from the station master that he was not to take part in any shunting operations. The accident was caused by Porter Chapman who was described as an experienced man of excellent character. He had neglected to check that the points were set correctly before signalling a train back into the up platform. Chapman was suspended for fourteen days.

The death of Alfred Augustus West at Wells East Somerset in 1916 has already been mentioned. He was knocked down by the engine of the Bristol goods that was running tender first. The driver had seen the man, who had raised his hand in acknowledgement and was some yards ahead of the train. The driver was then alerted by someone else shouting at him and stopped the train as soon as he could. West had been run over by the train and a doctor was called immediately but it was too late and West died within minutes of the doctor's arrival. The verdict was accidental death, although it was never explained why a man in his twenties in good health with some years railway experience would have crossed the line in front of a train in that manner.

The final accident occurred on Saturday, 12th August 1961. Ivatt Class 2MT No.41208 was working the 6.55am Yatton-Wells passenger train running bunker first when a blow-back occurred between Draycott and Lodge Hill. A blow-back is a sudden interruption in the normal flow of the hot combustion products in the firebox that results in a sheet of flame entering the locomotive cab instead of travelling though the boiler tubes and out through the chimney. The causes are various and it could be that the exhaust blast in the smokebox was momentarily interrupted by some freak wind blowing down the locomotive's chimney. In any case, the Bristol driver George Whitman and his fireman Michael James jumped off the locomotive to avoid the flames. The guard, Derek Palmer, was no doubt alerted by the fact that the train had run through Lodge Hill station without stopping, and he eventually stopped the train just before Easton cutting.

Paul Fry, whose father was a guard on the Somerset & Dorset and had been a railwayman himself, was a volunteer for the Somerset County Ambulance Service. He has a vivid memory of this incident and his very graphic account of it is transcribed here in his own words:

"During the 1960s the Somerset County Ambulance Service only employed one full-time ambulance driver in Wells – the late Mr. Bert Rendall, and all assistance was given by us the volunteers. We were on call during the night from 11.00pm to 8.00am and responded to all emergency calls during those times.

It was on 12th August 1961, a Saturday morning to be precise. I had been detailed to do a duty for the Wells Division St. John Ambulance but, before I could start, things took a rather sudden change of direction. At about 7.30am we received an emergency call.

The Wells Ambulance driver, a very experienced ambulanceman, and I set off not knowing what we we going to find. All we had been told, "There has been an accident on the railway line between Draycott and Lodge Hill", other than the fact, "There would be someone waiting on the main road to show us how to get to the nearest point to the line."

We did in fact see a man sitting on a gate by the main road but he gave absolutely no sign to us, or even looked as if he had recognised us, so we went on. We spent some time going down the various tracks and lanes, climbing up banks, etc, looking for the incident. Eventually, having found nothing, we backtracked to where the man was.

When we stopped he calmly said, "It be down there," and pointed across a large field. Fortunately the grass was dry, otherwise we would not have been able to drive down to the fence above the cutting - the ambulance, a Bedford Wyvern conversion (BYC433), was certainly not a cross country vehicle. We did actually find out later we had lost the spare wheel crossing the field.

We arrived at the fence and looked over and down a cutting, only to see the enginmen lying by the side of the permanent way, both in a bad way. The driver Mr. Whitman was complaining of an intense pain in his leg – he, in fact, had a broken femur - and the fireman was huddled up shivering, complaining loudly of being cold. On examination we found that he was terribly burned down one side, with the skin of his face hanging down like curtains. The smell of burnt flesh and oily clothes was most horrible, it took me months to get the smell out of my nostrils.

Just as we arrived three strong gangers fortunately came up the line and with their help we carried the fireman up the steep cutting side, through the fence and to the ambulance, no mean feat. A radio message had been sent to ambulance control for assistance. We returned to the driver and immobilised his leg as best we could before getting him up off the track.

We really were on the horns of a dilemma. What to do? A decision had to be made and it is hoped we made the right one. The burnt man was in a very bad condition, as indeed was the driver. Both men were suffering from shock (loss of body fluid), the fireman from his burns and the driver from loss of blood from his fracture.

A decision had to be made quickly, we could only take one casualty. Bert Rendall decided we would return to Wells with the fireman, doing what little we could on the way. Mr. James just complained all the way he was cold and wanted a drink – however he could only be given sips of water to moisten his lips, in case an anaesthetic was needed on arrival at hospital.

The driver was made as comfortable as possible and had to wait for the back-up ambulance from Shepton Mallet, to turn up. He was left in the hands of a ganger - one who fortunately was first-aid trained.

Another radio message was made asking for a doctor to be waiting at his surgery in Chamberlain Street in Wells when we went through on the way to hospital.

We made contact with the doctor, who gave the casualty an injection to ease the pain and I was relieved by another ambulanceman, who went to Frenchay Hospital with the patient.

I was certainly very glad to be relieved, as I was physically sick and exhausted by this time, what with the tension and the smell of burnt flesh and also with the frustration that there was very little that we could do. I suppose the fact that he was a fellow railwayman made matters worse. There was no such thing as counselling in those days. I was told that it was all part of the job and to get on with it. Which I did."

Meanwhile back to the train; Harry Viles and another member of the Wells shed staff came out by car. When they found the train and climbed aboard, No.41208 was blowing off steam. They also found evidence of the blowback in that there was some waste rag and a locoman's cap alight on the footplate. They drove the train onwards to Wells station where they detached the coaches and ran onto Wells shed. The locomotive was later checked out back at Bristol but nothing was found to be wrong with it. Fortunately both footplatemen recovered and afterwards the fireman came back to work but the driver left the railway.

Chapter Fourteen

CAMPING COACHES

Camping coaches were a feature of branch lines in rural and holiday areas during the middle years of the twentieth century. They remained common up until the 1960s, after which they declined with the increased availability of relatively cheap holidays abroad, but there are still one or two places where they survive to this day.

It was the London and North Eastern Railway that thought of the original idea, introducing the first camping coaches under the title of 'Railway Caravans' in 1933. The company was probably in the worst financial situation of the four groups during that period, so that it comes as no surprise that the idea came from that quarter. It was a well conceived scheme to make money by renting out life-expired vehicles as holiday homes. The cost to the company was fairly small for the conversion of the vehicles into what was pretty rudimentary accommodation lacking running water and sanitary facilities. By that time road transport was beginning to eat into the traffic on branch lines and so it was probably fairly easy to find siding space at rural stations. In the event, the other three main line companies were eager to copy the idea.

The Great Western Railway followed suit in 1935 and many of the stations on the Cheddar Valley section received them during the GWR era. There was a lull after 1939, no doubt caused by the hostilities of the 1940s, but the idea was revived in 1952 and many stations, including a number on the Cheddar Valley line, were allocated camping coaches once more. Congresbury was allocated a camping coach every year up until and including 1962 which, like many others, was fashioned from a 55ft clerestory first/second composite coach. In 1959 vehicle number W9901W was in use here and it is believed that the same vehicle was resident at Congresbury throughout the period in question. This vehicle was certainly noted there in September 1962. Photographs show that it was originally situated in one of the sidings on the up side at the Sandford end of the station. Later it was moved into the loading dock on the goods shed road behind the down platform.

Sandford and Banwell never had a camping coach because of the heavy stone traffic. Winscombe had one up until 1939 and then again from 1952 to 1960. Vehicle number W9909W was noted here during the 1950s and it was located in the goods loop headshunt just north of the station platform. Axbridge hosted camping facilities until 1939, whilst Cheddar had a camping coach allocated every year up till 1963 except for 1953. It was situated in the down sidings behind the goods shed. No. W9902W seemed to be the incumbent there as it was noted on four separate occasions between 1956 and 1963. Draycott never had a camping coach, no doubt because of the fact that the small goods yard could be very busy in the strawberry season. Lodge Hill hosted one from 1936 to 1939 but after the resumption in 1952 it had one for that year only and so may be judged as not being a great success. Wookey had a camping coach between 1935 and 1939 and, although official records do not show any allocation after the war, local knowledge has it that it did return for at least one year. Harry Viles of Wells shed recalls that when he was made up to fireman and was transferred to Swindon for a few months in 1941, one of his first turns there was to take the Wookey camping coach to the Highworth branch for storage. Wells had a camping coach in 1952, after which there was a five year gap until one was allocated again in 1958. Wells then had one every year up until and including 1963. It was kept on the goods shed dead end road. Vehicle number W9927W was noted there on 15th September 1962.

In 1939 6-berth camping coaches were at Congresbury, Winscombe, Axbridge, Lodge Hill and Wookey whilst that at Cheddar had 8 berths. Blagdon on the Wrington Vale line also had a 6-berth camping coach in 1939, even though the passenger service on the branch had finished in 1931.

Plate 253 - Winscombe station on 21st June 1958 as 0-6-0PT No.9729 is at the head of an up train. Note the camping coach in the siding headshunt, probably W9909W.
Camera flare precludes the use of any more of the foreground.
Bob Griffiths

Chapter Fifteen

MEMORIES OF A BRANCH LINE

One of the aspects of railway operation that, along with the branch line itself, has more or less disappeared from the modern national railway network is the sense of community. There was a sense of purpose in everything that was done and everybody worked together to provide a good service to the local population. A spin-off from this is the number of stories, anecdotes and even legends that accumulated down the years and the Yatton to Witham line was no exception.

The steep gradients on the East Somerset section, in particular the stretch of 1 in 46 that was over three miles in length between Shepton Mallet and Wells, caused a number of incidents. A couple of these are related here and although both were probably quite frightening to those involved at the time, they are not without an element of humour.

In 1942 a Government stores train conveying several wagons loaded with high-octane aviation fuel in five-gallon jerry cans bound for an American store at Highbridge was on its way down from Shepton Mallet. All unfitted goods trains were supposed to stop at the top of the 1 in 46 bank going down to Wells in order to pin down a sufficient number of brakes to ensure a safe descent. The on-board inspector was concerned that if the brakes were applied, the wheels would become too hot with the possibility of a fire and potentially disastrous consequences. The driver agreed to descend the bank using just the locomotive brakes alone but gravity soon took over and the train sped down the bank.

The signalman at Wells East Somerset signal box, having heard the locomotive whistling continuously down the bank realised that something was wrong and opened the level crossing gates and sent the 'Train Running Away' bell code to Priory Road box. The signalman here controlled the junction of the lines to Glastonbury and Yatton and so had the option of which way to send the train. Under normal circumstances the train, being bound for Highbridge, would have been signalled for the Glastonbury route. However the signalman set the road for the Yatton direction and passed the 'Train Running Away' signal on to the signalman at Tucker Street.

Meanwhile the train, now travelling at well over twice the permitted line speed, shot through Priory Road and Tucker Street stations and into Portway cutting where it was finally brought under control, assisted by the rising gradient. It was fortunate for all those concerned, and indeed many of the residents of that part of Wells, that the line was clear through both stations, that the East Somerset signalman managed to open the level crossing gates in time and that the train stayed on the road through some very sharp curves.

Naturally there was an enquiry following this incident. All three signalmen were interviewed and congratulated on their quick thinking and prompt action. However, when the Somerset & Dorset signalman was asked why he had decided to send the train on to Tucker Street instead of to Glastonbury his reply was, *"Twas their train so I let 'em have it."* He had concluded that as the Great Western had created the problem in the first place it was up to them to come up with a solution. The animosity between the Great Western and the Somerset & Dorset was still strong in spite of the fact that there was a war on and everyone was supposed to be fighting a common enemy!

A later incident involved a passenger train consisting of a B-set hauled by a BR Standard Class 3MT 2-6-2T (82000 Class). There was a crew change at Shepton Mallet and the driver,

Plate 254 - Looking under Burcott Road bridge at Wells showing the goods yard and impressive goods shed. In the distance is the rising ground leading to Portway cutting, which acted as the 'over-run' for a runaway train carrying aviation fuel in 1942 after the driver and travelling inspector misjudged the braking power of the engine.
J Moss; Roger Carpenter collection

Plate 255 - Undated view taken from a train arriving at Shepton Mallet High Street from the Witham direction.

J Moss; Roger Carpenter collection

being a die-hard Great Western man, without thinking sat down in the right hand seat on the footplate. When the fireman reminded him that this was a standard engine and that the driver's controls were on the left hand side of the cab, he moved over muttering derogatory remarks about what he referred to as 'Midland engines'; was he not aware that this class was actually built at Swindon and fitted with a Swindon boiler? The train duly set off in the direction of Wells.

After a brief climb out of Shepton Mallet for a mile or so, the head of the 1 in 46 bank down to Wells was reached. Its position was marked by a stop board requesting all down goods and mineral trains to 'pin down' before proceeding. Passenger trains were fully fitted with continuous automatic brakes and so did not have to comply with this procedure. However, it was the general practice to apply the locomotive hand brake sufficiently to help check the speed of descent in addition to the vacuum brake that was applied to every vehicle in the train. On this occasion our driver refused to do this saying, *"The handbrake is no good on Midland engines,"* and, in spite of the fireman reminding him that it was a Standard engine, the handbrake remained firmly off. He chose to rely solely on the vacuum brake; or at least what he thought was the vacuum brake.

The former Great Western locomotives had only one brake handle on the footplate in addition to the handbrake. This applied the automatic vacuum brake to both the locomotive and to any vacuum fitted vehicles in the train. On the other hand, the British Railways Standard locomotives were fitted with a steam brake that was applied only to the locomotive itself and a vacuum brake that operated on any vacuum fitted vehicle in the train and also applied the steam brake on the locomotive via a graduable steam brake valve. The driver thus had two brake handles on the footplate. The first applied both the vacuum brake to the train and the steam brake to the locomotive, whilst the second applied the steam brake only. The former would be used when operating a passenger or other vacuum fitted train and the latter when running light or hauling an unfitted train

As it turned out on this occasion, our driver was only using the steam brake and thus was trying to check the entire train using only the locomotive's brake, which was quite inadequate on a 1 in 46 gradient! As the train gathered speed the fireman realised what had happened and hastily told the driver that he needed to use the vacuum brake. This was done and the train was brought to a halt by Wells East Somerset signal box just short of the level crossing. The driver was heard to say, *"That was lucky,"* but what was not recorded were his views on the braking performance of BR Standard locomotives.

Over-inflated egos could soon be deflated and the person concerned brought back to earth with a bang. This fate befell a rather self-opinionated porter who was acting as a guard on a goods train heading into Wells on the Cheddar Valley section. His flamboyant flag waving when giving the 'right away' had been noticed by, and was no doubt becoming an irritation to, other railwaymen. When stopped at a wayside station he noticed the station master in conversation with an inspector and, wishing to make himself prominent, left his guards van. Meanwhile, one of the signal and telegraph linesmen and the

MEMORIES OF 'STRAWBERRY LINE' PASSENGER POWER

Plate 256 - 4500 2-6-2T No.5542 shunts East Somerset yard on 7th May 1959. Probably still a Westbury engine at that time - where it was allocated a year earlier - it has now been preserved.

Rex Conway collection

(Below) Plate 257 - A Cheddar Valley branch passenger train leaves Yatton behind 4500 2-6-2T No.5528 on 10th June 1957. The mineral wagons are standing in the goods loop.

Mark Warburton

Opposite page

(Upper) Plate 258 - A view of Wells station from Burcott Road bridge. BR Standard Class 3MT 2-6-2T No.82009 pauses with the 3.17pm Frome-Bristol Temple Meads on 8th April 1960. Advantage is being taken of the water column between the tracks, a legacy of the original broad gauge spacing.

Brian Arman collection

Plate 259 - 4500 2-6-2T No.4595 stands in the down platform at Axbridge. The date is not known.

Robin Russell

THE EAST SOMERSET AND CHEDDAR VALLEY RAILWAYS

train driver conspired to play a trick on the guard. The linesman gave the driver the nod and slipped along the blind side of the train and quietly uncoupled the brake van. The guard, not suspecting that anything was wrong, gave the 'right away' in his usual exaggerated fashion and the train moved smartly out of the station leaving the brake van behind and the guard running down the platform shouting for the train to stop in full view of the station master and the inspector. Needless to say, there was a sufficient number of witnesses around to ensure that the whole event was quickly relayed to everybody up and down the line!

The winter of 1962-3 was one of the worst in living memory and all forms of transport were badly hit after heavy snowfalls. The bad weather started on Saturday, 29th December and on Monday 31st the early morning trains did get through, although they did run late. Colin Forse, formerly of Yatton shed, recalls that the first goods did get to Wells that day. Although Colin still lived in Yatton he now worked from Barrow Road shed in Bristol. On the Monday night he caught the train from Yatton to Bristol to go to work. When he arrived at the shed the foreman asked him to work the early Wells goods with fireman Clive Joslin. They ran light engine to West Depot to pick up the goods with Ivatt Class 2MT 2-6-0 No.46506.

The weather was very bad and after some discussion with Control they decided to run to Wells light engine. The thought was that they would be more likely to get through without a load behind. When they got to Yatton, Clive filled up with water and threw some coal off the tender for the fire devil whilst Colin found some shovels and sheeting. Congresbury signal box was open so the Yatton West signalman was able to get line clear and obtain the token for the section. No.46506 set off for Congresbury but when they arrived there they found that the road was set for the Wrington line and the points were frozen, so they used the steam lance to clean out the points and free them up. They were about to set off for Sandford when the signalman told them they had to wait at Congresbury because there was another locomotive coming down with a snowplough attached. Whilst waiting they took the opportunity to have some breakfast. The engine that arrived was a Collett 0-6-0 No.2277 and had an inspector on board who, it turns out, had never been on the line before. It was decided that the two locomotives would proceed with No.2277 in front (as it had the snowplough attached) and when they came across a snow drift they would 'go for it' and hope to get through.

They got to Sandford and exchanged tokens with the signalman. As they passed Winscombe they noticed a solitary man stood on the platform in the falling snow looking somewhat like a flour grader from the well known television advertisement. Presumably the optimistic gentleman was waiting for the first up passenger train to arrive! It was not until after Cheddar that they found the line blocked with snow. Leaving Cheddar station the line ran on an embankment first and then into a cutting near the Draycott down distant signal. Colin advised the inspector that the cutting would be full of snow and that they should uncouple the two locomotives so that the first one could rush into the drift at speed and the second one could pull the first out when it could move no further. They would continue this procedure until they broke through the drift. The inspector did not agree with this idea and went to get off the footplate. Colin called to him not to get off but it was too late and the inspector disappeared into a snow drift. They pulled him out of the snow and back onto the footplate. By now it was mid-morning on Tuesday, 1st January and it was snowing again. The depth of snow in the cutting was such that both locomotives were now stranded. They lit a fire in the locomotive cab itself to keep warm and built up a wall of snow to keep the blizzard out.

The inspector wanted to send a man back to Cheddar to explain the situation and to obtain assistance. Eventually it was agreed that it would be much safer for two men to go. Some children appeared by the railway from a nearby farmhouse and asked for some coal. In exchange, the children said that their mother would provide the railwaymen with a meal. The two men who walked to Cheddar returned later in the afternoon, by which time it was dark. The farmer's wife came over and told them the meal was ready. The men went over to the farmhouse

Plate 260 - The train shed at Cheddar Train shed viewed from the down platform in May 1948. Note that the old-style gas station lamps are still in situ.

J Moss; Roger Carpenter collection

and saw the table laid with a large spread. The farmer's wife said, *"Where are the rest of you?"* at which the five men looked puzzled as they were definitely all there and wondered why such a large spread had been put out for them. She told them that she had heard on the radio that upwards of one hundred men were trying to clear the railway. As it turned out, this was on the Somerset & Dorset line where the early morning goods from Bath to Evercreech Junction had also been abandoned in the snow! The men also found out later that an attempt had been made to clear the line from the Wells direction but they had become stuck in a snow drift in Easton cutting.

There was nothing else that could be done so they had to wait to be rescued. They spent Tuesday night, all day Wednesday and Wednesday night waiting. The locomotives were running short of water so the fires were let out. On the Thursday a Hymek diesel arrived and that became stuck. Walking alongside they could tell that something was wrong since the sandboxes appeared to be very high. In fact the locomotive was off the road. Compacted snow had lifted the front clear of the track! On the Friday morning, 4th January, a 2251 0-6-0 appeared. All of the men went back on the footplate leaving the two stricken steam locomotives and the one diesel to their fate! Colin Forse booked off duty at 12.20pm on Friday having booked on Monday evening. When his pay packet came through he had only been paid for two days and it took two weeks to get his pay sorted out. By the following week the ordeal had caught up with the men; Colin himself was off sick for two weeks afterwards.

Keeping the Memory Alive

Two projects of recent years will ensure that the existence of the Yatton to Witham line will not fade entirely from everybody's memory.

The first of these came about when, some twenty years after the last train had passed, it was decided that the track bed through Wells would form a major part of a Relief Road scheme. Although the road had been very much needed for many years, some of the citizens of Wells were none too happy to see the virtually complete destruction of what remained of Wells' once extensive railway infrastructure. After the opening of the relief road in the 1990s all that remained were the former goods shed at Tucker Street (that now incorrectly bears the name 'The Engine Shed') and a group of cottages at the bottom of Tucker Street called 'The Cheddar Valley Buildings'. To the observant these cottages are instantly recognisable as being of Bristol & Exeter Railway origin by their barge boards. There is also some railway fencing nearby that had originally lined the station approach road.

In the mid-1990s, Paul Fry (whose railway pedigree has already been established) and John Parsons, both of whom live in Wookey Hole, thought that it would be appropriate to mark the site of the three stations at Wells in some way. They approached Somerset County Council to see if they could help permanently mark these sites so as to commemorate the lives of all of the men and the women who had worked over the years on the local railways.

Fortunately the County Council Engineer at the time, Mr. Jim Olney, had had the foresight to preserve some of the stone from Burcott Road bridge that had stood immediately on the Cheddar side of Tucker Street station. This stone was used to construct three substantial markers, one on each station site. Each marker was topped with a Draycott marble slab into which was set a stainless steel plaque showing a map of the course of the old lines through Wells. Miniature railway totems bearing the name of each station were also mounted on the markers.

The original plan was to hold the official unveiling ceremony for the new markers on 29th October 2001 so as to coincide with the fiftieth anniversary of the closure of the Glastonbury to Wells line, but unfortunately the project was delayed. Eventually the design was completed and work started under the direction of Mr. Nicholas Wall of the Council's Environmental and Property Department. Mr. Wall saw the project through to its conclusion.

The project's completion was marked by an unveiling ceremony held on the site of the former Somerset & Dorset Priory Road station at midday on Wednesday, 6th March 2002. Somerset & Dorset enthusiasts will, of course, recognise that this date 36 years previously had witnessed the last passenger trains on that line. A group of invited guests assembled at the site. The unveiling was performed by Mr. Roger Bennett of BBC Radio Bristol and Mrs. Phyllis Hayes, widow of the last station master at Wells. Other invited guests included the Mayor of Wells, Cllr. David Anderson; Dr. Peter Cattermole, Somerset & Dorset Railway Trust; Mr. David Stephens, Chairman of the Wells Railway Fraternity; Mr. Alan Cooper, President of the Wells Civic Society; Mr. Keith Donaghue, Wells Town Clerk plus members of the Wells Railway Fraternity and the Somerset & Dorset Railway Trust. The total number present amounted to about fifty. The Wells Town Crier, Mr. Len Swailes, called the group to order and Roger Bennett welcomed those present and Mrs. Hayes removed the red and green guard's flags from the top of the marker. After the ceremony a small buffet sponsored by the two railway societies was held in the nearby Sherston Hotel, where a bouquet of flowers was presented to Mrs. Hayes. Also to mark the occasion Roger Bennett was presented with a railway book, and railway badges were presented to Nicholas Wall and the two stone masons, Andy Stevens and Ian Lewis.

The second project to keep the memory of the line alive is that of the Winscombe Millenium Green. Peter Knight's book *A Parish and the Railway* devotes a complete chapter to the subject but a brief account is included here.

The first meeting of the Winscombe and Sandford Millenium Green Trust was held on 21st July 1997. Its aim was to create a public amenity on the site of Winscombe station. In order to achieve this it was proposed to obtain a Millenium Commission grant to acquire the land, to obtain Charitable Trust status to be able to raise funds and to ensure that the land is held in perpetuity for public access and use. It was also proposed to gain local support in the community and form a management group to maintain and manage the land.

At this time the whole site was overgrown apart from the narrow path of the Cheddar Valley Walk that followed the track bed. There were some remaining railway artefacts that included the crane base and the station platform, although the platform

Plate 261 - An undated view of the Somerset & Dorset goods yard taken from the Sheldon Jones' grain silo. Priory Road itself runs from right to left just beyond the wall that defines the yard boundary. West Street is the road with houses bathed in sunshine. The big white 'block house' in the distance on the right of the picture is the World War II cold store, just east of the East Somerset yard and locomotive shed, so it can be seen how the railway curved through almost ninety degrees to the south of the city. *Gordon Scammell*

coping stones had been removed to Didcot by the Great Western Society many years before.

In 1998, the Countryside Commission, later the Countryside Agency, was promoting the establishment of village greens in celebration of the impending Millenium. In order to attract funds from this source the community at large would have to be involved, so it was at this point that a number of other local groups and individuals were enlisted. The project progressed when on 4th November 1998 the trust became a registered charity. A number of local groups, charities and businesses contributed to the cost of the project. Planning permission was granted by North Somerset Council on 13th January 1999 and the land purchase was completed on 19th February.

The official launch of the project was on 27th February 1999 when Mrs. Sue Gunn cut the first sod, an event that was witnessed by more than 200 people. Mrs. Gunn's great-grandmother was none other than Mrs. Yatman, who had cut the first sod of the railway back in 1867. The same ceremonial spade was used on both occasions.

The plan was to restore the platform and outline the station building with bricks set into the ground at surface level. A start was made to clear the accumulated undergrowth but at the same time ensuring that suitable habitats were retained in the locality for any wildlife that had been disturbed in the process, particularly for protected species. Once the platform surface had been cleared, an exercise worthy of an archaeological dig revealed evidence of the position of the structures that had once occupied the platform. The platform surface was subsequently restored, the new surface being partly grass and partly gravel except, of course, where the plan of the second station building was marked out with brickwork. The platform was edged with new coping stones obtained from the Sandford Stone company that had until recently occupied the site of Sandford and Banwell station. Much of the station area away from the platform was also turfed.

The official opening of the Green was on Sunday, 6th May 2000 and was attended by a number of local celebrities as well as around one thousand local inhabitants. It was a day of fine sunny weather and the green was bedecked with various stalls and a Maypole. The Weston Brass Band was present to complete the festivities. In the evening those with sufficient energy left repaired to the Woodborough Hotel for a celebratory dinner and, as Peter Knight said in his book, all that was left to be done was to maintain it!

Lastly, mention must be made of the Cheddar Valley Railway Path that is supported by the Cheddar Valley Railway Walk Society. At present it is possible to walk the course of the railway for much of the distance between Yatton and Cheddar with gaps just north of Congresbury and more notably north of Sandford. The eventual aim is to have a footpath on as much of the former track bed as possible between Yatton and Wells, and possibly further to meet up with the still extant section of the East Somerset Railway. What better way would there be to keep the memory of the railway alive!

Plate 262 - BR Standard Class 3MT No.82039 crosses the Somerset & Dorset line with a train bound for Witham on 4th May 1963. Shepton Mallet (S&D) station is visible to the right of the engine's smokebox, a final reminder of the animosity between the two companies.
Michael Mensing

Plate 263 - A month or so after the withdrawal of passenger services between Yatton and Witham, the Home Counties Railtour is near Axbridge on 6th October 1963. Two 2-6-2Ts, Nos.4103 and 6148, worked the train. *Ivo Peters*

FINAL MEMORIES OF A BRANCH LINE

Appendix 1

STRAWBERRY TRAFFIC

It was for the strawberry traffic that the line is probably most fondly remembered, particularly by the local population. The source of this traffic was confined to the section of the Cheddar Valley line from Draycott to Axbridge. Prior to the introduction of more modern cultivation methods the local strawberry season was relatively short, lasting no more than a few weeks from the second week of June until the beginning of July. This brought additional traffic to the line for just a few weeks but, unfortunately, this was not sufficient to maintain the line for very many years after the cessation of passenger traffic in 1963.

Fortunately some documents survive that give us some insight into the importance of the strawberry traffic to the line in the early years of the twentieth century. The provision of additional vehicles and staff on what was a single track branch line required a great deal of organisation on the part of the railway company, who regarded this traffic to be of sufficient value to require a working notice that ran to several pages.

The railway management were clearly concerned that fruit traffic should be delivered on time so as to reach the markets in the best possible condition and measures were put into place to ensure that this was the case. Instructions were issued to railway staff to ensure that trains conveying fruit traffic were not delayed:

'Every exertion must be made to ensure the trains conveying fruit traffic keeping time, and at all stations where shunting is done every endeavour must be made to ascertain how the trains are running, so that shunting operations may be suspended in good time to allow them to pass without delay.

Excursion and local stopping trains should be shunted for them to pass when delay is likely to be caused to the fruit specials by the former running in front.'

These instructions were printed in bold face type to emphasise their importance. On completion of each journey, guards of trains conveying fruit traffic were obliged to submit detailed reports to the appropriate divisional superintendents and to the line superintendent at Paddington for further scrutiny.

In 1905 a total of 279 vehicles loaded with strawberries were dispatched in 24 special trains between 12th and 29th June. In 1906 the number was 231 vehicles in 17 specials between 12th June and 1st July. A footnote indicates that a bad storm destroyed the early blossom in 1906. In 1905 the railway made £1,603 from the specials but this had dropped to £1,376 in 1906. The note makes no reference to any traffic conveyed by scheduled train services. In 1907 the strawberry traffic was recorded as totalling 476 tons, with proceeds to the railway of £1,982.

In 1906 strawberries were conveyed by passenger train to a variety of destinations. Departure times were from Draycott at 5.11pm, Cheddar 5.21pm and Axbridge 5.30pm. In order to avoid transfer on the journey, through vans were attached to various services departing from Bristol Temple Meads, including one running to Banbury and then via the recently opened Great Central Railway London Extension to Leicester, Nottingham, Sheffield and other destinations in the north-east to arrive at Newcastle at 4.42am the next morning. It is not clear whether this service was through from Bristol or involved an exchange of traffic with the Great Central at Banbury. Another train ran via the Severn Tunnel to destinations in the north-west, Edinburgh, Glasgow and an arrival time was even quoted for Dublin. A Sunday special would run if there was sufficient traffic.

Plate 264 - A mouth-watering prospect at Axbridge as strawberries are loaded into vans. The ventilated van at extreme left appears to be chalked for Sheffield; the 'S' is obscured but the rest of the name is legible. The 6-wheel Siphon apparently being supported by the porter appears to have racking inside to prevent undue movement of the baskets of fruit.

Lens of Sutton Association

Plate 265 - These vehicles stabled in the up sidings at Congresbury in the late 1950s appear to be awaiting the call to form a 'strawberry special'. The date of the photograph is vague, but the trees appear in full leaf and it is probably high summer, just the right time for the soft fruit season.
J Moss; Roger Carpenter collection

The 1907 working notice gives details of a special fruit train to run from Cheddar to Bristol Temple Meads as required (Saturdays and Sundays excepted) departing from Cheddar at 5.33pm calling only at Axbridge and arriving at Bristol at 6.30pm. A footnote indicates that the 5.25pm mixed from Blagdon was to be kept clear, strawberries clearly being more important to the railway than passengers off the Wrington Vale line. Traffic from Draycott was to be forwarded by the 4.55pm from Wells and transferred at Cheddar. Presumably starting the special from Draycott would have occupied the single line section for too long. The footplate crew and guard for this train would travel from Bristol to Yatton on the cushions and work the empty stock train which departed from Yatton at 3.45pm and arrived at Cheddar at 4.25pm.

Strict instructions were issued that Mr. Tucker at Cheddar, after consulting with Draycott and Axbridge, must wire Bristol as soon as possible after 11.30am if the traffic available was sufficient to require the special to run. If there was sufficient traffic this train would be extended to Crewe running via the Severn Tunnel, Maindee Junction at Newport, Hereford and Shrewsbury. The booked arrival time at Crewe was 11.08pm. This train would also convey perishable traffic from Devon and Cornwall which was attached at Bristol.

On days when fruit traffic was particularly heavy the 5.33pm would be duplicated either from Cheddar or Axbridge. When evening fruit traffic was heavy the 8.10pm passenger train from Wells to Bristol would run in two portions. The first portion conveyed all of the passenger traffic and some milk whilst the second conveyed the rest of the milk and all of the fruit. The stipulated maximum load for a tender goods engine between Draycott and Yatton was 25 six-wheel milk vans.

Loading of vehicles was a potential problem for the station staff. Without any separate facilities, the strawberries would have to be loaded at the platform, as illustrated in *Plate 264*. Any activity such as that, especially when loading small baskets of fruit, could take a considerable time and pose a threat to the smooth running of the booked passenger trains. To mitigate the effects, the baskets were grouped in fours, apparently fixed to a pole that ran through the handles. Even so, the photograph of Axbridge shows 40 baskets to a platform barrow, with some barrows having at least two tiers. Having said that, the station staff appear to have help from the growers and feel they have time to pose for the camera! The British Railways 1960 Sectional Appendix to the Bristol District working timetable issued specific instructions for loading vehicles at Axbridge and these are reproduced below.

AXBRIDGE

When it is necessary to bring a vehicle or vehicles to the Up Platform at Axbridge to stand for loading milk or other traffic, without an engine being attached, this must only be done under the personal authority of the Station Master or person in charge.

Should such vehicle or vehicles have to remain after sunset the Station Master or person in charge will be responsible for seeing that a lighted red lamp is on the last vehicle showing towards Cheddar.

This working must not be resorted to during fog or falling snow, but special arrangements must be made for the vehicle or vehicles to be attached to the train which has to take the traffic forward to be loaded whilst the train is at the Platform.

Such vehicle or vehicles must not be allowed to stand on the Up Loop any longer than is absolutely necessary for the loading of the traffic, but must be placed in the Siding in readiness to be taken on by the train intended to be used.

Appendix 2

SINGLE LINE WORKING

The essential feature of single line working is to ensure that there is only one train on any section of single line at any one time. In the early days, before the widespread adoption of the electric telegraph when there was no communication between the opposite ends of a single line section, this was difficult to achieve and many lightly used branch lines resorted to the 'One Engine in Steam' method of working. It was also known as 'One Train Working'. To work an entire line with only a single train, although 100% safe, was inflexible and as traffic grew proved to be unacceptable. The East Somerset Railway was worked under one train regulations when it opened but it was not long before the growth in traffic demanded something better.

Railways were quick to see the benefit of installing the electric telegraph in order to provide communication between stations and the controlling office. This enabled them to operate the timetable in a more flexible and safe manner. Some companies used train orders (or crossing orders) in conjunction with the electric telegraph as the means of providing safe operation on longer single line railways. Other companies required the driver to carry some form of 'token of authority' to proceed through a single line section. This led to the development of the absolute block system of operation in association with a train staff. The requirement of the absolute block system was that only one train could occupy a section of line between two signal boxes at any one time, thereby eliminating the risk of a collision. On a double line the use of the absolute block system was in itself sufficient but on a single line the adoption of train staff working was necessary to ensure safe operation.

The essential feature of this method of operation was, as its name suggests, the train staff. This was nothing more than a piece of wood about eighteen inches in length and of regular section (eg. round, square or octagonal). The names of the two signal boxes between which the staff was valid were inscribed upon a metal (usually brass) plate fixed to the staff. As an additional aid to its identity the staff was painted an unmistakable colour such as red or blue. Staffs in use on adjacent single line sections would be of different colour and different shape in order to prevent confusion; eg. red round section followed by blue square section followed by green triangular section and so on.

To enable a signalman to send a train into a single line section he would have to be in possession of the appropriate train staff. Before the train could proceed he would contact the signalman at the other end of the section using the telegraph and ask for 'Line Clear'. Provided that the line was clear to a designated point called the clearing point, typically the starting signal for the next section in advance, the signalman receiving the 'Is Line Clear' request would give a 'Line Clear' response. If there was an obstruction within the clearing point such as a train standing at a station platform, he would respond with 'Line Blocked'. Sending and receiving messages in English on the telegraph was time consuming and could lead to misunderstandings, so a system of 'Bell Codes' was adopted. For example, a signalman would ask for line clear by a bell code of 3-1 (the hyphen indicating a pause). This system of bell codes is still in use in semaphore signalled areas and on preserved railways.

Having received the 'Line Clear' response, the first signalman would give the train staff to the driver and clear the required fixed signals to authorise the train to proceed into the single line section. It was the driver's responsibility to ensure that he had the correct staff for the section before departing. He would not be permitted to pass into the single line section without the train staff even if the signals had been cleared. It was also the guard's responsibility to ensure that the driver had the correct staff and that the correct signals had been cleared before giving the 'Right Away'. Thus, provided that all concerned (ie. signalmen, driver and guard) all carried out their duties correctly, there was no possibility of a single line collision. There was only one train staff for the section, and the driver had to have it in his possession whilst in the section so that there could never be two trains in the same section at the same time.

The main problem with the train staff is that it is inflexible. It only works if successive trains pass through a single line section in opposite directions. If successive trains require to pass through a section in the same direction then the staff had to be carried back through the section by some other means after the first train and before the second. One solution was to use a divisible staff so that successive trains running in the same direction could each take a part of the staff through the section. A train would not be permitted to enter from the other end until all of the portions of the staff had arrived there.

The solution that enjoyed the most widespread adoption was the train staff and ticket system. In this system a key was attached to the train staff that unlocked a box containing numbered tickets by which the signalman could authorise the driver to proceed through a single line section without carrying the train staff. Knowing that two successive trains were to enter the single line section from his end and having received 'Line Clear' from the signal box in advance, the signalman would obtain a ticket from the box. He would write the details of the train on the ticket before handing it to the driver of the first train. At the same time he would show the train staff to the driver to indicate that it was in his possession. It was the driver's responsibility to ensure that it was the correct staff for the section. When the fixed signals were cleared, the train could proceed. Once the first train had cleared the section at the other end and 'Is Line Clear' had been requested and accepted, the signalman would hand the train staff to the driver of the second train as his authority to proceed.

The train staff and ticket system allows for any number of trains to proceed successively through a single line section in the same direction, each but the last carrying a ticket as authority to proceed, the last carrying the train staff. The train staff and ticket system is simple and reliable to the extent that its use has continued into the twenty-first century. It does, however, suffer from one essential drawback in that it cannot handle sudden alterations caused by late running or additional workings. For example, if a train is running late it would be desirable to change the booked crossing places so as to minimise the delay to trains running in the opposite direction. If the signalmen involved are given sufficient notice, then it may be possible to alter the staff and ticket arrangements accordingly but if this is not the case then the train staff may be at the wrong end of one or more of the sections involved. If this situation occurs it is very difficult to recover from late running particularly on busier lines. It would, of course, be possible to transfer the train staff from one end of the section to the other by some other means. However, with long single line sections in rural areas any time gained by altering the crossing arrangements would probably be lost in the time taken to carry out the transfer. Another disadvantage of the train staff and ticket system is that if the signalman gives the driver the train staff by mistake when he should be issuing a ticket (or vice versa) then a staff transfer will have to be made and late running will result.

On busier cross-country lines the train staff and ticket system was too restrictive. What was needed was some means of being able issue the staff at either end of the section at any time, provided that it was not already occupied by a train. Such a system would allow alterations to be made to the running of trains at very short notice. This need led to the development of the electric train tablet, the electric train staff and the electric key token systems of operation. The basic operation of all three systems is very similar but the electric key token system, being the most modern, is the one described here. An instrument containing a number of key tokens is electrically connected to an identical instrument at the other end of the single line section that also contains a similar number of key tokens. The electric circuit and associated components is known as the token circuit. As their name would suggest, the tokens are shaped like a key and are held in a magazine within the body of the instrument. The other main features of the instrument are an electrically operated lock, a plunger and an indicating needle. A block bell in each signal box also forms part of the token circuit.

If the signalman at box 'A' wishes to send a train through the single line section to box 'B' he will send the call attention bell code (1) using the plunger on his token instrument. This will cause the block bell in box 'B' to ring, to which the signalman there will respond thus ringing the block bell in box 'A'. The signalman at 'A' will then send the appropriate 'Is Line Clear' bell code for the train concerned. If the line is clear and the signalman at 'B' can accept the train he will repeat the code back to 'A'. Having entered the last beat of the code he will keep his plunger depressed. This will be indicated to the signalman at 'A' by the needle on his token instrument being deflected. The signalman at 'A' may then lift a token from the magazine and engage it in the electric lock. The act of the signalman at 'B' keeping the plunger on his instrument depressed frees the lock in the instrument at 'A' so that the signalman there may rotate the token by 180 degrees in order to release it from the instrument. The token is then given to the driver of the train in the normal way. The train may then proceed through the single line section from 'A' to 'B'.

The barrel of the electric lock contains a number of electrical contacts known as a commutator. As the token is rotated in the lock some of the contacts on the commutator are made and some are broken. The token circuit is arranged so that the lock is only released when the commutators in both instruments are so positioned as to complete the electrical circuit. In this situation the instruments are said to be 'in phase'. Once one or the other of the commutators is rotated the circuit is effectively broken, the lock is inoperable and the instruments are said to be 'out of phase'. As a result, once a token has been withdrawn from either instrument it is impossible to obtain another one.

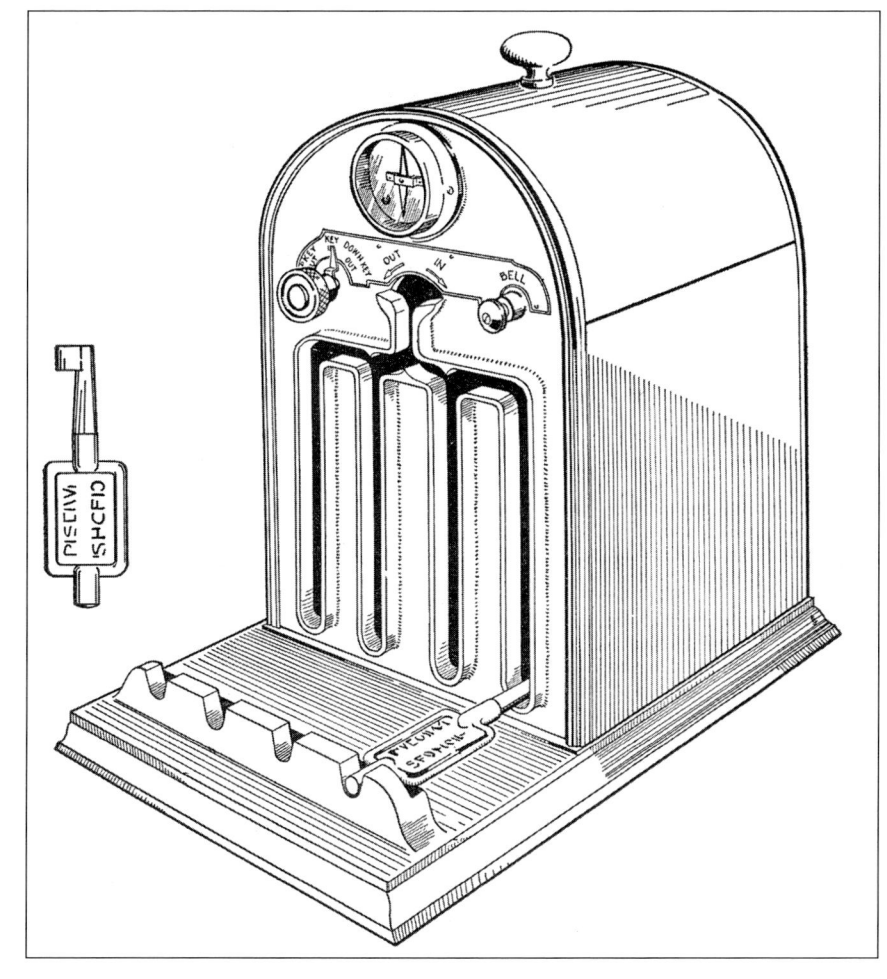

Figure 54 - The Electric Key Token instrument which can be seen in *Plate 242*. The older Staff Instrument is illustrated overleaf. *Author's collection*

Figure 55 and Plate 266 - The Electric Train Staff instrument similar to that in *Plate 248*. The photograph is of a disused machine at Roscrea, in Ireland. *Author's collection*

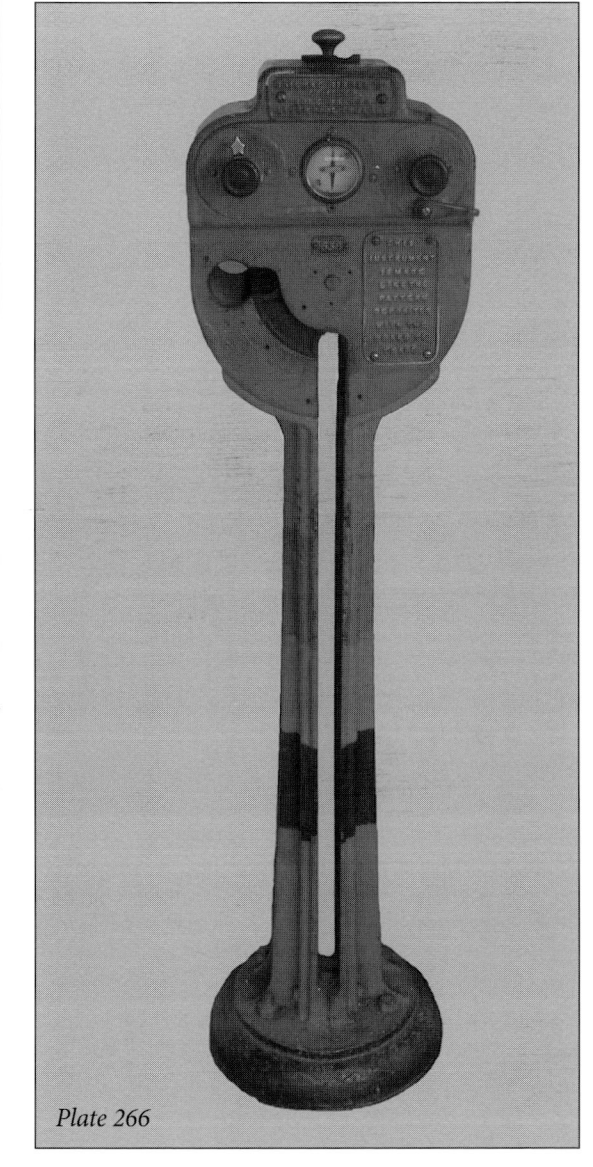

Arrangement'. The signalman will ensure that the driver understands this before allowing the train to enter the section. 'Normal Acceptance' indicates that the line is clear to the clearing point of the signal box in advance, but 'Warning Acceptance' indicates that the line is clear only as far as the home signal. This allows the signalman at the box in advance to authorise shunting operations within station limits confident that the driver of the approaching train expects to be stopped at the home signal (although in this particular case he will never get that far). The warning arrangement is also used for non-passenger trains that may run right through the section. This will allow the signalman in advance to carry out non-passenger train movements within his clearing point.

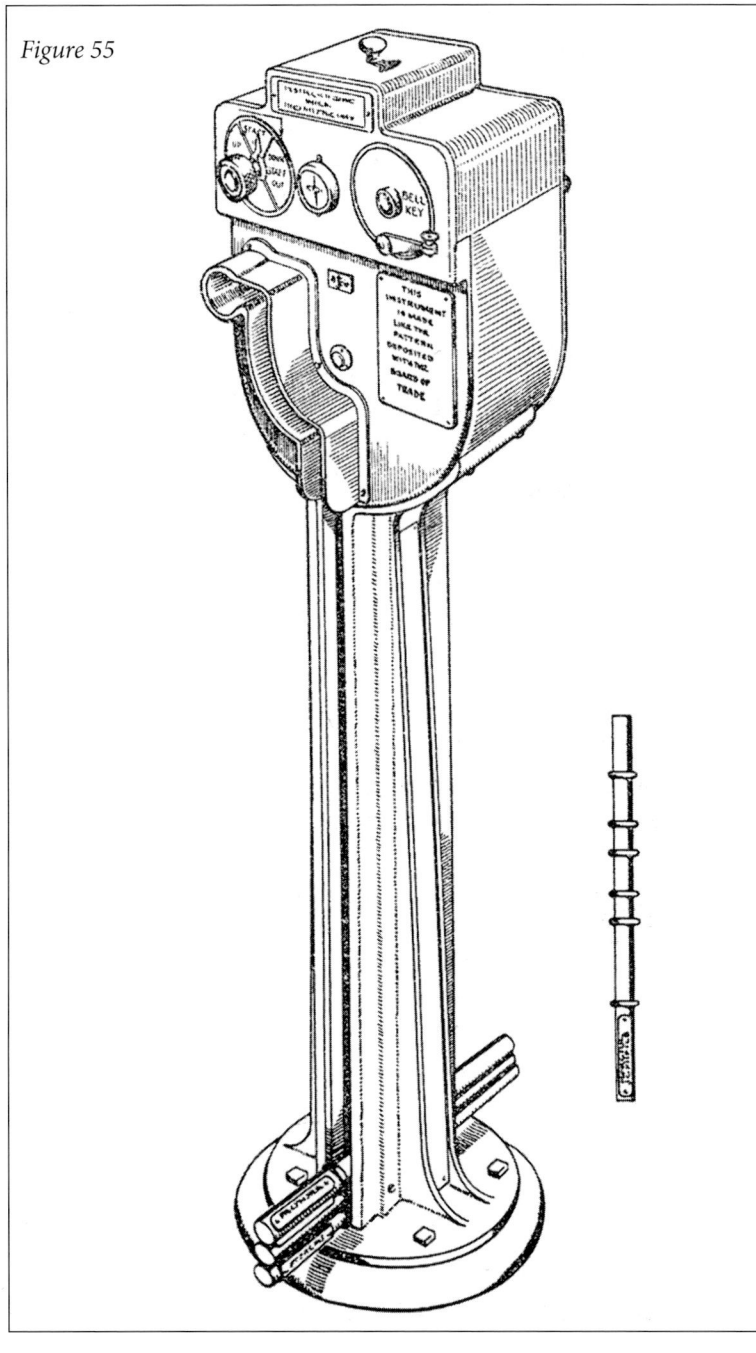

When a token has been withdrawn it may be replaced in either instrument again in order to put them back into phase. This is useful if a signalman withdraws a token for a train that is subsequently cancelled for some reason. In this case the signalman will just put the token back into his own instrument and send the appropriate bell code to the other signalman to indicate that the train has been cancelled. Another instance would be where a train enters a single line section in order to shunt at sidings controlled by an in-section ground frame and afterwards returns to the same end of the section from which it entered. In this case the train would be offered, accepted and the token given to the driver as normal. Once shunting is complete and the train has returned and cleared the single line section, the token would be placed back into the instrument and the cancelling signal sent to the other box.

When it is known that a train is going to return to the end of the section from which it originally entered, it will be accepted under the 'Warning

Appendix 3

SIGNAL BOX DIAGRAMS AND LOCKING TABLES

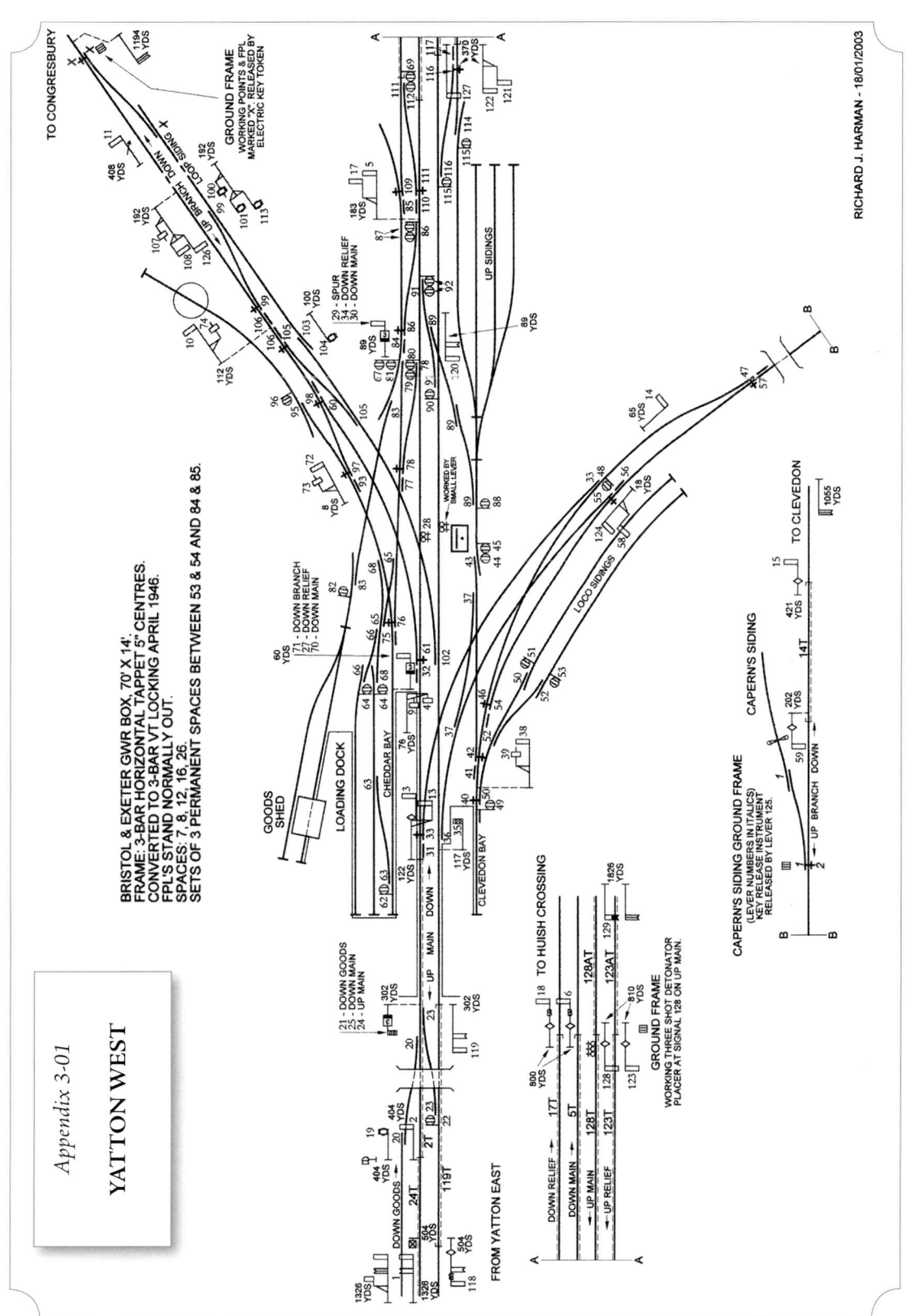

Appendix 3-01

YATTON WEST

App 3-01 - Although reproduced to a reduced scale, the diagram is included for completeness and to show the complexity of the junction layout.

RICHARD J. HARMAN - 18/01/2003

Appendix 3-02
CONGRESBURY
SANDFORD AND
BANWELL

CONGRESBURY

GWR TYPE 5 BOX, 30' 6" X 12' ELEVATED 8'.
OPENED 14/04/1901 TO REPLACE ORIGINAL.
FRAME: DOUBLE TWIST STUD 5¼" CENTRES
CONVERTED TO 5-BAR VT LOCKING 04/07/1949.
FPL'S STAND NORMALLY OUT.
SPACES: 1, 2, 9, 10, 11, 20, 21, 24, 25, 30, 34, 35, 36, 37, 41, 43.

ORIGINAL DRAWING S428/2 - DATED APRIL 1948
REDRAWN FROM INFORMATION IN P.R.O. REF: RAIL/282/199

SANDFORD AND BANWELL

GWR TYPE 7D BOX, 29' X 12' ELEVATED 8'.
OPENED 12/12/1905 TO REPLACE ORIGINAL.
FRAME: STUD 5¼" CENTRES.
FPL'S STAND NORMALLY OUT.
SPACES: 1, 8, 9, 23, 24, 25, 31.

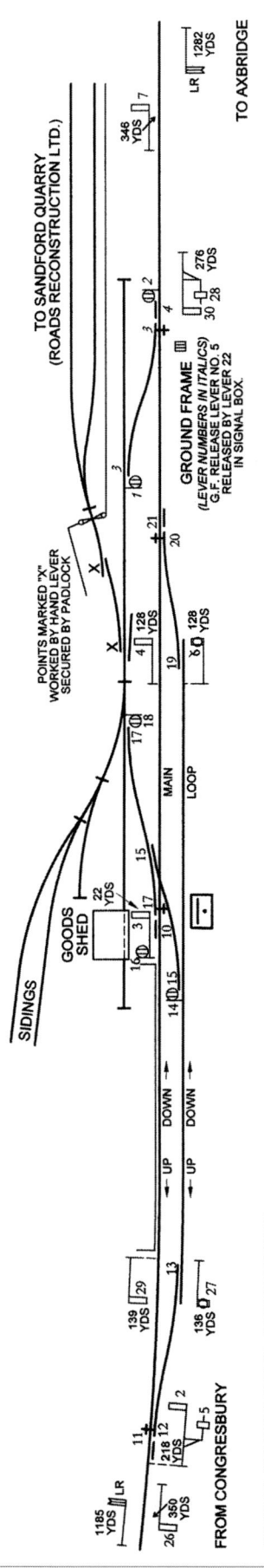

POINTS MARKED "X"
WORKED BY HAND LEVER
SECURED BY PADLOCK

GROUND FRAME
(LEVER NUMBERS IN ITALICS)
G.F. RELEASE LEVER NO. 5
RELEASED BY LEVER 22
IN SIGNAL BOX.

ORIGINAL DRAWING S427/2 - DATED 5/11/1934.
REDRAWN FROM INFORMATION IN P.R.O. REF: RAIL/282/198

RICHARD J. HARMAN - 06/01/2003

CONGRESBURY S.B. - LOCKING TABLE

No.	RELEASED BY	LOCKS NORMAL	LOCKS B/W	RELEASES
1	X			
2	X			
3	12, 22	13, 38, 42, (32W23N)		
4	22	15, (32W23N)	12, 13	
5	22, 23			
6		29, 42	23, 27, 28, (15W27N), (18W23N0, (27W23N)	
7	22, 33	40, (39W15R)	15	
8	12, 13^S, 14	38		
9	X			
10	X			
11	X			
12			13	3, 8
13		3		8, 15, 18, 39, 14
14	(22,33W15R,16N), 13	19, 39, 40, 42 (17W16R), (23,27W15,18N)	12, 13^S, 15, 16, 18 (28W15,18N)	8
15	13	4, 18, 23, 32, 42		16, 40
16	15	33		
17		31, (14W16R)	16, 32	
18	13	15, 27, 42		19
19	18	14		
20	X			
21	X			
22			23	3, 4, 5, 7, (14)
23		15, 27, 28, 33, (14W15,18N)		5
24	X			
25	X			
26	27	29	28	
27		18, 23, 42 (14W15,18N)		26, 29
28		23	27	29, 42
29	27, 28	6, 26		
30	X			
31		17	16, 32	
32		15, 33, (3,4W23N)		
33		16, 23, 32		7, 40 (14)
34	X			
35	X			
36	X			
37	X			
38		3, 8	12, 13	
39	13	14, (7W15R)	12, 15, 16, 18, (27W15R,16N), (23,27,28W15,18N), (33W15R)	
40	15, 33	7, 14	22	
41	X			
42	28	3, 6, 14, 15, 18, 27		
43	X			

Appendix 3-03: Reproduced from original locking table ref. S/428/3 dated 23rd November 1948; TNA RAIL 282/199 (Richard Harman, 19th January 2004)

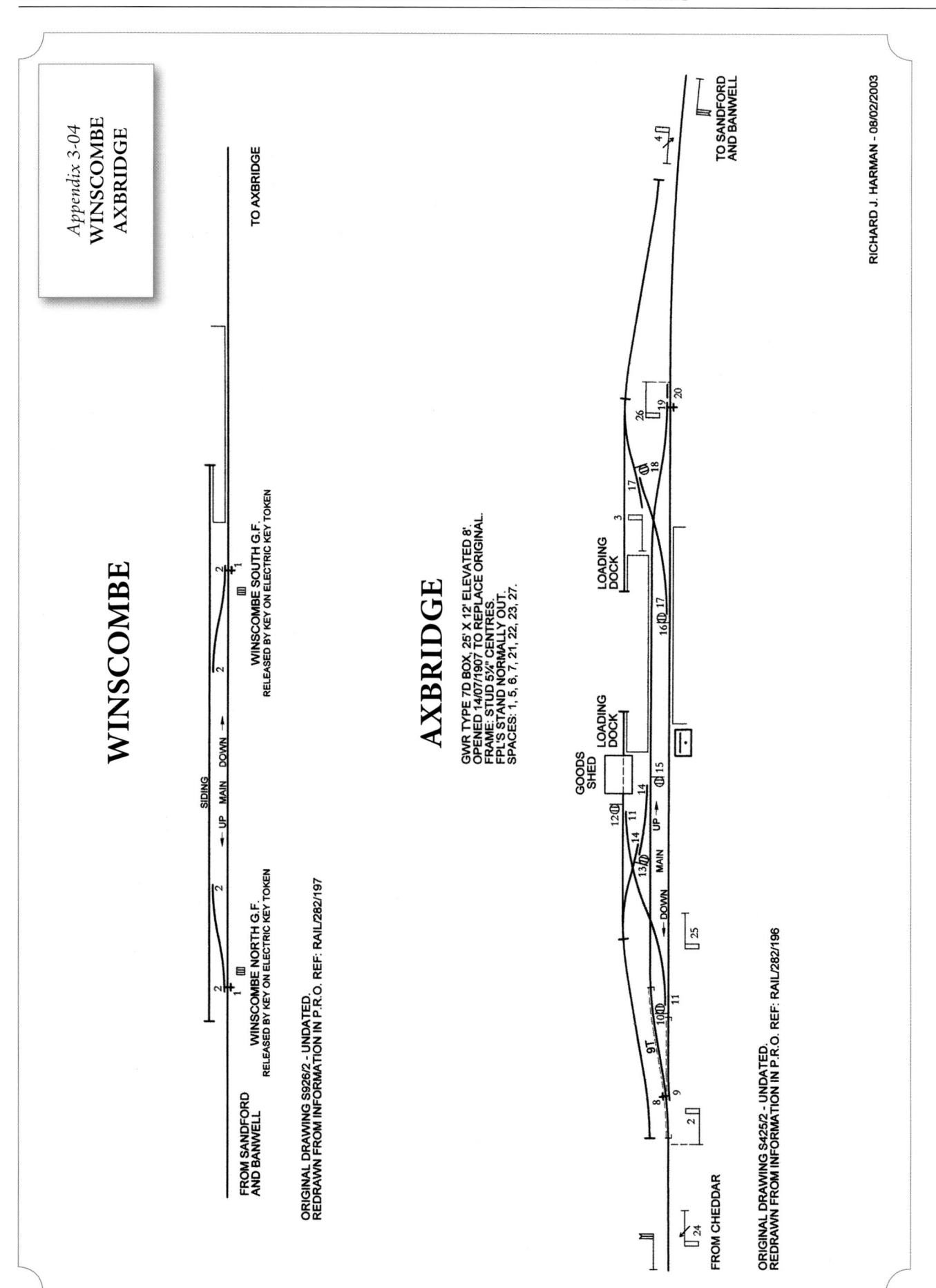

248 THE EAST SOMERSET AND CHEDDAR VALLEY RAILWAYS

Appendix 3-04
WINSCOMBE
AXBRIDGE

WINSCOMBE

WINSCOMBE NORTH G.F.
RELEASED BY KEY ON ELECTRIC KEY TOKEN

WINSCOMBE SOUTH G.F.
RELEASED BY KEY ON ELECTRIC KEY TOKEN

TO AXBRIDGE

FROM SANDFORD AND BANWELL

ORIGINAL DRAWING S926/2 - UNDATED.
REDRAWN FROM INFORMATION IN P.R.O. REF: RAIL/282/197

AXBRIDGE

GWR TYPE 7D BOX, 25' X 12' ELEVATED 8'.
OPENED 14/07/1907 TO REPLACE ORIGINAL.
FRAME: STUD 5¼" CENTRES.
FPL'S STAND NORMALLY OUT.
SPACES: 1, 5, 6, 7, 21, 22, 23, 27.

TO SANDFORD AND BANWELL

GOODS SHED

LOADING DOCK

LOADING DOCK

FROM CHEDDAR

ORIGINAL DRAWING S425/2 - UNDATED.
REDRAWN FROM INFORMATION IN P.R.O. REF: RAIL/282/196

RICHARD J. HARMAN - 08/02/2003

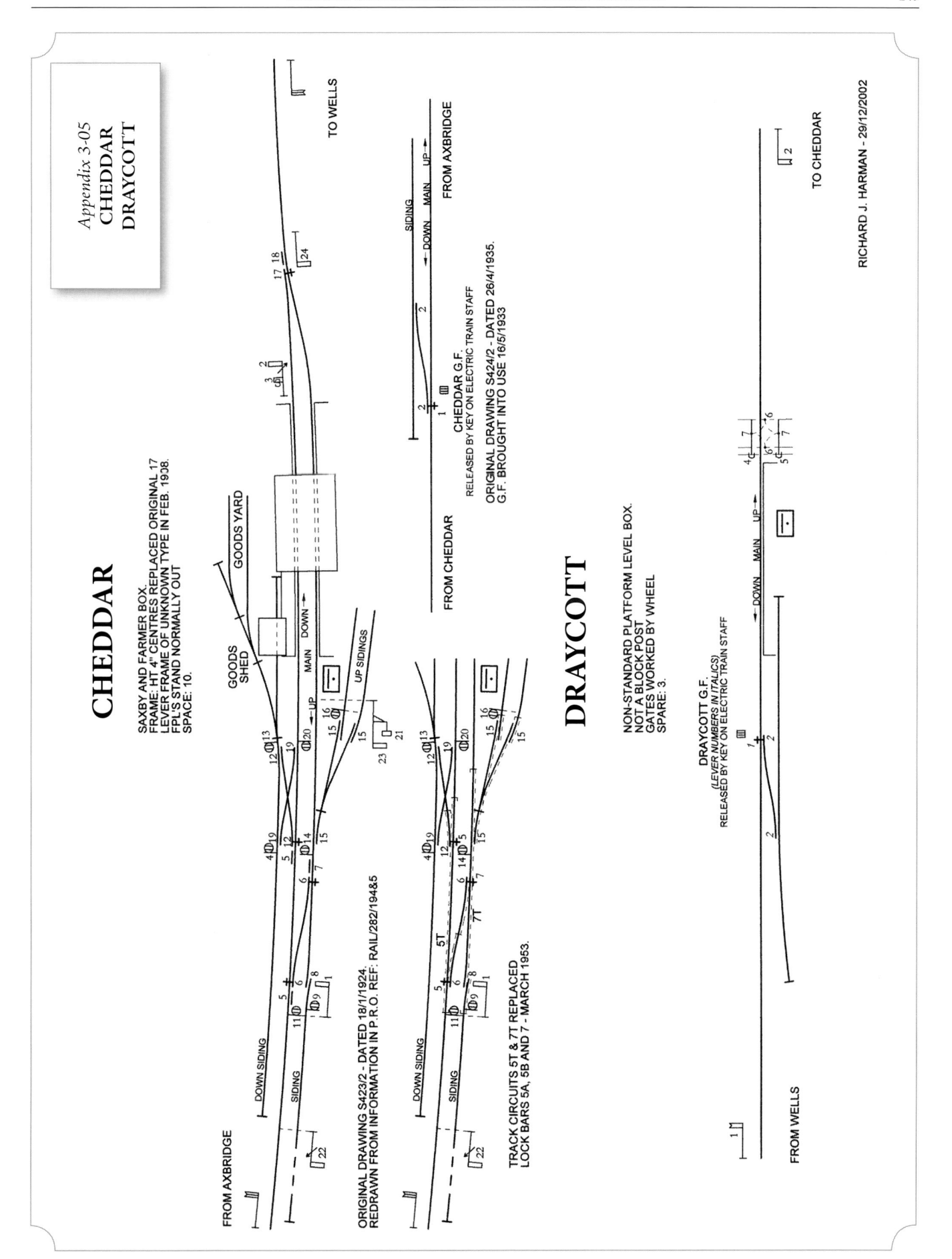

Appendix 3-05
CHEDDAR
DRAYCOTT

CHEDDAR

SAXBY AND FARMER BOX.
FRAME: HT 4" CENTRES REPLACED ORIGINAL 17 LEVER FRAME OF UNKNOWN TYPE IN FEB. 1938.
FPL'S STAND NORMALLY OUT
SPACE: 10.

TO WELLS

FROM AXBRIDGE

ORIGINAL DRAWING S423/2 - DATED 18/1/1924.
REDRAWN FROM INFORMATION IN P.R.O. REF: RAIL/282/194&5

TRACK CIRCUITS 5T & 7T REPLACED
LOCK BARS 5A, 5B AND 7 - MARCH 1953.

FROM CHEDDAR

CHEDDAR G.F.
RELEASED BY KEY ON ELECTRIC TRAIN STAFF
ORIGINAL DRAWING S424/2 - DATED 26/4/1935.
G.F. BROUGHT INTO USE 16/5/1933.

DRAYCOTT

NON-STANDARD PLATFORM LEVEL BOX.
NOT A BLOCK POST
GATES WORKED BY WHEEL
SPARE: 3.

DRAYCOTT G.F.
(LEVER NUMBERS IN ITALICS)
RELEASED BY KEY ON ELECTRIC TRAIN STAFF

FROM WELLS

TO CHEDDAR

RICHARD J. HARMAN - 29/12/2002

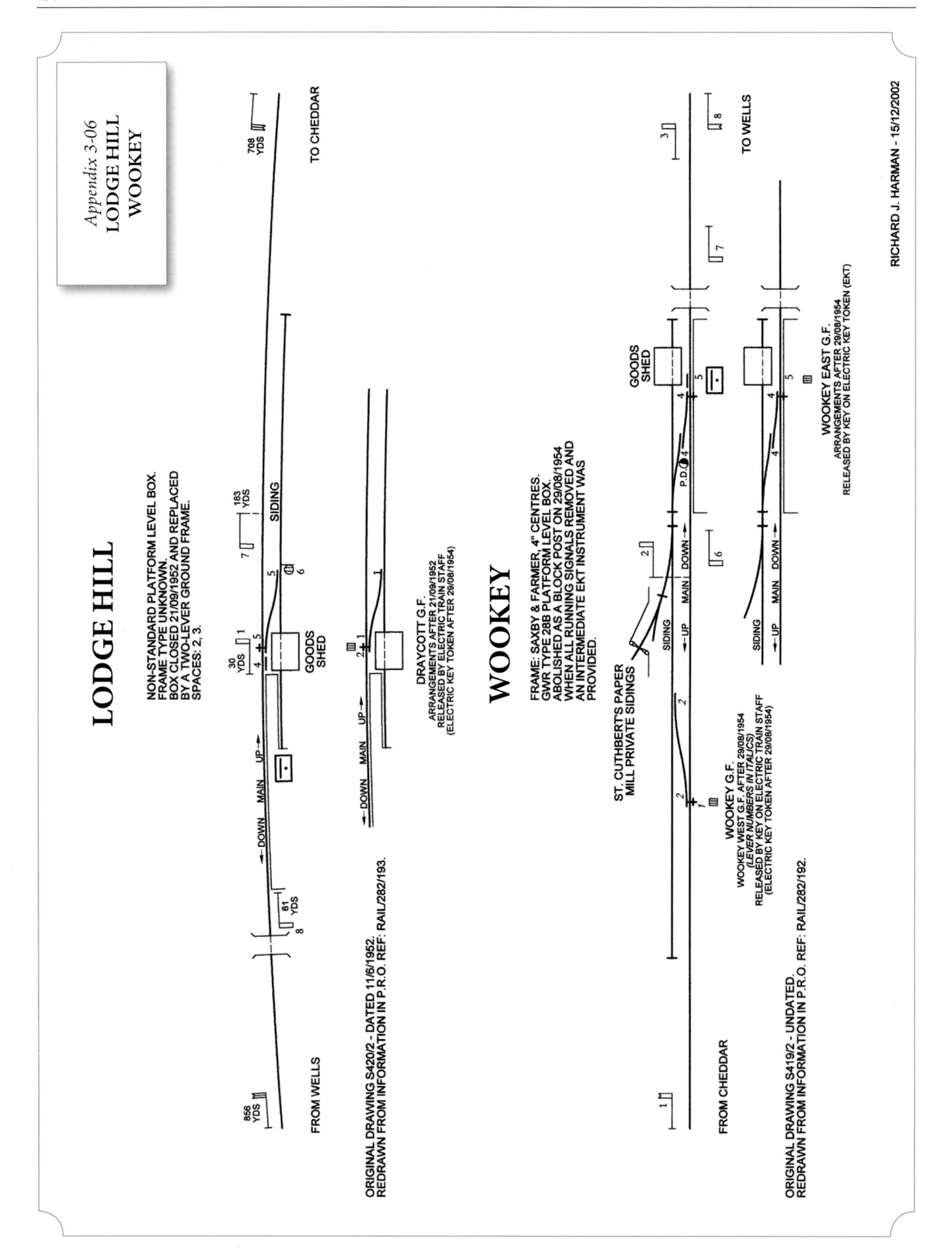

Appendix 3-06
LODGE HILL
WOOKEY

LODGE HILL

NON-STANDARD PLATFORM LEVEL BOX.
FRAME TYPE UNKNOWN.
BOX CLOSED 21/09/1952 AND REPLACED
BY A TWO-LEVER GROUND FRAME.
SPACES: 2, 3.

DRAYCOTT G.F.
ARRANGEMENTS AFTER 21/09/1952
RELEASED BY ELECTRIC TRAIN STAFF
(ELECTRIC KEY TOKEN AFTER 29/08/1954)

ORIGINAL DRAWING S420/2 - DATED 11/6/1952.
REDRAWN FROM INFORMATION IN P.R.O. REF: RAIL/282/193.

WOOKEY

FRAME: SAXBY & FARMER, 4" CENTRES.
GWR TYPE 28B PLATFORM LEVEL BOX.
ABOLISHED AS A BLOCK POST ON 29/08/1954
WHEN ALL RUNNING SIGNALS REMOVED AND
AN INTERMEDIATE EKT INSTRUMENT WAS
PROVIDED.

WOOKEY WEST G.F. AFTER 29/08/1954
(LEVER NUMBERS IN ITALICS)
RELEASED BY KEY ON ELECTRIC TRAIN STAFF
(ELECTRIC KEY TOKEN AFTER 29/08/1954)

WOOKEY EAST G.F.
ARRANGEMENTS AFTER 29/08/1954
RELEASED BY KEY ON ELECTRIC KEY TOKEN (EKT)

ORIGINAL DRAWING S419/2 - UNDATED.
REDRAWN FROM INFORMATION IN P.R.O. REF: RAIL/282/192.

RICHARD J. HARMAN - 15/12/2002

Appendix 3-07
WELLS STATION
GATE LANE
GROUND FRAME

WELLS STATION

GWR TYPE 7B SIGNAL BOX: BRICK 23' 6" X 10' 8" X 5' 0"
FRAME: GWR DOUBLE TWIST, 5½" CENTRES, INSTALLED 1900.
FPL'S STAND UNBOLTED, 2 HOLE (NO. 7 - 1 HOLE).
SEQUENTIAL LOCKING NOT PROVIDED.
ILLUMINATED DIAGRAM: NIL.
ELECTRICAL REFERENCE: E43.
SPACES: 1, 4, 5.
SPARES: 23.

✲ TOKEN RELEASE AFTER 2/12/1955 IN CONNECTION WITH THE INTRODUCTION OF EKT WORKING BETWEEN WELLS STATION AND WELLS EAST SOMERSET BOXES

ORIGINAL DRAWING S417/2 - DATED 4/1/1955
REDRAWN FROM INFORMATION IN P.R.O. REF: RAIL/282/191

GATE LANE GROUND FRAME

INSTALLED IN 1942 TO SERVE MINISTRY OF FOOD COLD STORE, CLOSED 1966
RELEASED BY KEY ON WELLS EAST SOMERSET TO SHEPTON MALLET ELECTRIC KEY TOKEN

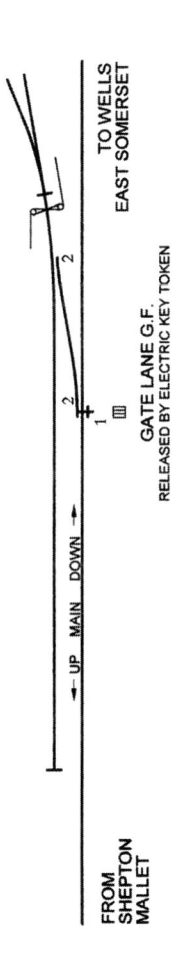

GATE LANE G.F.
RELEASED BY ELECTRIC KEY TOKEN

ORIGINAL DRAWING S415/2 - DATED 13/3/1942
REDRAWN FROM INFORMATION IN P.R.O. REF: RAIL/282/189

RICHARD J. HARMAN - 26/12/2002

WELLS EAST SOMERSET

Appendix 3-08
WELLS EAST SOMERSET

DIAGRAM 1 - 1912 TO 1955

GWR TYPE 27C SIGNAL BOX.
FRAME: GWR STUD, 5¼" CENTRES.
GATES WORKED BY WHEEL.
FPL'S STAND UNBOLTED.
SPACES: 7, 8, 18, 19.
CLOSING SWITCH: NIL.

ORIGINAL DRAWING S48/120 - DATED 12/11/1921
REDRAWN FROM INFORMATION IN P.R.O. REF: RAIL/282/190

DIAGRAM 2 - 1955 TO 1965 (After closure of S&D box)

FRAME: BR(WR) 5-BAR VT, 4" CENTRES
GATES WORKED BY WHEEL
FPL'S STAND UNBOLTED.
SPACES: 7, 8, 18, 19.
CLOSING SWITCH: NIL.

INFORMATION COURTESY BRIAN HILLIER

RICHARD J. HARMAN - 10/02/2003

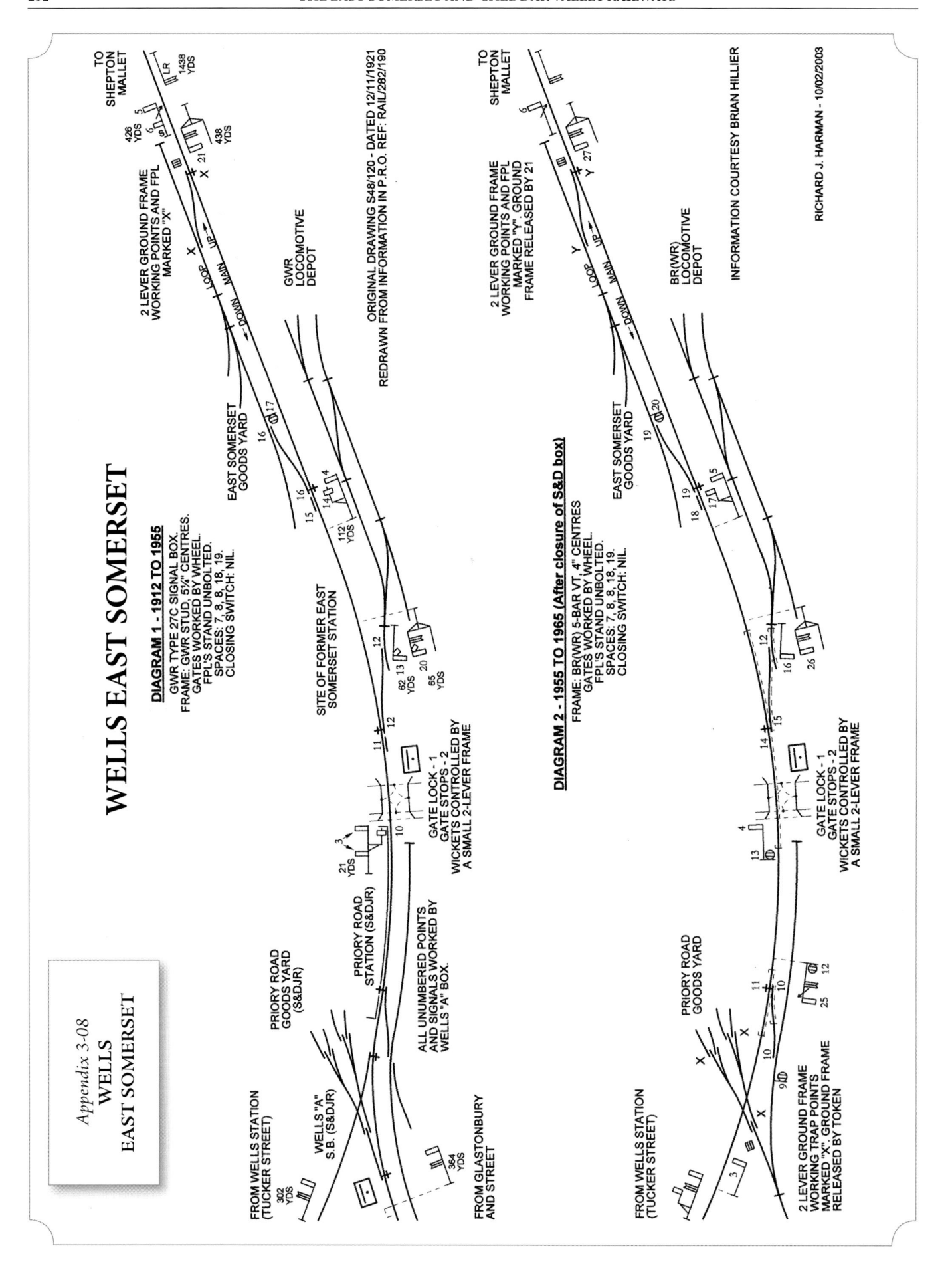

No.	DESCRIPTION	RELEASED BY	LOCKS NORMAL	LOCKS B/W	RELEASES
Wheel	GATE WHEEL	1			2
1	GATE LOCK		4, 15, 20, 26, 27, (9W10R)		Wheel
2	GATE BACK STOP	Wheel			
3	UP HOME	14	10, 16, 20, 25, 26, 27		
4	UP INNER HOME	14, 18	1, 12, 15, 20, 21, 25, 26, 27	10	
5	UP STARTING	18	19, 21, 26, 27	1, 15	
6	UP ADVANCE STARTING		27	18, 19, 21	
7	SPACE				
8	SPACE				
9	DISC - PRIORY ROAD SDGS. TO UP MAIN	(14W10R)	12, (1, 16, 20, 26, 27W10R)	10	12
10	CROSSOVER - DOWN MAIN TO PRIORY RD. SDGS.		3, 25		
11	FPL FOR 10A			10	12, 16, 25, 26
12	DISC - DOWN MAIN TO PRIORY ROAD SDGS.	10, 11	4, 9, 13	1, 15	
13	DISC - UP MAIN TO DN SIDINGS/LOCO	14, 15	12, 16, 25	10	3, 4, (9), 13
14	FPL FOR 15A			15	13, 16
15	CROSSOVER - UP MAIN TO DN SIDINGS/LOCO	11, 15	1, 4, 19, 26, 27		
16	DOWN SIDINGS STARTING	11, 15	3, 13, (9W10R)		
17	SHUNT SIGNAL - UP MAIN TO UP SIDINGS	18, 19	20, 26	1	
18	FPL FOR 19A		5, 15, 21, 27	19	4, 5, 17
19	CROSSOVER - UP MAIN TO UP SIDINGS.		1, 3, 4, 17, (9W10R)		17, 20
20	DISC - UP SIDINGS TO DOWN MAIN	19		18	
21	RELEASE LEVER FOR EAST SOMERSET G.F.		4, 5, 19, 27		
22	SPACE				
23	SPACE				
24	SPACE				
25	DOWN STARTING	11	3, 4, 10, 13	1, 15	
26	DOWN INNER HOME	11	1, 3, 4, 5, 15, 17, (9W10R)	18, 19, 21	
27	DOWN HOME		1, 3, 4, 5, 6, 15, 19, 21, (9W10R)	18	

REDRAWN FROM ORIGINAL LOCKING TABLE REF. S/416/3 DATED 14/2/1955 (P.R.O. REF. RAIL 282/190). APPLIES TO NEW FRAME INSTALLED IN 1955

RICHARD HARMAN - 21/09/1999

WELLS EAST SOMERSET

LOCKING TABLE

Appendix 3-10
**SHEPTON MALLET
KILVER STREET CROSSING**

SHEPTON MALLET

GWR TYPE 5 SIGNAL BOX: 27' 9" X 12' 0".
FRAME: GWR DOUBLE TWIST, 5¼" CENTRES.
OPENED 1894.
FPL'S STAND UNBOLTED.
CLOSING SWITCH: NIL
SPACES: 1, 29, 31.

ORIGINAL DRAWING S413/2 - DATED 6/4/1926
REDRAWN FROM INFORMATION IN P.R.O. REF: RAIL/282/188

KILVER STREET CROSSING

NOT A BLOCK POST
GATES WORKED BY HAND

ORIGINAL DRAWING S412/2 - DATED xx/xx/xxxx
REDRAWN FROM INFORMATION IN P.R.O. REF: RAIL/282/187

RICHARD J. HARMAN - 14/12/2002

Appendix 3-11
CRANMORE
WANSTROW

CRANMORE

GWR TYPE 7B SIGNAL BOX: 29' X 12' X 8'.
FRAME: GWR DOUBLE TWIST, 5¼" CENTRES.
OPENED 1904 TO REPLACE ORIGINAL
FPL'S STAND UNBOLTED.
CLOSING SWITCH: NIL
SPACE: 27.
SPARE: 24.

WANSTROW

ORIGINAL DRAWING S410/2 - DATED 25/11/1926
REDRAWN FROM INFORMATION IN P.R.O. REF: RAIL/282/188

RICHARD J. HARMAN - 15/12/2002

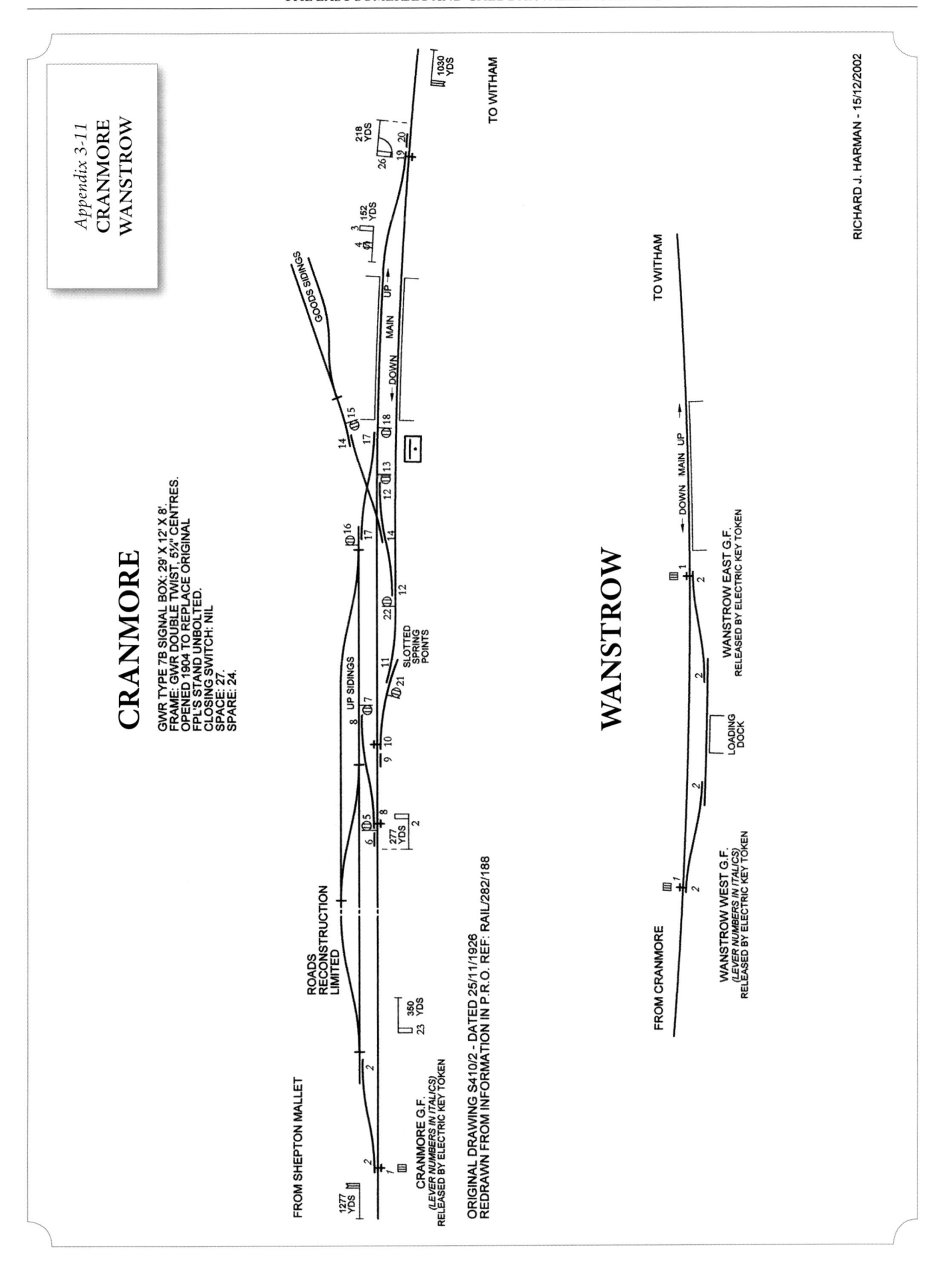

Appensix 3-12
WITHAM

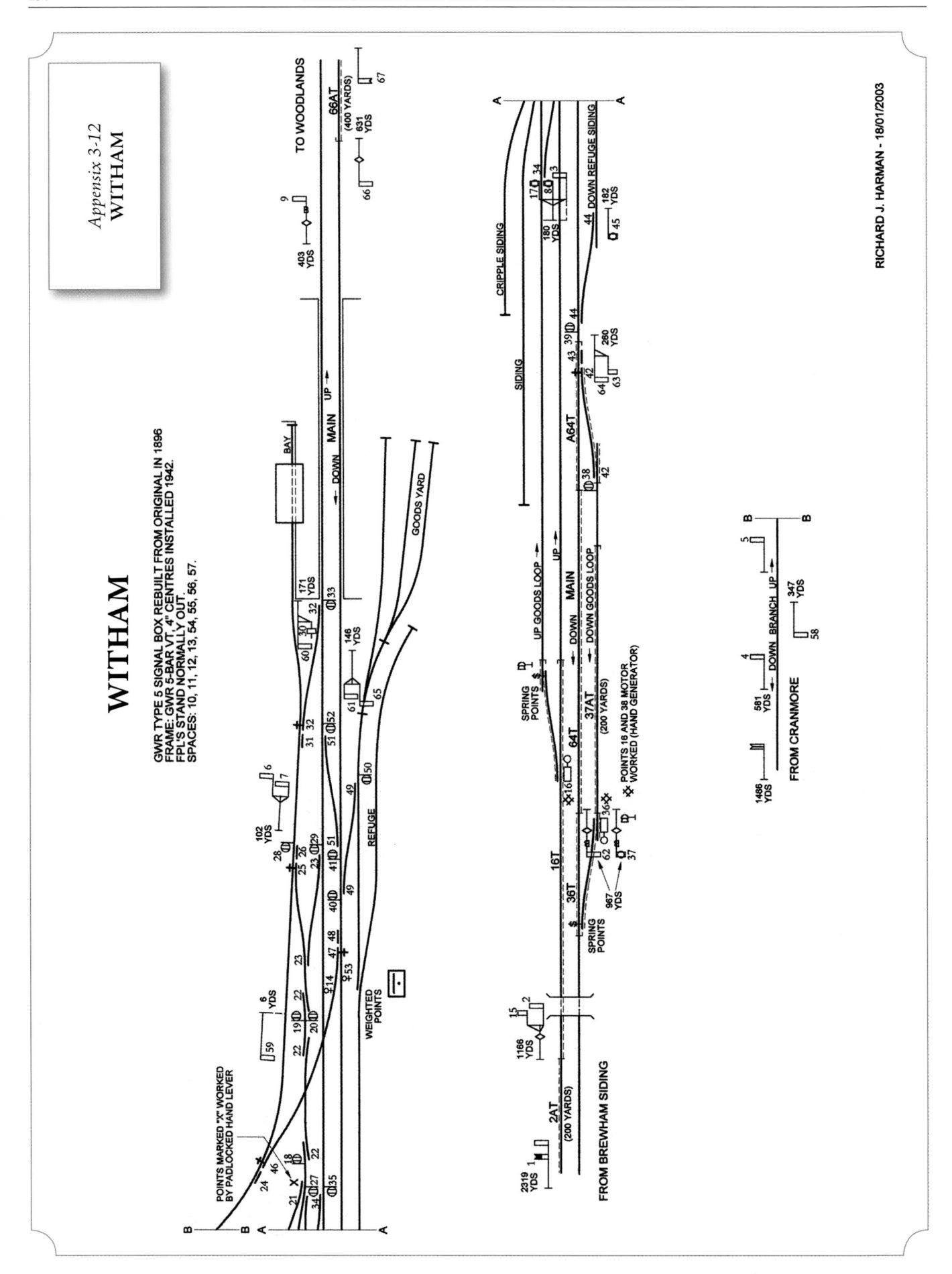

Appendix 4

BRISTOL DIVISION TRAFFIC RECEIPTS, 1906 - 1911

Stations	Year 1906 Passenger & Parcels	Year 1906 Goods	Year 1906 Total	Year 1907 Passenger & Parcels	Year 1907 Goods	Year 1907 Total	Increase / Decrease	Remarks
	£	£	£	£	£	£	£	
Congresbury	1119	1263	2382	1055	1227	2282	- 100	
Sandford and Banwell	1811	6936	8747	1702	2917	4619	- 4128	
Winscombe	2791	2000	4791	2960	1876	4836	+ 45	
Axbridge	4615	1973	6588	4826	2152	6978	+ 390	
Cheddar	4503	4762	9265	4204	3890	8094	- 1171	
Draycott	1683	639	2292	1803	741	2544	+ 252	
Lodge Hill	1766	251	2017	1699	267	1966	- 51	
Wookey	542	7032	7574	514	7523	8037	+ 463	
Wells	7156	5068	12224	7316	5327	12643	+ 419	
Shepton Mallet	3844	19040	22884	3925	19451	23376	+ 492	
Cranmore	1817	13164	14981	1539	13378	14917	- 64	
	31,617	62,128	93,745	31,543	58,749	90,292	**- £3,453**	Net decrease

Stations	Year 1910 Passenger & Parcels	Year 1910 Goods	Year 1910 Total	Year 1911 Passenger & Parcels	Year 1911 Goods	Year 1911 Total	Increase / Decrease	Remarks
	£	£	£	£	£	£	£	
Congresbury	985	1225	2210	1038	1309	2347	+ 137	
Sandford and Banwell	1570	2079	3649	1461	2169	3630	- 19	
Winscombe	3002	1440	4442	2749	1458	4207	- 235	
Axbridge	4607	2069	6676	4253	2165	6418	- 258	Strawberry traffic
Cheddar	4998	3893	8891	4507	3639	8146	- 745	Strawberry traffic
Draycott	1768	553	2321	1663	581	2244	- 77	
Lodge Hill	1824	289	2113	1733	309	2042	- 71	
Wookey	451	7529	7980	498	7647	8145	+ 165	
Wells	7736	5836	13572	6962	5814	12776	- 796	Military camp 1910
Shepton Mallet	3856	19145	23001	3674	19623	23297	+ 296	
Cranmore	1673	12605	14278	1807	10903	12710	- 1568	Stone traffic
Wanstrow	792	-	792	971	-	971	+ 179	
	33,262	56,663	89,925	31,316	55,617	86,933	**- £2,992**	Net decrease

Milk traffic and Staffing levels on the line, 1910

Stations	1910 Milk Traffic Churns	1910 Milk Traffic Amount £	1910 Staffing Salary	1910 Staffing Wage
Congresbury	9454	275 - 13 - 3d	-	5
Sandford and Banwell	6659	364 - 14 - 3d	-	5
Winscombe	13041	732 - 6 - 9d	-	3
Axbridge	31337	2197 - 9 - 6d	-	7
Cheddar	15571	1068 - 0 - 5d	2	5
Draycott	12894	813 - 5 - 9d	-	3

Stations (cont)	1910 Milk Traffic Churns	1910 Milk Traffic Amount £	1910 Staffing Salary	1910 Staffing Wage
Lodge Hill	20281	1299 - 7 - 8d	-	2
Wookey	-	-	-	4
Wells	8115	601 - 15 - 5d	3	19
Shepton Mallet	4152	303 - 9 - 0d	4	10
Cranmore	13580	1104 - 3 - 7d	-	5
Wanstrow	6355	496 - 6 - 3d	-	1

Appendix 5

PRIVATE TRADERS ON THE LINE

Yatton

Yatton Gas Consumers Company Ltd

Horsecastle, Yatton, Somerset.

Was operating in 1933 since the company signed up to 1933 RCH Scheme. No further details.

Barber Bros.

Yatton, Somerset.

The firm was listed in the 1928 *Colliery Year Book*, at the same address, and listed as coal merchants in the 1938 *Colliery Year Book*. That year the firm was noted at Railway Wharf, Wrington.

On or about 14th September 1914 the Gloucester RC&W Co. agreed to supply this firm with a single second-hand 10-ton wagon on seven years' terms.

Two wagons appear in a postcard view of Wrington station.

W. Counsell & Company

Yatton; also at Congresbury and Wrington.

In the 1901 Census, Walter Counsell is noted as being 41 years old, having been born at Winscombe and at the time of the Census was trading as a coal and timber merchant. He had a son, Robert C., who later appeared in *Kelly's Directory* (1926 and 1933) as trading from Railway Wharf, Yatton.

The firm appears in 1909 ledger of coal merchants with an account with the London & North Western Railway.

On 14th September 1914 Gloucester RC&W Co. supplied one new 10-ton wagon on three years deferred purchase. Counsell were to arrange a repairs agreement, which they contracted with GRC&W Co. for seven years. The wagon was photographed in September 1914, painted black, lettered white with red shading; *Plate 232*.

Winscombe

Alfred G. Weeks & Sons

Winscombe, Somerset; also with premises at Sandford and Banwell.

Listed in the 1928 *Colliery Year Book* and as coal merchants in the 1938 *Colliery Year Book*, at the Garage, Winscombe.

New 10-ton wagon built and photographed in 1913 by Ince Waggon & Ironworks Co. of Wigan; paint colour unknown; *Plate 233*.

Cheddar

Alfred Perry

'Nyland View', Station Road, Cheddar.

Alfred Perry was a coal merchant between about 1896 and 1927. The firm is not listed among coal merchants in the 1938 *Colliery Year Book*.

Posed but undated photograph of wagons Nos.31, 32 and 33; *Plate 29*.

A. W. Andrews

Cheddar, Somerset.

Two 8-ton wagons Nos.8 and 9 were built by the Somerset Engineering Company, Radstock in 1878. They had dead buffers and were built for the Western Wagon Company who

Figure 56 - Sketch of Crow, Catchpole vehicle - see text.

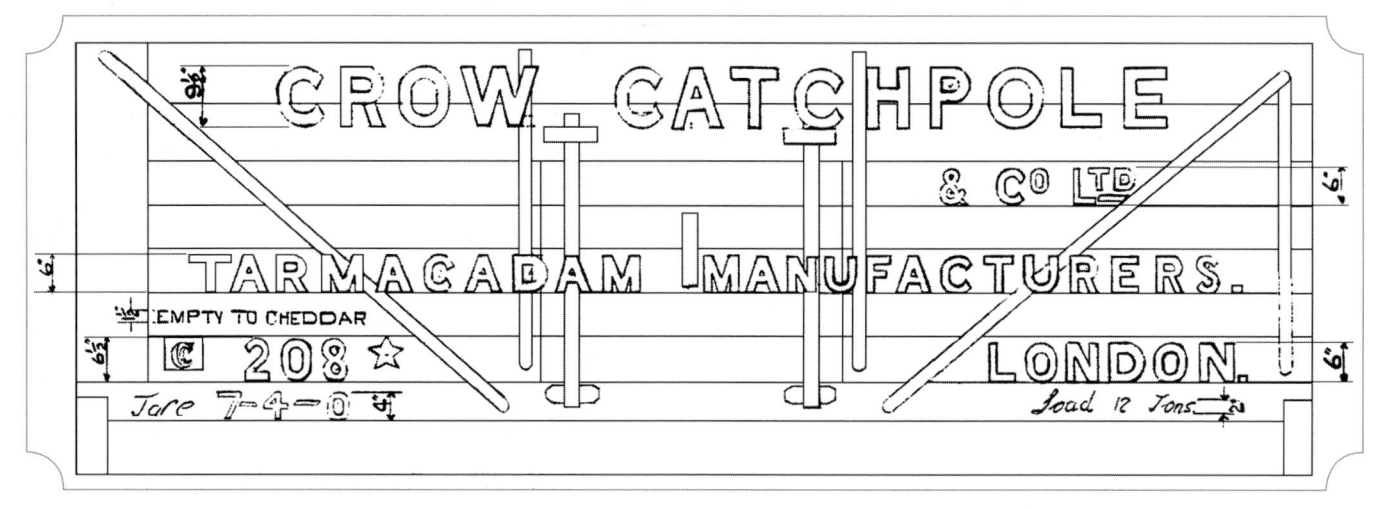

hired them to Andrews. They were registered by the GWR. However, there is no record of this in the Western Wagon Company's minutes, so the wagons were possibly on simple hire only.

On 21st November 1879 the *London Gazette* recorded:

> 'In the Matter of Proceedings for Liquidation by Arrangement or Composition with Creditors, instituted by Albert William Andrews, of Cheddar, in the county of Somerset, Coal Merchant. NOTICE is hereby given, that a First General Meeting of the creditors of the above-named person has been summoned to be held at the George Railway Hotel, Victoria-street, in the city of Bristol, on the 4th day of December, 1879, at half-past twelve o'clock in the afternoon precisely. Dated this 18th day of November, 1879.'

Batts Combe Quarry Company Ltd

Cheddar, Somerset.

Registered in 1935, the company owned fifteen 10-ton wagons in 1946. Being specifically for tarmacadam they were not included in the general pool of wagons. Of these, No.43 (and perhaps others) was taken over by British Railways in 1949 as part of Lot 1594 and renumbered M360264M. A 12-ton tar tank wagon was also bought by BR and renumbered in the 'M' series; it might have been Batts Combe No.49.

Crow Catchpole & Company Ltd

Shipham Hill, Cheddar.

Crow, Catchpole & Company Ltd was formed in October 1920 by the amalgamation of Thomas Crow & Sons Ltd, of West Ham, and E. Catchpole & Sons (London) Ltd of Rotherhithe, each of whom had been in the tar distilling business since the 1870s and 1880s. The registered office was in Harts Lane, Barking, Essex.

The company's main works were in Barking and Rotherhithe, but there were branches at Deptford, Rochester, Newhaven, Littlehampton, Creekmouth, Dover, Wandsworth, Hayes and Ipswich. There were two quarries in which the company had an interest; Craster in Northumberland and Shipham Hill, Cheddar. The need for stone possibly indicated a move to tarmacadam production instead of pure tar distillation.

In 1959 the company was acquired by Tarmac Limited and Crow, Catchpole was wound up in December of that year.

As well as a fleet of tank wagons for tar, there is evidence of conventional open wagons for stone traffic. The sketch (*opposite*) of a 12-ton 7-plank wagon was taken from a Wagon Repairs Ltd drawing, which indicated that the vehicle was painted black with white lettering.

Wells

Foster Yeoman

Fifty 12-ton wagons were built by Gloucester RC&W Co. in 1925 and numbered 101-150. They were registered by the GWR and were on hire from the Gloucester company.

The quarry company had numerous dealings with GRC&W Co. which reflect the rapid expansion of Dulcote New Quarry's output:

> 12th March 1923: financing proposed not settled; 100 x 12-ton. Possibly the order covered by this entry was unfulfilled because of the lack of agreement over financing.
>
> 9th April 1923: 100 new 12-ton wagons, deferred purchase over seven years;
>
> 30th July 1923: 100 new 12-ton wagons, deferred purchase over seven years;
>
> 10th November 1924: 50 new 12-ton wagons, deferred purchase over seven years;
>
> 24th November 1924: The agreement that Foster Yeoman had entered into with the Gloucester Co. for the hire of, and with option to purchase, 100 x 12-ton wagons was to expire on 30th September 1929.
>
> It was agreed to cancel that agreement and re-let the wagons from 1st October 1924 for seven years @ £18 10s per wagon per annum, repaying £10,320 4s 5d.

Photographs

> Builder's photograph: 'Foster Yeoman Ltd' No.36;
>
> Painted black, white lettering, September 1923; *Plate 200*.
>
> Builder's photograph: 'Foster Yeoman Ltd' No.126;
>
> Painted black, white lettering, January 1925; *Plate 202*.

A sketch of wagon No.119 appears in Vol.1 of *The Modeller's Sketchbook of Private Owner Wagons* by A. G. Thomas.

Somerset County Council

Underwood Quarry,

Wells, Somerset.

29 x 12-ton high goods wagons were built by Stableford Ltd, Coalville, in March 1926. They were numbered 88-116 and registered by the GWR.

Appendix 6

WORKING TIMETABLES

Plate 267 - Six years into the nationalised era, this shows the branch working timetable for the Yatton to Witham direction. The timings apply on weekdays (Mondays to Saturdays) between 14th June and 19th September 1954. Note the last conditional train of the day, the 9.50pm fruit from Axbridge with a path to Birmingham Moor Street.

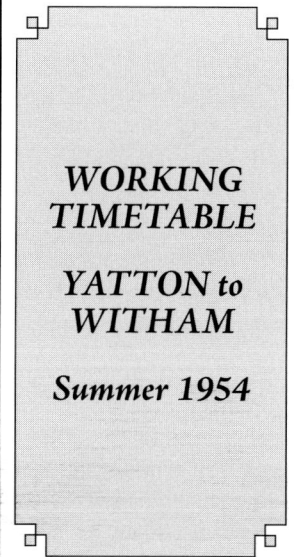

WORKING TIMETABLE

YATTON to WITHAM

Summer 1954

YATTON, WELLS AND WITHAM — WEEK DAYS

Station		K 3.55 a.m. Bristol (West Depot) Freight	B Pass.	K Freight SX	B 7.25 a.m. Bristol to Frome Pass.	G Engine and Van to Frome SO	K Freight SX	B Pass	B Frome Pass	K 9.30 a.m. Bristol (West Depot) Freight SX	B Pass SO	G Engine	B Frome Diesel SX Pass SO	K Westbury Freight SX	K Freight	B 5.20 p.m. Bristol Pass	B Frome Pass	B Pass.	C Birmingham (Moor St.) Fruit RR SX
		a.m.	a.m.	a.m.	a.m.	a.m.	a.m.	a.m.	a.m.	a.m.	p.m.	p.m.	p.m.	p.m.	p.m.	p.m.	p.m.	p.m.	p.m.
YATTON	dep.	4.50	6.55	7.10	7.58			11.12		10.33	1.11		2.52			5.47	6.10	8.08	
Congresbury	arr.	4.56	6.59	CR	8.02			11.15		CR	1.14					5.50	6.13	8.11	
	dep.	5.06	7.00	-	8.03			11.16			1.15		2.56			5.51	6.14	8.12	
Sandford & Banwell	arr.	5.17	7.05	7.25	8.08			11.21		10.48	1.20					5.56	6.19	8.17	
	dep.	5.27	7.06		8.09			11.22		11x45	1X21		3.02			5.57	6.20	8.18	
Winscombe	arr.	5.34	7.09		8.12			11.25		11.53	1.24					6.00	6.23	8.21	
	dep.	5.44	7.10		8.13			11.26		12.00	1.25	1↑30	3.06			6.01	6.24	8.22	
Axbridge	arr.	5.55	7.14		8.17			11.30		12.11	1.29	-	3.10		Cheddar to Wells (SX)	6.05	6.28	8.26	9.50
	dep.	6.10	7.15		8x20			11x31		12.20	1.30	CS	3X12			6.06	6x29	8.27	9.55
CHEDDAR	arr.	6.17	7.19		8.24			11.35		12.27	1.34	1↑50	3.16			6x10	6.33	8.31	10.05
	dep.	6.35	7x22		8.26			11.36		1.55	1.35		3.19		4.45	6.11	6.34	8x33	10.10
Draycott	arr.	-	7.26		8.30			11.39½		CR	1.39					6.14½	6.38	8.36½	10.10
	dep.	CS	7.27		8.31			11.40			1.40		3.23			6.15	6.39	8.37	10.18
Lodge Hill	arr.	-	7.31		8.35			11.44		2X08	1.44				CS	6.19	6.43	8.41	-
	dep.	6.55	7.32		8.36			11.45		2.16	1.45		3.28			6.20	6.44	8.42	CS
Wookey	arr.	7X10	7.36		8.40			11.49		2.25	1.49					6.24	6.48	8.46	-
	dep.	-	7.37		8.41			11.50		2.30	1.50		3.33		5.05	6.25	6.49	8.47	CS
WELLS	arr.	7.14	7.40		8x44			11.53		2.36	1.53		3.36		5.30	6.28	6.52	8.50	10.40
	dep.	7.31			9.05				12.03	2.45			3x49	4.25	5.37		7.00			10.45
Wells (East Somerset)					CS				CS	2.50			CS		6.15		CS			CS
Dulcote Siding		Engine and Guard to work trip to Wells				10↑10			12.16					4.02	6.32		7.13			-
Shepton Mallet	arr.				9.19	10X21		N 11.10	12.18				4X04	4.47	6.42		7X16			CS
(High Street)	dep.				9.21	10↑35		11.35					4.13	5.05	6X59		7.23			CS
Cranmore	arr.	Cold Store			9.28	CS		Dulcote Sidings arr. 11.21 a.m. RR between Cranmore and Witham	12.25				4.14	5.22	7.45		7.24			CS
	dep.				9.29			11.49					4.20	6.10	7P54					-
Stop Board Wanstrow	arr.	Depot if required			9.35			11.59	-				4.21	6P19	-		7.31			CS
	dep.				9.36			12.16	12.33				-	CR	-		-			CS
Stop Board	arr.				-			12.45						6P30	8P06					-
WITHAM	arr.				9.42	11.10		1P06	12.39				4.26	6.41	8.15		7.36			11.17

Plate 268 - The summer 1954 service shown here and overleaf was fairly typical of the service up until September 1958, when both the pasenger and goods services were subjected to major surgery as detailed in the text. The Sunday service by 1954 was for the summer timetable only, the winter Sunday services having been withdrawn in 1950. Even in the summer the Sunday service was not for the faint hearted. The outward journey from Yatton to Witham took nearly two hours and the return journey took 2 hours and 24 minutes, which included a wait of 1 hour and 6 minutes at Wells at a time when the local hostelries were probably not open.

Passengers would have been well advised to take a book and a flask of tea, although this is not mentioned in the timetable!

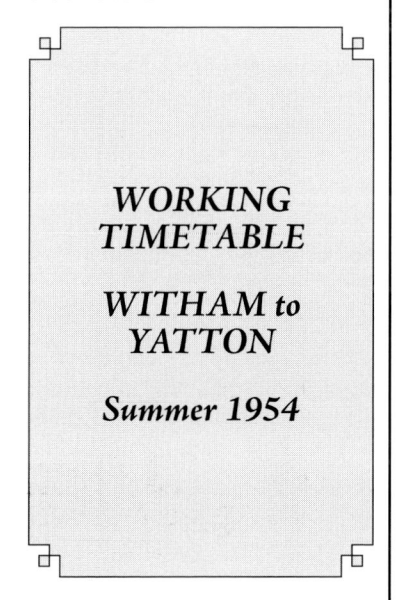

WORKING TIMETABLE

WITHAM to YATTON

Summer 1954

WITHAM, WELLS AND YATTON — WEEK DAYS

		Pass. B	Engine and Van G SX	Pass. B	Bristol (West Depot) Freight K	5.20 a.m. Westbury Freight K	7.53 a.m. Trowbridge to Bristol pass. B	9.25 a.m. W'g'tn Freight RR K SX	9.47 a.m. Westbury to Bristol Pass. B SO	9.57 a.m. Westbury to Bristol Pass. B SX	Bristol Pass. B SO	Bristol Pass. B SX	Pass. B SO	Engine and Van G SX	Freight K SX	3.20 p.m. Frome to Bristol Pass. B SX	3.27 p.m. Frome to Bristol Pass. B SO	St. Philips Marsh Freight. K SX	Bristol Pass. B SX	5.20 p.m. Bristol Pass. B	8†20 p.m. Frome Engine & Van RR G SX	Pass. B
		a.m.	a.m.	a.m.	a.m.	a.m.	a.m.	a.m.	a.m.	a.m.	p.m.	p.m.	p.m.	p.m.	p.m.	p.m.	p.m.	p.m.	p.m.	p.m.	p.m.	p.m.
WITHAM	dep.	..	..	..	..	6.35	8.25	..	10.10	10.20	1.10	1.30	..	..	11¶45	3.30	3.37	4.40	..	6.53	8†30	9.20
Vanstrow	arr.	..	..	..	..	-	-	..	-	-	-	-	..	..	-	-	-	-	7.00	7.01	-	9.28
	dep.	..	..	..	..	-	8.32	..	10.17	10.27	1.17	1.37	..	..	2.25	3.38	3.45	4.45	7.02½	7.08	-	9.37
Cranmore	arr.	..	..	..	..	6.57	-	..	-	-	-	-	..	..	2.35	-	-	4.55	7.03	-	8.45	9.38
	dep.	..	..	..	..	7.10	8.39	..	10.27	10.37	1.24	1.44	..	..	-	3.46	4.53	5.00	7.07	-	-	-
Stop Board	arr.	..	..	..	..	7P21	-	..	-	-	-	-	..	..	2P46	-	-	5.15	7.08	-	-	-
	dep.	..	..	..	..	7.30	8.46	..	10.34	10.44	1.31	1.51	..	..	2.55	3.54	4.01	5.23	-	7X15	-	9.45
Shepton Mallet (High Street)	arr.	..	..	..	..	7.55	8.47	..	10.35	10.45	1.32	1.54	..	..	3.13	4X03	4X03	5.30	7.13	7.17	-	9.46
	dep.	..	..	..	..	8P03	-	..	-	-	-	-	..	..	3P31	-	-	5.38	-	-	-	-
Stop Board	arr.	..	..	..	..	8.17	-	..	-	-	-	-	..	..	CR	-	-	5CR43	-	-	-	-
Dulcote Siding	dep.	..	..	..	..	8.25	8.58	..	10.45	10.55	1.42	2.02	..	2.45	3.35	4.12	4.12	5X50	-	7.26	-	9.57
WELLS (East Somerset)	arr.	..	..	..	..	8.28	-	..	-	-	1X55	2.06	..	CS		4.17	4.22	6.15	7.18	8.15	9†01	
	dep.	..	7.05	..	7.55	-	9X15	..	11.12½	11.12½	1.57½	2.08½	..	CS		4.19½	4.24½	6.23	7.22	8.17½	9†07	
WELLS	arr.	..	7.07½	..	7.58			..					..									
	dep.	..	7X08	..	8.04		9.17½	..	11.13	11.13	1.58	2.09	2.42	-		4.20	4.25	6X38	7.23	8.18	CS	
Wookey	arr.	..	7.12	..	8.09		9.18	..	11.17	11.17	2.02	2.13	2.50	CS		4.24	4.29	6.48	7.08	8.22	-	
	dep.	..	7.13	..	8.03		9.22	..	11.18	11.18	2.03	2.14	2.55	CS		4.25	4.30			8.23	CS	
Lodge Hill	arr.	..	7.16	..	8.07		9.23	..	11.21	11.21	2.06	2.17	-	-		4.28	4.33			8.26	-	
	dep.	..	7.17	..	8.08		9.26	..	11.22	11.22	2.07	2.20	2.59	-		4.31	4.34		7.13	8.27	-	
Draycott	arr.	..	7.20	..	8.11		9.27	..	11.25	11.25	2.10	2.23	3.02	3.09	Between Witham and Cranmore. Merehead Quarry Siding if required. 2.2 - 2.15p.m.	4.35	4.38			8.30	CS	
	dep.	..	7X21	..	8.12		9.30	..	11.26	11.26	2.11	2.26	3.04	-		4.38	4.-			8X32	-	
CHEDDAR	arr.	..	7.24	..	8.15		9.31	..	11.29	11.29	2.15	2.29	3.08	To work 4.45		4.41	4.43		7.18	8.35	CS	
	dep.	..	7.25	..	8.16		9.35	..	11.32	11.32	2.16	2.32	3X11			4.44	4.44		7.22	8.36	9†27	
Axbridge	arr.	..	7.29	..	8X22		9.36	..	11.36	11.36	2.20	2.36				4.48	4.48		7.23	8.40		

YATTON, WELLS AND WITHAM

SUNDAYS | SUNDAYS

	B			B
	2.10 p.m. Bristol Pass.			Bristol Pass.
	p.m.			p.m.
YATTON .... dep.	2.30	WITHAM .... dep.		5.40
Congresbury .... dep.	2.34	Wanstrow .... ,,		5.47
Sandford and arr.	2.39	Cranmore .... arr.		5.53
Banwell dep.	2.40	dep.		5.54
Winscombe .... arr.	2.43	Stop Board .... ,,		-
dep.	2.44	Shepton Mallet arr.		6.01
Axbridge .... arr.	2.48	(High Street) ...... dep.		6.04
dep.	2.49	Stop Board .... ,,		-
CHEDDAR .... arr.	2.53	Dulcote Siding .... ,,		-
dep.	2.54	WELLS arr.		CS
Draycott .... dep.	2.58	(East Somerset) ..... dep.		-
Lodge Hill .... arr.	-	WELLS .... arr.		6.14
dep.		dep.		7.20
Wookey .... dep.	3.07	Wookey .... ,,		7.23
WELLS .... arr.	3.10	Lodge Hill .... arr.		-
dep.	4.00	dep.		
Wells arr.	CS	Draycott .... arr.		7.32
(East Somerset) ..... dep.	-	dep.		7.33
Dulcote Siding .... ,,	-	CHEDDAR .... arr.		7.37
Shepton Mallet arr.	4.13	dep.		7.38
(High Street) ...... dep.	4.16	Axbridge .... arr.		7.42
Cranmore .... arr.	4.23	dep.		7.43
dep.	4.24	Winscombe .... arr.		7.47
Stop Board .... ,,	-	dep.		7.49
Wanstrow .... arr.	4.30	Sandford and arr.		-
dep.	4.31	Banwell dep.		7.54
Stop Board .... ,,	-	Congresbury .... arr.		7.59
WITHAM .... arr.	4.26	dep.		8.00
		YATTON .... arr.		8.04

Plate 269 - Working timetable for the single train each way on summer Sundays, 1954.

Plate 270 - The Wells transfer trips between Tucker Street, East Somerset and the Somerset & Dorset are mentioned in the text. This GWR timetable is for 1933.

WELLS. TRANSFER TRIPS BETWEEN G.W. & S. & D.

		S. & D. Engine.		S. & D.		S. & D.		S. & D. Engine.		S. & D.		
		p.m.		p.m.		p.m.		p.m.		p.m.		
East Somerset ...... dep.	....	12‖17	....		....	2 8	....	4‖27	....	5 32	....	
S. and D. .... arr.	..	12‖19	..		..	2 10	..	4‖29	..	5 34	..	...
S. and D. .... dep.	....		....	1 45	....		....		....		....	...
Tucker Street ...... arr.	..		..	1 47	..		..		..		..	..

		S. & D.		G.W.		S. & D. Engine.		S. & D. Engine.		S. & D.		S. & D. Engine.
		p.m.		p.m.		p.m.				p.m.		p.m.
Tucker Street ...... dep.	....	....	....	12 50	....	1‖50	....	....	....	....	....	....
S. and D. .... arr.	..		..	12 52	..	1‖52	..		..		..	
S. and D. .... dep.	..	12 10	..	12‖57	..		..	1‖50	..	4 20	..	5‖25
East Somerset ...... arr.	..	12 13	..	12‖59	..		..	1‖52	..	4 23	..	5‖28

In addition to above, special trips are arranged as desired with live stock, meat and urgent traffic.

Plate 271 - The first of three pages from the Great Western Railway's working timetable for 11th July to 25th September 1927. The last train on a Saturday, the 9.30pm from Yatton, is noted as an Excursion although there is no similar outbound train in the Witham to Yatton pages. It may be that outbound day excursion tickets were issued for use on a variety of trains earlier in the day and this late train was to enable travellers to return home from destinations far and wide.

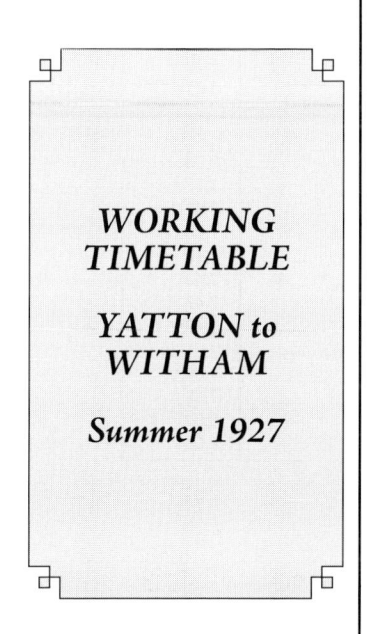

WORKING TIMETABLE

YATTON to WITHAM

Summer 1927

Plate 272 - The Witham to Yatton timings from the summer 1927 timetable.

One point to note is that the empty Excursion coaching stock working from Shepton Mallet to Wells has been suspended, although the suspension of the Excursion working itself is not evident in the Yatton to Witham pages.

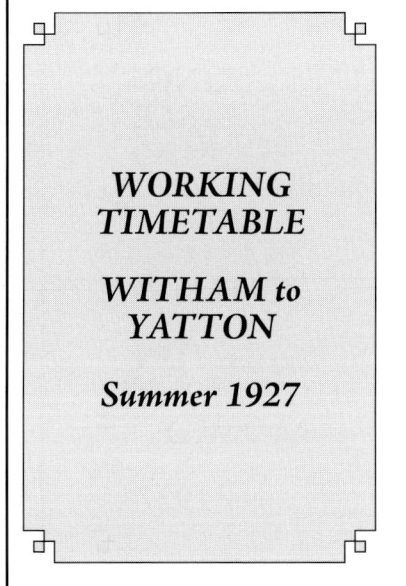

WORKING TIMETABLE

WITHAM to YATTON

Summer 1927

Plate 273 - The Sunday service for the Yatton to Witham line as well as the full timetable for Congresbury to Blagdon branch, which retained its passenger service until 1931.

There is one anomaly in the table; the final sentence under the Wrington Vale section reads:
'The Engineers have absolute occupation of the Branch each morning from 5 a.m. until 15 min. before the first train is due to leave Blagdon.'

The first train from Blagdon is 8.55am, intimating that the Engineers have possession until 8.40am. However, the branch is already being traversed by the 8.15am Yatton, due into Blagdon at 8.45am.

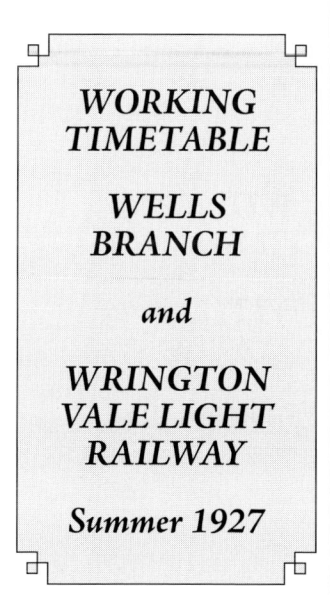

WORKING TIMETABLE

WELLS BRANCH

and

WRINGTON VALE LIGHT RAILWAY

Summer 1927

Appendix 7

CHRONOLOGY

Important dates in the history of the Yatton to Witham line and associated railways, 1835-1864

1835	31st August	Great Western Railway Act of Parliament (London to Bristol).
1836	19th May	Bristol & Exeter Railway Act.
1840	31st August	Great Western Railway opened between Bristol and Bath.
1841	14th June	Bristol & Exeter Railway opened to Bridgwater.
	30th June	Great Western Railway missing link between Bath and Chippenham opened.
1844	1st May	Bristol & Exeter Railway main line completed and opened to Exeter.
1845	30th June	Wilts, Somerset & Weymouth Railway Act.
	31st July	Bristol & Exeter Railway Act for Clevedon Branch.
1847	28th July	Clevedon Branch opened for traffic.
1848	22nd July	Bristol & Exeter Railway Act for a branch from Uphill to Wells, Glastonbury and Street. (Never built although revived in the 1860s)
1852	17th June	Somerset Central Railway Act (Highbridge to Glastonbury).
1851	3rd July	Act confirming the take-over of the Wilts, Somerset & Weymouth by the Great Western Railway (actual take-over had taken place in 1850).
1854	28th August	Somerset Central Railway opens for traffic from Highbridge to Glastonbury. (Formal opening on 17th August)
1855	30th July	Somerset Central Railway Act for the Wells Extension.
1856	5th June	East Somerset Railway Act (Witham to Shepton Mallet).
	21st July	Somerset Central Railway Act for the line from Glastonbury to Cole (Bruton Extension).
	29th July	Dorset Central Railway Act (Wimborne to Blandford Forum).
	1st September	Wilts, Somerset & Weymouth Railway Frome to Yeovil section opened for traffic.
1857	27th July	East Somerset Railway Act for the extension from Shepton Mallet to Wells.
	10th August	Dorset Central Railway Act (Cole to Blandford Forum).
1858	9th November	East Somerset Railway opens from Witham to Shepton Mallet.
1859	15th March	Somerset Central Railway opens for traffic from Glastonbury to Wells. (Formal opening 3rd March)
1860	14th June	East Somerset Railway Act for a revised route from Shepton Mallet to Wells. (The original extension line authorised by the 1857 Act was abandoned along with the connection to the Somerset Central at Wells)
1861	21st June	Agreement by the Great Western Railway to work the East Somerset Railway.
	28th August	Bristol & Exeter lease of the Somerset Central Railway expires. Somerset Central obtains an Act (actual date not known) to build Bruton Extension to standard gauge and link up with the Dorset Central rather than the Wilts, Somerset & Weymouth. Somerset Central subsequently lays third rail between Burnham and Wells.
1862	3rd February	Somerset Central and Dorset Central opens between Glastonbury and Templecombe. Somerset Central commences running standard gauge services.
	28th February	East Somerset extension opens from Shepton Mallet to Wells (East Somerset) with connection to the Somerset Central.
	7th August	Somerset Central and Dorset Central Act of Amalgamation.
	1st September	Somerset & Dorset Railway comes into being.
1863	31st August	Somerset & Dorset opens missing link from Templecombe to Blandford Forum.
1864	27th May	Agreement between the Somerset & Dorset and Bristol & Exeter Railways for the latter to subscribe to the former's proposed line from Yatton to Wells.
	14th July	Cheddar Valley & Yatton Railway Act.

Appendix 7

CHRONOLOGY (continued)

Important dates in the history of the Yatton to Witham line and associated railways, 1865-1975

1865	19th June	Act of Parliament transferring the powers to build the Yatton to Wells line from the Somerset & Dorset to the Bristol & Exeter Railway. The Bristol & Exeter's proposed line from Uphill was abandoned.
1867	26th February	Cutting of the first sod on the Cheddar Valley & Yatton Railway.
1869	3rd August	Cheddar Valley & Yatton section from Yatton to Cheddar opening ceremony.
	4th August	Midland Railway opens its branch from Mangotsfield (on the Bristol to Gloucester) to Bath.
1870	5th April	Cheddar Valley & Yatton section from Cheddar to Wells opens to traffic.
1871	21st August	Somerset & Dorset Act for the Bath Extension.
1874	14th June	Act authorising the take over of the East Somerset Railway by the Great Western Railway (formal take-over in December 1874).
	21st June	Gauge conversion of the East Somerset Railway completed (started on 19th June).
	20th July	Somerset & Dorset Bath Extension opens for traffic.
1875	15th April	Colonel Yolland of the Railway Inspectorate inspects the arrangements at Wells following the completion of the link between the three stations.
	23rd April	Colonel Yolland's report refuses to allow passenger traffic to use the link at Wells.
	1st June	Bristol & Exeter main line became mixed gauge from Bristol to Highbridge.
	1st November	Somerset & Dorset Railway leased jointly to the London & South Western and Midland Railways for 999 years.
	18th November	Gauge conversion of the Cheddar Valley line completed (started on 15th November).
1876	1st January	Great Western Railway absorbs the Bristol & Exeter Railway.
	13th July	Act confirming the lease of the Somerset & Dorset Railway.
1878	1st January	Link between Cheddar Valley and East Somerset sections at Wells finally opened for passenger traffic and East Somerset passenger station closed.
1879	28th September	Clevedon Branch converted to standard gauge.
1892	23rd May	Broad gauge abolished.
1898	18th March	Light Railway Order granted for the construction of the Wrington Vale Light Railway.
1901	4th December	Wrington Vale Light Railway opens for traffic.
1923	1st January	The Grouping of Britain's railways.
1931	14th September	Wrington Vale Light Railway closes for passenger traffic.
1934	1st October	Great Western trains call at Wells Priory Road station for the first time.
1948	1st January	The Nationalisation of Britain's railways.
1950	1st November	Wrington to Blagdon closed completely.
1951	29th October	Glastonbury to Wells branch closed for all traffic.
1963	10th June	Congresbury to Wrington and the Clevedon Branch close to goods traffic.
1963	9th September	Yatton to Witham line closed for passenger traffic.
1963	6th October	Home Counties rail tour runs from Yatton to Witham.
1964	1st October	Yatton to Cheddar closed completely.
1966	7th March	Somerset & Dorset closed for passenger traffic.
1966	3rd October	Clevedon Branch closes completely.
1969	26th April	Stone traffic from Cheddar ceases.
1969	31st May	RCTS rail tour to Cheddar forms the last revenue earning train to Cheddar.
1975	20th August	Line officially closed between Cranmore and Dulcote Quarry sidings.

Bibliography

Sources and Suggestions for Further Reading

Beisly, P., *The Northmarsh of Somerset*, Weston-super-Mare Heritage Centre 1996.
Birmingham Locomotive Club, *Industrial Locomotives of Southern England*, The Birmingham Locomotive Club 1958.
Christensen, M. & Turner, C., 'Congresbury', *Great Western Railway Journal* No.15 p.618, Wild Swan 1995.
Clarke, R.H., *An Historical Survey of Selected Great Western Stations* Volume 1, Oxford Publishing Company 1976.
Clinker, C. R., 'The Cheddar Valley Railway', *The Railway Magazine* No.588, p.224, 1950.
Clinker, C. R., *Register of Closed Passenger and Goods Stations*, Avon-Anglia 1978.
Congresbury History Group, *The Railway at Congresbury*, Congresbury History Group 1986.
Cooke, R. A., *Atlas of the Great Western Railway as at 1947*, Wild Swan 1988.
Cooke, R. A., *Track Layout Diagrams of the GWR and BR, WR, Section 16 (Second Edition)*, R. A. Cooke 1990.
Dando, Compton, 'The Cheddar Valley Line in BR days', *Railway Bylines* March 2001, Irwell Press 2001.
Down, C. G. & Warrington, A. J. 'The Newbury Railway, Appendix 3: Waterlip Quarry', *Industrial Railway Record* No.82, Industrial Railway Society 1979.
Edwards, W. E., 'The East Somerset Railway', *Railway Magazine* July 1921.
Farr, M., Maggs, C. G., Lovell, R. & Whetmath, C., *The Wrington Vale Light Railway*, Avon-Anglia 1978.
Frost, K. A., 'The Railways of Wells', *Backtrack* Volume 12 No.1 pp.70-76, Atlantic Transport Publishers 1998.
Fry, P., *Railways into Wells*, The Somerset & Dorset Trust 1998. (3)
Harrison, I., 'Dulcote, A Tale of Two Quarries', *British Railway Journal* No.54, Wild Swan 1995.
Hayes, R. & Shaw, M., *Railways in Wells*, HST 1982.
Hillier, B., 'S&T Maintenance on the Cheddar Valley', *Great Western Railway Journal* No 54 p.303, Wild Swan 2005.
Hutton, E., *Highways and Byways in Somerset*, Macmillan and Co. 1912.
Jenkins, S., 'Life before Preservation 25: The East Somerset Railway', *Steam Days* No.145, Redgauntlet Publications 2001.
Kidder, D. & Brading, A., *Cheddar Valley Railway Walk*, Ex Libris Press 1999.
Knight, F. A., *A History of Sidcot School*, publisher unknown (1908).
Knight, P., *The Parish and the Railway*, Knight 2000. (2)
MacDermot, E. T., *A History of the Great Western Railway* Vol. 2 1862-1921, (1927) Ian Allen as revised by C. R. Clinker 1964.
Madge, R., *Somerset Railways*, Dovecote 1984.
Maggs, C. G., *The East Somerset Railway 1858-1972*, East Somerset Railway Co. Ltd / Avon-Anglia 1977.
Maggs, C. G., *The Clevedon Branch*, Wild Swan 1987.
Marsden, C. J., *Foster Yeoman - The Rail Story - 75 years of aggregate by rail*, Channel AV Publishing 1998.
McRae, A., *British Railways Camping Coach Holidays* Part Two, Foxline 1998.
Mitchell, V. & Smith, K., *Branch Line to Cheddar including the Wrington Vale Light Railway*, Middleton Press 1997. (1)
Phillips, D., *Steaming along the Cheddar Valley*, Ian Allan 2001. (4)
Pryer, G. A., *Signal Box Diagrams of the Great Western & Southern Railways Volume 10*, G. A. Pryer (Undated).
Railway Clearing House, *Junction Diagrams 1914*, reprinted by Ian Allen.
Railway Correspondence & Travel Society, *Locomotives of the Great Western Railway* series.
Smith, M., 'The Strawberry Line', *British Railways Illustrated* Summer Special No.3, Irwell Press 1995.
de Viggiani, M. C., *A Cranmore Chronicle*, de Viggiani 1985.
de Viggiani, M. C., *Two Estates*, de Viggiani 1988.
Vincent, M., *Lines to Avonmouth*, Oxford Publishing Company 1979.

The numbers in parentheses are to assist the reader in locating the references in the Introduction

❀ Sources ❀

Other Sources of Information

Public Record Office, Kew; now The National Archives
Somerset County Record Office, Obridge Road, Taunton
Somerset Studies Library, Paul Street, Taunton
Wells & Mendip Museum, Wells
Wiltshire and Swindon Record Office, Chippenham
Wells Journal
Railway Observer

❀ Acknowledgements ❀

I should like to thank the following for their assistance and as sources of information in the preparation of this work:

Brian Hillier, who worked on S&T on the branch; the late Peter Knight, a local historian of the Winscombe area; Chris Osment, Ray Caston, John McCrickard and the late John Morris of the Signalling Record Society; Paul Fry of the Wells Railway Fraternity and local expert on the railways of Wells; Andy Viles, whose father, Harry, was a driver at Wells, Colin Forse who was a driver at Yatton and Bristol Bath Road; Chris Pratt who provided some more information on signalling; Mark Bailey for information on Cheddar; Brian Arman, Hugh Ballantyne, Ivan Beale, Rod Blencowe, Roger Carpenter, Rex Conway, Hugh Davies, John Spencer Gilks, Michael Hale, Bert Colbourn of the HMRS, Kidderminster Railway Museum, the Lens of Sutton Association, Michael Mensing, Warwick Burton, Terry Nicholls, Colin Nash, Julian Peters, Gordon Scammell, John Alsop, Ian Pope, Neil Parkhouse, Tony Miller, F. A. Wycherley, Robin Russell, D.P. Leckonby, Mike Barnsley, Mike Esau, John Edgington, the Industrial Locomotive Society, Geoff Fitton and Brian Murless of SIAS, R.E. Toop; the staffs of the Somerset County Record Office, the Somerset Studies Library, the Wiltshire and Swindon Record Office; Wells & Mendip Museum; the National Monuments Record Centre in Swindon and the National Archives at Kew (formerly the Public Record Office).

I should also like to thank Gerald Nichols, John Uncles, Mark Warburton, Bob Griffiths and the late Jack Burrell, all long-standing members of the Bristol Railway Circle for their assistance.

Last but not least thanks to my wife, Andrea, for proof reading and pointing out my grammatical errors.

Efforts have been made to trace the copyright holders of all photographs and other material used in this publication. If we have failed in any way to do this correctly for any reason then please contact us.

❀

Subject Index

Accidents   41, 52, 64, 191, 195, 228-230
     Fatalities   191, 228, 229
Acts of Parliament   14-18, 21, 35, 38
Andesite   179

Board of Trade
     Inspections   18-19, 40-41, 44, 46, 50, 52-53, 59-61
     Inspectors
         Major Druitt   61
         Major General Hutchinson   50, 53
         Major Marindin   59
         Major Pringle   59
         Colonel Rich   46, 181, 229
         Captain Tyler   44
         Colonel Yolland   18-19, 40-41, 52-53
         Colonel Yorke   60, 62
Bridges
     Over S&D at Shepton Mallet   162
     Drawing of bridge over S&D   161
Bristol Waterworks   60, 63
Bristol Waterworks Siding   113
British Transport Commission   74

Camping coaches   231
Celebratory events   19, 26, 28, 31
Cold Store, Wells   65
Contractors
     George Bevan   25
     Brock   100
     Rowland Brotherhood   18-19, 27
     Green and King   24
     John & William Pickering   30
     Smith and Knight   24
     Saxby & Farmer   215, 217, 218, 220

Doulting Stone Siding   47, 68, 162, 176-177
     Layout plan 1903   176
Downhead Quarry   178-179
Dulcote New Quarry   183-185
     Layout plan of sidings 1923   184
     Train working   211
Dulcote Quarry   152, 181-186
     Layout plan of sidings 1903   182
     Siding signalling   183

Gasworks, Wells   147
Gate Lane Level Crossing   60, 147, 194, 209, 211
Gradient profile   80
Ground Frames *see Signal Boxes and Ground Frames*

Kilver Street Crossing   19, 160

Locomotives
     Broad gauge   18
     Locomotive turntables   190
     Locomotive workings   186, 188-207
     Midland Railway locomotives   194

     Waterlip Quarry tramway   178-180
     Gamecock   178-179
     Horwich   178-180
     Keighley, Tattoo   78
     Medway   179

Maps
     Cheddar Valley Railway   29, 33
     East Somerset Railway   20, 151
Marcroft Wagons Ltd   164
Memorials to the railway   237
Merehead Quarry   181, 186
Merehead Quarry Siding   164

Permanent way
     Bristol & Exeter Railway   41, 44
     British Rail   186
     Cheddar Valley & Yatton Railway   30
     East Somerset Railway   19
     Great Western Railway   194, 229
Personalities
     Lord Bath   19
     W. B. Beauchamp   177
     William Chester Berryman the Younger   18
     I. K. Brunel   18
     Cyrus Clark   14
     James Clark   14
     Edward Clarke   19
     Charles Clinker   104
     Edmund Hugh Clerk   18
     Earl of Devon   31
     Viscount Dungarvon   18
     T. S. Foxwell   19
     John Gould   147-148
     C. H. Gregory   215
     John Hamblin   178
     Sir Edward Strode Knight   18
     John Moore Paget   18-19
     Arthur C. Phipps   19
     James Curtis Somerville   18, 25
     J. G. Somerville   19
     Edward Charles Chetham Strode   18, 177
     Hon. Henry Thynne   18
     John Wason   18
     Foster Yeoman   183
Promotional literature   48-49, 194
Proposed railway lines   10-15, 17, 24, 37, 60

Quarries
     Chelynch   27, 176-177
     Doulting Stone Siding track plan 1903   176
     Downhead   178-179
     Dulcote   21, 77, 152, 181-186
         Layout plan of sidings 1903   182
         Dulcote New Quarry   183, 208
         Layout plan of sidings 1923   184
     Merehead   164, 181, 186, 208

Sandford	61, 173-177
Layout plan post-1915	175
Train working	211
Shipman Hill	259
Underwood	133, 259
Waterlip	46, 177-180
Locomotives	178-180
Tramway layout at Cranmore	178
Railway Clearing House	147
Railway companies	
Bristol & Exeter Railway	12, 14, 35
Bristol & North Somerset Railway	17
Cheddar Valley & Yatton Railway	16, 28-37
Acts of Parliament	16
Maps	28, 33
Officials	
Francis Fox	28, 35
John Hingston Fox	28
Signalling	215
Dorset Central Railway	14
East Somerset Railway	7, 16, 18-27, 38
Acts of Parliament	52
Maps	18, 23, 151
Officials	
G. M. Mackay	19
R. J. Ward	19, 24-25
Great Western Railway	12, 18, 38
Acts of Parliament	60
Officials	
John Grant	43
James Grierson	44
Alexander Wood	43
London, Midland & Scottish Railway	63
London & South Western Railway	11-12, 17
Midland Railway	7, 15, 17
Somerset Central Railway	14-15, 24-25
Somerset & Dorset Railway	7, 14, 16-17, 35, 63
Southern Railway	7, 63
Wilts, Somerset & Weymouth Railway	7, 12, 18
Wrington Vale Light Railway	50, 60
Railway time	8
Rolling stock	
Diesel railcars	195
Foster Yeoman vehicles	181, 183, 186, 259
Passenger vehicles	197
Royal Edward Dock, Avonmouth	173
Sandford Quarry	61, 173-177
Layout plan post-1915	175
Sheldon Jones Ltd	135-136
Shute Shelve Tunnel	30, 105
Sidcot School	104
Signal boxes and Ground Frames	
Axbridge	217
Signal box diagram	248
Cheddar	77, 218-219
Signal box diagram	249
Congresbury	60, 93, 215-216
Locking table	247
Signal box diagram	246
Cranmore	77, 165, 224
Signal box diagram	255
Doulting Siding	224
Draycott	218
Signal box diagram	249
Gate Lane Level Crossing	60, 147, 194, 209, 211
Signal box diagram	251
Kilver Street Crossing	224
Signal box diagram	254
Lodge Hill	220
Signal box diagram	250
Sandford and Banwell	217
Signal box diagram	246
Locking table	247
Shepton Mallet	77, 224
Signal box diagram	254
Wanstrow signal box diagram	255
Wells East Somerset	52-53, 77, 144, 222-223
Signal box diagrams	252
Locking table	253
Wells Priory Road (S&D)	66, 221-223
Wells Tucker Street	140, 220
Signal box diagram	251
Winscombe	217
Signal box diagram	248
Witham	224
Signal box diagram	256
Wookey	220
Signal box diagram	250
Yatton Junction	60
Yatton West	86, 215-216, 245
Signal box diagram	245
Signalling	45, 47, 50, 61, 183, 209, 215-227
Annett's Key	217
Electric Key Token working	226
Electric Train Staff working	226
Single Line Working	242-244
Wells, between signal boxes	223
Somerset County Council	133
St. Cuthbert's paper mill	50, 130-131, 208, 220
Stations	
Axbridge	28, 41, 44, 62, 76, 106-112
Layout plan	107
Cheddar	32, 41, 73, 76-77, 113-122
Bristol Waterworks Siding	113
L. W. Bryant Quarries Ltd Siding	117
Layout plan c.1905	114, 116
Layout plan 1940	116-117
McAlpine's Siding	113, 211
Congresbury	41, 76, 86-94, 228
Accidents	228, 229
Layout plan	88
Signal box	93
Cranmore	41, 46, 55, 59, 162-166, 180
Layout plan, c.1910 and 1927	163
Mendip Mountain Quarries Ltd	178, 211
Stone traffic working	211
Draycott	74, 123-125
Layout plan	125
Train working	218
Lodge Hill	35, 73, 125-128
Layout plan	126
Train working	220

Sandford and Banwell	34, 61, 76, 94-99
Layout plan	96
Stone traffic working	211
Shepton Mallet (High Street)	19, 41, 59, 153-161
Down platform waiting room drawing	156
Layout plan 1930	153
Train working	211
Wanstrow	19, 62, 166-168
Layout plan	167
Wells	
Joint station proposal	51
Layout plan of stations 1936	134
Wells East Somerset	24, 38-41, 50, 144-150
East Somerset yard layout plan 1929	146
East Somerset yard layout plan 1942	149
East Somerset locomotive shed	188-191
Layout plans	189
Wells Priory Road	25-26, 40-41, 45, 55, 142-143
Layout plan 1936	130
Level crossing	50, 52-55
Wells Tucker Street	40-41, 44, 55, 133-141
Layout plan 1936	134
Sheldon Jones Ltd	135-136
Up platform waiting room drawing	139
Winscombe	35, 61, 76, 100-104
Layout plan	101
Signalling	100
Witham	78, 169-172
Layout plan 1903	171
Woodborough (*see also* Winscombe)	28, 35, 100
Wookey	50, 61, 129-132
Accidents	228
Layout plan	130
St. Cuthbert's paper mill	50, 130-131, 208
Wookey Stone Siding	133
Yatton	44, 60, 79-86
Layout plan	82
Signalling	85-86
Steamer services	15
Strawberry traffic	240-241
Telegraph	8-9
Traders	
A.W. Andrews	258
Barber Bros.	258
Batts Combe Quarry Company Ltd	259
L. W. Bryant Quarries Ltd	117
Callow Rock Lime Company Ltd	77, 117
W. Counsell & Company, Yatton	213, 258
Crow, Catchpole & Company Ltd	258-259
E.C.C. Quarries Ltd	77
Foster Yeoman Ltd	77, 183-186, 259
John Aird & Company	173
Sir John Jackson Ltd	174
Marcroft Wagons Ltd	164
McAlpine's Siding	76, 113, 117, 211, 224
Mendip Black Rock Stone Company	177
Mendip Granite and Asphalte Company Ltd	178
Mendip Mountain Quarries Ltd	178
Alfred Perry	258
Roads Reconstruction Ltd	174, 178
Sheldon Jones Ltd	77
A. G. Weeks, Winscombe	213, 258
Yatton Gas Consumer's Company Ltd	258
Traffic	
Bitumen	74, 77
Goods	18, 44, 70, 74-75
Perishable	9, 74-75, 208, 240-241
Passenger	18, 74-75
Receipts, 1908-1911	257
Stone	47, 74, 76-77, 174, 183-186, 208, 210
Train services	
British Railways	67-69, 71-72, 76, 193-207
1954 service timetable	260-262
Cheddar Valley & Yatton Railway	32-34, 38-39
East Somerset Railway	19, 26-27, 38
Excursions	69-70, 187, 194
Glastonbury branch	66
Great Western Railway	
1879 service	46-48
1886 service	55-59
1927 service timetable	263-265
1933 service	63-65
1944 service	198-199
Post WWII	192, 198-199
Wrington Vale branch	63, 265
Train working	
Bristol & Exeter Railway	187
British Railways	71, 73-77, 186, 191-207, 209, 211
Cheddar Valley & Yatton Railway	30, 39
Disruption by weather	236
East Somerset Railway	18, 26
Goods	65, 197
Great Western Railway	43, 45-46, 65, 183, 191-199, 213-214
Mixed trains	46-47
Passenger	21
Perishables	208, 240-241
Runaways	232-233
Wells goods transfer trips	213-214, 262
Wookey	220
Wrington Vale branch	217
Transport Users' Consultative Committee	74-75
Turnpike Trust	38
Underwood Quarry	133
Waterlip Quarry	46, 177-179
Locomotives	178-179
Mendip Black Rock Stone Company	177
Mendip Granite and Asphalte Company Ltd	178
Mendip Mountain Quarries Ltd	178
Roads Reconstruction Ltd	178
Tramway layout at Cranmore	178
Water supplies	66, 156, 191
Wells Cold Store	65
Wells Gasworks	147
Wells Town Council	50-55
Working timetables	56, 260-265